THE BAD TRIP

THE BAD TRIP

DARK OMENS, NEW WORLDS AND THE END OF THE SIXTIES

JAMES RILEY

ICON

Published in the UK in 2019 by
Icon Books Ltd, Omnibus Business Centre,
39–41 North Road, London N7 9DP
email: info@iconbooks.com
www.iconbooks.com

Sold in the UK, Europe and Asia by
Faber & Faber Ltd, Bloomsbury House,
74–77 Great Russell Street,
London WC1B 3DA or their agents

Distributed in the UK, Europe and Asia by
Grantham Book Services
Trent Road, Grantham NG31 7XQ

Distributed in Australia and New Zealand by
Allen & Unwin Pty Ltd,
PO Box 8500, 83 Alexander Street,
Crows Nest, NSW 2065

Distributed in India by
Penguin Books India,
7th Floor, Infinity Tower – C, DLF Cyber City,
Gurgaon 122002, Haryana

Distributed in South Africa by
Jonathan Ball, Office B4, The District,
41 Sir Lowry Road, Woodstock 7925

ISBN: 978-178578-453-8

Typeset in Warnock by Marie Doherty

Printed and bound in Great Britain
by Clays Ltd, Elcograf S.p.A.

Contents

About the Author

James Riley is Fellow of English Literature at Girton College, University of Cambridge where he works on modern and contemporary literature, popular film and 1960s culture. Widely published, he has written for *The i*, *Fortean Times*, *Vertigo*, *Monolith* and *One+One*. He has contributed chapters to books on the fiction of the 1960s, ghosts, psychedelia, and contemporary protest. James has lectured internationally and has performed spoken word shows in London, Vienna and Coney Island, New York. He likes coffee, makes films and is the author of the blog *Residual Noise*.

Prologue: *Apotheosis*

In early September 1969, a small group of people arrived at an airfield in Hampshire close to the south-east coast of England. The weather was warm, but a thick bank of cloud had muffled the sun, creating a cold zone in the middle of the runway. As the group discussed their plans a large helium balloon inflated alongside them. It was not unusual to see weather balloons drifting across the sky in this part of the world, but the team that convened that day were not meteorologists. The group consisted of a musician, an artist, a cinematographer and a sound engineer, and their interest in balloons was not so much scientific as creative: they had turned up at the airfield to shoot a film.

The musician – tall with shoulder length hair, an obsessive stare and professorial glasses – was John Lennon of the Beatles. The artist – small with shoulder length hair, an obsessive stare and an aura of formidable intelligence – was Yoko Ono, avant-gardist of international repute.[1]

Lennon and Ono had recently married. They had met at an exhibition of Ono's work at London's Indica Gallery in mid-1966. They stayed in touch, gradually feeding each other's fascination until, in May 1968, they began a musical collaboration. Released as *Unfinished Music No. 1: Two Virgins* (1968) the album consisted of tape-loops, whistles and shrieks; it was a shock to most listeners matched only by the record's cover: Lennon and Ono naked, staring blankly at the camera. *Two Virgins* clearly, strategically and intentionally, told a different story to that of *Please Please Me* (1963). This was not a record made by four cheeky lads from Liverpool; this was a record made by two artists unafraid to challenge expectations of what 'music' should sound like and what musicians should look like.

Standing on the airfield as the balloon started to rise, Lennon would have been well placed to reflect on the differences between the albums, the stories they told and the versions of himself they represented. Indeed, since the recording of *Two Virgins* he had completely rebooted his life. He had left Cynthia and Julian, his wife and young son, to be with Ono; he had embarked on a new musical direction with the Plastic Ono Band, and he had left the Beatles, his musical partners of the last ten years. Their last public concert had been in January 1969, a jam-session on the roof of the Apple building in London's Savile Row. Forty minutes of noodling through 'Get Back' (1969) ended with the police turning up to complain about the volume.

Ono meanwhile had been catapulted from the relative obscurity of the contemporary art scene into the celebrity aura of her new husband. Along the way she experienced all the sexism and racism that came from being a Japanese-American woman in the public eye in the late 1960s, to say nothing of the ire she generated as the 'cause' of the Beatles' break-up.

Although the Beatles would publicly dissolve in April 1970 with McCartney's departure, it was at the start of September 1969, mere days before the airfield rendezvous, that Lennon had privately announced his intention to leave. Life in the band had become increasingly frustrating. The sessions for what would turn out to be their final two albums, *The Beatles*, aka the 'White Album' (1968) and *Let It Be* (1970), had been fractious and divisive. It felt like the four members – Lennon, McCartney, George Harrison and Ringo Starr – had been pulling in different creative directions.

There were other reasons, of course. Money, legal issues, the decision to stop touring, the mutual burnout that comes from spending more than a decade living with four other people. Lennon was also coming down following the Beatles' trip to India in 1968. Transcendental Meditation under the Maharishi Mahesh Yogi was not all that it had been cracked up to be and Lennon was left in a spiritual void. A void of enormous wealth and rock star privilege, but a void nonetheless. He was looking for something and someone to fill it. Shortly after their marriage, Lennon and Ono bought Tittenhurst Park, a mansion near Ascot in Berkshire. Away from London, the gaze of the media and the dying days of the Beatles, Lennon and Ono drifted further into their private world as intertwined artists. As Lennon would put it in a 1971 letter, they were now JOHNANDYOKO.[2]

Their day in Hampshire was part of this metamorphosis. They were there to make what became the short film *Apotheosis* (1970). The idea was simple: a camera attached to the balloon would record the flight until the film ran out. Lennon and Ono wanted a single shot that would show them gradually disappearing as the balloon flew higher.

The word 'apotheosis' means the process of ascent into the figure of a god: it's an acceptance of the divine. Some of Lennon's more conservative critics may have expected such arrogance from the man who, in 1966, had said the Beatles were 'bigger than Jesus', but in terms of Lennon and Ono's relationship, the film has a more personal message. *Apotheosis* depicts a movement beyond, a stark visual statement of rising above *everything*. Here are Lennon and Ono, stood at the crossroads of their personal and artistic lives, offering a clear sign that a new story is about to begin.

For all its simplicity though, if *Apotheosis* is about an escape or 'a release from earthly life', then it's a release that's never fully granted. The balloon ascends and goes elsewhere, Lennon and Ono do not. They remain on the ground, static and shrinking as the camera rises. Rather than a way of waving goodbye to the world and its concerns, the film speaks of the *desire* to depart: an act of incredible longing that's left unfulfilled.[3]

All of which begs the question, why was this desire so strong? Yes, they had personal problems and were embroiled in business matters, the likes of which they would continue to encounter in their life together. But apart from such tensions, what might Lennon and Ono have wanted to fly away from? Had the world become so terrible by September 1969 that they would want to leave it all behind? Why would anyone else, for that matter, want to try to escape from the sixties?

PART I

Demons Descending

CHAPTER I

The Devil's Business

On 9 August 1969, the actress Sharon Tate hosted a small party at 10050 Cielo Drive, the Los Angeles home she shared with her film director husband, Roman Polanski. With Polanski working in London, Tate, who was eight and a half months pregnant, had gathered her friends and house guests for the weekend. Present on the night were the celebrity hairdresser Jay Sebring who was Tate's long-term confidant and former boyfriend, Abigail Folger, heiress to the Folger Coffee Company, and her partner, the actor Wojciech Frykowski. Tate had met Polanski in 1966 and it was while working with him on *The Fearless Vampire Killers* (1967) that they became close. They had married in London in January 1968, just as Polanski was completing his second American feature: the Satanic horror movie *Rosemary's Baby* (1968). Based on Ira Levin's 1967 novel of the same name and featuring Mia Farrow as the young New Yorker Rosemary Woodhouse, the film charts her nightmarish pregnancy in the shadow of an occult conspiracy emanating from the city's sinister Bramford Building. For the newly-wed Polanskis, life could not have been more different. The expected arrival of their baby was a source of great joy and, far away from the noise of New York, 10050 Cielo Drive had become Tate's 'love house'. Since moving in in February 1969, much effort had gone into preparing the nursery.

Cielo Drive is an affluent residential area on the west side of Los Angeles. A classic retreat for the wealthier members of the city's entertainment industry, the drive has always been verdant, quiet and isolated. It's also close enough to Beverly Hills to enjoy the area's bustling social life. On the evening of the ninth, Tate and her friends had dined at El Coyote, a Mexican restaurant on Beverly Boulevard. Returning to the house, they spent the rest of night talking before retiring to bed. Everyone in the party would have drifted to sleep with every reason to feel safe in that house. In 1969 the villa at 10050 had the security that came with money and influence. It occupied a gated, three-acre site the entrance to which was at the peak of the drive, nestled into a cul-de-sac. Perfect for all the relaxed, celebrity gatherings the Polanskis had hosted since moving in. The perfect place, it seemed to Tate, to raise a child. Perfect, precisely because it was not the kind of place that you might wander by of an afternoon: you would only be there if you had a reason to be there. Which is why the night-time appearance of a carload of black-clad young people carrying ropes, knives, wire cutters and a gun should have caused concern. It should have, but it didn't. The privacy of Benedict Canyon was also its downside. People mind their own business in the LA hills.

It was shortly after midnight when Frykowski woke to the sound of movement in his room. He found a tall man looming over him. This was Charles 'Tex' Watson and he had arrived at the party with *his* friends: Susan Atkins, Patricia Krenwinkel and Linda Kasabian. They were members of the Family, a commune-cum-cult held together by the con man, criminal and sometime musician, Charles Manson. 'Who are you?', asked Frykowski, confused and disorientated. 'I'm the devil,' replied Watson. 'I'm here to do the devil's business. Give me all your money.'[1]

*

Towards the climax of *Rosemary's Baby* there's a scene in which Rosemary – exhausted from an apparent miscarriage and months of psychological distress – begins to hear a baby crying through her bedroom wall. She realises it is coming from the neighbouring apartment, the home of Minnie and Roman Castevet, the weird old couple who had been supportive at the start of her pregnancy but whose behaviour in the latter, traumatic, days had become sinister and threatening. Rosemary follows the noise and finds a strange partition in the hallway closet: a door that joins the two apartments. Brandishing a knife Rosemary creeps through and comes upon a dark gathering. Her husband Guy, the Castevets and the rest of the coven that populate the Bramford attend the presence of a baby: her baby. To Rosemary's horror it is put to her that the baby was born safely but Guy is not the father. The child has a more ominous parentage: he is the son of Satan, the devil born on Earth. It's a terrifying reveal but there's something about that partition door that carries a greater, more intimate horror and which goes some way to describing the horror that Frykowski must have felt when he encountered Watson. All the terrible things that have happened to Rosemary in the film have happened because of that door, because her private space has not been private. Finding the door confirms all of Rosemary's worst fears: your house is not your own, your body is not your own, your child is not your own. The devil has dominion everywhere.

Unfortunately for Frykowski and the rest of Tate's party, 'the devil's business' was not merely an act of theft. Watson, Atkins and Krenwinkel heeded Manson's order to 'destroy the house and everyone in it'. They had already killed Steven Parent, a young man who had come to see William Garretson, the caretaker at Cielo Drive. Garretson had spent the summer living in a cottage on the property: tending the garden, looking after the dogs, smoking weed. Parent had hung out with Garretson that evening, and when he left after midnight he ran right into Watson. They faced each other on the driveway for a few seconds before

Watson raised the gun he was holding and shot Parent four times. Garretson apparently heard none of this, nor did he hear the gunfire, screams and sounds of struggle that later came from the main house. Manson-lore has him listening to 'The End' (1967) by the Doors late into the night.[2]

Frykowski, Folger, Sebring and Tate were lined up in the living room. Frykowski had been bound in nylon rope. Watson told them all to get down on their stomachs. He was still asking for money at this point. Sebring made a lunge for him, received a gunshot to his side and was later beaten and stabbed to death. Meanwhile Tate, Folger and Frykowski were trussed with a rope that had been thrown over the ceiling beam, as if they were about to be hung. Frykowski struggled free and attacked Atkins before running for the front lawn to shout for help. He was stabbed and shot multiple times by both Atkins and Watson. Folger also got free and made for the back-porch door that led to the swimming pool but was killed by Krenwinkel. Multiple stab wounds. That left Tate who had witnessed the deaths of her three friends. She was stabbed sixteen times by Atkins, Watson and Krenwinkel. Watson then tied a joint noose around the necks of Tate and Sebring's bodies while Atkins used some of Tate's blood to smear 'PIG' on the wall.

The carnage at Cielo Drive was matched only by the deaths of Leno and Rosemary LaBianca the following night, 10 August. Manson decided to personally lead the death squad of Watson, Krenwinkel, and fellow Family member Leslie Van Houten. 'Doing' the Tate house had been far too disorganised, he thought. This time the proceedings would have some discipline. After setting out from their base of operations, the dilapidated Spahn Ranch on the Santa Susana Pass Road, they prowled the streets of central Los Angeles for an hour or two. Following Manson's lead Watson drove to the wealthy district of Los Feliz, close to Griffith

Park, finally alighting outside 3301 Waverly Drive, the LaBianca residence.

Dispensing with the inconvenience of unreliable firearms, Manson entered the house armed with a cutlass, as if leading a pirate raiding party. Sitting in his lounge, enjoying a beer in the early hours of Sunday morning, Leno looked up from his newspaper and found Manson – short, bearded and intense – looking at him, sword by his side. Leno looked at Manson, Manson stared back at Leno. Rosemary pottered in the bedroom. Another diabolical encounter, but this time there was no introduction, just a curt instruction from Manson: 'Be calm, sit down and be quiet.' Leno watched, in shock, as Manson went to the bedroom and retrieved Rosemary. She struggled and protested as Manson tied them together with long leather cords. 'Everything will be okay. You won't be hurt,' he said to them both as he took Rosemary's purse and walked back out the front door. A short time later, Watson and the others entered the house. They greeted the couple and quickly made it clear that this was not just a robbery.

The LaBiancas were separated, Leno remained in the front room, Rosemary was taken back to the bedroom. Using a carving knife taken from the kitchen, Watson killed Leno with multiple wounds to his chest and body. Rosemary, face down on the bedroom floor was killed next, stabbed by Krenwinkel and Van Houten. Leno's corpse was then mutilated. Watson cut a large 'X' into his chest before adding 'WAR'. Krenwinkel went at both bodies with a fork and then shoved it into Leno's abdomen. Emblazoned, and with the fork still sticking out, Leno was hooded with a pillow case. Just as they had done with Tate, the murderers then began to write in the blood of their victims, scrawling 'DEATH TO PIGS', 'RISE' and, most enduringly, 'HEALTER SKELTER' (sic) around the living room and the kitchen.[3]

Savagery. It is difficult to describe the Tate–LaBianca killings in any other terms. They speak of the violent loss of loved ones and murder at its most senseless. That said, as unpalatable as it seems, there was a certain kind of logic informing the deaths, albeit an extremely twisted logic. The motive had little to do with theft, despite the small amounts taken from each scene. Manson knew the house at Cielo Drive and had something of a grudge against its former resident, the music producer Terry Melcher, but killing Tate and her friends had little to do with revenge.[4] Instead, as was revealed during his protracted trial of 1970–71, the key was in the writing left behind. 'HEALTER SKELTER' was a reference to 'Helter Skelter', a Lennon and McCartney song from the 'White Album' which Manson had heard shortly after its release in November 1968.

'Helter Skelter' along with Lennon's 'Happiness is a Warm Gun' and George Harrison's 'Piggies' became touchstones for Manson and the Family. As he listened to the songs on a daily basis, Manson got a clear message of imminent societal breakdown. 'Look out', says 'Helter Skelter', things are 'coming down fast'. Life's 'getting worse', says 'Piggies', because the 'bigger piggies' in their 'starched white shirts' are 'Stirring up the dirt'. They need 'a damn good whacking', the realisation of which would lead to the empowerment, satisfaction and 'happiness' of the 'warm gun'. The aggression of these songs would have made it easy for someone like Manson to 'receive' an invitation to violence, and he came to believe that the Beatles were using their music to communicate with him directly. That said, Manson was neither a survivalist-in-waiting nor an earnest class warrior seeking a validation of his politics. Instead, the event he called and prepared for as 'Helter Skelter' was one part of a weirdly messianic personal narrative which far exceeded the themes and ideas dealt with on the 'White Album'.[5]

Whether he *really* believed this pitch or not, the outline, as prosecutor Vincent Bugliosi discovered during Manson's trial proceedings, went as follows. The *modus operandi* of the Family was to incite an apocalyptic race war between black and white America. They would do this by committing atrocious acts of murder in the homes of affluent white people, leaving suggestive evidence that the perpetrators were black. In the ensuing street battles and general chaos as decades of racial tension and mutual distrust came to the fore, the Manson Family would retreat to the desert of Death Valley in a convoy of high-powered dune buggies and descend into a secret subterranean world. There, in the imagined company of the Beatles themselves, the Family would sit out the destructive black revolution. They would remain hidden until the members of newly sovereign black nation inevitably faltered in their unfamiliar role as leaders. At which point Manson, his multiplied disciples and the Beatles would re-emerge from 'the bottomless pit' and assume their rightful place as rulers of the new dawn. This was 'Helter Skelter': the moment when the world as we, the squares and the straights, knew it would end and all that remained would come down to Manson as his rightful inheritance.[6]

The writer and journalist Joan Didion was living in Los Angeles at the time of the Tate–LaBianca murders. Her house on Franklin Avenue, in a once-opulent part of Hollywood, was large and roomy. She lived there with her husband and daughter; she played music there; held parties there and often hosted Sunday lunches that ran on into Monday. Rock bands lived across the street, Janis Joplin would drop by, and during the long weekend gatherings there was much talk of auras, zen and philosophy. The perfect sixties household: a space of togetherness, communality and free thinking. But for Didion this was to be a fleeting vision of the sixties. As the summer of 1969 came around things began to change. 'Everything had been so loose', recalled fellow writer Eve Babitz to journalist Barney Hoskyns, 'now it could never be loose again'. Where 'a guy with long hair' had been a 'brother' in 1967, by late 1969 'you just didn't know'.[7] On first reading, Didion's account of this period, her long essay 'The White Album' (1968–78), makes it clear that, whatever the apocalyptic ideas of Manson himself, the Tate–LaBianca murders marked out another 'end', one that was just as catastrophic but more specific. The work of the Manson Family, it seems, announced not the end of the world *per se*, but the end of a particular way of thinking and acting. The end of an era.[8]

The Family may have looked like hippies and talked like hippies, but unlike the peaceful flower children they were less interested in the expansion of consciousness than the pursuit of a collective death trip. Put into practice at Cielo Drive, this project had a seismic impact on the cultural landscape in the months that followed. Up and down the Sunset Strip, once-bustling clubs lost their clientele, and across the canyons the doors to previously open houses slammed shut. And it wasn't just a sense of fear that descended. The emergence of Manson and his followers seemed to ignite an attitudinal shift within the youth culture of Los Angeles and beyond. As Lennon remarked to *Rolling Stone* shortly after the murders became public, the Family exemplified a new generation of 'aggressive hippies', the 'uptight maniacs wearing peace symbols' who increasingly turned up at his door with bizarre interpretations of his lyrics.[9]

Such talk of 'aggressive hippies' in the national press would have likely brought to mind the wild-eyed picture of Manson that appeared on the cover of *Life* magazine on 19 December 1969. Staring out from underneath the headline 'The Love and Terror

Cult', like Rosemary's Satanic baby catapulted into adulthood, Manson was used to introduce America's reading public to 'the dark edge of hippie life'. Two years earlier, *Time* magazine had dispatched Robert Jones to report on the hippie scene, an assignment that resulted in the cover story: 'Hippie: The Philosophy of a Subculture'. In outlining what he took to be a consistent, coherent worldview, Jones spoke of 'young and generally thoughtful Americans' who were hoping 'to generate an entirely new society, one rich in spiritual grace that will revive the old virtues of agape and reverence'. Now here was Manson held up by *Life* as a dark glass to that new society. As a terrifying distortion of the popular images associated with the much-vaunted 'Summer of Love' and a figure who simultaneously confirmed the establishment view that nothing good could come from this new culture of the young, Manson thus came to signify the devil's business done; the traumatic cancellation of the hippie project; the dashing of the decade's utopian hopes: the end of the sixties.[10]

Charles Manson, formerly Charles Milles Maddox, arrived in San Francisco in March 1967. He was 32 years old and fresh out of prison. Manson had spent most of his life up until that point behind bars. His longest and most recent stretch – a ten-year sentence of which he served the best part of seven – was for violating an earlier set of parole terms and for trafficking women across state lines. Locked up from 1961 in Washington and then California the thief, hustler, con man and now pimp came under the sway of the usual prison influences. He learnt how to survive within the general population of gangsters and murderers, while also quietly learning from them: how to coerce, how to intimidate, how to control. Manson also threw himself into a period of self-improvement, taking courses on Dale Carnegie's *How to Win Friends and Influence People* (1936), participating in group therapy and reading up on psychiatry.

Prisons are petri dishes just as much as they are containers, and the varied methods used to deal with the problems of society often find their test beds among the incarcerated. The psychic landscape of post-war America was a heady mixture of individual effort and individual scrutiny – Benjamin Franklin meets Sigmund Freud – and in its attempt to cultivate the penitent, the prison system drew heavily on the techniques of this psychotherapeutic climate, aiming first for punishment and then for reprogramming. That Manson was taking to the library, rather than engaging in the violence that had marked his earlier stints in jail, seemed a validation of this rehabilitative American Dream. However, his interest in the psychology of self-improvement was professional just as much as it was personal. It helped with his depression and taught him to cope as a prisoner, but Manson was also fascinated by the insights it provided into the techniques of persuasion and suggestion, the various ways a personality could be broken down and rebuilt, and how a therapist could establish a subtle but dominant authority over an individual or an entire group. Having navigated the physical dangers of the prison yard, Manson turned to the inner world of the mind. He was, in other words, learning how to coerce, how to intimidate and how to control.

According to his biographer Simon Wells, Manson encountered three other points of influence while an inmate at McNeil Island prison, a trio of texts, ideas and images that would resonate with him for years to come. He read Robert Heinlein's science fiction novel *Stranger in a Strange Land* (1961); he learnt about L. Ron Hubbard and Scientology from his cellmate Lanier Ramer;

and, in February 1964, he saw the Beatles perform on *The Ed Sullivan Show*.[11]

An eclectic range of influences but not without points of overlap. *Stranger* tells the story of Valentine Michael Smith, a human born during a manned spaceflight to Mars. Raised as a Martian, Smith returns to Earth possessing extreme wealth, strange abilities and childlike innocence. Over the course of Heinlein's parable, Smith establishes the Church of All Worlds, a commune-style congregation that combines human religion, esoteric beliefs and aspects of Martian life. Smith is eventually killed as a heretic by members of a rival religious group, but his sexually charged, very wealthy followers continue the work of his church, setting forth at the close of the novel to transform human culture.

In 1950 Hubbard, a friend and sometime correspondent of Heinlein's, had published *Dianetics: The Modern Science of Mental Health*, a book that located the cause of psychological and physical ailments to the retention of 'engrams': traces of painful or traumatic memories stored in the unconscious or 'reactive' mind. *Dianetics* stated that through the application of an analytic technique called 'auditing', engrams could be erased from the mind – like recordings from magnetic tape – thus enabling the subject to become a 'clear', free of burdensome neuroses and fully able to pursue a life of high achievement. By 1954 Hubbard had developed his self-help system into the Church of Scientology, a religious organisation that promoted the spiritual significance of mental and physical health and used the principles of *Dianetics* as its central 'technology'.

Opinion differs as to whether Heinlein had Hubbard in mind when he wrote about Smith and the Church of All Worlds, but if you did harbour messianic fantasies, you could do worse than to transform your work of pop psychology into a fully fledged religion. Scientology promised much to its flock, clear minds and new beginnings; but within its deeply hierarchical structure, it also promised much to its auditors, the ability *to* clear minds and to offer new beginnings. As Ed Sanders said of Manson's enthusiasm for the discipline, his interpretation of its practices was of great use 'when he began to re-organise the minds of his young followers.'[12]

And the Beatles? How do they fit into this? Watching the *Ed Sullivan Show* in 1964 along with 73 million other viewers, Manson was presented with a curious spectacle. Here were four young men who had appeared from nowhere and yet seemed able to bring American culture to its knees. They could stop traffic, bring the nation to a halt and reduce crowds of teenagers to a screaming mass. If Heinlein and Hubbard offered the fictional and practical techniques necessary for the cultivation of a messianic mindset, for Manson the fame of the Beatles was the goal. Manson believed he could achieve their level of power and influence with the careful application of these tools.[13]

Manson initially gravitated towards San Francisco's Haight-Ashbury district out of necessity. With cheap housing and a range of free community services, the microclimate that revolved around the intersection of Haight and Ashbury Street was the ideal location for a parolee to find his feet. At the turn of the century, Haight-Ashbury had been a prosperous, middle-class area well served by the city's cable-car network. However, by mid-century the combined effect of the Great Depression and the threat of a proposed freeway project had reduced the area to a virtual ghost town. With residents moving out to the suburbs, the grand Victorian properties were turned into flats and boarding houses. At the same time rents were rising in North Beach, the city's beatnik enclave. The abandoned, dilapidated Haight thus became the go-to area for those wanting to live on the fringes.[14]

Economic shifts influence the fabric of every city, but what made the mid-sixties resettlement of Haight-Ashbury notable was the speed and extent to which its residents generated a vibrant culture. Shops, rock bands and various forms of social enterprise proliferated, with groups like the Diggers working to maintain the area's infrastructure. From 1966 the Haight also had its own newspaper, the *San Francisco Oracle* edited by Allen Cohen. As Danny Goldberg has recently outlined, these various interests did not always co-exist in harmony. The Diggers, led by Emmett Grogan and Peter Cohon, took their name from the 17th-century English radicals who cultivated common ground in defiance of laws regarding land rights. The Diggers of Haight-Ashbury similarly advocated a mode of communality in which everything could and should be free. They were into redistribution and recycling: taking the unwanted food from San Francisco's markets and cooking it up into a daily stew they distributed to the community. They also gathered up and gave away clothing in spaces they operated as 'free shops'. Such altruism was a boon to the large number of travellers, drifters and runaways who converged on the area as it – and its fame – grew. However, for the entrepreneurs and small businesses who attempted to cater to the same crowd, the Diggers' social agenda caused problems. Grogan saw any kind of commercialism as anathema to what his group were trying to achieve, and he was not afraid of letting shopkeepers and promoters know, even if they were bringing in vital revenue to local artists and producers. For the Diggers, the spectre of capital had no place in the Haight; instead they encouraged a gift economy, a collective of mutual support and a much more nebulous but no less pervasive currency of 'love'.[15]

These ideological differences aside, those who lived within and contributed to the ecology of the Haight saw it as a city within a city, one that attempted to exist away from the social obligations and financial expectations that governed post-war America. To this 'outside' world Haight-Ashbury was, by 1966, a zone of autonomous existence that exemplified the type of activity that has come to be known as the 'counterculture'.

Writing in 'Youth and the Great Refusal', a March 1968 article for *The Nation*, the American sociologist Theodore Roszak described the counterculture as:

> the effort to discover new types of community, new family patterns, new sexual mores, new kinds of livelihood, new aesthetic forms, new personal identities on the far side of power politics, the bourgeois home, and the Protestant work ethic.[16]

At least from an American perspective, the hippie was the stereotypical example of this 'effort'. In his report for *Time* Robert Jones described 'the cult of hippiedom' as those who:

> are unable to reconcile themselves to the stated values and implicit contradictions of contemporary Western society and have become internal émigrés seeking individual liberation through means as various as drug use, total withdrawal from the economy and the quest for individual identity.[17]

Roszak and Jones were both suggesting that at some point in the early to mid 1960s, a portion of America's 'youthquake' – its under-25 age group – morphed into a sector recognisably different from so-called 'mainstream' society. This was a separation made possible by the relative security that greeted the baby boomers as they came of age. Rather than claim the material benefits of this post-war affluence – the stereotypical suburban house, new car and solid white-collar job – this demographic eschewed such rewards in favour of communal experimentation. Alternative living patterns and alternative ways of thinking; minds opened not just by drug use but also through exposure to Eastern literature and a revival of interest in mysticism.

Jones and Roszak were not alone in their attempts to map this new post-war field. The word 'hippie' had emerged from a miasma of tabloid reporting between 1963 and 1967 which had in turn drawn upon jazz slang of the 1930s and 40s. 'Hippie' was taken from 'hipster' and 'hepcat', words for someone 'in the know', but which latterly became all-purpose labels to describe drug users, social misfits and 'beatniks' (yet another media term, from the late 1950s). This 'reportage' went hand in hand with works of popular sociology like Harrison E. Salisbury's *The Shook-up Generation* (1958) that applied a language of deviancy to visible trends in post-war youth culture. This generic grouping pulled together a wide range of activities under easily identifiable umbrella terms. As a diminutive 'hippie' is an extremely reductive term, while words like 'subculture' describe something 'lower' than, and by implication inferior to, 'mainstream' society.[18]

In contrast, Roszak's preference for '*counter*culture', particularly in the title of his 1969 book, *The Making of a Counterculture*, makes a very different claim. Looking over the events of the decade Roszak did not recognise a 'phase' of youthful rebellion but rather the strategic adoption of an alternative lifestyle. A lifestyle that was not just existing in parallel with but was at odds to the culture – the taste, the manners, the artistic and intellectual values, the maintained conventions – of the dominant socio-political landscape. To back up this claim, Roszak argued that the activities he described were not isolated examples, but markers of a widespread change of mood. Between 1965 and 1969, parallel behaviour could be seen on an international scale, in London, Liverpool, Paris, Amsterdam, Berlin and Tokyo: all urban centres with high concentrations of educated, creative and, crucially, disaffected young people. As Joseph Berke put it in his book *Counterculture* (1969), what lay behind the stoned stereotypes was a wave of youth-led, politically-orientated attempts to move away from 'the parental stem.' This was meant literally in terms of the nuclear family and metaphorically in terms of the governmental, economic and psychological structures of 'Western' (i.e. white middle-class) society.[19]

In January 1967 Golden Gate Park, the green and pleasant space that the Haight fed into, played host to 'a gathering of the tribes,' the Human Be-In. Spearheaded by Cohen and the *Oracle*'s art director Michael Bowen, the Be-In was part festival and part rally that attempted to unify the varied groups that made up San Francisco's complex subculture. Diggers, anti-war protesters, members of the *Berkeley Barb* and free speech activists were convinced by the 'heads' of the Haight to join in the public demonstration of a shared community ethos. The event involved speeches, blessings, group chanting and performances by a host of San Francisco bands including the Grateful Dead and Jefferson Airplane. Overall though, the crowd (which peaked at around 30,000) *was* the event.

It was at the Be-In that Timothy Leary, ex-Harvard academic turned LSD proselytiser encouraged the crowd to 'turn-on, tune-in and drop-out.' Although this invitation to a kind of radical solipsism jarred with the far-left rhetoric on display elsewhere during the day, it was perfectly in sync with the mantras and peace invocations of poets Allen Ginsberg and Gary Snyder who opened the event. Stalwarts of the 1950s Beat scene, in the intervening years Ginsberg and Snyder had undergone a deep immersion in Hindu and Buddhist religious practices. Resplendent with beards, prayer beads and ritual conch shells, they looked like holy men, and by bookending the event with such sacred sentiments, they symbolised what has become the enduring image of the Be-In and the culture it reflected. This un-anchored 'new society' of the young was embarking on a spiritualised separation from mainstream society.[20]

While the 'crusades' of evangelist Billy Graham rumbled on and the American Bible Society's *Good News for Modern Man* (1966) became the text of choice for the Christian Church, the proceedings of the Be-In indicated that the counterculture was developing a kind of ground zero religion. This melange of Eastern spirituality, 'alternative' living and consciousness expansion would soon reside under the indistinct umbrella of 'New Age', but for the collective counterculture that took the Haight as its base, these ideas were crucial to its growing mythology and public status as a burgeoning social movement.

The astrologer Gavin Arthur laid much of the philosophical groundwork for the Be-In via his regular column for the *Oracle*. He had also been consulted during its planning and had determined 14 January as the most astrologically congenial date for a harmonious mass gathering. Aged 66 in 1967, Arthur was something of an elder statesman among the San Francisco counterculture: a mystical teacher with an eventful life behind him that had involved gold prospecting, commune leadership and, as detailed in his book *The Circle of Sex* (1962), esoteric sexology. Drawing on various sources including the theosophist Madame Blavatsky, he came to see the 1960s as marking a great and long-lasting change in the direction of human culture. This optimistic tribe of the young bringing forth messages of peace and happiness held up a way of life that rejected the violence and warfare that had dominated the lives of previous generations. As Gary Lachman explains, Arthur looked forward to a coming era of 'brotherhood' and 'universality', dubbing the 1960s 'The Age of Aquarius'.

Behind this popular image lies a long history of stargazing and prediction, a tradition of speculation that relates to nothing less than change of cosmic significance. 'Astronomically', as Lachman continues, the Age of Aquarius is 'the effect of a wobble in the Earth's rotation, part of a curious phenomenon known as the "precession of the equinoxes"'. Roughly every 2,000 years, 'the constellation against which the sun rises [...] at dawn on the vernal equinox changes'. In the 20th century it rose against Pisces, having shifted from Aries just prior to the birth of Christ. The next constellation would be Aquarius, which should occur sometime around the year 2000, 'give or take a century or two'. Arthur could not have made a grander claim about the 1960s. To be entering the Age of Aquarius meant to be embarking on 'a massive change in consciousness, a return, in short, to the Golden Age'.[21]

The 'Golden Age' refers to a mythical, prelapsarian state of unity between men and gods. It is described in *Works and Days*, an essay on agricultural life written around 700 BC by the Greek poet Hesiod. Hesiod imagines a rural idyll 'remote from toil and misery' in which golden fields of grain yield harvest after harvest. There's no strife in the Golden Age. Everyone is free to spend their time feasting and enjoying the world's abundance. However, it doesn't last. Hesiod goes onto describe a long period of decline across four successive ages of human culture, each one further lacking the lustre and luxury of the first: the Silver Age, the Bronze Age, the Heroic Age and the Iron Age. The last, the Iron Age, is the most recent and corresponds to Hesiod's own time in the late 8th and early 7th centuries BC. He describes a climate of toil, conflict and distress. According to Hesiod the Iron Age is one of enmity in which brothers turn on each other and violence prevails. Scholarly opinion differs as to whether he was describing a period of actual crisis or if he was offering cautionary instruction on the responsibilities of the farmer. Either way, in *Works and Days*, the Golden Age stands as a shining symbol of society at its best. It's an image of a wonderful, lost world, but Hesiod suggests its joys can be revived if we humans choose to live in harmony with the land, the gods and each other.

In the *Oracle*, Gavin Arthur was not writing about the agricultural landscapes of ancient Greece, but he was tying a predicted astronomical shift to a hoped-for change in society at large. If the Age of Pisces coincided with the birth of Christ, the Age of Aquarius was a new dawn rising, a potential step away from the behaviour and attitudes associated with Christianity: patriarchy, hierarchical beliefs, suffering, guilt, repression, the pain of Christ on the cross. With Haight-Ashbury flourishing before him and the new millennium approaching on the horizon, it seemed to Arthur the right time to shed these beliefs, re-write the rulebook and rebuild something like the Golden Age; to live, as Hesiod would put it, 'like gods with carefree heart'.[22]

Arthur was not the only one to make such pronouncements, nor was he the only writer to have an impact on the esoteric thinking of the counterculture. As Lachman has shown, the 1960s saw a revival of interest in previously obscure magicians and mystic writers. Thanks to the availability of mass-market paperbacks like Louis Pauwels and Jacques Bergier's *The Morning of the Magicians* (1960), adventurous sixties readers were able to get a crash course in the work of Madame Blavatsky, P.D. Ouspensky and George

Gurdjieff, among others.[23] Another person of interest was the British writer and occultist Aleister Crowley. A regular name in the scandal sheets of the inter-war period, Crowley's public status as a ritual magician, drug user and general libertine earned him the enduring title of 'The Wickedest Man in the World'. In 1903 Crowley married Rose Edith Kelly and embarked on a long honeymoon trip that brought them to Cairo in the spring of 1904. There Crowley claimed to have established contact with his Holy Guardian Angel, a disincarnate entity he called 'Aiwass'. Aiwass allegedly spoke to him over the course of three days and Crowley incorporated these messages into his doctrinal text *The Book of the Law* (1904).

The Book of the Law became Crowley's mission statement in which he outlined his system of magic and the religious philosophy he called 'Thelema'. Named after the Greek word for 'will', Thelema directed its followers towards the realisation of their true 'will', a sense of calling, purpose and identity that exceeds one's own conscious desire. History, according to the Thelemic worldview moves through a series of religious phases or 'aeons' characterised by different spiritual practices. What Crowley announced with the publication of *The Book of the Law* was the latest shift in this cosmic calendar, the inauguration of a new aeon. Where Arthur plotted the shift of ages astronomically according the sign of the zodiac, Crowley took his cue from the Egyptian mythology linked to Cairo and the supernatural voice of Aiwass. The new aeon was dubbed the Aeon of Horus, and Crowley believed that it was his 'will' to act as its herald. In the Egyptian pantheon Horus is the offspring of Isis and Osiris, a falcon-headed god associated with the sun and the sky: a powerful deity of light who casts away all darkness. To Crowley, Horus was the 'crowned and conquering child', a dynamic, unruly deity who symbolised a movement away from the religious orthodoxies of previous aeons, the goddess worship of Isis and the patriarchal authority of Osiris. Although he was drawing on a very different mythology, in announcing the Aeon of Horus, Crowley was expressing a conviction similar to Arthur's hopes for the Age of Aquarius: the world was on the cusp of a great change, one that would see the old order come to an end and a joyous new way of life take its place.[24]

Crowley, who died in 1947, is one of the many famous faces chosen by the Beatles to appear on the album cover for *Sgt. Pepper's Lonely Hearts Club Band* (1967). He stands in the top left corner nestled between Swami Sri Yukteswar Giri and Mae West. Beyond this fleeting appearance, his work more readily fed into the fabric of the counterculture by way of another Haight resident, Kenneth Anger. Anger, a dedicated follower of Thelema, is a filmmaker and occultist who places himself firmly in Crowley's lineage. Anger's signature style is a combination of high-camp, esoteric symbolism and an abiding fascination with the inner workings of secret groups and coteries. His 1954 film *Inauguration of the Pleasuredome* shows LA's occult celebrities performing a series of luxurious rituals. In *Scorpio Rising* (1963) Anger fetishised the black leather and chrome that formed the erotic core of Marlon Brando's performance in *The Wild One* (1953). *Kustom Kar Kommandos* (1965) did much the same for hot rod enthusiasts, and both films displayed Anger's pre-MTV ability to match vivid images with choice cuts of pop music.

The mid 1960s found Anger in Haight-Ashbury living in the Russian Embassy – not the actual embassy – but one of the Haight's legendary palatial houses that also doubled as a venue, thanks to its large ballroom on the ground floor. Anger lodged there along with the usual crowd of musicians and artists, and he began work on a film called *Lucifer Rising*. It would be 1980 before the film was complete after undergoing numerous changes in direction and personnel. The version he worked on between 1966 and 1967 was to be an expression of his belief that cosmic history was about to move into a new phase. In throwing the name 'Lucifer' into the counterculture's melting pot of references and symbolism, Anger was invoking the rebellious archangel of Christian myth and John Milton's epic poem *Paradise Lost* (1667). Lucifer is a fallen angel, the bright star who is cast out of heaven after challenging the authority of God. Landing in hell, he becomes Satan, God's adversary. Like Horus then, Lucifer is a figure of disobedience, another deity who goes against the law of the father. For Anger though, the attraction of Lucifer lay in his ambivalence. He is both angel and devil, the ultimate bad boy, good precisely because he is so wicked: a kind of biblical James Dean.

With *Lucifer Rising*, Anger was celebrating the power of this beautifully defiant attitude. If the new dawn was to come it would require such a shining star, or better still a cadre of such figures to light the way forward for the rest of the world. Anger found such heralds in the Haight's vibrant artistic scene. In particular, a young musician called Bobby Beausoleil seemed to Anger to typify the rebellious Luciferian spirit. Depending on which source you read, Anger first met Beausoleil at 'The Invisible Circus', an orgy organised by the Diggers at Glide Memorial Church in February 1967, or at the Brave New World, a gay bar in Los Angeles, sometime in 1965. Either way by early 1967 Beausoleil had become Anger's protégé and a fixture of his life in San Francisco. Beausoleil opened the city to Anger and brought like-minded people into their developing circle. With Anger's encouragement, Beausoleil took on the film's central role of Lucifer, and he began to work on a suitably epic soundtrack for the project, a potent mix of Wagner and psychedelic rock. In September 1967, the pair celebrated the autumnal equinox with 'Equinox of the Gods', a live show that featured Anger performing magical rituals alongside Beausoleil's music. The event was filmed, and Anger originally planned for the footage of him in full flight to be included in *Lucifer Rising*. He intended for this material, coupled with footage taken at the Russian Embassy showing a 'Wand-Bearer' presiding over a group of acolytes, to show that within America's post-war demographic, ancient knowledge had become indigenous to the children of Horus. In other words, the Age of Aquarius would be brought about by the new culture of the young.[25]

Landing in March 1967, Manson would have benefitted from the day-to-day markers of the Haight's cultural independence – crash pads, street charity, legal clinics – but he also would have been able to bask in this harmonious sense of goodwill, the positive energy generated as the area transformed into the *symbolic* capital of the counterculture. He looked the part, he carried – along with practically every other new arrival – a guitar on which he played his own songs, and with a headful of the Beatles, Robert Heinlein and L. Ron Hubbard, he quickly tuned into the Haight's wavelength. With its communes, its cosmic mysticism, its emphasis on free sex and its clear desire to challenge the social mores of the day, *Stranger in a Strange Land* already had its place in the Aquarian mindset when Manson arrived. Indeed, one of Heinlein's Martian coinages, the verb 'grok', meaning to know or to understand something to the point of absorption, had by 1967 become part of what Jay Stevens has called the 'hippie *sprecht*'. This 'charged code' helped to mark out one's membership of the counterculture while also succinctly expressing its key ideas. Manson grokked the Haight and the Haight grokked him back.[26]

That said, a listen to Manson's music indicates that his thinking was moving in a different, darker direction than that plotted by the Be-In and Gavin Arthur's speculations. Early songs like 'Sick City' with its 'restless' speaker desperate to leave the uncaring, miserable town that's 'killing' them initially seems like a straightforward blues number. Having taken to the guitar while in prison before honing his style busking on the streets, it's not surprising that Manson's initial efforts would comfortably fit within a tried and tested mode: a song about the misery of privation and the desire for a better life. Where other songs of this type, Bob Dylan's 'Down the Highway' (1963) for example, involve the singer stating their problems to move beyond them, the lyrics of 'Sick City' boil with rage and confusion. The 'restless people / From the sick city' are said to have 'burnt their houses down', a spectacle that makes 'the sky look pretty'. On one level this is restlessness taken to the extreme: people set fires across the city because there's simply nothing better to do. On another, Manson seems to be singing about an ominous social divide. Shut out of the city's affluence, the restless take destructive revenge upon those who seem to have it all.

'Cease to Exist', a song Manson wrote and recorded in 1968, lacks the overt aggression of 'Sick City' but is equally sinister in its evocation of a smothering psychodrama between its speaker and a 'pretty girl'. With such unremarkable platitudes as 'I love you pretty girl / My world is yours', there's initially little to separate the lyrics from any number of sugar-sweet pop songs. Just as he had heard the Beatles do it on *The Ed Sullivan Show* with 'I Want to Hold Your Hand' (1964), Manson expresses his love and looks for it in return. With the Beatles though, however intense the hormonal rush is that propels the song forward, the address remains politely chaste. In asking 'please … let me be your man' and 'please … let me hold your hand', their song is about permission just as much as it is about desire. Not so with 'Cease to Exist'. Here, the expression of love is not just hyperbolically overwhelming but an outright act of domination. The invitation is for the pretty girl to 'Give up [her] world' by recognising that 'Submission is a gift'. There's a fair amount of grokking going on, but it's an annihilating process in which the identity of Manson's speaker eclipses that of the girl: 'I'm your kind / I'm your mind / I'm your brother'. 'Cease to Exist' is the Beatles filtered through Heinlein, Hubbard and the group mind that was taking shape in Manson's Family: a pop song designed for a cult.[27]

Compare both 'Sick City' and 'Cease to Exist' with Jefferson Airplane's 'Somebody to Love' (1967) and Manson's divergence from the general ethos of the counterculture becomes clear. Recorded for the band's second album *Surrealistic Pillow* (released one month after the Be-In in February 1967), 'Somebody to Love' has, together with 'White Rabbit' (1967), become one of the classics of the era. Written by Darby Slick for his band the Great Society, the track was originally recorded in 1966 as 'Someone to Love' before vocalist Grace Slick graduated to Jefferson Airplane and took the song with her. Combining folk music and psychedelic rock alongside a soaring vocal performance, 'Somebody to Love' conjures up a scene of discord and despair: truth found to be lies, joy dying inside and gardens of dead flowers. Darby Slick had just broken up with his girlfriend when he wrote the lyrics and was clearly working through his angst. Out of this misery though, having 'somebody to love' becomes a matter of survival, a necessity when times are bad. Across the song's catalogue of problems that range from black moods to false friends, a bond with 'somebody' else is offered as the all-purpose solution. It's a simple message that would be utterly naïve were it not for its relevance and applicability at the time.[28]

By 1967 American troop deployment in Vietnam stood at 485,000. Despite this heavy presence it appeared that little strategic progress was being made and American, South Vietnamese and North Vietnamese forces were merely becoming bogged down in a protracted and increasingly bloody conflict. In response, domestic anti-war protest and equivalent movements in the UK were becoming vociferous in their opposition. While 1968 would see these passions boil over into aggressive public demonstrations, 1967 was marked by some exemplary acts of non-violent protest. 'Flower Power' (1967), a photograph by Bernie Boston originally published in *The Washington Star*, shows a young man placing a flower in the barrel of a rifle held by a military policeman. The confrontation occurred in October 1967 during a march on the Pentagon organised by the 'Mobe' or National Mobilization Committee to End the War in Vietnam. This was the event documented by Norman Mailer in *The Armies of the Night* (1968) during which Allen Ginsberg, Ed Sanders and a contingent of the amassed protestors attempted to 'levitate' the Pentagon building as a means of 'exorcising' the 'evil' it contained. As well as neutralising conflict on the day, the offer of flowers also helped to set out the Mobe's political standpoint: violence was not an inevitability, it was a choice. This is beautifully captured in Boston's image. The gesture of the young man is a refusal to engage in violence, an attempt to show that empathy and compassion can win out over combat.[29]

Although any mention of 'love' in a countercultural context invariably suggests vague ideas of 'free love' and sexual indulgence, the line of thought leading from Jefferson Airplane to 'Flower Power' was much more expressive of a humanitarian philosophy. The same potency coloured phrases like 'Summer of Love'. Overused as a media caption, it is often unclear exactly what this describes or even if it took place at all. That said, as the Haight swelled to bursting point during the middle of 1967 with travellers, tourists and college students alike making it a site of pilgrimage, the hastily convened 'Council for the Summer of Love' tried to ensure that the community could cope. As Danny Goldberg describes, notices in the *Oracle* 'exhorted all new visitors to bring warm clothing, food, ID, sleeping bags and camping equipment.' This was not the invitation to the orgy that new residents may have expected or hoped for. Instead, the encouragement was towards a duty of care. To love one another means to live in harmony, to make the experimental community work and thereby demonstrate to all who care to look, that another way is possible. Treat the next person along as your sister or brother, show them respect rather than suspicion, and there will be no need for words like 'enemy.'[30]

That's not how it worked with Manson. When he gathered Watson, Atkins, Krenwinkel and the other members of the Family together there was talk of love and care. Manson's oft-repeated claim was that he was lord of the 'garbage people'; that he was taking under his wing the misfits and the outsiders, those whom society had cast aside. In reality, he worked by reinforcing in his followers a sense of their own worthlessness, separating them from forms of possible support and in turn assuming the role of a dominant father figure, one who demanded obedience to the point of self-erasure. By encouraging a state of hypervigilance, Manson also fostered within the Family a sense of impending hostility. It was a matter of 'Us' against 'Them.' What the Family called 'Creepy Crawls' were the perfect breeding ground for this group mentality. Sent out in squads on overnight raids, Family members were instructed to break into houses, move furniture and damage stuff. Nothing was to be stolen, but enough was to be done to make homeowners know someone had been there. In their house. In their beds. Part power trip and part training exercise, 'Creepy Crawls' also helped to cement the Family's outsider mentality. Comfortable living rooms, pictures of the grandkids, nice dinner tables: these were things other people had. Not satisfied with living in communal separation from this world in the space they had created at Spahn Ranch, the Manson family would restlessly creep in and out of the suburbs, aiming to scupper its sense of security with a gnawing sense of unease.[31]

Creepiness was a feeling that Joan Didion knew well. Living in her Franklin Avenue home, slowly processing the thoughts that would become her essay 'The White Album', it was the crawl *towards* suspicion and the nagging sense that – contrary to what the *Oracle* might say – enemies were *all around*, which made her think the sixties were coming to an end. In the essay, she describes phone calls from a musician acquaintance who tells her she can be saved 'through Scientology'; a 'stranger from Montreal' who is concerned that 'Big Brother' might be listening on the phone tries to enlist her 'in a narcotics operation'; and a former school friend turns up in 'the guise of a private detective from West Covina' and encourages Didion to meet her 'very close friends in law enforcement'. These were not 'atypical encounters of the period' reflects Didion, but the 'Sixties were over' before it 'occurred to [her]' that the visits, particularly the last, 'might have been less than entirely social'.

Across the essay Didion deftly paints a portrait of a culture in crisis. As well as the Manson murders that haunt the text like malevolent ghosts, she also mentions the funeral of Senator Robert Kennedy following his assassination on 6 June 1968 and her reactions to the first reports of the My Lai massacre of March 1968. Also known as 'Pinkville', this was the incident in which US troops were suspected of unlawfully killing 500 inhabitants of a South Vietnamese village. Later, Didion recounts an encounter with Huey P. Newton, founder of the Black Panther Party following his arrest for allegedly shooting the Oakland Police Officer John Frey in October 1967. Other isolated but no less disturbing incidents embellish the picture such as 'the story of Betty Lansdown Fouquet' a young woman who 'put her five-year-old daughter out to die on the centre divider of Interstate 5 some miles south of the last Bakersfield exit'. None of these images matches the day-glo optimism and peace sentiments we have come to associate with the Age of Aquarius, and for Didion, writing with a mix of incredulity and horrified puzzlement, they refuse to 'fit into' any narratives she was aware of. Around these events Didion weaves a personal account of her nervous breakdown, an attack of 'vertigo and nausea' which she comes to see as a not 'inappropriate response to the summer of 1968'. Within this panorama, the events of Cielo Drive carry such an impact not because they disturb the peace of a hitherto untroubled decade but because they legitimate Didion's anxiety. They tell her that she *should* be worried. For Didion, the 'tension broke' on 9 August 1969, the 'paranoia was fulfilled.'[32]

Whatever the sense of energy, optimism and *communitas* we might associate with Haight-Ashbury and the diverse counterculture of 1967, reading Didion's 'The White Album' it seems that by 1969 something had gone very wrong. Or, more likely, what *Time* magazine presented in July 1967 as the hippy 'subculture' was soon revealed to be a small sector in a much wider national and international scenario of violence, intolerance and human damage. Either way, when Didion writes of Manson, and how news of the deaths at Cielo Drive marked the 'precise moment' when 'the Sixties came to an end', she has in mind not the close of the decade but the evaporation of what 'the Sixties' had come to signify.[33] For the denizens of the Haight 'the Sixties' signalled the birth of a new, youth-led society that plotted out a levelling agenda of social activism. For Didion, the period gave rise only to a pervasive sense of fear and confusion. Didion writes at a very personal level, about herself and her subjects, but her essays, not least 'The White Album', chase the bigger fish. Coming in and out of focus as the essay develops, Didion's Manson is a catalyst, a presence in the essay that's alluded to in order to mark an ominous sense of social and political change.

Other writers dealing with the late 1960s have since followed Didion's lead and have presented Manson as a figure emblematic of the end of the sixties. For the investigative journalist Maury Terry, he is the 'ultimate evil', personally and individually responsible for the decade's decline. For Simon Wells, Manson's role is much more symbolic. As he puts it, 'the Manson saga brought the 1960s to a deeply unhappy close' because the horror of his acts cancelled the counterculture's hopes for a revolution that could 'free mankind and build a world based on peace and love'. James Parks makes a similar point when describing how Manson's 'peculiar cocktail of black magic, drugs, sex and rock 'n' roll' demonstrated 'that the fragrance of love hanging over the 1960s was mutating into violence and barbarity'. Writing in *Acid Dreams* (1985), their social history of LSD, Martin A. Lee and Bruce Shlain combine each of these views. They see the 'Manson affair' as an act so terrible that it shatters the dream of the sixties; it refutes 'the sixties myth that anyone who took LSD would automatically become holy or reverential'. At the same time, they present Manson as a mirror, someone who merely reflected attitudes that already circulated during the decade. In their words the tendency of 'certain segments of the counterculture' to 'canonize' Manson 'was a measure of how desperate and bitter people had become in the final days of the 1960s'.[34]

Manson clearly casts a long shadow in the popular history of the sixties, but the fact does remain that the Tate–LaBianca murders were not the only terrible acts that loomed large over the decade. Even if you look beyond the assassinations of John F. Kennedy, Robert Kennedy and Martin Luther King, the American sixties remains a decade of violence, one populated, for example, by a brigade of serial killers responsible for deaths that far exceed the body count associated with the Manson Family. Between 1962 and 1964, Albert DeSalvo, the so-called 'Boston Strangler' killed thirteen women in and around the city, and 1968 saw the trial of Ed Gein, the notorious 'Butcher of Plainfield'. As the Tate–LaBianca murders took place, the never-caught and still never fully identified 'Zodiac Killer' was roaming round the San Francisco Bay Area heavily armed, just as the 'Co-Ed Killer', Edmund Kemper, began to look for hitchhikers along the roads of California.

That said, few of these cases have the enduring resonance of Manson and the Family. By the time Manson's trial had reached its conclusion in 1971, the murders had become inextricably linked to the aura of Sharon Tate, Roman Polanski and the LA celebrity elite as well as the Beatles, the Californian counterculture and the hinterlands of the music industry that stood in between. Add to this the apocalyptic overtones of Polanksi's *Rosemary's Baby*, to say nothing of Tate's earlier film role as a witch in J. Lee Thompson's *Eye of the Devil* (1966) and the tempting haze of an occult conspiracy begins to emerge. Early accounts of the Manson case, such as Ed Sanders' *The Family* (1971), highlighted alleged links to esoteric groups such as Anton LaVey's Church of Satan and

Robert de Grimston's the Process Church of the Final Judgement (of which more later). Ninth of August, as more than one commentator has been keen to point out, also coincides with the date of the American detonation of the plutonium bomb over Nagasaki in 1945. Pull these strands together and Manson appears as the portentous enemy of the sixties, a demon in the truest sense of the word: an evil spirit of the age that embodies all its anxieties and works for its downfall. In *Rosemary's Baby* it is predicted that Adrian, son of Satan will 'overthrow the mighty and lay waste their temples.' Accounts of the sixties that present August 1969 as the decade's terminal end, consciously or not, cast Manson in a similarly diabolical role. It is as if, in orchestrating the devil's business at Cielo Drive, with this weight of uncanny expectation behind him, Manson becomes a dreadful dark star. Somehow, in fuelling the murder of Tate and her friends, he manages to snuff out all the light that had previously radiated from the counterculture.[35]

'We tell ourselves stories in order to live,' writes Didion at the start of 'The White Album.' The sixties have inspired and continue to inspire an enormous number of stories. Whether you were there or not, whether you can remember them or not, the sixties remain a vibrant and difficult decade. That the end of the sixties should appear so notable, particularly when the curtain appears to fall in such disastrous terms, speaks volumes about the exceptionalism of the period as a whole. An oasis of colour between the drab fifties and hungover seventies, the sixties continually stand alone in the public imagination. Framing their closure as a point of personal and cultural tragedy helps to generate the nostalgia upon which this status relies. If only the sixties hadn't ended, if only we could go back. For all the horror it brings to mind, Manson's face on the cover of *Time* magazine is an important part of this rose-tinted view. What else could be expected from such a supernova of a decade like the sixties than a spectacular burnout?

Of course, the reality of the situation is somewhat different. The 1960s were neither glorious nor doomed. During the decade plenty of things happened the likes of which had neither been seen before nor since and, as 1969 approached, the atmosphere in various quarters did indeed take a turn for the weird. However, much the same could be said about any other decade of the 20th century. Also, no one person or event managed to bring the sixties to a definite close. Despite the protest, the experimentalism and the creativity, things merely moved on, and that's probably more unpalatable a thought than imagining the sixties blowing up and filling the screen with smithereens. The end of the sixties is thus one story among many but, as Didion's words imply, it's a story that serves a particular function. To unpack what is meant by the stories of Manson and a constellation of fellow dark stars who circulated through the decade it is necessary to look back to an earlier vantage point. Not exactly the start of the decade but something harder to pin down: the point of overlap where the decade and the era started to blur, and the sixties rose up out of the 1960s.

CHAPTER II

Bomb Culture

On 11 June 1965, a 28-year-old filmmaker called Peter Whitehead set out from his studio in London's Soho and walked over to South Kensington. It was a glorious summer's evening, Hyde Park looked beautiful, and he was on his way to the Royal Albert Hall, the city's grandest venue. Whitehead had spent the past few days pulling in favours and gathering equipment: for £10 he had rented a portable 16mm camera from the cinematographer Louis Wolfers; and a loan of £90 from the writers Brian and Elinor Shaffer had bought him four rolls of black and white film. That night the Albert Hall was playing host to the International Poetry Incarnation, a hastily organised large-scale poetry reading featuring American Beat poets Allen Ginsberg, Lawrence Ferlinghetti, Gregory Corso and an array of British and European performers. Whitehead was there to record the proceedings.

Since enrolling at the embryonic film department at the Slade School of Art in 1963, Whitehead had made two short films, worked on an educational documentary about microscopes for the Nuffield Foundation and had otherwise paid his dues as a newsreel cameraman for Italian and Greek television and by making promotional films for *Top of the Pops*. The Albert Hall would be Whitehead's biggest gig yet, a chance to shoot some of the key names in the underground literature scene live on stage and maybe put a documentary out under his own name. That is, should the event go as planned; should anyone actually turn up.[1]

A month earlier on 19 May, Whitehead had seen Ginsberg read at Better Books, a bookshop on Charing Cross Road that served as a magnet for anyone interested in alternative literature. The shop had close links with San Francisco's Beat-hub City Lights Books, and so when Ginsberg arrived in London, having been elected King of May in Czechoslovakia before being deported for 'subversive activities', Better Books was an obvious port of call. For the network of readers, writers, poets and artists who revolved around the shop – among them Jeff Nuttall, Barry Miles, Alexander Trocchi and Michael Horovitz – Ginsberg's arrival was a major event. The author of *Howl* (1956) was an already legendary figure, a poet whose intertwined life and work had broken taboos, pushed against the law and told a generation of readers that they need not accept the status quo.

Whitehead arrived to find Better Books packed to the rafters. Andy Warhol was in attendance, as was another visiting luminary of the American avant-garde, the filmmaker Barbara Rubin. As Whitehead sat at the back snapping still photographs of this glittering crowd, Ginsberg read from his journals and recited polemical poems like 'King of May' and 'Who will Take over the Universe'. These missives bore witness to Ginsberg's belief in poetry as a critical, progressive force. In declaring that 'the revolution in America had begun' while denouncing 'Communists' who 'have nothing to offer', Ginsberg was making it clear that poetry was about far more than the craft of rhetoric. For Ginsberg, poetry could, and should, make things happen.

Although the world didn't change that night, the effect of Ginsberg's presence was nonetheless catalytic. The reading made things happen: people started to talk about another gig and a larger venue, the largest one possible. As Whitehead remembers it, these plans came together *immediately*. While Ginsberg circulated in the afterglow, Whitehead wandered over to one of the room's excited huddles and made the acquaintance of John Esam.

Esam was an American poet living in London who was good friends with another expatriate writer, Dan Richter. Whitehead thought Esam was 'a bit of an operator', certainly when he started talking about the Albert Hall, of all places, but not wanting to miss an opportunity, he offered his services on the spot. 'Look, I'm a cameraman,' said Whitehead, 'I've made films before ... and if you're really going to do this, I'll come along and film it.' There was a handshake, and everyone dissolved merrily into the night. A few weeks passed and then out of the blue Whitehead got a phone call from Esam. The Albert Hall was booked, Ginsberg would be reading along with poets from all over the world, and they did indeed want Whitehead to film it all. Oh, and it was going to happen in about two days' time. How does that sound? 'Well ... fine OK,' responded Whitehead with classic understatement, his mind already racing through lists of all the gear he'd need to borrow.[2]

On the other end of the phone things were equally hectic for Esam, but there had been rather more organisation involved than Whitehead's account gives credit for. Esam had in fact been working with Richter as part of the Poets' Co-operative, a loose collective formed with the Better Books crowd that had taken on the task of bringing the Albert Hall event to fruition. According to Sue Miles, who along with her then-husband Barry was hosting Ginsberg in their Hanson Street flat, the idea was conceived in the days that followed the May reading. Various venues were considered before Rubin, who had been staying on in London as part of Ginsberg's entourage, asked the obvious question: 'What's the biggest hall in town?' One phone call later and the Albert Hall's next available date on 11 June was booked. It was a mere ten days away. Dan Richter's wife Jill put up the £450 booking fee. While the Americans in the group got on with the important task of promotion and logistics, the English contingent got on with the important task of hand-wringing and worry: will anyone come? Will we fill it? Will Jill ever get her money back?

The word went around the London poetry scene and, as manager of Better Books, Barry Miles was happy to handle ticket sales from the shop. This would have been fine for the usual poetry audience of about 25 or so, but the Albert Hall held a few more (about 7,000), so it fell to Rubin and company to forge ahead with the publicity campaign. Press releases were sent to all the major newspapers and a series of press conferences were held with Ginsberg and the ever-increasing catalogue of poets who'd got wind of the event and wanted to perform. The reading was going to be anchored around Ginsberg, Ferlinghetti and Corso, with Ginsberg as the headliner. Trocchi was going to be the compere and, somehow, he had to hold together a burgeoning, all-male rota that included Horovitz, Esam, Richter, Christopher Logue, Harry Fainlight, Adrian Mitchell, Ernst Jandl, Anselm Hollo, George MacBeth, Tom McGrath, Spike Hawkins, Simon Vinkenoog and Paolo Lionni. In among this list of wildly different poetic styles, traditions and temperaments, there was talk of getting the exiled Russian poet Andrei Voznesensky to read. Jeff Nuttall, along with his friend the artist John Latham, were planning to paint themselves blue and throw books at each other as a sort of 'happening'. Add to this the inventor Bruce Lacey who wanted to have his automata roaming up and down the aisles during the evening, and the Incarnation promised to be quite a show.

On 10 June a gathering was held on the steps of the Albert Memorial, London's sacred temple of national pride. Ginsberg, Trocchi, Horovitz and the rest of the gang hung out as the BBC came to record an item for the *Nine O'Clock News*. In lieu of an official statement or final running order, the group announced the event via an 'Invocation', a jointly composed poem that described the International Poetry Incarnation as a 'Spontaneous planet-chant Carnival!' The text was prefaced by six lines from William Blake's poem 'Jerusalem' (1804):

England! awake! awake! awake!
  Jerusalem thy Sister calls!
And now the time returns again:
  Our souls exult, & London's towers
Receive the Lamb of God to dwell
  In England's green & pleasant bowers.

'You could not have asked for better publicity', remembers Christopher Logue. The ten-minute item 'announced the show and the whole of the South of England saw it, that this poetry reading was going to take place at the Albert Hall from six o'clock onwards the following day'. In the event Jill did indeed get her money back: 7,000 people turned up to the reading and the Albert Hall was full. As six o'clock came around flowers were given out to the crowd, booze flowed from shared bottles, and a cloud of marijuana smoke started to engulf the auditorium.[3]

When Whitehead arrived, he realised he'd have to draw on all his newsreel experience to cover it. The Éclair camera was perfectly portable, but the size of the hall meant that he would have to keep mobile and choose his shots carefully. His four rolls of film equated to just 40 minutes. Every shot was going to have to count. He decided to save an entire roll for Ginsberg and use the other three to catch as much of the other poets as possible. Over the course of the next four hours, Whitehead crawled, crept and crouched through the hall as the poets appeared and disappeared from the central podium.

People shouted out from the audience, the poets openly bickered with one another, and most of the performances overran. When Harry Fainlight got up to read he was visibly twitching and agitated. He heroically ploughed through his long poem 'The Spider' (1965), allegedly about a terrible LSD experience in New York, but rather than letting the images of mutating spiders resonate for themselves he tried to explain things as he went along. 'Read the poem!' shouted his friend Ginsberg as the audience started to heckle. Eventually Fainlight was ushered off the stage. Poems unread, he looked like a man excoriated by shock treatment.

Somewhere backstage Nuttall's 'happening' was also not going as planned. He and Latham had covered each other in paint, but Latham had passed out because the thick blue mixture had blocked his pores. Nuttall then scooped him up and shoved him into a bath in one of the dressing rooms. Getting in, Nuttall proceeded to throw water everywhere to revive his friend and get the paint off, much to the shock and consternation of the Albert Hall's caretaker.

If he thought Nuttall was weird, the caretaker should have stuck around for Ernst Jandl's performance. Jandl, an Austrian sound poet, specialised in poems that revelled in the power and plasticity of the human voice: not oratory, but the reverberant vibrations of the throat and larynx. To hear Jandl perform was like listening to a machine invent its own language from the sound of its clanking components. After taking the audience through '*Schmerz durch Reibung*' ('pain through friction') and '*im Anfang war das Wort*' ('in the beginning was the word'), Jandl enlisted Horovitz and Pete Brown to assist him in a three-way poetic rendition of a sneeze. As their yelps, grunts and glottals flowed forth with rising intensity, the audience responded in kind, first clapping, then shouting. According to writer Alexis Lykiard, the audience 'successively turned football crowd, Boy Scout rally and wolfpack.' When the final 'choo' was delivered, a thunderous cheer rang around the hall. Whitehead got a beautiful shot of Jandl, relieved at having orchestrated such a potentially disastrous piece, leaving the stage, as Pete Brown, bearded, rotund and very drunk, raises a massive glass of wine to the applause like a lord addressing a feast.

For Harry Fainlight the reading was a disaster. Ginsberg too, had little good to say about it. He was drunk by the time he got up to read and later claimed, no doubt in the cold, self-disgusted light of a massive hangover, that he'd given a terrible performance. For other observers though, it was precisely this sense of undisciplined spontaneity, creative passion and borderline chaos that gave the reading its verve. The poet Robert Gittings wrote admiringly of the event as 'a play impromptu,' while the *Times Literary Supplement*, under the leader 'Stirring Times,' praised the organisers for making 'literary history by a combination of flair, courage and seized opportunities.' Before the year was out Whitehead had released his footage as *Wholly Communion* (1965), a documentary that won the gold medal at the 1966 Mannheim Film Festival. Of the 40 minutes taken from the four-hour event, he had crafted a brisk half-hour film which, with the aid of a soundtrack taken from a BBC recording of the night, captured the varied voices of the poets and the cacophony of the crowd.[4]

Despite Whitehead regarding *Wholly Communion* as a highly selective document, vastly different in its truncated form from the event it resembled, reviews of the film continued to celebrate the cultural impact of the Poetry Incarnation. Writing in *Films and Filming* in 1966, the esteemed critic Raymond Durgnat called it a record of 'the first big eruption of the too-long-quiescent poetic volcano.' There was a definite sense of occasion surrounding the Albert Hall reading. Other venues like London's Institute of Contemporary Arts hosted Ginsberg and his fellow poets before and after the Albert Hall, and Horovitz went on to stage similar events there in the years that followed. Few of these were able to cultivate quite the sense of a watershed moment as the Poetry Incarnation and its cinematic double, *Wholly Communion*. When Ginsberg read 'King of May' at Better Books he talked teasingly, beratingly of the 'revolution' that was yet to begin in England. The Poetry Incarnation felt like the explosive, rapid-fire response to this challenge: an importation of American Beat poetry into the heart of the British establishment and a supercharging of the powerful energies held in the traditions of English verse. The symbolic proximity of the Albert Hall to Poets' Corner at Westminster Abbey was not lost on the participants. The Poetry Incarnation was a means of kicking up the dust of this history to revivify its ghosts for a new generation. It created a propulsive sense that things were starting to *happen*. As Nuttall put it in his memoir *Bomb Culture* (1968), after the Albert Hall, he wrote to his friend Klaus Lea: 'London is in flames. The spirit of William Blake walks on the water of the Thames [...] Come and drink the dew.' If Charles Manson's traumatic fade to black marked the end of the American sixties, to many eyes *Wholly Communion* and the event it recorded signalled the fabulous, true, beginning of the British sixties.[5]

In 1960 London was still living in the shadow of the Second World War: rationing had ended only six years prior in 1954, national service was still in effect, and impact craters punctuated the city streets. Rather than calling to mind the idea of a counterculture, any talk of the 'underground' would likely have brought up stories of nights spent huddled in Tube stations as the Blitz rained down from above.

Twenty thousand bombs had fallen on London between 1940 and 1941, and these caused irreparable damage to more than 100,000 buildings. Most were fine examples of Victorian architecture. Townhouses were reduced to rubble, terraces were obliterated and, as was the case with All Saints Notting Hill, churches were reduced to lonely spires standing amid the dust. Apart from a few scratches and scrapes though, the Albert Hall avoided destruction allegedly because the *Luftwaffe* pilots used it as a navigational landmark during their flights. As with St Paul's Cathedral, memorably captured amid bomb-smoke in Herbert Mason's photograph 'St. Paul's Survives' (1940), the Albert Hall took on an important symbolic value during the Blitz. Aerial bombing was not just confined to London, but as the Hall played host to the 1941 Proms concert following the destruction of the Queen's Hall on Langham Place, it came to exemplify the heady mix of fortitude, defiance and melancholia that marked the mind-set of the British home front during the period.[6]

Faced with this destruction in the capital city and a nation-wide loss of up to 4 million houses across the entire war, Winston Churchill's coalition and later Clement Attlee's Labour government spearheaded a massive programme of post-war reconstruction. This drew on pre-war projects relating to sub-urban 'overspill' estates and garden cities and attempted to move residents away from heavily bombed centres. There was also a drive to develop new, 'modern' housing based on post-war infrastructure and the country's expanding motorway network. Enter, the post-war New Town: functional settlements of con-crete walkways and landscaped gardens that began to pepper the map as the 1960s began. Utilitarian in its design and utopian in its outlook, Lancashire's Skelmersdale welcomed its first residents in October 1961. By 1964 other readymade communities like Telford, Redditch, Runcorn and Washington in Tyne and Wear had also established themselves as comfortable commuter belts. The thinking was that high-quality accommodation would go hand in hand with a push for full employment, thus stoking the economy as Britain found its feet in the new post-war landscape.[7]

Speaking ahead of the 1951 General Election, Attlee saw the roll-out of such projects as part of his party's plan for 'a society of free men and women – free from poverty, free from fear, able to develop to the full their faculties in co-operation with their fellows, everyone giving and having the opportunity to give service to the community'. This was placed in contrast to the stance of the British Conservative party led by Churchill who, according to Attlee, 'regard the economic process primarily as the giving an opportunity to the individual to advance his own interests; community interests, national interests, are regarded as a hypothetical by-product.' Churchill eventually won the 1951 election which resulted in thirteen years of Conservative rule under Prime Ministers Harold Macmillan and Alec Douglas-Home. Although it was Labour's opponents who dominated the 1950s and steered the country into the 1960s, aspects of Attlee's egalitarian vision found form in the early years of the new decade. The growth of New Towns shadowed the development of the tripartite education system consisting of grammar schools, secondary modern and secondary technical schools. Although selective and elitist in its designation of the grammar school as the premiere mode of education, as a state-funded institution the system provided opportunities for working-class students to enter what had once been an Old Boys' Club.[8]

Peter Whitehead was the classic 'guinea pig' in this regard. Born in Liverpool in 1937 'without prospect or privilege into a working-class family', he won a scholarship to attend Ashville College, Harrogate in 1949. This '"posh", expensive fee-paying public school' taught Whitehead how to speak 'proper' and how to fit in while also furnishing him with a classical education. A scholarship to Cambridge after two years of compulsory national service completed the transformation. By 1962 Whitehead had received a gentleman's education and as he considered his next move – an offer to write for the *Guardian*, a place at the Slade School of Art to study film, a little art collecting perhaps – it seemed as if he had all the opportunities that went with it. For Whitehead and all the other beneficiaries of the 1944 Education Act, this social mobility was evidence of a successful experiment. What remained obscure was the precise purpose of the experiment. Whitehead had, in one sense, been initiated into the world of the English elite, but he also remained by dint of birth something of an outsider in the camp. Why then was he there? Maybe, as Whitehead came to see it, he had been trained as a kind of secret agent, an unconscious member of a post-war sleeper cell sent in to 'subvert the pernicious class system that structured English society'.[9]

As the decade opened, other secret agents were chipping away at once rigid class boundaries. In 1960 Penguin Books won a much-publicised obscenity trial over their decision to publish an unexpurgated version of D.H. Lawrence's novel *Lady Chatterley's Lover* (1928). *Lady Chatterley* is, depending on your taste, either a modernist classic, a heated story of love across the class divide; or a work of barely-concealed pornography, the *summa theologica* of posh-bird fantasies. For the presiding judge, John Mervyn Guthrie Griffith-Jones, *Chatterley* was very much the latter, but the issue was not the racy content so much as the format Penguin were proposing. Reading Lawrence's novel as an expensive leather-bound volume with a cigar and a glass of port after an Oxbridge reunion dinner at the Old Boys' Club was fine; publishing it as a mass-market paperback certainly was not. As a paperback, *anyone* could read it, and who knows what would then become of England? 'Is it a book you would even wish your wives and servants to read?', Griffith-Jones asked in his now famous opening statement, almost spluttering at the thought of it. The eventual success of Penguin's case was a victory against this type of snobbery. It brought literary eroticism out of the drawing room and put it into bookshops, newsagents and train stations across the country. This coupled with the parallel rise of British rock 'n' roll, then the Beatles and then the Rolling Stones, meant that in the opening years of the 1960s frank, uncoded and unapologetic sexuality could be found at the heart of British popular culture.[10]

*

Philip Larkin memorably mapped out this climate in 'Annus Mirabilis' (1974), a poem in which the speaker offers 'nineteen sixty-three' as the year that 'Sexual intercourse began', somewhere between 'the end of the *Chatterley* ban / And the Beatles' first LP'. That said, given that it marks such a seismic event, the much purported 'invention' of sex in the 1960s, Larkin's poem is remarkably restrained. Full of understatement, self-deprecation and reserve, it works hard to reign in the very forces it appears to announce. Larkin's verse was typical of the so-called 'Movement' poets: university educated, largely middle-class and white male writers including Robert Conquest, Thom Gunn and Donald Davie who, as Conquest put it, 'refused to abandon a rational structure and comprehensible language even when the verse is most highly charged with sensuous or emotional intent'.

Dominant in the British literary scene from the mid 1950s onwards, particularly in the wake of the anthology edited by Conquest *New Lines* (1956), the poetic conservatism of the Movement reflected that of the wider social and cultural sphere. On the surface it seemed as if the conformism of the 1950s was evaporating and the old orders were crumbling but, in reality, Britain remained as hierarchical as ever. The rate and extent of the country's post-war reconstruction had in part been fuelled by a late-1950s 'property boom which had been unleashed in London by the relaxation of building and rent controls, [and which was by the 1960s] accelerating by leaps and bounds.' Sowing the seeds for today's housing crisis, these Conservative policies provided an opportunity to individual landlords and developers but, in Attlee's terms, came at the cost of community interests. The scars of war also lay deep. Just as unexploded bombs were often unearthed during the rapid reconstruction of London, so too did the repressed psychic damage of the conflict regularly make itself known.[11]

One figure who exemplified this combination of post-war opportunism and post-war trauma was the infamous landlord Peter Rachman. Born in Poland in 1919, Rachman arrived in London in 1948 after seeing combat throughout Europe and the Middle East. Finding work as an estate agent, Rachman quickly began to buy and manage rental properties. Focusing on heavily bomb-damaged areas like Notting Hill, Rachman brought buildings back into use but as subdivided flats, an enterprise that by the time of his death in 1962, had netted him great wealth. He had targeted the large number of West Indian immigrants who had answered the call of Attlee's government and filled much needed vacancies in Britain's post-war industries. Many of those who arrived on the *Empire Windrush* in 1948 and those who followed did find work, but they also found racism, prejudice and in some cases violence. As Sam Selvon described in his novel *The Housing Lark* (1965), West Indian immigrants also faced enormous difficulties when it came to accommodation. Rachman, unlike other landlords who cheerfully announced, 'No dogs, no blacks, no Irish', had no qualms about who he rented to but cared little for the conditions of his properties; he was keen to extract as much money as possible for his flats and would violently pursue monies owed. Thanks to Conservative policies regarding rent controls his residents had little in the way of guarantees and protection. Rachman the model entrepreneur was, by contrast, able to own six cars, an opulent house for his wife and an elegant flat for his string of mistresses which included the model Mandy Rice-Davies. He also had a habit of squirrelling away pieces of food under his bed. This was the legacy of the horrors he experienced while interned in a Serbian labour camp during the winter of 1940.

Rachman had met Rice-Davies through another of his girlfriends, Christine Keeler, a model who in 1961 had a brief liaison with John Profumo, then Secretary of State for War. Thanks to the social connections of her friend, the wealthy osteopath Stephen Ward – a man who could charm royalty and court gangsters alike – Keeler had also been seeing Yevgeny Ivanov, a Soviet naval attaché. When details of this complicated social whirl began to emerge, first through political whispers and then in the gossip columns of the tabloid press, questions arose about sex, security and pillow talk. Once the whole thing became a full-blown scandal in 1963 the concern was that nuclear secrets and matters of foreign policy may have been finding their way, consciously or not, from Profumo to Ivanov via Keeler.

From private psychological dramas to major political incidents, from demobbed soldiers trying to navigate suburbia to the vertigo of a new immigrant's first days in London: as the 1960s moved through its first act, the war seemed to be ongoing, albeit in a colder, ghostlier fashion. Where you lived and who you slept with, the job you did and the money you earned: the matter of daily life, so tinged in the early 1960s with a veneer of the 'modern' and an ideology of post-war progression, remained overtly and covertly rooted in the conflict of the preceding years. *Please Please Me* may have been a standout pop record of 1963, but probably the most critically acclaimed release of the year was the recording of Benjamin Britten's *War Requiem* (1962). Britten's composition was dedicated to the reconsecration of Coventry Cathedral, a building that had been destroyed by bombs that fell in November 1940. Filled with a sense of loss but marking also an act of triumphant reconstruction, Britten's piece served as an accurate barometer of the national pulse. The country would prevail not because of its transformative embrace of the modern, but because its traditional structures and institutions would remain. Similarly shored up by Conservative rule, Britain's political and social establishment, despite concessions to reform, also remained secure: as strong and steadfast as the Albert Hall during an air raid.[12]

If the political climate of the early 1960s was marked by tradition, reserve and the rule of the establishment, 'the sixties', at first glance, seem to open out to a completely different territory. The difference between the decade and the era is as stark as that between black and white and blazing technicolor. Rather than bomb-damage, concrete and New Towns, the British sixties bring to mind *Ready Steady Go*, mod-badges, mini cars and miniskirts; Diana Rigg in *The Avengers*; Peter Wyngarde in *Department S*; Simon Dee driving off with a girl in kinky boots at the end of *Dee*

Time. In this zone the cultural landscape has less to do with the guiding lights of the Conservative party and *War Requiem* than such rising stars as Mary Quant and Vidal Sassoon, as well as artistic milestones like Sir Peter Blake's kaleidoscopic cover for the Beatles' *Sgt. Pepper's Lonely Hearts Club Band* (1967).

There is a sequence of photographs taken by Adam Ritchie of Pink Floyd playing at Joe Boyd and John 'Hoppy' Hopkins' UFO nightclub on Tottenham Court Road in December 1966. The band are depicted playing on a crowded stage bathed in Boyd's polychromatic projections. If you look at the photos taken from stage front – all beautifully blurred and often double exposed – it is as if Ritchie has managed to capture the ectoplasmic essence of the sixties. They are spirit photographs of sensory overload, mind expansion and the great Pink Floyd in full flight. In the photos taken from the side of the stage, which show clearer images of the band, the sheet they used as a projection screen and the club's grubby back wall underneath, Ritchie has caught something else, the point where this mask slips, the cold surface of the 1960s. The lights of the séance room have gone up and we see a gigging band who have yet to release an album playing all night in the basement of the Blarney Club for 150 quid.[13]

Every decade generates its own myths and stories. The pathway from the historical reality of the 1960s to the matrix of fictions that make up the sixties is paved with the usual mix of culture, fashion and politics. As the decade progressed Britain did reap the benefits of its reconstruction programme with continued economic growth, high employment and record levels of home ownership by 1969. The idea of the sixties, though – the halcyon view of the decade as one of pleasure, decadence and youthful freedom – has ostensibly little to say about actual, material gain. It speaks more of a sensibility, an attitude: the notion that despite the surrounding context the decade gave birth to a dynamic community of the young; a generation who would leave war, rationing and the conformity of the fifties far behind. What is peculiar about this view is the rapidity with which it took hold and the extent to which it superimposed itself – like Boyd's lightshow – onto the walls of the period.

Much of this traction is thanks to *Time* magazine, which in April 1966 published its famous cover story 'London: The Swinging City'. With its focus on the likes of the Robert Fraser Gallery, Carnaby Street and nightclubs including the Ad Lib and the Scotch of St James, the article was essentially a map of the city's elite, affluent centre: Mayfair, Belgravia, South Kensington, a world as alien to the rest of Britain, and indeed to most Londoners, as it would have been to *Time*'s American readership. As Jonathon Green is quick to remind us, similar stories had already appeared in the *Daily Telegraph* in 1965 and *The Sunday Times Colour Supplement* in 1962. The London-based British press were just as keen as the American media to frame the city as one driven by a young and vibrant demographic: one that also embodied, as is implied by the winking sobriquet of 'swinging', a casual sexual availability.

That said, *Time* magazine had the advantage of landing just as Whitehead's *Wholly Communion* started to gain traction, and just as the celebrated Italian filmmaker Michelangelo Antonioni was in London working on *Blow-Up* (1966), his first English language feature. *Blow-Up* featured David Hemmings as Thomas, a hip Kensington photographer who may or may not have documented a murder in London's Maryon Park. To 'solve' the mystery Thomas embarks on an existential odyssey through the scenes and boutiques of sixties London. This includes a guitar-smashing club sequence in which the Yardbirds (then featuring Jimmy Page and Jeff Beck) play to an audience who are, by stages, static, nonplussed and riotous.[14]

For all its art-house credentials and cerebral provocations *Blow-Up*, released in America in December 1966 and Britain in March 1967, accurately channels the energies that according to *Time* had 'switched on' London. From costume designer Jocelyn Rickards' attempts to produce utterly contemporaneous fashions, to David Hemmings removing them from Jane Birkin and Gillian Hills during the film's threesome, *Blow-Up* shows what *Time*, with barely concealed lasciviousness, celebrated about 'swinging' London: its transformation from a 'once sedate world of faded splendour' into a scene full of 'everything new, uninhibited and kinky'. For those who cared to look, films like *Wholly Communion* provided the kind of evidence that may well have reiterated this fiction. Although London's fashion world was not the same milieu as that populated by the city's experimental poets, the Albert Hall reading was another event that appeared to blast away the city's 'faded splendor'. Seen as artefacts of the sixties, the *Time* story, *Blow-Up* and *Wholly Communion* connect the flowering of the era to the emergence of a demographic very much alternative in its actions and outlook to preceding generations.

This mythic but nonetheless resonant perspective underpins the idea of London's 'counterculture'. As Green puts it in his book *Days in the Life* (1988), the British counterculture is to be understood as 'a cultural subset of the era', a movement that sprang from 'an eclectic fusion of beats, mods, the New Left, black music and white teenagers'. He continues: 'It flourished in its most visible manifestation from the Albert Hall poetry reading of June 1965 to the *OZ* trial of July 1971' and achieved 'its most powerful period between 1966 and 1969'. For this 'brief but influential period' young people attempted 'to step outside the bounds of established society and exist within a world whose only limits were of their own definition.'[15]

Wholly Communion provides the perfect example of this self-definition. In the latter half of the film, part way through Ginsberg's set, Whitehead's camera falls on the image of a young woman dancing ecstatically as he reads. The woman was a patient of the 'anti-psychiatrist' R.D. Laing who was in attendance on the evening with a group from the experimental therapy centre Kingsley Hall. She is a model of spontaneity and unselfconsciousness, who breaks away from the passive reserve of the British audience. At one point it becomes delightfully unclear whether the woman is an embodiment of Ginsberg's verse or if Ginsberg is somehow vocalising her shamanic display.

The moment works so well in the film because it is precisely in-sync with the poetic ideology underpinning the event. In citing William Blake as part of their 'Invocation' on the steps of the Albert Memorial, Horovitz and company were not drawing on the nationalistic implications of Blake's preface to 'Milton', his long epic poem written and published between 1806 and 1808. This preface was set to music by Sir Hubert Parry in 1916 under the title 'Jerusalem' at the suggestion of Poet Laureate Robert Bridges. Bridges wanted a stirring hymn that could inspire patriotism at a time when support for the terminal drive of the First World War was beginning to wane. When politicians like Clement Attlee invoked England's 'green and pleasant land' as part of their reconstruction project, when Promenaders at the Albert Hall and congregations in parish churches speculate on Christ's visit to Glastonbury with the question 'And did these feet in ancient time / walk upon England's mountains green?' they are quoting these verses. Horovitz, by contrast, had little time for such establishmentarianism. His point of reference was the poem that

Blake had intentionally titled 'Jerusalem: The Emanation of the Giant Albion', a long, occult text from 1804. 'Jerusalem' is one of Blake's most complex lyrics. It presents a version of the Fall myth in which mankind, 'Albion', is divided before being reborn in unified harmony. For Horovitz, it was this essence of imaginative, creative and artistic revival that the 'Invocation' and by extension the Poetry Incarnation were attempting to generate.

As he described in his 'Afterwords' to the anthology he edited for Penguin Books, *Children of Albion* (1969), Horovitz saw Ginsberg, Ferlinghetti and Corso as 'catalysts', poets who could 'purge the atmosphere of slick or ambiguous non-sounds'. Horovitz may well have had the constrained verse of the Movement poets in mind here, but he was also making a wider point about the social function of poetry. In a world dominated by what Horovitz called the 'goliaths of advertising', the powerful voices of Ginsberg *et al* had the ability to reinvigorate the language and break away from the 'deathly stupor of materialism'. Just as Theodore Roszak presented the American counterculture in opposition to the 'technocracy' and its associated mercantile interests, so too was Horovitz claiming that English verse, if properly amplified via the energies of American Beat poetry, had the potential to counter the forces that govern 'normality': commerce, commodification and literary conservatism. In describing this form of poetry Horovitz was outlining a literary subculture, a scene that ran in parallel to the artistic establishment while also standing in opposition to its orthodoxies. The writing of this poetic and cultural 'underground' would not encourage its readers to buy things they didn't need. It was not made up of the slogans and ad copy that flowed through *The Sunday Times Colour Supplement*. Instead, it would liberate the imagination and get its readers to think differently.[16]

It is easy to be sceptical of such grand claims, but beyond Horovitz's elevated rhetoric, the Poetry Incarnation did prove to be catalytic, inspiring more than mere lofty words and intoxicating ideas. The event provided the impetus for the pioneering underground newspaper *International Times*, and several alumni of the Poets' Co-operative, among them Barry Miles, joined its editorial board. Launched in 1966 and edited by the writer Tom McGrath, *International Times* was, in part, born out of a desire to maintain the momentum of the event by providing this now visible community with a mouthpiece and information source.

In March 1967 the paper was subject to a police raid following a complaint to the Department of Public Prosecution. Thousands of copies were seized on the grounds of the classic, catch-all accusation of obscenity. Widely seen as an act of authoritarian intimidation, the raid generated an immediate protest spectacle, 'The Death of *IT*.' Roused into action by Harry Fainlight, various *International Times* staff members and supporters spilled out from the UFO nightclub and acted as 'pallbearers'. They carried a coffin containing Fainlight down Tottenham Court Road and onto Charing Cross with the intention of noisily weaving their way through Trafalgar Square and Whitehall to eventually meet with photographers and journalists at the Cenotaph. In addition to the press this colourful, traffic-disrupting group also attracted the attention of the police. According to author, musician and one-time *International Times* editor, Mick Farren, the procession avoided a confrontation by quickly escaping into a tube station. The 'underground decanted into the Underground', continues Farren, 'and rode around with coffin and noise spreading alarm'. Re-emerging at Notting Hill Gate, the group headed towards Portobello Road, 'to the obvious displeasure of the market traders who had just set up for Saturday, the big business day'.

The London Underground once again offered a space of refuge. Rather than avoiding the Blitz, this carnivalesque procession used the tube stations like wormholes, evading the police by getting off the 'all too historic streets' and causing them at the same time 'a good deal of jurisdictional confusion'. In Farren's terms the 'underground' is a form of collective cultural energy that stands apart from the everyday routines of the marketplace, uses existing services in unexpected ways and defiantly obstructs attempts to curtail or contain its movements. Where Horovitz used 'underground' to speak of a particular kind of poetry, Farren had in mind a model of public activism. *International Times* provided a bridge between the two types.

In the aftermath of the raid, *International Times* and the culture it supported was given a further boost by another now legendary event, the 14 Hour Technicolor Dream, a psychedelic festival-cum-fundraiser held at London's Alexandra Palace in April 1967. Antonioni was there, soaking up the atmosphere as *Blow-Up* neared completion, as was Whitehead, camera in hand, recording the proceedings for his semi-sequel to *Wholly Communion*, *Tonite Let's All Make Love in London* (1967). John Lennon took time out from the recording of *Sgt. Pepper* to attend, and when the album was released a month later in May 1967, it seemed to have brought into the public eye the style, graphics and attitude of the underground. With its mix of Englishness and the European avant-garde combined with a sharp sense of humour and a cast of iconic characters on its cover, including such regular *International Times* contributors as William Burroughs, *Sgt. Pepper* quickly assumed its place as the soundtrack of 1967, the British Summer of Love. A month later, in parallel with the events and sentiments coming out of San Francisco, the Beatles broadcast 'All You Need is Love' to a world audience. The studio was full of sundry Rolling

Stones and their respective entourages: jamming, hanging out, smoking. After the Albert Hall, the *International Times* and the 14 Hour Technicolor Dream, this was the next mass gathering. To the 25 million who tuned in and saw the show, this was Swinging London; this was the underground going global; this – until the tragedy of the Manson murders – was the future.[17]

Somewhere at the edge of all this stood Jeff Nuttall. Poet, artist and raconteur, Nuttall was heavily involved in the British counterculture (paint and bathtub exploits notwithstanding), but in contrast to Horovitz's Blakean optimism Nuttall saw the world through a much darker lens. In 1963 he started *My Own Mag*, a little magazine which by its second issue was publishing writing by the controversial American Beat author William Burroughs. An irreverent and often scatological mix of comic strips and experimental writing, *My Own Mag* was the unruly animal in the pack of British literary magazines published during the 1960s: imagine *The Beano* seen through a surrealist lens. Drawings and eccentric typography interspersed the dense typescript; one issue was published with a cover singed at the edges; and, thanks to Nuttall making cuts and tears, the magazine's pages seemed to spill open like slit guts.

For Nuttall art was a matter of obscenity. It was a way of shocking the system out of its complacency and calling out the cruelty of human life, the violence and degradation that happens every day but which we try hard not to think about. Just as Burroughs did in his abject masterpiece *Naked Lunch* (1959), Nuttall often dealt with the human body *in extremis*: the body breaking down, the body in pain, the sweaty intensity of the primal body. For all his provocation though, Nuttall remained a deeply humanitarian artist. His work compelled its audience to acknowledge the base meat out of which human culture grows while screaming in rage at the inhuman damage that is so often inflicted upon it. When he came to write *Bomb Culture* in 1967, such damage was at the forefront of Nuttall's mind. Over the preceding years he'd seen the underground flourish, but all this talk of 'love' jarred with the state of the world as he saw it. With the thought of mushroom clouds looming in the post-war period and in the shadow of the ongoing conflict in Vietnam, such sentiments began to sound achingly hollow. Nuttall's map of a 'post Hiroshima, napalm-scorched world' contained no flowers, just public executions, burning monks and the horror of entire cities blasted into dust.

Although the Albert Hall event was a spectacular success, one evening featuring 'a few poets trying to be natural', as Trocchi put it, was a far cry from what Nuttall saw as the activist origins of the decade's counterculture: the Aldermaston marches of 1958–63 and the work of CND, the Campaign for Nuclear Disarmament. As Nuttall describes in *Bomb Culture,* the first march was organised by the predominantly left-leaning Committee for Direct Action, a group that involved leading pacifist thinkers and anti-nuclear campaigners. It took place on Good Friday 1958 and saw a procession trudge for four days from Trafalgar Square to the perimeter fence of the Atomic Weapons Research Establishment in Aldermaston, Berkshire. Those involved were acutely aware that the appearance of the H-Bomb was a high price to pay for the 'security' of peace time. 'We had', intones Nuttall in *Bomb Culture,* 'ended the war with the power to destroy the world'. The scale of the marches grew considerably over the following years and, with the route reversed, the annual arrival of a noisy, passionate, chanting procession in Trafalgar Square crystallised the large public opposition to nuclear armament and continued nuclear testing. By 1959 CND, headed by the philosopher Bertrand Russell, had taken over the organisation of the march, and this large-scale demonstration became one of the group's key campaigning tools. Given the mainly left-wing make-up of the anti-nuclear campaign, pressure was placed on the Labour party to formally adopt a policy of disarmament. A Labour victory was expected in 1959 and the hope was that Britain's nuclear reliance could be phased out once a sympathetic government came into power. In the event it would be 1964 before Labour's election victory, and the trajectory of their thinking on domestic policy in the interim was far from satisfactory as far as CND was concerned. The Labour party conference adopted a resolution on disarmament in 1960 but this was overturned only a year later, highlighting that while anti-nuclear sentiment was strong among the grassroots, the party leadership were not in favour. There was simply too much money, Cold War angst and political capital invested in Britain's nuclear sector for it to be scaled back.

Although the international Test Ban Treaty of 1963 responded to a number of CND's demands, for activists like Nuttall, Labour's failure to officially support the anti-nuclear cause was a bitter disappointment. It robbed the cause of political legitimacy at the precise moment it stood poised to institute significant change within Britain's modern political landscape. For Nuttall this refusal was the beginning of the end as far as post-war activism was concerned: 'it left us stranded in the unbearable'. Growing up during in the 1950s, Nuttall had seen how a generational 'hunger for a cause' had manifested itself in the anti-nuclear movement. With the decline of its potency, what remained was a distrust if not hostility towards the establishment coupled with the residual anxiety regarding the threat to life that nuclear devices continued to pose.[18]

*

Meanwhile, Labour were optimistically setting into motion their plan for the country. Just as Nuttall was beginning to lament the failure of the radical centre-left, Prime Minister-in-waiting Harold Wilson was giving his now famous 'white heat' speech at the party's October 1963 conference in Scarborough. Claiming that Britain's future as a modern nation lay in harnessing the power of 'the scientific revolution', he added that the country should be prepared to 'make far-reaching changes' in its 'economic and social attitudes'. Where Clement Attlee had looked forward to a green and pleasant land, Wilson envisaged a glowing crucible, and the new Britain that was to be 'forged in the white heat of this revolution' would be 'no place for restrictive practices or for outdated methods on either side of industry'.

Over the course of the Labour government that followed (1964–70), this agenda of modernisation found its parallel in a series of social reforms regarding contraception, abortion, homosexuality and theatre censorship. For historians like Arthur Marwick, these measures rather than the advocacy of an active counterculture were the real scaffold of the sixties. As Marwick puts it:

> There was never any possibility of a revolution; there was never any possibility of a 'counter-culture' replacing 'bourgeois' culture. Modern society is highly complex with respect to the distribution of power, authority, and influence. Just as it was *not* formed by the simple overthrow of the aristocracy by the bourgeoisie, so, in its contemporary form, it does not consist simply of a bourgeois ruling class and a proletariat.

He goes on to state that the recognisable social transformations evident in the sixties were not due 'solely to counter-cultural protest' but 'to a conjunction of developments, including economic, demographic, and technological ones, and, critically, to the existence in positions of authority of men and women of traditional and enlightened outlook who respond flexibly and tolerantly to counter-cultural demands.' Harold Wilson and his Home Secretary Roy Jenkins were such traditional, enlightened and tolerant men.[19]

The British counterculture was born out of this climate of permission and advancement rather than any of the ripples caused by events like the Poetry Incarnation. By the time *Wholly Communion* was being screened throughout 1966, social progressivism was joining technological advance as an equal part of Britain's drive towards modernity. The same economic and industrial forces that Wilson invoked in 1963 gave rise to major infrastructural and communications projects such as the Post Office Tower, officially opened in 1965, and it was this investment in telecoms that enabled the Beatles to broadcast their message of love from London to their record-breaking international audience.

Whitehead's film *Tonite Let's All Make Love in London* (1967) takes an accurate sounding of this period of economically driven social change. Subtitled a 'Pop Concerto for Film,' the documentary takes a kaleidoscopic look at the London-based youth culture of the later sixties. On the surface, *Tonite* is the perfect continuation of *Wholly Communion*. Taking its name from a line in 'Who Be Kind To' (1965), the poem Ginsberg read at the Poetry Incarnation, it moves out from the Albert Hall and explores the dazzling cornucopias of Carnaby Street, Biba, UFO and other quintessentially hip scenes across the city. Whitehead interviews the happening 'faces' of the time, Michael Caine, Julie Christie, David Hockney, Mick Jagger and 'Pop artist' Alan Aldridge. The whole package throbs along to the sound of 'Interstellar Overdrive', Pink Floyd's stunning instrumental from *Piper at the Gates of Dawn* (1967), a piece the band had not put on to record until Whitehead organised and paid for the necessary studio time to include it in the film.

As one watches *Tonite* there's plenty of evidence to suggest that Britain's dusty old traditions are being cast off. Marriage, work, respect for authority, respect for cultural and artistic heritage: it all seems to have been replaced by a new, young and utterly liberated generation who make their own rules out of a spirit of possibility and experimentation. If this sounds like the pitch of 'London: The Swinging City', that is because it is *Time*'s view of London that Whitehead is interested in – and critical of – not the city itself. For all the energy and professed freedom discussed in the film, Whitehead is keen to show that this is a world of commerce, commercialism and commodification. The London of the film is a fabulous product, one born straight out of the 'white heat' of Wilson's modern industrialism and consumed by its young customers without question. It is beautiful and exciting but ultimately superficial: everyone in the film agrees that London is where 'it's at', but no one can really say precisely what 'it' is.

At one point, Whitehead balances himself precariously on a fairground skyride and interviews a self-identifying 'Dolly Girl' in an adjacent car. As the conversation takes place, the ride begins, and the girl flies through the air as utterly unburdened as the lifestyle she describes:

> GIRL: A Dolly Girl is someone who dresses how she feels, she does what she likes, she's free, she doesn't care about convention. [...] She does what she likes and has a wonderful time [...] Probably young.
>
> INTERVIEWER: Where do Dolly Girls go? Which clubs?

> GIRL: Oh well the clubs, I suppose the Scotch and Dolly's and I think Birdland is a new one, which I've been to once or twice, it's quite swinging [...] Otherwise there aren't really that many with-it clubs in London. The ones that are, are great. You know, you can just go there, drink, talk, relax. Do what you like. No one cares. Do what you like.

And off she floats. With all the energy of a robot programmed to say, 'Do what you like', the Dolly Girl announces her freedom as if she's advertising the few 'with-it clubs' in London. Hers is a freedom that consists of a very limited number of options: drinking and talking, that's it. As with the tone of the *Time* article, the independence of Whitehead's interviewee also belies its obvious economic dependence. It takes money to be as 'free' as this, because 'swinging' clubs like the Scotch of St James, quite simply, were not.[20]

In *Bomb Culture*, Nuttall focuses less on the commercialism of the sixties and more on the continued, reverberant presence of the H-Bomb and its cultural after-effects. For Nuttall, the 'white heat' of scientific progress had been realised long before the start of the decade and it led not to the productive drive of cultural advancement, but to the blinding flashes of a bomb detonating at the Trinity test in New Mexico and then over the massive population centres of Hiroshima and Nagasaki. Within such circumstances, the post-war underground was, according to Nuttall, a spontaneous occurrence. It represented neither a failed attempt at 'revolution' nor the adoption of a popular style but was instead indicative of a much more instinctual response to a world of endless conflict and imminent nuclear fire. Where the Dolly Girls of Swinging London appeared content to insulate themselves in the city's fashionable bubble, the activists of the underground assumed a much more global and engaged outlook. As Nuttall put it, the underground was 'simply what you did in the H-bomb world if you were, by nature, creative and concerned for humanity.'[21]

Nuttall was not alone in offering these sentiments. In Balfour Place deep in the heart of London's Mayfair, the dead centre of *Time*'s map of Swinging London, a group of young people dressed in long flowing cloaks held strange events in their penthouse like Sabbath Assemblies and telepathy workshops. Known as the Process, and by the end of 1967 as the Process Church of the Final Judgement, the group were led by two ex-Scientologists, Robert de Grimston and Mary Ann MacLean. They had met in 1963 in London and established Compulsions Analysis, a therapy group that drew on various aspects of psychoanalysis and Scientology. By the time they were using the name 'the Process' in early 1966, the group had become much more spiritual in its outlook. 'Patients', as Arthur Goldwag puts it, 'had become disciples', members of a cultish, aloof and deliberately mysterious religion that mixed Christianity and Jungian psychology together with an apocalyptic worldview.

The Process espoused a theology of unification. If Christ's main teaching was to 'love thine enemy' then Satan, Christ's enemy, must also be loved. Through this love, wrote de Grimston in one of his many doctrinal texts, Christ and Satan can destroy their enmity and 'come together for the End. Christ to judge, Satan to execute judgement.' For any evangelical Christians encountering Process material, these beliefs would have recalled the last book of the New Testament, the Revelation of St John the Divine.

Here, the Second Coming also involves the meeting of Christ and Satan, but they do not unify; they come together in battle. Satan is defeated at Armageddon before a further, final battle vanquishes him forever. It's at this point that Christ comes to judge the living and the dead. In their version of the end times, the Process did not see the Final Judgement in quite such epic, polarised terms; it would not be a war between the embodiments of 'good' and 'evil'. Rather, what they called 'the Final End' would mark the point at which these opposing forces would be reconciled within the individual. As they would chant at their Sabbath Assemblies, the final reckoning would be an 'End and a New Beginning', the point at which Christ and Satan would be joined and 'all conflicts resolved'.

When they spoke about Christ and Satan, and the other names in their pantheon, Lucifer and Jehovah, the Process were not referring to deities but what they saw as competing personality types. To them, Satan represented a will towards evil and violence, Lucifer the fallen angel represented hedonistic indulgence, while Jehovah embodied stern authority. According to de Grimston, these 'three great gods' symbolise the impulses that are continually at war in each of us. Processians were encouraged to follow the god that best exemplified their personality and explore the insights raised by this identification. The ultimate goal was to achieve a sense of reconciliation, for each member to resolve the archetypal conflicts within their own psyche. Reflecting on Christ was the key to this resolution because in Process teaching he was the intermediary, the figure of unification, the Lord of understanding who taught compassion.

For all these therapeutic intentions, the language used by the Process remained distinctly apocalyptic. De Grimston describes the unification of Jehovah, Lucifer and Satan as 'the End of the world as we know it'. Writing with the force of a fire and brimstone preacher, de Grimston claimed that human values, endeavours, creations and ambitions will be destroyed in the pursuit of their religious mission; everything will have to go 'to make way for a New Age and a new way of life'. Aleister Crowley had said much the same thing when announcing the Aeon of Horus. He claimed it would be heralded by a time of catastrophe, a 'great war' and 'Bloody Sacrifice' that would proclaim Horus as 'Lord of the Aeon'. While Haight-Ashbury was celebrating the imminent Age of Aquarius as a time of approaching harmony, the Process, like Crowley, saw the shift to this new age as dependent upon a preceding period of chaos. The Process were promising a new beginning, but this would only come once the world as we know it had arrived at its 'Final End', a period, according to one of their hymns, of shrieking wind and boiling seas in which 'man' is struck from the face of the Earth.

The Process were not fundamentalists but so vivid is their imagery that it is often hard to tell if they believed in the reality of the apocalypse or not. For a group that tried to offer its deities as personality traits, calling out that the end of the world is nigh may seem like a far too literal embodiment of their beliefs. That said, de Grimston was encouraging his members to change their personalities, to undo a lifetime of neuroses, tensions and hang-ups. Processians were called upon to reject tendencies so ingrained in human consciousness that to move beyond them could well have seemed like the end of the world *as they knew it*. The Process also saw themselves as a religion suited to the post-war climate of global conflict and nuclear threat. Such was with the amount of death and destruction on display across the world, it would have been hard to think of the future in any other terms. Thus, the Process assumed the role of catalysts of the 'Final End'. Their role was to prepare for, if not precipitate into, the apocalypse so that in the aftermath those who had successfully resolved their inner warfare could step into 'the Beginning of Peace'.

Members of the Process circulated and recruited at the 14 Hour Technicolor Dream. Edward Mason, who joined the group in 1967, remembers Processian Timothy Wyllie looming out of the gloom at Alexandra Palace, resplendent in his purple-lined cloak, handing out copies of the *Process* magazine, a typical issue of which was filled with images of death, fear and torture. Jeff Nuttall was not particularly religious, and he was too headstrong and independent to be involved in anything akin to a cult, but in many ways the Process were the perfect embodiment of what he was trying to say with *Bomb Culture*. Seated right at the fashionable heart of the sixties, emerging like a vapour from the underground, here was a hip, creative and adventurous coterie who were acutely aware of and fully prepared to greet the imminent latter days.[22]

Their outlook mirrored the work of contemporary artists like Colin Self, a painter whose images expressed the deep domestic anxieties of the Cold War period. Famous pieces like 'Guard Dog on a Missile Base, No. 1' (1965) found Self matching an assembled missile array with the feral form of a growling hound. Full of looming menace, the painting connects the engines of war to primal, lycanthropic forces. Whatever level of sophistication stands embodied in the modern weapon, Self suggests that the work it does is a matter of animal, almost atavistic, violence. Using the tools of war, however 'advanced' they might be, does nothing more than bring out the beast in us.

Another kindred spirit was John Latham, Nuttall's blue partner from the ill-fated Albert Hall performance. He offered an even starker image than 'Guard Dog' in his painting 'Full Stop' (1961). Magnificently abstract, the image is that of a black circle dominating the otherwise blank canvas, a punctuation mark magnified into an unquestionable void. Beyond this formal experimentalism the image takes on a more figurative significance when we pause to consider the other implication of the title 'Full Stop', the point at which everything comes to an end. The ominous black hole announces an absolute termination. It's hard not to think of the Trinity tests here, particularly the attempts made to photograph the detonation. High sensitivity photographic film was trained on the explosion from the limits of the exclusion zone, but even at this great remove the intense heat burnt straight through the surface of the film. The result was a series of dark scorches that look like miniature studies towards Latham's painting: jet black circles framed by canvas-white halos. Read in this way, the deep silence of 'Full Stop' is that conjured up and inscribed by the bomb, a weapon so terrible it exceeds any attempts to record its effects.

There was also the poetry of Adrian Mitchell, who in his celebrated performance at the Poetry Incarnation, spoke of a different but no less devastating form of bombing, the American use of napalm in the then escalating war in Vietnam. His poem 'To Whom It May Concern' (1964) was a coruscating response to a sight that was new to British television, the grisly spectacle of fire-bombed Vietnamese villages. Vietnam was the first truly televised war and Mitchell, enraged and disgusted, castigates the temptation this might bring to simply look away from images of such violence. 'Tell me lies', his voice repeats as the images of bodily damage pile up:

> I smell something burning, hope it's just my brains
> They're only dropping peppermints and daisy-chains
> So stuff my nose with garlic

Coat my eyes with butter
Fill my ears with silver
Stick my legs in plaster
Tell me lies about Vietnam

In wishing to be insulated from the images of Vietnam, Mitchell creates an image of the body as mangled and as traumatised as the burnt corpses at the heart of the conflict. The voice of the poem ties itself in eviscerating loops: wishing not to know about the conflict and yet torturing itself for such a refusal. Just as Nuttall would regularly do in the pages of *My Own Mag*, the body becomes the battlefield and Mitchell wants us, the audience, to be aware of every painful twist in this confrontation of the war. The poem was later absorbed into *US* (1966), the satirical anti-war play that Mitchell developed with director Peter Brook for the Royal Shakespeare Company. Filmed by Whitehead as *Benefit of the Doubt* (1967), *US* expanded on the revulsion and rage of 'To Whom it May Concern'. It featured spectacular destruction, bodies in agony and repeated calls for the violence of Vietnam to be brought 'home' to polite English gardens.[23]

What each of these works shares with Nuttall and the world-view of the Process is a palpable sense of horror. They regard the end of the Second World War not as a point of closure, but a moment that brought devastating weapons into the world and left a legacy of ongoing conflict. By the mid 1960s this climate had plunged the world into a state of almost perpetual combat: skirmishes, escalations, guerrilla operations, civil war and – despite the treaties, protests and public objections – continued nuclear tests. 'Peace' in this world was a flimsy concept and so too was human care. While Michael Horovitz may have celebrated the proliferation of poetry readings during the period as events that emphasised the power of 'the human voice and body', in Nuttall's view it was the human voice and body that was being silenced and destroyed by the clamour of perpetually falling bombs. It was this carnage that he felt artists and writers should be emphasising. Nuttall was not suggesting that art should revel in the cruelty of warfare, but he was arguing that it should present the human body in all its precious fragility. For Nuttall, art that revealed and spoke about the screeching obscenity of violence was art that carried out a vital social function: it reminded us to cherish human life and to call out the terrible injustice of any damage done to it. 'Faced with the end of man', he claimed in *Bomb Culture*, the artist of the late 20th century should strive for a 'reaffirmation of life by orgy and violence'.[24] One could almost hear something of Charles Manson in Nuttall's outrage at the state of the world were it not, of course, for his deep and committed humanitarianism. There was nothing misanthropic about Nuttall. At the same time, he believed the artist working in the shadow of the mushroom cloud had a duty to stare right into the abyss and soak up the darkness. The Beatles could keep their love.

CHAPTER III

Surrender to the Void

'The radiator is beginning to throb; pounding as if with some huge entrapped insect beating to get out'. In the glare of the overhead lights of the Albert Hall, surrounded by his peers and an audience as big as an ocean, microphone hanging heavy round his neck like an albatross, Harry Fainlight soldiered on with his reading of 'The Spider'. Captured in *Wholly Communion*, it's excruciating to watch the tide of the crowd turn against him but mesmerising to see the performance Fainlight is able to muster in the face of such hostility. With the conviction of a man who knows he's drowning, he makes every word count: '– a cavern full of / wicked sisters, a whole new breed of them mutated by this / new hallucogenic vitamin which I hereby christen SPIRITLECT'.

Michael Horovitz called 'The Spider' a 'rather nightmare poem'. Monstrous and panic stricken, it is full of witches, bad magic and creatures pulled straight from the id. For all its supernaturalism though, the poem has a more chemical point of focus. As Fainlight's use of 'hallucogenic' (sic) indicates, the poem deals with the confusion and sensory overload that accompanies the use of a mind-altering (or psychotropic) substance. For the speaker in Fainlight's long, lyrical poem, this overload is a deeply unpleasant experience, one in which the body itself starts to convulse and revolt: 'My stomach is throbbing too. / I WANT TO VOMIT UP A SPIDER'.

By the time he came to read at the Albert Hall, Fainlight had just returned from three years living in America. While there he had become heavily involved in the New York experimental poetry scene, he had met and become friends with Allen Ginsberg and had been involved with the work of fellow poets like Ed Sanders who ran the Peace Eye Bookstore on the city's Lower East Side. Drug use had also been part of this sojourn with Fainlight sampling marijuana, mescaline and lysergic acid diethylamide, more commonly known as LSD. 'The Spider' is a dispatch from this period of experimentation. When he insisted on pausing to explain the poem to his audience, it was the 'horror' of this 'acid vision' that Fainlight was trying to communicate: 'these drugs' he is reported to have said, 'aren't all sweetness and light'. Spike Hawkins, another of the poets on the Albert Hall bill, recalls that this admission 'dropped a grenade into the audience'. For Fainlight to say that 'he'd written his piece under the influence of LSD' was 'considered extremely risqué at the time – especially at the Albert Hall'.[1]

It was 'extremely risqué' because although in 1965 LSD was not illegal, it was widely misunderstood. Having previously been used in professional medical and psychiatric contexts, its emergence as a 'social' drug and the appearance of such semi-official institutions as the World Psychedelic Centre in London's Belgravia stirred concerns regarding the possible danger it posed to the public. British tabloids gleefully exercised their imaginations when picturing the moral degradation and sexual debauchery that apparently took place at high-class 'acid parties', while heavyweight American publications like *Time* and *Life* also began to report on the cultural significance of LSD's seemingly inexorable rise.

Life assigned their story to the writer–photographer team of Gerald Moore and Lawrence Schiller who provided the magazine with its March 1966 cover story: 'The Exploding Threat of the Mind Drug that Got Out of Control'. Compared to *Time*'s article a month later, 'Drugs: The Dangers of LSD', their piece was reasonably even-handed despite its sensationalistic title. In the article Moore opined that LSD, 'No longer just a promising psychological research tool', was 'out in the open' and used by college students, theologians and at least one (conveniently anonymous) 'hard-headed, conservative, Midwestern, Republican businessman'. Although he happily termed LSD a 'remarkable drug', Moore's general tone was cautionary. Overall, the point was made that anyone brave or foolhardy enough to use LSD stood on a knife-edge; set to receive, with little chance of prediction or control, either 'beatific serenity and shimmering insight' or, as Fainlight put it in the 'The Spider', 'frenzy and terror'.

When conducting their research Schiller and Moore were keen to speak to as many active users as possible. In Los Angeles they met a man named Brian (surname unknown) who agreed to an experiment. Schiller wanted an audio recording of an LSD session to go with his photographs 'of ordinary people, not kooks or beatniks, reacting to the drug'. He thought Brian, a confident veteran of 33 acid trips, would be the perfect subject. He received no mention in the article, but edited sections of Brian's twelve-hour trip were later released as *LSD* (1966) an album on Capitol Records produced by Schiller that purported to be 'a documentary report on the current psychedelic drug controversy'. On the record Brian initially sounds like he's pleasantly stoned before the trustworthy voice of Richard Warren Lewis, the album's narrator, informs us that 'Brian's mood is gradually changing'. He becomes paranoid, he starts to shout and, as Lewis intones, 'He sobs as his joy turns to fear'. Moore described a similar situation in the *Life* article, with the case of 'a teen-age girl at an "acid party" near Hollywood's Sunset Strip', who slipped into a terrifying state, 'a sudden vision of horror or death which often grips LSD users when they take it without proper mental preparation'. It seemed that Brian had found himself in the same zone. Just as Fainlight had done before him, Brian was having a 'bummer' and there was nothing he could do about it. After all his experience, here it was at last: a bad trip.[2]

*

Someone who definitely had the 'proper mental preparation' for LSD was British author Aldous Huxley. Born in 1894, Huxley began his writing career with sharply observed social satires like *Chrome Yellow* (1921) and *Antic Hay* (1923). He remains best known for his classic work of dystopian fiction *Brave New World* (1934), a novel that envisaged a future society regulated by a government sanctioned drug called Soma. From 1937 onwards, Huxley lived in Southern California where he was part of an expatriate circle that included fellow writers like Christopher Isherwood.

Throughout his time in California, Huxley practised meditation, but he began to seriously experiment with altered states of consciousness when he started to use mescaline and then LSD. Huxley encountered both drugs via his friend, the British psychiatrist Humphry Osmond. Osmond, along with his colleague John Smythies, had conducted research in the early 1950s into the use of mescaline as a treatment for schizophrenia. Based on his experiences with the drug, Osmond surmised that when reporting extreme psychosis and hallucinatory symptoms, schizophrenic patients were not using analogies, but describing the world as they found it. He theorised that schizophrenia was an existential state which 'conventional' medicine chooses to pathologise, and what is experienced under the influence of mescaline is this worldview made fully manifest. Like the work of the mysterious Tillinghast Resonator in H.P. Lovecraft's short story 'From Beyond' (1934), a machine that 'generates waves acting on unrecognised sense organs' and which opens 'vistas unknown to man', it was as if mescaline was making visible another world: one that is *there* but which had so often gone unseen or underappreciated.

Reading their work, Huxley found that the theoretical and philosophical implications of this view chimed with his own intellectual project regarding human consciousness. Huxley believed that access to the full capacity of the brain – a kind of cosmic consciousness, an evolutionary step beyond human self-consciousness – was possible if the filters regulating blood access to the brain and the reception of external stimuli could somehow be opened or removed altogether. This, according to Huxley, was the feat achieved by mystics and shamans, who through various types of inebriation and sensory deprivation were able to walk on a higher plane. If, as Osmond and Smythies were suggesting, it was possible to inhabit the extreme psychological state that has come to be known as schizophrenia simply by taking mescaline, then it seemed to Huxley that the drug was the key he had been looking for. His interest was not therapeutic, he was not looking for a chemical 'cure' for schizophrenia; rather he was keen to explore the altered state of consciousness that mescaline seemed to provide access to.[3]

In May 1953 at home and in the company of Osmond, Huxley took a dose and waited patiently. Colours started to flicker before everything in his field of vision took on a clarity and significance the likes of which he'd never previously experienced. It seemed that as his vision intensified, Huxley's sense of ego dissolved, like a wall crumbling to dust. Writing up the experience as *The Doors of Perception* (1954) Huxley, just as Michael Horovitz would do when describing British underground poetry, turned to William Blake. Quoting Blake's *The Marriage of Heaven and Hell* (1790),

Huxley felt that under mescaline the doors of perception had been 'cleansed', resulting in everything appearing 'as it is, infinite'. Beyond the aesthetic pleasure of the experience Huxley also felt a looming sense of pressure. It was as if he had exposed his mind to sensory overload, a space of 'madness' that he felt could be difficult to control.[4]

Further mescaline experiments continued until in 1955 Osmond introduced Huxley to the entrepreneur, businessman and chemical adventurer, Al Hubbard. Hubbard had a supply of LSD that came direct from its place of manufacture: Sandoz Laboratories, a pharmaceutical company in Basel, Switzerland. It was here that chemist Albert Hofman first synthesised LSD in 1938. He was working with the fungus ergot in an attempt to produce 'new drugs that would ease labor and childbirth'. LSD-25, the 25th derivative produced during a series of routine syntheses was at first seen as largely unexceptional before Hofman returned to it for further examination in 1943. For five years it had waited, patiently. After accidentally ingesting a tiny amount he stumbled on the chemical's primary quality: it was a hallucinogen of extreme potency. Additional tests confirmed this, and LSD was no longer considered as a painkiller but was made available by Sandoz under the trade name Delysid and recommended for use in psychiatric contexts.[5]

When Hubbard offered LSD to Huxley on Christmas Eve 1955, he did so not just out of experimental, that's to say scientific, interest. Hubbard was deeply immersed in Catholic mysticism and what William James, the 19th-century psychologist (and enthusiastic user of peyote), would call the varieties of religious experience. For Hubbard, LSD offered a sensory experience of profound religious significance. When Huxley finally came down from his first trip sometime on Christmas Day morning, he was of much the same view: where mescaline had been a visionary tool, LSD was a gateway to spiritual ecstasy. Indeed, when he first used it, he felt that something had come 'through the closed door' and had thus afforded access to what he called the 'Clear Light', not a maddening wave of stimuli, but a presence that bordered on the divine.

While Huxley pondered the philosophical implications of this peak experience, one thing became clear: words like 'hallucination', with their implication of seeing what isn't there, were simply not sufficient to describe the effects of mescaline, to say nothing of LSD. In psychiatric and therapeutic circles both drugs were touted as *psychotomimetic* because they were seen to mimic the symptoms of psychosis. For Huxley the power of these drugs had little to do with simulation. Rather, they were agents of manifestation, bringing to the surface that which was hitherto unknown. As an alternative, Huxley offered 'phanerothyme', a typically erudite Huxley-ism that meant 'to make the soul visible'. Osmond, replying to Huxley in a letter offered the slightly more user-friendly adjective of 'psychedelic', a conjunction of '*psyche*' meaning 'mind' and '*delos*' meaning 'clear' or 'visible' that produced a word suggestive of 'mind-clearing' or 'mind-manifesting'. It is thus thanks to Osmond that we don't have to describe the music of bands like the Doors (who took their name from *The Doors of Perception*) as *phanerothymic rock*.

In 1960 Huxley was diagnosed with an aggressive form of cancer. He continued to work but his health deteriorated until he died on the morning of 22 November 1963. That morning, at his request, Huxley's wife Laura administered two doses of LSD. In what has now become one of the most iconic moments in the cultural history of the drug, he went on one last trip. Just as news of President John F. Kennedy's death circulated around the world and Lyndon Baines Johnson was hurriedly sworn into office,

Huxley drifted away, delightfully lost in a moment of epiphanic serenity.[6]

⁂

Although it raised some eyebrows in intellectual circles, Huxley's late-career turn to drugs gave subsequent adherents of psychedelics a healthy shot of highbrow legitimacy. Most notably, the spirit of Huxley's optimistic experiments fed into the controversial but high-profile work of ex-academic Timothy Leary. Headquartered at the Hitchcock Estate in Millbrook, New York from 1963 onwards, Leary embarked on a programme of proselytisation – part charm offensive, part media baiting – that continually argued for the cultural value of LSD's mind-expanding potential. Along with his colleagues Ralph Metzner and Richard Alpert he established the journal *The Psychedelic Review* (1963–71) and published something of a 'user's guide' to LSD, *The Psychedelic Experience* (1964), which was dedicated to Huxley and placed heavy emphasis on the drug as a kind of sacrament. Leary, Metzner and Alpert 'adapted' *The Psychedelic Experience* from W.Y. Evans-Wentz's edition of *The Tibetan Book of the Dead* to furnish the LSD experience with both a narrative framework and a spiritual paradigm.

Leary appeared on Schiller's *LSD* album, cautiously introduced as a sort of pied-piper figure: charming, smooth-talking and – at 45 years of age having lost that most coveted of jobs, a lectureship at Harvard, due to his interest in drugs – probably not the role model most readers of *Life* would want for their children. Speaking on the album, Leary unapologetically lived up to this role, combining the spiritual speculation of Huxley's approach to LSD with a hip, classically countercultural emphasis on the idea of a psychedelic revolution:

> The LSD trip is a pilgrimage far out beyond your normal mind into that risky and revelatory territory which has been explored for thousands of years by mystics and visionary philosophers. In the last year we are told that perhaps a million Americans – most of them young people – had made the LSD experience part of their lives. Is this a social menace and a cause for alarm? I don't think so. I see nothing less than the speedy evolution of a new, indigenous religion.

By 1966 Leary was using LSD and marijuana on an almost daily basis and his slow, aphoristic speech audible on the record make him sound, unsurprisingly, stoned out of his mind. His statement follows on from another of the album's counterbalancing voices of reason, the physician and pharmacologist Sidney Cohen, author of *The Beyond Within: The LSD Story* (1964). Where Leary is effusive, encouraging both 'risk' and 'revelation', Cohen, then Chief of Psychiatry at Wadsworth Veterans Administration Hospital in Los Angeles, offers a note of warning. Cohen had been working with LSD since the early 1950s, his work often overlapping with that done by Osmond with Huxley. Trying the drug for himself, Cohen found it to produce a pleasant and insightful experience.

As a medical researcher he was particularly interested in its therapeutic applications when dealing with schizophrenic patients, recovering alcoholics and traumatised veterans. By 1959, though, Cohen was beginning to see LSD used as a social drug, and the rise of the acid parties that *Life* would later report on became a matter of grave concern. That people enjoyed the effects of the drug was not what worried Cohen. Rather, he was anxious about the spread of LSD beyond the boundaries of controlled, medical contexts. In his view LSD was not a drug to be used lightly. Its potency, unpredictability and the often extreme nature of its psychotropic effects raised serious questions regarding the safety of its users. Cohen believed that taking LSD could cause significant psychological harm if it was not prepared, applied and its effects monitored with the necessary amount of scientific rigour.

Leary would have argued that his convivial LSD sessions at Millbrook had just as much rigour as Cohen's hospital-based trials in Los Angeles, only he preferred to follow *The Psychedelic Experience* rather than the techniques of psychiatry. For his part, Cohen would have agreed with the relative value of these different approaches. On the *LSD* album he does speak about the 'scientific investigation of LSD' and the value of experiencing 'madness in miniature' before discussing Leary's approach, what Cohen calls the present 'idyllic, psychedelic, evangelical era' in which LSD is touted as a tool to 'free us from life's games so we can enter into non-game ecstasy'. What he has a problem with is what he calls 'Acid-Heads', those who use the drug with no preparation or guidance whatsoever. For Cohen, when LSD becomes a party drug taken in unmeasured doses or – worse still – in spiked drinks, and when it's sold on the street alongside marijuana and amphetamines, there is no way of regulating or properly responding to its strange effects. It then becomes difficult to help people who run into trouble. One can endlessly pontificate on the spiritual significance of LSD but, as Cohen implied when reflecting on the recordings of Brian's bad trip, this is of little use to someone lost in the infinite darkness of their Los Angeles apartment.[7]

Charles Manson first took LSD in June 1967, three months after he had arrived in San Francisco on parole. He was at the city's Avalon Ballroom where he saw a concert by the Grateful Dead. What Pink Floyd were to the London scene and the UFO club, the Grateful Dead were to San Francisco and Haight-Ashbury. Dedicated residents of the Haight, the Dead were led by singer and guitarist Jerry Garcia and had formed in 1965 as the Warlocks. Things moved fast: they gained a local following and developed a dense, improvisatory style. By the end of the year the Warlocks had become the Grateful Dead and, rather than gigging round local bars playing background music for drinkers, they were performing extended jams at a rather different set of engagements: Ken Kesey's Acid Tests.[8]

Writer, wrestler and rebel, by the mid 1960s Ken Kesey was riding high on the critical and financial success of *One Flew Over the Cuckoo's Nest* (1962). An anti-authoritarian classic, the novel drew on his experiences as a student volunteer in 1960 on a Stanford University research programme dealing with psychotomimetic drugs. Like Huxley before him, Kesey found LSD to be truly mind-expanding and was keen to spread it around as much as possible. More so than the stoned philosopher routine of Timothy Leary, Kesey's joyful, anarchic approach to LSD brought it firmly out of the shadow of medical research and into the Bacchanalian sphere of fun and kicks: very much the social phase of the drug that so concerned Sidney Cohen. Gathering together the 'Merry Pranksters', a band of friends and fellow travellers, Kesey purchased an old school bus and transformed it into 'Furthur', a mobile commune-cum-laboratory, and set off to spread the good news. Where the American Pentecostal Church had their tent revival meetings, Kesey and the Pranksters had the Acid Test. Between 1965 and 1968, they mounted large-scale immersive concerts across California. Using walls of sound equipment, light shows and acid-laced punch, the aim was to initiate and to amplify: to provide a hyper-stimulated environment in which to take LSD and a reverberant space in which to exacerbate its effects. The Grateful Dead were the perfect band for these hedonistic but also strangely ceremonial gatherings. By 1966 American garage bands like the Blues Magoos, the Deep and the 13th Floor Elevators were beginning to use the word 'psychedelic' in their music. The Dead, however, with their jamming, their elongated solos and their uncanny ability to vibe off each other, made music that felt psychedelic and fed straight into the flow of a peaking trip. What Kesey wanted with the Acid Test was much more of ritual atmosphere than what was found at participatory demonstrations like the Human Be-In. He wanted to generate a kind of organic, communal feedback loop in which the environment would be conducive to acid use, the effects of which would then infuse the atmosphere as a whole, thereby creating an environment conducive to more acid use. And so on. As the British band Spacemen 3 would later put it, the central dynamic was thus a matter of taking drugs to make music to take drugs to.[9]

Manson's evening at the Avalon ballroom was not billed as an Acid Test but it nonetheless carried most of the trappings: the Dead, light projections, loads of people already tripping and plenty of free LSD going around the hall. Most of the acid, including Manson's dose, would have likely come from Stanley Owsley III, a gifted chemist and underground businessman who was the main supplier of black market LSD around the San Francisco area. In 1966 Sandoz had ceased to promote LSD following pressure from the American Medical Association and the Food and Drug Administration. Since 1962 they had been raising concerns regarding the difficulty in properly assessing the effects, use-value and safety of the drug which resulted in a series of restrictions placed on its manufacture and research availability. It would be 1968 before possession and sale of LSD were fully criminalised, but the measures imposed by 1966 had effectively stemmed the flow from 'official' channels. By spotting an opportunity and stepping into the fray outlaw chemists like Owsley responded to the growing demand. Such underground enterprise also helped to foster an active psychedelic culture, exactly what the government restrictions were attempting to prevent. The sale of LSD supported the Haight's network of bands and events and 'Head' shops appeared selling psychedelic regalia like beads, posters and incense. The shared experiences of the drug helped bind the community together, inspiring its psychic life while also fuelling its economy.

Arriving at precisely the right time, Manson met this culture head-on, and his first trip was a textbook example of sensory overload and visionary intensity. Getting caught up in the swirl of the Grateful Dead, Manson later described how 'the acid, the music and the loss of inhibitions opened up a new world for me'. As Manson's biographer Simon Wells picks up the story, the experience culminated in Manson falling to the floor after having an 'earth-shattering' vision of 'the crucifixion'.[10]

In the terms offered by *Life* magazine, this would have been every inch the bad trip. What could be more indicative of a 'sudden vision of horror or death' than an image of the crucifixion followed by a state of physical collapse? Other sources at the time used similar accounts of burnout, and visions almost too terrible to contemplate, to strengthen the argument against LSD use. According to Gerard DeGroot, in 1968 reports started to emerge concerning the work of one Dr Yoder of the Pennsylvania Institute for the Blind. He claimed that six students from the University of Pennsylvania had permanently lost their sight after taking LSD and staring at the sun for hours on end. Although extreme, Yoder's claim was in keeping with the tone of other references to LSD in popular culture. The drug was to be approached with caution and fear.

One of LSD's earliest public appearances was in Terry Taylor's British novel, *Baron's Court All Change* (1961). A modish portrait of early sixties youth culture, *Baron's Court* features a scene at a party in which the talk of drugs flows as easy as the alcohol. Speaking with a 'junkie friend', Taylor's unnamed narrator is asked about his current drug use, 'Bennies, L.S.D., or Nems?' The narrator has no real problem with Benzedrine or Nembutals, but its LSD that makes him nervous: 'I wouldn't touch that stuff if you paid me to', he says, adding that he is not 'made for it psychologically'. In Roger Harris' *The LSD Dossier* (1966), a novel that was substantially ghostwritten by British author Michael Moorcock, this sense of psychological danger is taken much further. An Ian Fleming-esque spy thriller featuring MI6 agent Nick Allard, *The LSD Dossier* presents the drug as a potential mass weapon with hallucinatory and incapacitating effects. Moorcock renders Allard's experience as one of intense colour, spatial distortion and elongated time: all noted sensory effects of the drug. However, Moorcock's writing carries none of the wonder one finds in *The Doors of Perception* and much more of the cosmic horror of Lovecraft's 'From Beyond'. With the doors swung open, Allard is adrift and vulnerable:

> For an eternity Allard was alone in an icy limbo where all the colours were bright and sharp and comfortless. For another eternity Allard swam through seas without end, all green and cool and deep, where distorted creatures drifted, sometimes attacking him.

He goes on to feel 'supremely powerful' but eventually descends 'Into hell. Into fire. Into torture of the most dreadful kind.'

It turned out that the 'torture' experienced by Yoder's students was something of a smokescreen. Nobody went blind; the story was the work of a psychology professor adding to the anti-drug debate. That said, where Taylor and Moorcock prefigure the negative swing of *Life*'s pendulum, the dreadful threat that LSD might bring on a horrifying, psychologically damaging bad trip, there remains something pleasingly psychedelic about Yoder's scenario, even in view of the warning it attempts to sound. It is virtually a parable appropriate to, rather than critical of, the acid generation, hovering as it does somewhere between fact and myth; playing with its suggestions of blindness and insight. Most acid users at the time would likely say 'yes, that's exactly what LSD is supposed to do'. Like the blinding light seen by Paul the Apostle on the road to Damascus, acid clears your mind, lifts the veil, opens your third eye. If perception of only the phenomenal world is what you call 'sight', then let me become 'blind' and look inward.[11]

For Leary, the loss of one's ego was a key aspect of the journey undertaken when one uses LSD. So too for Manson. Writhing around on the floor of the Avalon Ballroom having lost not just his inhibitions but also control of his body, Manson recalled that this potentially catastrophic collapse was a moment of deep personal significance: a watershed. He felt as if he was 'experiencing a re-birth'. Writing with Alpert and Metzner, Leary defined the 'psychedelic experience' in very similar terms. It was a 'journey to new realms of consciousness' but one that required the traveller to jettison a fair amount of previously essential baggage, being that it involved the 'transcendence of verbal concepts, of space-time dimensions, and of the ego or identity'.

For Leary, this 'transcendent experience' is not the 'magic' work of the drug itself but is instead the result of LSD operating at a neurochemical level, 'free[ing] the nervous systems of its ordinary patterns and structures'. Such a 'liberation' is not so much a rewiring of the nervous system as a powering down of its operation to a state of abeyance, 'devoid of mental-conceptual activity'. 'Whenever in doubt', Leary encourages at the start of *The Psychedelic Experience*, 'Turn-off your mind, relax, float downstream.' By letting go in this way the regulating power of the ego can somehow be dissolved. At which point the user of the drug would be left unanchored and ecstatic. In various meditative and religious practices this loss of attachment describes an abandonment of self-centredness, a self-denial that brings one closer to God, spirit, the divine. Leary goes on to clarify such a state of tranquillity as one of spiritual significance: 'Realization of the Voidness, the Unbecome, the Unborn, the Unmade, the Unformed, implies Buddhahood, Perfect Enlightenment – the state of the divine mind of the Buddha.'[12]

By the time Leary was writing, numerous scientific trials by the likes of Humphry Osmond, Sidney Cohen and Oscar Janiger had produced responses that would generally concur with *The Psychedelic Experience*. Despite the difficulties LSD presents to analysis due to its extremely subjective effects, use of the drug was generally linked to an experience of depersonalisation. The 'unfixing of perceptual restraints' would place the user in a sensory whirlpool, within which the 'I' would lose its anchorage. As Martin A. Lee and Bruce Shlain write in *Acid Dreams*, when seeing the world through this augmented perspective, 'Existence is no longer a riddle to be solved but a mystery to behold.' What Leary adds to these descriptions of the effects of LSD is a philosophical and religious imperative. In rewriting *The Tibetan Book of the Dead*, a text that ostensibly describes 'the experiences to be expected at the moment of death', Leary is keen to emphasise that the original was a book 'for the living as well as the dying', an esoteric initiatory guide 'into the Buddhist mystical doctrines'.

When speaking of death and re-birth in this context, 'death' does not mean 'of the body' but relates to a paradigm shift, a movement from one way of seeing to another, very different, worldview.[13]

John Lennon turned to *The Psychedelic Experience* as a guide for his own trips after first taking LSD unawares. He and George Harrison along with their wives Cynthia Lennon and Patti Boyd were spiked by Harrison's dentist John Riley in April 1965. Lennon found the effects to be distressing but intriguing enough to try more, which he did while on tour with the Beatles in America, later in the year. It is often claimed that these incidents, along with Lennon's further drug use, inspired the surreal lyrics and complex arrangements in the music the Beatles would produce after 1965. It may well be debatable whether 'Lucy in the Sky with Diamonds' (1967) is a cheeky acrostic describing LSD, but 'Tomorrow Never Knows' from *Revolver* (1966) with its elongated drones and reverse tape loops certainly *sounds* like an LSD trip. The song also draws on *The Psychedelic Experience*. 'Turn off your mind, relax and float downstream', Lennon chants in an eerie channelling of Leary's opening comments. 'Lay down all thoughts, surrender to the void', comes next, echoing a portion of 'Instructions for Use During a Psychedelic Session', the long poetic text that closes the book. During the course of 'Instructions' Leary addresses a 'Voyager' who is about to encounter 'the Clear Light':

> Remember:
> The light is the life energy.
> The endless flame of life.
> [...]
> Do not fear it.

Surrender to it.
Join it.
It is part of you.
You are part of it.
Remember also:
Beyond the restless flowing electricity of life is the
ultimate reality –
The Void.

With 'Tomorrow Never Knows' Lennon was selective in what he took from 'Instructions', but the song still managed to boil down the essential message of *The Psychedelic Experience*, the idea that the perceptual loss of one's 'self' under LSD was tantamount to a kind of spiritual transformation. For Leary, the 'game' could also be transcended through this process, and by the 'game' he meant the quotidian merry-go-round of social roles, responsibilities and expected patterns of behaviour. The rat race. Fed up with your job? Not getting the life you feel entitled to? Preaching from the pages of *The Psychedelic Experience* Leary suggested that another, higher form of existence was possible through LSD: better living through chemistry.[14]

This classically 1960s mix of Eastern philosophy and Dale Carnegie-esque self-help is what we might call the 'heroic' psychedelic narrative. It is best exemplified by another artefact from 1965, Frank Herbert's epic science fiction novel *Dune*. A space opera of power and politics set in the far future, *Dune* features two Imperial Houses, the Atreides and the Harkonnens who battle to control the desert planet Arrakis. Otherwise known as 'Dune', Arrakis is a nigh-on inhospitable wasteland which would be of little strategic value were it not for a unique aspect of its ecology. Arrakis is the only known natural source of 'the greatest treasure in the universe', the narcotic substance *melange*, also known as 'spice'. Spice flows through the novel as a gaseous haze, rich with the aroma of cinnamon. Addictive and euphoric in its effects, spice is also used in massive quantities by the novel's most mysterious characters, the Guild Navigators. As Herbert gradually reveals later in the *Dune* series, the Navigators are continually immersed in tanks of spice gas. From these private oceans the navigators control interstellar travel by 'folding' space.

Against the backdrop of this strange, exotic planet, *Dune* charts the archetypal story of heroic development in which Paul Atreides succeeds his father as head of the House Atreides and eventually claims his destiny as the religious, military and political leader of Arrakis. This journey is accelerated through his ritualistic use of massively concentrated spice called 'The Water of Life', which activates Paul's psychic powers, ignites his genetic memory and elevates him to the level of *Kwisatz Haderach*, the long prophesised male messiah whose 'organic mental powers' allow him to 'bridge space and time'. Herbert's writing is suffused with a deep ecological sensitivity based on his observations of and concern for the sand dunes of the Oregon coast. Allegedly he also drew on his own experiences with psilocybin or 'magic' mushrooms when developing the novel's spice culture.

Paul's transformation certainly sees him rise above 'the game': he abandons his former life in various apprentice roles as child, son and student and assumes through a visionary process – one that results in death for many others – an advanced, if not superhuman identity on Arrakis. The spice blows his mind wide, 'ripping open the curtains to let them see the distant grey turmoil of his future', just as Leary's 'voyager' must 'turn off' their mind, let it 'rest without distraction' to 'see the truth'. *Dune* won the Hugo and Nebula awards in 1966 and, by the time Herbert published the sequel

Dune Messiah in 1969, the first novel had become a cult classic read, in Hari Kunzru's words, 'in squats, communes, labs and studios anywhere where the idea of global transformation seemed attractive.' Where *Dune* is 'the paradigmatic fantasy of the Age of Aquarius,' *The Psychedelic Experience* was the practical guidebook. Both volumes linked the use of psychoactive substances to transformational, transcendental states of being. You could blast off and leave the world behind. All you had to do was embrace the void.[15]

*

The 'void' also turns up in *Bomb Culture*, but when Jeff Nuttall uses the word, he does not talk about the cosmic void of deep space and ancient memory that Paul accesses in *Dune*, nor does he talk of the void of 'non-mind' that Leary celebrates in *The Psychedelic Experience*. Instead, Nuttall is thinking of a much broader meaning. When surveying the cultural climate of the mid-to-late 1960s, he claims, with sweeping absolutism, that 'the future is a void.' In the post-war period, nothing was assured. The fall of the nuclear curtain that ended the war had, to some, ushered in an era of peace and unparalleled technological sophistication, but for others, like Nuttall, the only result was the increased risk of global annihilation. Either way, from the standpoint of the 1960s, whether the world was moving triumphantly forwards or merely awaiting the imminent end, the future was unwritten. Nuttall argued that, thanks to the destruction, cynicism and cruelty of the war, there were no longer any comfortable stories or certainties to cling to and guide the way. The rules of the game no longer applied. Thus, for the artist faced with such a void, the only reasonable response was to devise their own. In a world of Mutually Assured Destruction, one that had become truly 'mad,' the artist had the opportunity to fill the waiting void as they saw fit.

As Leary's 'indigenous religion' spread out from the palatial surroundings of the Millbrook Estate, he seemed to be trying to fill the psychedelic void in a similar way. For all his interest in ego-loss, Leary remained a consummate egotist. In his increasingly visible role as a spiritual leader for the acid generation, and with *The Psychedelic Experience* in hand, he stood in an uneasy position somewhere between that of gatekeeper and guide. While Leary often spoke eloquently about the deeply subjective effects of LSD, his handbook was at the same time clearly setting down a road-map for the acid trip, one that included detailed accounts of what the 'Voyager' should be feeling and experiencing at each stage of the process. *The Psychedelic Experience* was, in one sense, a great work of imaginative exploration. Like the artists Nuttall discussed in *Bomb Culture* Leary was leaping into uncharted territory. In the absence of a satisfactory language with which to talk about the intense psychological and spiritual impact of LSD, Leary was developing his own. When it came to taking acid, though, there was much more at stake than writing a book and what Leary had to say was not necessarily going to reflect what every LSD user experienced. As Lee and Shlain recount, several in the Millbrook camp, including Leary's co-author Ralph Metzner, came to see the attempt to 'program' an acid trip as essentially futile. There were far too many variables at play to offer such a prescriptive model, not least the interaction between what Leary called the 'set and setting': the context in which one takes LSD, and the individual proclivities and mindset of the user. Taking acid undoubtedly placed the user in a vulnerable position and having someone more experienced around was a sound principle. But for that guide to become something of a guru, a conduit through which all the myriad acid-experiences are interpreted seemed to defeat the object of taking the drug in the first place. Why fill the void with all the social and psychological problems – ego, authority, control – that LSD initially looked set to dissolve?[16]

*

When Manson had his first acid trip at the Avalon Ballroom he was living with Mary Brunner, a young assistant librarian at the University of California, Berkeley. Manson had been playing guitar around campus and had seen Brunner walking by during her lunchbreak. When they got talking he quickly noticed that Brunner was quiet, shy but nonetheless appreciative of his attention. For Manson this was the perfect combination. Using the con man's classic formula of charm, flattery and manipulation, Manson easily gained Brunner's trust. Then her affection. And then her loyalty. Before she knew it, Brunner and Manson were lovers and he was comfortably installed in her city centre apartment. Then the other women started to turn up and move in, among them Lynette Fromme and Susan Atkins, both nineteen. Manson, the expert pick-up artist, was spending his days ranging through San Francisco striking up casual conversations with any woman who fit the bill: young, alone, a little lost-looking. Within weeks Brunner's apartment had become something resembling a harem lorded over by Manson.

By August 1967 Brunner was pregnant with Manson's child and had quit her job at the library. As Simon Wells recounts, she had also given up the lease on her apartment and had moved with Manson – and everyone else – to a new place on Cole Street, deep in Haight-Ashbury. Their new digs were a few doors down from a place rented by one Victor Wild, better known as 'Brother Ely', a member of the Process Church. He had been sent from London along with a contingent of other members charged with the task of setting up an outpost on the West Coast. In addition to hanging out at the Avalon, it is likely that Manson looked in on his new neighbours and learnt about the core beliefs of the Process: the unity of Christ and Satan, the imminent end of the world and the duty of the church members to bring it about.[17]

It would prove to be an influential but ultimately brief point of contact. The group, then numbering about eighteen women, soon loaded onto a school bus that Manson had bought and kitted out as a mobile commune and painted black. They left Haight-Ashbury and travelled through California for much of the following year, picking up more members – like Charles Watson and Paul Watkins – along the way. They slept in the bus, occupied any dilapidated buildings they happened upon and drifted through LA's network of canyon communities. In April 1968 Valentine Michael Manson was born, named after the lead character in *Stranger in a Strange Land*. Around the same time, the Family met and became friendly with Dennis Wilson, drummer with the dysfunctional but nonetheless quintessential American pop group, the Beach Boys. Wilson was then in the middle of recording the band's fourteenth album *Friends* (1968) when a chance meeting with some of the Family hitchhiking through Malibu led to all the occupants of the black bus taking up residence in his Beverly Hills home for much of the summer.

Taking over Wilson's house was a good break for Manson, but given the Family wrought havoc on the musician's life, it was inevitably a bridge that was soon burnt. In August 1968 though, the Family's restless wandering came to a halt. They moved into the Spahn Ranch, a rundown movie ranch and hiking spot nestled in the Santa Susana Pass, about twenty miles out from central Los Angeles and close to the laid-back bohemian community of Topanga Canyon. In February 1968 Spahn Ranch had been used as the location for *The Ramrodder*, a cowboy-themed porn film that featured the musician Bobby Beausoleil as a Native American. Beausoleil was living a semi-nomadic existence after having 'split' from Kenneth Anger and the scene at the Russian Embassy. Beausoleil had packed up his car, hit the road and ended up in Topanga where he became friends with the music teacher Gary Hinman. Later he would meet another of the canyon's occasional residents, an intense charismatic guy who passed through with an ever-increasing gaggle of hippie girls: Charles Manson. Meanwhile, Anger started to put out the story out that Beausoleil had stolen all the footage from the unfinished *Lucifer Rising* and buried it in the desert. There was little evidence for this, but in retaliation Anger put a curse on Beausoleil, claiming that it would turn him into a toad.[18]

Where Beausoleil left San Francisco to get away from Anger's weirdness, Manson spoke of his own exodus, 'The Way of the Bus', in much grander terms. In *Helter Skelter* (1974), Prosecutor Vincent Bugliosi's account of the case, Manson claims to have left Haight-Ashbury in 1967 because he 'foresaw' its decline 'even before it came into full flower'. Among the free concerts and the free acid, he saw 'police harassment, bad trips, heavy vibes, people ripping-off one another and OD-ing in the streets'. It is true to say that busloads of tourists and triviallising media reports were not the only factors that soured the area's brief community experiment. By late summer amphetamines were beginning to replace LSD as the area's drug of choice and with this change came a very different atmosphere. Although in some ways faster and more immediately gratifying than the meditative effects of LSD, amphetamines are ruinous, addictive and prone to inducing waves of paranoia. They are not the type of drugs which generate a harmonious community spirit. In late 1967, however, they were cheap and – to the influx of dealers who converged on the Haight

– very lucrative. This economic and chemical shift, coupled with the area's chronic overcrowding and lack of proper infrastructure (the heroic efforts of the Diggers notwithstanding), meant that the Haight quickly became a place of menace rather than refuge. Those who zeroed-in on the area after watching Roger Corman's *The Trip*, released in late August 1967, found something very different to the film's chic LSD parties. By September the Haight would have offered few mind-bending epiphanies on the balconies of expensive houses, just a few streets of hustlers and runaways who, in Laura Whitcomb's words, were 'anesthetizing themselves from the impending San Francisco cold.'[19]

Manson's decision to gather up his women and drive off was, in part, an attempt to 'find a place away from the Man.' Mainly though, it was a move that very much recalled his former career as a pimp in the late 1950s. Just before his stretch at McNeil Island prison, Manson had run 3-Star Enterprises on Hollywood's Franklin Avenue, a racket of a 'talent agency' that conned hopeful actresses into working for him as prostitutes. The key to this scam was first gaining the trust of his 'clients' before isolating them from their friends and families. Once they became dependent on Manson for money, food, shelter and 'work,' he had gained control. Driving off in the black bus was the same hustle, but this time the talk was not about johns and working girls, but the freedom and togetherness that came with life in the Family. The language may have been different, but as they pulled away from San Francisco and Brunner waved goodbye to her job and her apartment, the intent was the same. As he welcomed more members into the fold and the vestiges of their former lives disappeared into a whirl of new names, new routines and frequently changing locations, Manson established himself as the singular and central anchor point in their lives.[20]

In little over a year Manson had gone from homeless parolee to leader of what was, in essence, a personality cult. Such a transition requires more than just force of will and the con man's patter. For Manson, this extra 'something' was LSD. Dropping acid had been a key part of life with Manson since he started to build the group, but once settled at Spahn Ranch, psychedelic drugs became a formal part of the Family's working rhythm and internal group dynamic. George Spahn, the elderly, near-blind owner of the ranch, allowed the Family to live rent-free in exchange for a series of caretaking roles. They repaired the buildings, looked after the few horses and took care of Spahn himself: cooking for him, cleaning for him, dressing him. There were regular food runs into the city during which Manson's girls would pluck what they could from supermarket dumpsters which would then be brought back and cooked up in large communal meals. Afterwards there would be singing before Manson would sermonise at length. At least once a week the Family would then take LSD together.

In orchestrating this combination of ritual and routine Manson was self-consciously trying to connect communality with a sense of spirituality. Preaching from the Bible, Manson would explicitly identify himself as Jesus Christ, leaning heavily on passages that spoke about persecution and crucifixion. Manson's gospel, as it were, was one in which Christ was the heroic outsider, cast out and misunderstood by those he tried to save. Cherry-picking from the apocalyptic Book of Revelation, and sowing the seeds for 'Helter Skelter', Manson would present the End of Days as a great and imminent reckoning, the moment when the world, and particularly those who had doubted him, would become unavoidably aware of his true identity. More importantly as regards his hold over the group, this scenario dictated that if Manson was Christ, the Family were his disciples.

They were his fellow social outcasts who, by virtue of them now following 'Man's Son', had joined a special gathering of the elect. It was a clear and ennobling creed: the garbage people, those whom Manson had found among the trash, were now the chosen ones. If they stayed together and helped to usher in the apocalypse, the kingdom would be theirs.[21]

The communal use of LSD helped to reinforce this message. During the sessions Manson would often play with images of the crucifixion, sometimes going so far as to re-stage the vision he had at the Avalon Ballroom. Fully committing to the role of Christ, Manson would circulate among his followers as the acid took hold and whisper that he died for them. Would they now die for him? These group trips were talked up as a way to explore and expand the Family's collective identity: to break down the barriers of the self and for them all to become 'one'. Despite encouraging this, Manson always took care to remain in control. He would often take a smaller dose than everyone else, and frequently nothing at all. Manson was very much sure of himself and had no desire for that 'self' to be dissolved. This sobriety in the face of a room full of tripping and suggestive young people meant that Manson was at his most powerful precisely when his followers were at their most vulnerable. Seizing the opportunity, he would then set about darkening the atmosphere, bringing to the group experience a gnawing sense of fear and uncertainty. One minute Manson would be a voice of calm, the next he would be letting rip with threats of violence and death. Paul Watkins, who joined the Family in March 1968 and quickly assumed the role of second-in-command, recalls an incident during a group LSD session in which Manson lunged at his throat, grabbing him in a stranglehold. As he muttered that Paul was about to die, Manson's hands gripped tighter. Then, as suddenly as the confrontation had begun, Manson let go and drifted back into the shadows of the room. For Watkins this was a test, one alpha male psyching-out the other, an example of how Manson – the tough but wise guru – would push his followers to their limits, challenging them to acknowledge their fears in order to transcend them.

These evenings of LSD at the Ranch would often segue into orgiastic group sex, which again, Manson would very carefully orchestrate. As well as enthusiastically participating, he would dictate the positions and multiple couplings, taking care to ensure that members of the group acted against their 'normal' sexual proclivities. Such experimentation was right out of *Stranger in a Strange Land* and it was again offered as a liberating form of deprogramming, a way of allowing his flock to let go of their hang-ups and give themselves more fully to the greater cause, the group mind of the Family.

In reality, far from having the best interests of his charges in mind, Manson's abusive behaviour and the situations he engineered were strategically and intentionally manipulative. The incipient violence was designed to instil a deep sense of paranoia, the anxiety coming not from the threat of attack – the possibility that Manson could once again grab you by the throat – but from the very unpredictability of his actions: the fact that you simply didn't know what he was going to do next. Directing the Family's sex lives was as much a way of controlling their bodies as their minds. In both instances, Manson was carefully scanning for any points of weakness. He was attuned not just to the look of fear but to the slightest moment of hesitation, the ripples of unease that might point to an underlying psychological fissure.[22]

There was more than a hint of Scientology present in this technique. According to *Dianetics* 'auditing' involved the use of an 'E-meter', a sort of polygraph machine that would record electrical activity on the surface of the skin in response to a series of questions. If the subject of the audit gave an answer that caused the E-meter's needle to spike, this would signal to the auditor the unconscious presence of an engram. The topic of the question would then be repeated until the needle fell still. At which point it would be declared that the engram was neutralised and the interrogative search for more would continue. What Manson did was the reverse of this process. Like a human E-meter he took soundings of the intricate, often fragile psychologies of his followers and then, by way of the susceptibility afforded by LSD, he got to work crowbarring these tiny fissures into gaping voids. Manson had no interest in providing therapy to the Family, nor had he any intention of making anyone 'clear'. Instead, he wanted those within his unit to submit to the domination outlined in 'Cease to Exist'. In surrendering to the void, the Family would in return find no 'Buddhahood' as Timothy Leary promised in *The Psychedelic Experience*, but rather a terrible, lonely predicament: Manson would open their minds before striding in and filling up the black holes he found there. A new ego for the old.[23]

*

Vilified and feared; celebrated and made sacred: LSD was made to wear many guises following its emergence from Sandoz Laboratories. But throughout this ideological struggle the effects of acid remained the same. It continued its slow, patient work of chipping away at the monuments we build to ourselves. Whether one was made to, in Humphry Osmond's words, 'fathom hell or soar angelic' through the use of psychedelics, good and bad trips alike were generated by the same mind-cleansing properties of the drug. For all Timothy Leary's talk of 'Perfect Enlightenment', the total domination sought by Charles Manson was an equally possible outcome of LSD's use in a group setting. In 'The Spider' Harry Fainlight spoke of 'the new hallucogenic vitamin' causing a mutation, some kind of transformation. As the decade's psychedelic culture progressed, the nature of this mutation became a key question. If the self was to be dissolved, what would come next and would we, or should we, accept it? How, exactly, are we to live in the void?[24]

At the same time similar questions were emerging in politics, art and in the multiple cultures of protest that flowered in the post-war period. If the 20th century was indeed the century of the self, it was the idea of the 'self' that was shaken to the core in the 1960s. What to make of this violence and why might it be necessary became a question of pressing urgency, not least because there was so much at stake. In the case of LSD, the alteration of one's brain chemistry was not a move to be taken lightly. Back in the world of the *LSD* album, Brian learnt this the hard way. The recording ends with him still trapped in his oubliette in Los Angeles. His bad trip is more of a comedown than an experience of horror. There has been no great vision, no great awakening. As the sun rises he is left disoriented and exhausted in the empty apartment. The promise of his 33 previous doses of LSD now seem to have come to nothing. The album leaves Brian with his wonder turning to rage: 'Somebody's going to pay for this bum trip.'[25]

CHAPTER IV

The Art of Violence

The crypt of the Judson Memorial Church in Greenwich Village, New York, was a blank box. It had bright white walls, precisely the type that attract splashes of paint. This was very much the intention of the progressive ministry that ran the church. In the 1950s, the crypt had been converted into an experimental exhibition space, a place where artists were encouraged to present their work without fear of censorship. In this spirit the white walls had seen early shows of Pop Art and Abstract Expressionism, but on the evening of 21 November 1967 they played host to the 'Henny Penny Piano Destruction Concert' by Raphael Montañez Ortiz, a performance that did rather more than merely challenge established traditions of painting. It began with Ortiz, dressed in white and looking like an emanation from the walls of the crypt itself, sitting still gently caressing a live chicken he held on his lap. He then stood and walked over to an upright piano in the corner of the room. Suddenly the chicken was thrust headfirst onto the keys. Holding it by the legs, Ortiz repeatedly smashed the bird onto the keyboard as if it was a bludgeon, before dragging it by the body across the piano top. Feathers filled the air and the chicken simply fell apart. In a matter of minutes Ortiz was left holding nothing but a shapeless stump of meat. Next, an axe was produced, and Ortiz went to work on the piano. To the discordant sound of splintering keys, he tore into the instrument until its own guts of strings, wood and mangled hammers spilled out on the floor. Not finished, Ortiz then picked up the remaining chicken bits and draped them over the exposed lattice of piano wire. The small audience were silent as Ortiz, sweating, breathing heavily but otherwise calm, slowly returned to his chair and set down the axe. Behind him splashes of blood, not paint, could be seen on the white walls.[1]

Peter Whitehead was in the audience that night, filming. He had arrived in New York on 20 September to show *Tonite Let's All Make Love in London* and *Benefit of the Doubt* at the New York Film Festival under the billing, 'The London Scene'. The films opened to good reviews and shortly after, at a party hosted by Metro-Goldwyn-Mayer, he was approached by two theatre producers, Iris Sawyer and Elinor Silverman, who made an intriguing proposal. They offered Whitehead a budget of $20,000 to make a documentary about 'The New York Scene'. The pitch was that Whitehead would have full creative control, but there was an expectation that he would ultimately deliver a mondo-type film; an Englishman's view, a hip, sexy portrait of the city that never sleeps: *Tonite Let's All Make Love in New York*. Whitehead accepted the offer but immediately began to plan a different kind of film. Interviewed on American TV shortly after the festival screenings, he announced his intention to reveal a side of New York that New York was not even aware of.[2]

Writing in his diary during the flight back to London on 10 October, Whitehead fleshed out his ideas in more detail. He confessed to a 'Love / Hate for Americana', before adding, with characteristic modesty:

> This must indeed be a masterpiece and can be. It really has to be the definitive film at this historical moment in time in world History. Christ, there ought to be no other subject closer to me than where the power lies at the moment … "Successful Power Failure" might be the title.

Whitehead believed that a key part of New York's 'power' (and, by extension, that of America) lay in the operation of its mass media. This is what he had been trying to say with *Tonite*, a film which, despite its exclusive focus on London, 'was also about America.' It had tried to show how London was packaged by the American media and sold to its readers. As Whitehead would put it in a later essay, the contention of *Tonite* was that the 'Swinging London myth became "fact" because *TIME* said so; if *TIME* said London was swinging, trivial, vacuous, then it was.' This new project would confront the media machine head-on. It would be *Time* magazine in reverse, an analysis of the strange mechanisms that allow an image to be created which then takes root in the public consciousness as a kind of 'truth.' Rather than looking in on the New York scene, Whitehead wanted to enter the frame as a test subject so that he could document his own absorption into a world driven by media, advertising, television and film. It would not be an Englishman's view of the city, but 'Peter Whitehead by New York': a 'self-portrait,' a 'diary [...] written by the mass media screens [...] Through a glass darkly but then face to face.'[3]

Whitehead returned to New York in late October and filming began in earnest. By the end of November, he had recorded the events at the Judson Memorial Church as well as a performance by the radical theatre group the San Francisco Mime Troupe, a reading by the poet Robert Lowell and a 'happening' on the New York subway by the dancer Julie Bavarso. On 1 November he filmed footage of a visit to the city by Senator Robert Kennedy. With Whitehead scheduled to film more events and interviews as 1967 ended, he developed the project still further. In a diary entry for the 27 November he announced that 'The film must become a feature film.' It would no longer be a documentary but 'a combination of *La Dolce Vita*, *8½*, *Blow-Up*, *Tonite* and *Benefit*.'

With this decision made Whitehead, mainly in the company of his driver Angelo Mansraven, continued to film all around the city, but he also started talking about getting actors to star in the film. He wanted someone to play 'Peter Whitehead', and he was also keen to have Jill O'Hara on board, an actor he had seen playing 'Sheila' as part of the original New York run of *Hair*. The film was now going to be called *The Fall* and it would involve 'Jill' helping 'Peter Whitehead' commit an act of 'pre-meditated murder', the assassination of a '70-year-old dying man'. This idea came from 'Protest', an earlier film treatment Whitehead had written soon after completing *Benefit of the Doubt*. 'Protest' involved Stephen, a young man who commits murder after seeing shocking, traumatic images of the conflict in Vietnam. Regarding the murder as a 'sacrifice', Stephen uses the ensuing trial as a public platform to decry the ongoing violence of the war. What Whitehead was proposing with *The Fall* was this outline combined with his own current experiences as a filmmaker in New York: a combustible mix of underground art, radical politics and experimental cinema.

Producers Iris Sawyer and Elinor Silverman were not best pleased by this change of direction. They wanted an entertainment and they were somewhat unconvinced by Whitehead's claim that *The Fall* would make for a better film than *Tonite Let's All Make Love in New York*. Over the course of more than one awkward lunch Whitehead tried to make his case. *The Fall*, he told them, would be more than just a film, it would be a 'Requiem Mass'. Upon hearing this Sawyer and Silverman glanced at each other, one thinking, the other asking: a requiem for what, exactly?[4]

*

Whitehead's arrival in New York on 21 October coincided with the National Mobilization Committee's 'March on the Pentagon' in

Washington D.C. This was the event during which the Pentagon was levitated and exorcised by a crowd chanting 'Out demons, out!' It was the largest anti-war demonstration to date and for Whitehead, who assiduously followed the proceedings from New York, it was confirmation that the sentiments he had explored in *Benefit of the Doubt* were part of a rising tide of international antipathy towards the war in Vietnam. Norman Mailer would confirm this sense of significance the following year with his account of the march, *The Armies of the Night* (1968), a book that Whitehead read carefully as *The Fall* came together. In the immediate aftermath though, Whitehead was dismayed at how quickly the protest, despite its scale and spectacle, was triviallised and its energies dissipated by the media. The event did not lack coverage and it generated now-iconic photographs like Bernie Boston's 'Flower Power', but at the time Whitehead was more taken by a write-up in *Women's Wear Daily*, a magazine that published 'a full page of photographs [...] devoted to the clothes worn by the protestors.' Soon after, he saw New York department stores like Macy's selling 'Peace Dresses' for $25, 'appropriately decorated with CND signs on different coloured backgrounds.' Protest becoming fashionable was not a good sign. For Whitehead it indicated that 'the normal language of protest, as used by the press, the artists and the public, has become debased, even embarrassing; it is ridiculed, it has lost its meaning.' As he put it in his 'Treatment' for *The Fall*, written in 1968, this state of affairs:

> [...] also means that the artist has lost his power, as his usual forms and language for abusing injustice and hypocrisy have become so used and misused by the Mass Media that he is in danger of being accused of exploiting protest for his own ulterior purposes.

If *The Fall* was going to be a 'Requiem', then, it was to be a requiem for these twin impulses of activism and artistic radicalism. Coming so soon after the widespread coverage of the Summer of Love in San Francisco, *The Fall* was to be Whitehead's statement that, certainly from the perspective of New York in late 1967, America's nascent counterculture had quickly lost its potency. It had made a big leap forward in the summer, but by the time the chill of autumn came along, it had somehow stumbled, lost its footing and collapsed.[5]

Another factor influencing the tone of the project was the atmosphere of New York itself. As soon as he arrived, Whitehead felt it was 'a city saturated with pent up violence', and a night spent on a police patrol cruising around Greenwich Village confirmed this. He got all the grisly details including first-hand accounts of the 'Groovy murders', a case that had recently made the headlines. On 8 October, a janitor had found the bodies of Linda Fitzpatrick and her boyfriend James 'Groovy' Hutchinson, two well-known members of New York's hippie scene, in a boiler room at 169 Avenue B. They had been beaten to death. Fitzpatrick, eighteen, had come into the city's drug culture from the comfortable heights of a middle-class background in Connecticut while 'Groovy', 21, was the 'friendly neighbourhood dope-dealer' with links to countercultural hot-spots like Ed Sanders' Peace Eye Bookstore on the Lower East Side. Together they spent their time busking and panhandling on the streets between lengthy drug sessions in hotel rooms. Under Groovy's tutelage, Fitzpatrick quickly graduated from marijuana to heavy doses of LSD. In the late summer of 1967 she had spent time in San Francisco but became dismayed upon seeing just how quickly amphetamines had taken root in the Haight. Back in the Village, however, the situation was much the same. By the autumn of 1967, the streets were awash with cheap speed and it wasn't long before Groovy and Fitzpatrick were using it all the time. As in San Francisco, the local dealers knew they could target these placid hippies and make a killing, which is probably what led to the scene in the boiler room.

As Whitehead would have learnt from the police, there was nothing exceptional about murder in the city. New York would see 746 similar crimes by the end of 1967. What was considered noteworthy was the *symbol* of Linda Fitzpatrick, the 'good girl' from a 'good family' who went to the big city and got mixed up in drugs. Hers was the American Dream in reverse, a classic fall from grace which raised the inevitable and seemingly reasonable question: why would anyone want to leave the security of a middle-class home for a life on the fringes? After a summer that saw a stream of young people – hippies, truth-seekers, students, runaways – make a break for the Haight and other enclaves like the Village, the Groovy murders validated all the parental and establishmentarian anxieties this exodus caused. Filtered through J. Anthony Lukas' Pulitzer Prize-winning *New York Times* story, 'The Two Worlds of Linda Fitzpatrick' (1967), the senseless crime quickly became a cautionary tale. It gave weight to a million dinner table speeches in which parents told rebellious teenagers that leaving the suburbs in search of 'freedom' and other such nonsense would get them one thing: their heads bashed in on a basement floor. Reporting on the murders for their October 1967 issue, *Newsweek* caught the mood perfectly. A cover image of a dirty, exhausted-looking young couple carried a banner that spoke of alarm, concern and more than a hint of 'I told you so' smugness: 'Trouble in Hippieland'.[6]

The basement of 169 Avenue B was a short walk from the crypt at Judson Street Memorial Church. Between October and November, they had both become blank boxes with blood on their walls. For Whitehead, it seemed as if New York's underground art was just as violent as its streets and, as soon as he started work on *The Fall*, it was clear that the whole scene was a far cry from the Albert Hall and the Blakean poetry of *Wholly Communion*. In this hostile situation and faced with a pacifying media, Whitehead contended that the artists of the late 1960s had to revivify their methods to remain effective. They must 'evolve new forms which will again have the power to surprise, shock, hurt people and provoke them to some collective action'. In making such a statement Whitehead was not only describing what he hoped to film but also the type of film he hoped to make. If America's radical culture was indeed wilting just as it had come into bloom, Whitehead wanted to document it, but he also wanted his film to *do* something. He had no desire to stand on the sidelines and simply observe. As he put it in his 'Treatment', 'the time for Poetry Readings is over'.[7]

As 1967 ended and he continued to develop the project into 1968, Whitehead intended for *The Fall* to be an example of this 'new' form. To do this, he knew that it would have to go much further than either *Tonite* or *Benefit of the Doubt*. Influential magazines like *Variety* had heaped praise on both during the New York Film Festival, but they had also raised points that chipped away at his own concerns about the films. *Tonite*, with its parade of the young and the beautiful having a jolly old time was maybe too 'commercial' and ephemeral for its media critique to really hit home, while *Benefit*, because it was a documentary about the production of an anti-war *play*, was perhaps a little too distant to work as a protest *film*. *The Fall*, by contrast, would be different: harder, more aggressive. The plot would use murder as a revolutionary tool, an act of violence that shocks the dormant protest culture back into action.

With the project coming together as the end of the year approached, Whitehead's commitment intensified. He was enthused, fired up and keen to invest *The Fall* with as much radical agency as possible. His ongoing diary was full of this passion, but to such an extent that it was often hard to see where his own life ended and the world of the film began. The two seemed increasingly to blur together as if Whitehead were not only moving into the frame but was also plotting some act of violence himself. At midnight on 27 November, he wrote of his intentions for the film and for 'Peter Whitehead'. This character, his double, the man Whitehead was by then considering 'playing' in his film, was embarking on a dangerous trajectory; he would '*really* commit the act of assassination *really really*.'[8]

It was not uncommon for artists to *really* do it during the 1960s, particularly if *really* doing it meant *really* committing acts of violence. For all its terminal finality, Raphael Montañez Ortiz conceived of his 'Henny Penny Piano Destruction Concert' as only one in a series of what he termed 'Destructivist' art works. As he described in 'Destructivism: A Manifesto' (1962), art that 'utilises the destructive processes' is born out of a 'desperate need to retain unconscious integrity'; to be true to the compulsions and desires, the 'anger and anguish' of our inner lives. These are the impulses that society typically requires us to 'displace' or otherwise hide behind 'the quiet face', even though said societies are regulated by allegedly 'rational' governments who have the power to 'push a button and annihilate 200 million people'. For Ortiz, making art that is fleeting, that falls into ruin and which expresses the will to destroy that is 'inherent in the deep unconscious life', is a necessary safety valve in such constrained circumstances. It powerfully expresses the fear of monumental annihilation while at the same time laughing in its face. The Destructivist artist ecstatically seizes life in the very act of physical destruction. In destroying a man-made object, Ortiz sees himself as releasing it from and allowing it to transcend 'its logically determined form' and in so doing the artist, like the shaman at the point of a completed ritual, 'is also released from and transcends his logical self'.[9]

Just as Ortiz was composing his manifesto in Brooklyn, the Chilean born artist, director and writer Alejandro Jodorowsky was exploring similar territory with the Panic Movement, the radical theatre collective he instigated in Paris in 1962 along with the avant-garde dramatists Roland Topor and Fernando Arrabal. The Panic Movement staged long, semi-improvised 'happenings' which they called 'ephemeral panics'. These works of performance art were designed to collapse the barriers that existed in 'traditional' theatre between characters and actors, actors and audience. This was not just an attempt to reveal the artificiality of theatre as one would find in the work of Bertolt Brecht. Rather, Jodorowsky was driven by a desire to break down the distinction between representation and reality, to create a stunning authenticity: if a punch was thrown on stage, he would want it to land with the force it would carry in a street fight. Although often violent in content, the happenings nevertheless carried a transformative, if not ritualistic intent. The aim was to allow the participants to 'be' and 'exist' rather than merely 'act'. For Jodorowsky, this approach was essentially therapeutic. As with Destructivist piano smashing, ephemeral panics were intended as creative expressions of destructive energy that would otherwise be left to stagnate in the absence of any suitable outlet.

This desire for authenticity was also built into Panic's focus on the 'ephemeral'. Panic 'art' was not meant to last. The events were designed to be unscripted, physically exhausting and often involved large amounts of perishable goods: flour, fruit, meat. As such, they could only be performed once. The most (in)famous was the four-hour 'Melodrama Sacramental' staged in May 1965 at the second Paris Festival of Free Expression. Among other spectacles this featured Jodorowsky dressed in a leather biker suit and crash helmet running around with a whip while snakes and geese were let loose at his feet. As with the 'Henny Penny Piano Destruction Concert', such theatrical euphoria was bad news for the unfortunate animals involved. By the time the proceedings finally ended, all the geese had been killed and the snakes, much to their distress, had been repeatedly thrown around the performance space.

Some of the most intense ephemeral panics remained unrealised. When discussing his work Jodorowsky would often gleefully speculate upon epic events yet to come, as if using interviews as platforms to deliver spontaneous Panic monologues. Speaking about the Panic Movement in 1970, Jodorowsky let rip with a bravura display of provocation and imagination:

> Look, you are going to see the reactions of a nun whom I have tied up and put in a tub of beef blood to her chin. How will she talk to a great lawyer whom I have tied up and put in a barrel of excrement, which is put into the tub with the nun? We are going to strip them of the plastic shell that has covered them and then we are going to let some mothers loose from whom we have taken their babies, and the babies are going to be in a cage about thirty feet from the floor, and a blindfolded man at the same height on a platform will be swinging a spade so that there is a danger of cutting the ropes supporting the babies. All the mothers

> are immobile with their feet buried in enormous bricks of Camembert cheese ... What will they say?

Pausing to let this image of horror sink in, Jodorowsky simply added, 'That I would like.'[10]

Thankfully, Jodorowsky never got around to imprisoning mothers in cheese and nuns in beef blood, but one group who came close to the extremity he imagined were the Vienna Actionists. Active throughout the 1960s, the Actionists were a loose gathering of Austrian artists with shared interests who often collaborated in destructive, scatological and deeply transgressive performances. Although they consistently resisted being seen as a distinct 'group', the main, most prolific and visible participants were Hermann Nitsch, Otto Mühl, Rudolf Schwarzkogler and Günter Brus. The oldest of the four, Mühl (born in 1925) had served in the German *Wehrmacht* while Schwarzkogler (born in 1940), Brus and Nitsch (both born in 1938) grew up through the Second World War and its immediate aftermath. Their work traced the psychic and physical scars of this conflict and, like a scream in the night or a bloodstain on a white wall, it also railed against the smooth surfaces of Austria's post-war reconstruction, a ritualistic reminder of the potential for carnage that underpins any 'civilised' society.

The concept of the 'action' was intended as a denial of the distanced contemplation of the easel and the exhibition space in favour of creative acts that, once again, blurred the distinction between art and life; the representation of violence and its experience. But where Ortiz and Jodorowsky were on the offensive in the pursuit of this end, attacking or destroying their surroundings, the Actionists turned on themselves. They used their own bodies as their canvases and in the actions they performed, 'blood, sweat and excrement' became their 'art material'. For Schwarzkogler, his 'actions' were a series of intense, solemn performances that he mounted in private apartments around Vienna between 1965 and 1966. In the haunting images that emerged from these displays (taken by photographers Ludwig Hoffenreich, Franziska Cibulka and Michael Epp) one sees Schwarzkogler and sometimes his friend Heinz Cibulka bound in bandages. They appear to have received, or be in the process of receiving, a set of strange surgical procedures: blood seeps from beneath the gauze, dead fish and chicken intermingle with medical paraphernalia, and corkscrews look set to puncture exposed heads. At first glance the photographs speak of torture and intense pain, but in their solitary vignettes, the two bandaged figures also look like bodies undergoing acts of unprecedented transformation.

The same willingness to reorganise the body was evident in the comparatively more public work of Hermann Nitsch. In June 1963, Nitsch along with Otto Mühl mounted the 'Festival of Psycho-Physical Naturalism' in Mühl's basement studio in Vienna. In front of a white sheet Nitsch stood on a mattress and was engulfed in bucket loads of water, blood and animal intestines. He lay down on the mattress, and as he was covered in more and more of this offal, his physical form seemed to change. Once again, photographer Ludwig Hoffenreich was in attendance, and in his images of the action Nitsch initially looks like a man disembowelled, but, as more organic matter is accumulated, it is as if hitherto unknown organs begin to sprout from his body. The action was to conclude with Nitsch tearing apart the carcass of a lamb, but as he got stuck in the police arrived and shut down the event; a window around which the spectators were gathered had made the outrageous display visible to the street. Nitsch and Mühl were arrested for 'indecent behaviour and breach of the peace' and both would serve short prison sentences as a result. As they were hauled off in handcuffs that day, covered in blood and entrails, it became clear that their action had achieved a further level of transgression. As well as confusing the line between art and life, as well as collapsing the barriers between the inside and the outside of the body, in their affront to public decency Nitsch and Mühl had troubled the distinction between the role of the artist and the outlaw, a difference they would continue to peck away at in future performances.[11]

Destructivism, Panic, Actionism: their visceral, provocative radicalism was exactly what Jeff Nuttall had in mind when he wrote in *Bomb Culture* that 'Art has seldom been closer to its violent, orgiastic roots.' This was the 'reaffirmation of life by orgy and violence' he called for, and which he presented as the signature art form of a post-nuclear milieu. 'What has happened', he explained, echoing the idea of art-as-catharsis offered by the likes of Ortiz, 'is that the pressure of restriction has precipitated a biological reflex', an explosive formula in which 'the leftist element in the young middle class' joined 'with the delinquent in the young working class'. Here, Nuttall is keying into the long tradition of the artist as outsider or rebel. At the same time, he also draws deep on the well-established connection between art and delinquency: the sense of criminality that surrounds the work of multiple literary provocateurs ranging from the Marquis de Sade to Jean Genet. That said, what Nuttall adds to the discussion of post-1960s art is a distinct sense of class-consciousness. In so doing, he alludes to a much wider set of issues at play in the political culture of the post-war period. In particular, that Nuttall should connect transgressive underground art with a 'leftist element' is reflective of the seismic shifts that occurred within left-wing thinking during the 1960s, particularly the debates surrounding the so-called 'New Left', a term that gained wide exposure with the debut of the journal *New Left Review* in 1960.[12]

Although the term describes a wide spectrum of political thought and activism, at a base level 'New Left' refers to the widespread recalibration of Marxist theory in the light of the post-war social and political climate. Marxism, as understood from Karl Marx's foundational texts, the pamphlet *The Communist Manifesto* (1848) written with Friedrich Engels and the glorious three-volume door-stop *Das Kapital* (1867–83), saw industrial mass capitalism as a deeply exploitative economic system. Capitalism, according to Marx, dictates that those who own the means of production reap the largest share of the accumulated profits. Meanwhile, the workforce who fuel this industry, the proletariat, are objectified: as cogs in the machine they are ultimately alienated from the material and financial benefits of the commodities they produce. Handloom weavers in the cotton mills of the Industrial Revolution, for example, did not make clothes for themselves or for bartering in kind, but produced linen that was exchanged elsewhere, in often global markets, at a far higher value than the cost of production. It was then the mill owner, the company boss, the man at the top of the pyramid, who had the necessary capital to set up the venture in the first place, who pocketed the difference: the surplus value.

For Marx, such inequality was not an example of 'bad' capitalism but was very much the basis upon which the system operated and depended. The idea was to reap the maximum profit from the minimum outlay, and this basically boiled down to a matter of keeping things cheap, particularly the labour. What Marx and Engels hypothesised in response was communism, the collective ownership of the means of production in which the profits were circulated among the co-operative rather than hoarded by the masters. To effect this seismic change, it was necessary to enlighten and to weaponise the proletariat, to make them conscious of their predicament and to equip them with the tools necessary to make the leap from critique to action.[13]

Over the course of the century that followed, Marxism plotted a revolutionary pathway through socialism, advanced socialism and then state communism. The Russian Revolution of 1917 saw the aristocratic sovereignty of the Romanovs replaced by the workers' councils of Vladimir Lenin, and shortly after, in 1921, the Chinese Communist Party emerged under Li Dazhao, Chen Duxiu and the country's future Chairman Mao Zedong. By 1949, with Joseph Stalin installed as General Secretary and national Premier in Russia and the People's Republic of China working in accordance with Maoism, it was clear that communism had become a political superpower capable of rivalling that of Western capitalism. The skirmishes and pseudo-skirmishes of the Cold War, including the Korean War (1950–53), the Cuban Missile Crisis and the war in Vietnam, were mounted as part of this ideological conflict. It was one long tussle played out between the land-grabbing of the Soviet Union and the attempts of the West – principally America – to protect its empire.[14]

At the same time, across the spectrum of international left-wing thought there was much condemnation of the despotism that accompanied Mao and Stalin's rise to power. Both had established and violently enforced dictatorships within their one-party states and had led their countries into ill thought-out campaigns of economic 'development', the main results of which were often poverty and starvation. Where capitalism gave its adherents televisions and refrigerators, post-war communism delivered unworkable irrigation systems and failed crops. Upon the death of Stalin in 1953 his successor Nikita Khrushchev was keen to dismantle his regime, decentralise the party and establish a comparatively cordial relationship with America. Ironically it was on Khrushchev's watch that Russia very nearly went to nuclear war with Kennedy's America over Cuba, an event that would have had a human cost far in excess of Stalin's atrocities. That said, it was out of this period of relative revisionism that the New Left emerged: a form of theory and practice that sought to move away from communist orthodoxies and re-engage with the founding radicalism of socialist thought.[15]

By mid-century there was also the issue of the continued relevance of *Das Kapital* within an increasingly post-industrial world. While much of Marx's analysis was accurate and remained influential, capitalism was seen to have come a long way since the end of the 19th century. The workplace had changed beyond recognition and various forms of social mobility had blurred the traditional distinction between the proletariat and the bourgeoisie. This was the argument made by the sociologist Daniel Bell in his book *The End of Ideology* (1960). Bell claimed that advanced capitalism and the rise of the technocracy, the corporate synthesis of technical expertise and administrative prowess, had relieved the need for the type of revolutionary politics encouraged by *The Communist Manifesto*. In Bell's view, the rise of white-collar industry, relative post-war affluence and a materialist, consumer-led economy had 'met all the objections of the nineteenth century and the Thirties'. In other words, now that suburban families had decent jobs and enough disposable income to buy all kinds of labour-saving devices, what was there to complain about?

Other writers like C. Wright Mills, author of *White Collar: The American Middle Classes* (1951), were sceptical of this sweeping vision but nonetheless took the point that the working class no longer stood as 'the historic agency'. In the face of a 'massive assimilation of industry and technology' it was, according to Mills, necessary to move away from the industrial story plotted by 'Victorian Marxism'. There were, quite simply, other workforces and other spaces to which post-Marxist thinking could be applied.

One such sector was education, particularly the traditional factories of intellectual labour, the universities. Although they often purported to be open fora for learning and the exchange of knowledge, in the boardroom, America's universities tended towards conservatism, either in terms of direct political sympathies or through the execution of their role as pillars of the establishment, defenders of the status quo. During the 1960s though, universities became increasingly militant, with student activists pursuing off-campus agendas and interrogating the policies of their home institutions. In the case of Mario Savio, leader of the Berkeley Free Speech Movement, he saw the university administration as a system that treated its students as little more than raw material to be exploited. In December 1964, frustrated at the attempts of the University of California to block fundraising attempts for the ongoing civil rights movement as well as their general hostility towards political activism, Savio organised a mass demonstration. During an occupation of the university's Sproul Hall, he delivered a stirring speech that clearly recalled a scene of discontent on the factory floor. In Savio's words the university was an 'odious' machine, the operation of which 'makes you so sick at heart' that 'you've got to put your bodies upon the gears and upon the wheels [...] and you've got to make it stop'. In parallel, the continuing work of groups like the Student Nonviolent Coordinating Committee and Students for a Democratic Society further extended practical activism to areas other than the conditions of the industrial workforce. Combining the politics and tactics of the civil rights movement with the organisational zeal of workers' unions, these groups successfully wove ideas of equality and identity politics into the remit of left-wing thought.[16]

These topics and many more were discussed at the Dialectics of Liberation, a congress held in July 1967 at London's Roundhouse, a large venue in Chalk Farm. Bringing together a broad sweep of the political left – activists, critics, theorists, psychiatrists, anthropologists – the congress took as its central focus the 'cardinal failure of all past revolutions'. David Cooper, the 'anti-psychiatrist' and primary organiser of the event, clarified this theme, noting that such periods of political upheaval were typically concerned with 'liberation on the mass social level' rather than 'liberation on the level of the individual and the concrete groups in which he is directly engaged'. He contended that focusing on matters of the individual, their psychology, the politics of identity and the contexts in which they existed, was just as important as engaging with grand concepts of revolution linked to changes in material circumstances:

> If we are to talk of revolution today, our talk will be meaningless unless we effect some union between the macro-social and micro-social, and between 'inner reality' and 'outer reality'. We have only to think back about the personal factor in Lenin that made it possible for him to ignore so much of the manoeuvrings of the super-bureaucrat Stalin until it was too late. We have only to consider the limited personal liberation achieved in the 'Second World' (The Soviet Union and Eastern Europe). Then we get the point that a radical de-bourgeoisification of society has to be achieved in the very style of revolutionary work and is

not automatically entailed by the seizure of power by an exploited class.

In their song 'Won't Get Fooled Again' (1971), the Who would succinctly distil this problem into a single lyric: 'Meet the new boss, same as the old boss'. For the New Left 'revolution' means nothing if it merely repeats the modes of thought and behaviour deemed so problematic in the first place.[17]

Mills made a similar point in his 'Letter to the New Left' (1960). The essay was a clarion call to a largely youth-led, politically engaged demographic. It encouraged them to recognise the difference between the veneer of economic health and the conditions that such circumstances had created for the culture at large. Although the dominant political consensus was that the post-war West existed in a state of relaxed, suburban, employed affluence, Mills argued that marginal disparities remained. Problems of poverty and inequality had either been ignored or had become worse despite the apparent health of the coffers. In *One-Dimensional Man* (1964), Herbert Marcuse took this argument further, arguing that the plenitude of advanced capitalism had deadened critical activity, the actual ability to think through and to critique such matters.[18]

There was still, then, much to complain about, and rightly so. One of the most vociferous voices within this period was Stokely Carmichael. Born in Trinidad in 1941, Carmichael was raised in America. By 1961 he was participating in the Freedom Rides, a series of direct-action protests against racial segregation in the country's southern states. By 1966 he had assumed the leadership of the Student Nonviolent Coordinating Committee and was advocating a philosophy of 'Black Power'. This was not so much an argument for equality and integration as a call for a self-determining black culture. Carmichael first outlined this stance following the shooting of the civil rights activist James Meredith in June 1966 during his Tennessee-to-Mississippi 'March Against Fear'. Carmichael's main claim was that combating individual instances of racism was not enough to generate lasting change. Instead, a real revolution would depend upon a strike against the forces that generate the ideology of racism.[19]

Carmichael, along with Charles V. Hamilton, published the book *Black Power: The Politics of Liberation* in October 1967, and in July of that year he spoke on the subject at the Dialectics of Liberation. Addressing the issue of economic inequality in American cities, Carmichael claimed that it often fell along racial lines with poor, black, inner-city neighbourhoods living in the shadow of affluent, white, middle-class suburbs. The former communities are ghettos, argued Carmichael, in which the black people 'do not control' nor 'own the resources', the 'land, the houses or the stores'. These belong to the 'whites who live outside the community'. Amplifying this stark vision of racially segregated ownership, Carmichael added that 'it is white power that makes the laws and enforces those laws with guns and sticks in the hands of white racist policemen and their black mercenaries'. From city to city such power repeats itself and for Carmichael the key factor was the operation of capitalism, a system that 'automatically contains within itself racism whether by design or not'. If power goes to those who control the means of production, such ownership is invariably held in the hands of white America. What else could be expected of a country that had previously maintained a buoyant culture of indentured slavery, and which had regarded black men and women as human commodities? In seeking to 'free these colonies from external domination', the aim for Carmichael was not to reverse the system of accumulated profit but to adopt a new system altogether. The idea was not for 'black money' to go into 'a few black pockets' but to move away from 'an oppressive capitalist society' towards one in which such wealth would go into 'the communal pocket'.[20]

Between 1965 and 1970 other minority groups made claims similar to those of Carmichael. 'Black Power' was followed by calls for 'Red Power' from the Native American group Indians of All Tribes who occupied Alcatraz Island between 1969 and 1971. Nineteen sixty-nine saw the emergence of the Gay Liberation Front in response to the events at New York's Stonewall Inn between June and July of that year. Kate Millett's *Sexual Politics* (1970) and Germaine Greer's *The Female Eunuch* (1970) also extended the issue of identity politics to the sphere of gender. Despite advocating very different causes, these groups carried with them an overlapping set of concerns. They each expressed a desire for independence and self-sufficiency within the culture at large; they were each concerned with psychological and subjective advancement, with changing the way people thought about the issue at play; and they were each committed to change at a material level in relation to such varied matters as housing, political representation, use of 'community' spaces and so on. Whether seen as a spontaneous flowering of parallel concerns or a domino effect leading from one social cause to another, left-wing dissent was so pervasive and wide-ranging in the 1960s that it appeared as if the dominant status quo were facing a state of imminent, total and long overdue transformation.[21]

Seen within this context, the violent avant-garde art discussed by Nuttall in *Bomb Culture* works as an intense crystallisation of these calls for political shift. In dissolving the distinction between art and life, in challenging taboos and embracing the obscene, artists like Raphael Ortiz, Alejandro Jodorowsky and the Vienna

Actionists were expressing a powerful, primal desire for change. They may have lacked the targeted, *overtly* political focus of other agendas regarding race, gender, ethnicity and sexuality, but they nevertheless displayed the same will and intent to challenge the order of things. Nuttall spoke of this impulse as a 'sickness', a 'will to enact some definite ceremony of violence that would spend the aggression inherent in the collective subconscious, exorcise it and thus leave society cleansed of fear'. According to Nuttall, such catharsis would provide a 'clear way out for our over-accumulated frustrated energies'. In the case of Stokely Carmichael he was certainly sick: he was sick of having the weight of deeply ingrained racism continually bearing down on him. His call for Black Power was thus intended to carry the force of an axe smashing into a piano. It was an attempt to aim the 'over-accumulated frustrated energies' of America's black communities against the country's edifice of discrimination. If, in making this call, Carmichael was fanning the flames of revolution then it was the members of the artistic underground who could be found somewhere in the shadows, stirring the gasoline.

In September 1966, fire starters like Raphael Ortiz, Günter Brus, Otto Mühl and Hermann Nitsch – Destructivists and Actionists alike – came out of the shadows and converged in London. Along with other artists including Yoko Ono and John Latham, they were in town for DIAS, the Destruction in Art Symposium. This series of meetings and happenings was organised by the German artist Gustav Metzger, who specialised in what he termed 'auto-destructive art'. Often working in public and often wearing clothes more commonly associated with heavy industry (gas masks, gloves, boots and overalls), Metzger would 'paint' with hydrochloric acid. His nylon canvases would dissolve into vapour just as he made contact. Other auto-destructive works included plate glass sheets falling to the ground 'in pre-arranged sequence' and Latham's 'Skoob' sculptures, huge towers of books that when set alight would collapse into dust. Pete Townsend's ritualistic guitar-smashing in the Who was also said to be informed by Metzger's work. The symposium dealt with the 'principle of transformation by destruction' and, by bringing the Destructivist Ortiz together with the Actionist contingent of Brus *et al*, Metzger was implicitly aligning their varied work with his own auto-destructive methods and the project's political stance. For all its wilful, instinctual damage, Metzger saw auto-destruction as a targeted attack on 'capitalist values and the drive to nuclear annihilation.' As he had outlined in 'Manifesto Auto-destructive Art' (1960), the work was intended to re-enact 'the obsession with destruction' that underpins 'the chaos of capitalism and Soviet Communism': the 'immense productive capacity [...], the co-existence of surplus and starvation; the increasing stock-piling of nuclear weapons.' The aim was to show the harm done by such a state of affairs, the 'pummelling to which individuals and masses [were] subjected' and the 'disintegrative effect of machinery [...] on the person.' Buried within the clamour of auto-destructive art, then, is a concern for the exploited human individual, the same basic cause advocated by much of the New Left.[22]

As he shot *The Fall* throughout late 1967 and into 1968 Whitehead became increasingly aware of this overlap between experimental art and New Left politics. If the anti-war movement was protesting the obscene human damage of the war and the civil rights movement was protesting the obscene human damage of racism, it came as no surprise to Whitehead that the art which came out of this climate of discontent was similarly physical, bodily and (in all senses of the word) offensive. More and more Whitehead felt that if *The Fall* was to be effective as a protest film, it somehow had to occupy this same intersection point: the thin line between the documentation of radicalism and the performance of a radical act. He was fully aware of what this could mean for him as the proposed subject or, at least, the focus of the film. 'I am encouraging my own self-destruction,' he confessed to his diary in October 1967 just as he had come think of *The Fall* as a 'Requiem Mass.' Searching around for another phrase, one that would give this gesture the necessary sense of *gravitas*, Whitehead seized upon the perfect distillation of art, protest and violence: 'This film is auto-destructive.'[23]

*

'Everyone gets everything he wants.' Shortly after the extraordinary scene in the hotel room that opens Francis Ford Coppola's *Apocalypse Now* (1979), Captain Willard (played by Martin Sheen) reflects on his new assignment to find and to 'terminate with extreme prejudice' the mysterious Colonel Kurtz. Mired in the haze of the Vietnam war circa 1969–70, Willard has been languishing in his room waiting for a mission, watching the walls draw in. When the call comes he gladly accepts. It gets him out of Saigon, back into 'the jungle,' and means that he no longer must drink himself to death out of fear, boredom or paranoia. For all his willingness, though, Willard knows that whatever he is about to encounter in the heart of darkness will be far worse than the horrors he's previously faced (or perhaps perpetrated) during his time in Vietnam. He sets out knowing that the journey will be difficult, if not deadly; but maybe such a journey is not just what he needs but also what he deserves: 'I wanted a mission, and for my sins, they gave me one.'[24]

In April 1968, deep into the filming of *The Fall*, Whitehead was in Washington D.C., feeling a similar sense of vertigo. The early part of the year had been spent shuttling between London and New York collecting footage, raising extra funds and writing the film's detailed 'Treatment'. The document shows that Whitehead had hammered into shape the story of 'Peter Whitehead', a young English filmmaker in New York who commits murder as an act of political protest. Around this scenario he had also written a tight summary of everything he had seen and absorbed in New York since his arrival in late 1967: the Destructivists, the Bread and Puppet Theatre, the San Francisco Mime Troupe, Julie Bavarso on the New York subway, 'Robert Lowell reading his poem written about his participation in the Washington march', 'Bobby Kennedy [...] at a campaign meeting in the Bronx' talking to 'a crowd of young people'. Whitehead's wider reading also peppered the text with references to 'Camus' *The Rebel*, Stokely Carmichael's *Black Power*, Salinger's book on [John F.] Kennedy and the assassination, [Jean-Luc] Godard's scripts of *Made in USA* and *Le Petit Soldat* and *Alphaville* [...] *Ramparts* magazine'. Up to date, extremely personal and full of the detail of his time in New York, the 'Treatment' was not unlike the diary that Whitehead kept throughout the making of *The Fall*. What remained unique to the treatment however, was the murder scenario. This is what was separated the 'real' Peter Whitehead from his fictional counterpart. Forming the climax of the film, the murder plot would mark the point where *The Fall* ceases to be a documentary and moves into the more imaginative and provocative territory of the 'thriller'.[25]

The completion of the treatment is what had brought Whitehead to Washington D.C. on 4 April 1968. It was a launch party of sorts held for backers and investors in *The Fall*, a moment for Whitehead to talk up the work he had done before the final push towards shooting the fictional sections of the film. Everything was going well until news came that the leading civil rights campaigner and advocate of non-violence, Martin Luther King, had been shot and killed in Memphis. Shocked and saddened Whitehead felt as if his fictional assassination plot had suddenly been realised in the most awful way possible. 'Reality', said Whitehead, 'had far exceeded my worst expectations'.

Making his way back to New York, Whitehead quickly found himself in Newark, New Jersey in the middle of a wave of rioting prompted by King's death. This poor, predominantly black neighbourhood, very much the type of economic 'colony' Carmichael had decried in his analysis of capitalism and race, was a tinder box. Along with Harlem, Newark had been ghettoised by years of underinvestment, and the shooting of King was the spark that ignited this simmering discontent. Standing with his camera amid burnt-out cars and smashed property, Whitehead could sense the veneer of his fictional scenario starting to dissolve. He wanted to join in and 'burn the houses down'. At the same time Whitehead also began to feel strangely 'responsible' for King's death as if all his reflections on 'premeditated murder' had somehow brought it to pass. Going forward he resolved that *The Fall* could only ever be about participation. For Whitehead this uncanny turn of events 'pushed the film away from [the] fiction script into the subject of the necessary and to be wished for collapse of the protest movement and the beginning of anarchy on the streets'. Although his feelings of direct, personal responsibility were unwarranted, Whitehead nonetheless felt compelled to add his voice and his actions to the mounting outrage. It was no longer enough to be a witness. 'I had become an inevitable activist and soon an ardent anarchist'. Whitehead had wanted a mission, and for his sins, America had given him one.[26]

A few weeks later on 23 April, a group of students converged on the campus of New York's Columbia University. The gathering was organised by the Columbia chapter of the Students for a Democratic Society, the president of which was twenty-year-old Mark Rudd. Rudd had recently returned from an SDS trip to Cuba and, according to Mark Kurlansky, was fired up with the thought of revolution.

The university had recently staged a memorial service for Martin Luther King, which to Rudd and his fellow student radicals smacked of gross hypocrisy. It was well known that since the late 1950s the university administration had been buying up large tracts of land and real estate in Harlem to use as student accommodation. This was an aggressive, asset-led policy that drained the local black community of essential resources. The construction of a university gym in the nearby Morningside Park became a particular issue of concern. In addition to absorbing valuable green space, it was originally designed to be used exclusively by university members, and 'the people of Harlem were to be denied access.' Another key issue was the matter of Columbia's alleged ties to the IDA, the Institute for Defense Analyses, a government-funded military research body that drew heavily on academic consultancy. As Kurlansky outlines, requests for transparency from the student body and the SDS had previously been met with the standard script, the university 'refused to confirm or deny participation.' By April 1968, however, the SDS were claiming otherwise, stating that 'not only did the university belong [to the IDA]' but that its president Grayson Kirk 'and another Columbia trustee were on the board of organization.' This, then, was the university that had so solemnly celebrated King's life and work. It was an institution that from the perspective of Rudd and the SDS had performed discriminating land grabs on deprived black communities and which was actively funnelling its expertise into the orchestration of the war in Vietnam. So much for civil rights and non-violence.

The gathering on the 23 April was intended as a protest against these and other matters. However, in the charged atmosphere that followed the death of King, with the knowledge that Harlem had responded with riots just as much as Newark, it became clear that the will of the assembled group favoured action, not speeches. The decision was taken – organically, spontaneously – to hold a sit-in and occupy the university's property. In the spirit of Mario Savio's revolt against the machine, they were hoping to block the university's gears until their demands were met. First the crowd, which over the course of the afternoon had swelled from 300 to 500, tried to get into the Low Library. Finding it locked they moved on to the sprawling teaching and administration building Hamilton Hall. They surged in, along with a contingent of activists from Harlem and the university's dean, Henry Coleman. Rudd and the SDS had taken a building and, it appeared, a hostage. Over the next two nights more buildings were occupied including Mathematics and Fayerweather Hall. Barricades were put up, supplies were brought in and the university effectively shut down. No one was sure what was going to happen next, but some things everyone could agree on: action had followed words and a line had been crossed. It would not go unnoticed and there would be consequences.[27]

When word of the events at Columbia reached Whitehead on 24 April, he quickly gathered his gear and headed over to the campus with his assistant Sebastian Keep and his driver Angelo Mansraven. At first, they just watched the scene and the crowds of students who had assembled to 'protect' the occupied buildings. A day later Whitehead filmed Stokely Carmichael and H. Rap Brown, his successor as leader of the SNCC. They had arrived on campus to give speeches in support of the action. Both viewed the events solely through the lens of Black Power, with Brown emphasising that it was 'Black Columbia university students' who were in 'complete control of all occurrences within Hamilton Hall'. He added that further support was coming from 'the community of Harlem'. Thus, if the university administration 'don't want to deal with the brothers in here, they're going to deal with the brothers on the street'. The Whitehead of October 1967 would have left things here. Filming done, footage of the speeches could be added to the archive as 'evidence' that a protest had taken place and that Whitehead had attended. However, post-King, his priorities had changed.

Along with Keep, Whitehead returned to campus and approached the students to let them join the occupation of Fayerweather Hall. They were admitted, and as far as Whitehead was concerned he was no longer 'just' a documentarian but an active member of the cause: 'Once inside Sebastian and I were part of the revolution'. In among all the Che Guevara posters on the walls, the hastily drafted cleaning rotas and the long, often fractious policy meetings, Whitehead quickly realised there was little consensus between the students or, for that matter, between the occupied buildings. Each had become an individual 'microcosm of democracy'. Late on the Saturday the Fayerweather group were deep in discussion about who was going to empty the bins when one of the occupying students from the Mathematics building entered the room. He talked about their debates regarding the 'structure of the university they were going to build from the ruins of the old'. Where Fayerweather saw themselves as a temporary demonstration, it was clear that the Maths building were in for the long haul. They had 'voted to resist – until the end'.

Whitehead was exhilarated to hear of such militancy. 'Years of negotiation had been met with silence by the poker-faced Corporate front', he reflected in his diary, so 'finally' in light of the grievances regarding 'civil rights issues' and the IDA, the students had 'taken their destiny into their own hands and acted. They took over what they could. Their education. [...] No longer merely content to protest, they were stepping forward'. As Saturday moved into Sunday the Fayerweather group elected to end the protest and leave their building peacefully. Whitehead, meanwhile, snuck away and set up his base of operations in Maths. There he found a tightly run operation that reflected the commitment of the group's rhetoric, but this also came with a heightened concern for 'security'. After an initial burst of filming, Whitehead was met by Tom Hurwitz, a key member of the SDS and the occupation's 'head of defence'. Stood by a window, carefully monitoring the flow of traffic in and out of the building, Hurwitz wasted no time. 'Look man, I'm sorry – I know we let you in – but you'll have to go. There's no argument. We have decided.' Whitehead pleaded his case nonetheless. He spoke of his films: *Tonite*, *Benefit*, 'The London Scene'. 'I'm one of you', he argued. Much to his delight and surprise Hurwitz said he had seen the films at the New York Film Festival in September. 'The London Scene', it turned out was something of a hit among those now involved in the occupation. Once he'd properly introduced himself, Whitehead was welcomed back into the fold, no longer as a possible security risk but as a vital part of the cause. 'He has to be allowed to film', Whitehead recalls Hurwitz telling the committee.

From Sunday 28 until Tuesday 30 April Whitehead filmed the occupiers as they carefully maintained the building and continued to make plans for the university yet to come. Fostering other actions and establishing contact with the revolutionary contingents then active in European cities like Paris and Prague were other, much discussed priorities. Then word came in of the police 'bust'. The buildings were to be cleared by force and the action was expected for the early hours of Tuesday morning. Knowing there would be violence and that the police would be armed with 'pickaxes, night-sticks, guns [...] and knuckle-dusters', some of the group elected to leave. The others, around 250 students and Whitehead, remained and set about preparing themselves. With a single roll of film, Whitehead shot the building of barricades, students applying Vaseline as protections against Mace before the thousand-strong police force converged on the building. They lined the stairwells and easily broke through the top floor barriers. Just before the film ran out, Whitehead caught a shot of an axe coming through the barricade as the cops piled in. He quickly threw his film out of the window to where Keep was waiting below. The police grabbed him, threw him up against the wall before manhandling him out of the room. As he was taken down the stairs passing cop after cop, it seemed to Whitehead that every one of them tried to beat him. Outside Whitehead, still grasping his camera, managed to melt into the waiting throng of press and photographers. Thanks to another roll of film from Keep, he managed to get some shots of the other students leaving the building. A lot of them were injured, 'bleeding, weeping, hardly able to stand'. With the occupation neutralised and the 'Police State' made manifest, *The Fall* now had its ending.

Writing up the experience in his diary on Wednesday 1 May, Whitehead's discontent was palpable. 'I am no longer a free man', the entry began. Having lived through a 'revolution' which was 'suppressed by force', force sanctioned by the university administration against its students, Whitehead felt embattled but also keen for the situation to escalate. Writing in terms he had previously reserved for his 'Treatment', Whitehead boldly asserted that he was now 'capable of killing a man': he was 'capable of sitting behind a machine gun and killing a thousand men'. He spoke not of 'a question of violence and non-violence' but of the inevitability of 'war' and the question of 'what side to be on.'[28]

It was not long before Whitehead had his feelings validated. In Paris, a series of student occupations and discontent among its factory workforce had, by 13 May, escalated to the point of a debilitating general strike. More so than in New York, the scale of the action during May 1968 – including pitched battles on the streets of Paris between police and left-wing student groups – carried with it the real possibility of a civil war. In the event, President Charles de Gaulle only managed to remain in office thanks to his government retaining the support of the military. Meanwhile back in New York, Whitehead found that some of the footage he had sent to the processing lab had been mysteriously damaged. He then started to hear from various contacts that the CIA were after him, and his film, because of the Columbia material. It is easy for rumours to circulate in times of tension. For Whitehead, paranoid, angry and impassioned, simultaneously trying to work through his experiences of the previous month while observing what appeared to be an international wave of revolutionary action, a rumour was enough. The time seemed right to put his thoughts into action.[29]

Whitehead arranged to meet Angelo Mansraven; he put $75 in his hand and said: 'Get me a gun.' Looking down at the wad of cash and then back to the wired, exhausted figure standing in front of him, Mansraven quietly returned the money. 'Listen, Peter,' he counselled, 'go – my advice is, go.' Go Home. This was the dose of clarity he needed. Whitehead realised just how far he had been pushing himself. Getting involved with the protests was one thing, getting beaten up by the police was another. But a gun? Time to get out before he made a mistake he wouldn't walk away from. Whitehead packed up his operation and took the next flight back to London, landing at Heathrow on 6 June 1968. He was immediately greeted by the news: Robert Kennedy had been shot and killed in Chicago by Sirhan Bishara Sirhan, a 24-year-old Palestinian. Kennedy was on the campaign trail after having, in March 1968, announced his intention to run for President. When he had filmed Kennedy on 1 November the previous year, Whitehead had reflected in his diary for that day on how 'tired and lost' the Senator had looked. He noted that his appearance in the Bronx seem to have had more to do with 'survival' than political strategy as if Kennedy had 'started something he dare not and cannot escape'. With a sense of foreboding, Whitehead added, 'I believe he has already said goodbye to himself'. Now facing the news in 1968, Whitehead felt that, as with his reaction to the death of Martin Luther King, he had somehow predicted, if not influenced Kennedy's shooting. Again, Whitehead 'could no longer distinguish between fiction and reality' and, coming so soon after the events at Columbia, he felt both were 'intolerable'. It was more than Whitehead could bear: 'I collapsed. I fell to pieces.'[30]

*

'I had a complete nervous breakdown and didn't speak to anyone for three months', he admitted in 1997. The combined stress of two years shuttling between London and New York plus the pressure of 'trying to edit the huge mass of devastating, violent film material' had led Whitehead to a point of crisis. He had thrown himself into the manifold complexities of late-1960s America, he had faced armed police at the barricades, and he had struggled with the weird synchronicities between his own work and two major assassinations. As 1968 became 1969 Whitehead found himself at a precipice, what he called 'the treacherous interface' where 'fiction becomes fact and vice versa'. That said, although the hours of film were a source of unease, Whitehead nevertheless ploughed on towards a final cut. It was only by 'giving form' to *The Fall*, by 'making it make sense' Whitehead would later reflect, that he was able to 'put [himself] back together'.[31]

A year after his return from New York, *The Fall* was screened as part of the 1969 Edinburgh International Film Festival. Also appearing on the bill that year was *Easy Rider* in what became its UK premiere. According to Paul Cronin, Whitehead was 'apprehensive about audience response to his complex new work'. Wanting a break from the stuffy hubbub of the festival and to 'calm himself [...] before the screening', Whitehead took to the Edinburgh streets. He eventually found 'refuge in a quiet leafy square'. Moments later the air was filled with the noise of fluttering birds as an old man appeared with a pocket full of seed. One by one, the man fed the birds, calling each of them by name. Whitehead sat entranced and watched this scene for half an hour. Suddenly, filmmaking didn't seem so important any more. This simple gesture of care with its almost psychic connection to a species other than the human carried infinitely more power than any of the auto-destructive acts he had seen over the past two years. There was no longer any need to tear a bird to pieces in the crypt of the Judson Memorial Church. 'At that moment', says Whitehead, 'I realised I would sooner have this old man's talent than the talent to make *The Fall*'. Guided by visions of birds, and flushed with the overwhelming desire to fly, Whitehead pushed open the walls of the white box, and disappeared.[32]

CHAPTER V

The Dark Side

According to the psychoanalyst Carl Gustav Jung, founder of analytical psychology, when birds appear in dreams and visions they represent 'thoughts and the flight of thought'. In the case of specific birds like the eagle, this ecstatic idea of the unconscious taking flight carries the additional gloss of 'spiritual aspiration'. Thus, in dreams of ocean voyages, the presence of eagles guiding the way indicates that the journey is an 'odyssey in search of wholeness'. Jung was fascinated by the appearance of these images in alchemical texts, and those who followed his psychoanalytic method would have found much to mull over in this interpretation of their dreams. In the psychic battlefield of the Cold War, the same analysis could also be applied to the desires, anxieties and symbolism of entire institutions, especially the American space agency NASA.[1]

Ever since President Eisenhower had formed the National Aeronautics and Space Administration as a knee-jerk response to the Russian launch of *Sputnik* in 1957, NASA had fought for results, and validity. As a civilian organisation they had faced hostility from the Air Force, and as a well-funded organisation they had, from the start, faced political pressure to justify the large amounts injected. After Soviet cosmonaut Yuri Gagarin's pioneering orbital flight in 1961, such pressure became even more intense, with every success, failure and disaster incurred by the *Mercury*, *Gemini* and *Apollo* programmes subject to intense scrutiny. And so, when NASA's very own *Eagle*, the lunar module of the *Apollo 11* mission, finally landed on the surface of the Moon on 20 July 1969, there was a definite sense that a collective set of aspirations – technical and political – had been fulfilled.

In reaching the Moon before the end of the decade NASA had not only honoured the wishes of the late President John F. Kennedy but had also far surpassed the technical capabilities of the Soviet Union and healed the wounds caused by the early successes of *Sputnik* and Gagarin. The spectacular launch of the *Saturn V* rocket – the massive vehicle that had carried the *Eagle* and the command module *Columbia* into space – had also demonstrated to any potential combatants a continued prowess in the field of long-range missiles. Victors in the space race, pioneers on the new, lunar frontier and renewed leaders on the world's political stage: if NASA had entered into the confidence of Carl Jung, they could comfortably have read the achievements of July 1969 as a momentary completion of America's 'odyssey in search of wholeness'.[2]

The two men inside the *Eagle*, commander Neil Armstrong and co-pilot Buzz Aldrin, were well aware of the significance of their mission, but just after touchdown on the Moon, their main feeling was one of relief. Just as it was for their wives, families and the entirety of NASA's mission control back on Earth, this immediate relief was rather more personal than political. Despite the unprecedented difficulty of the mission; despite everything that could (and did) go wrong; despite the deaths (confirmed and unconfirmed) both Russian and American that had been involved in the space race up to 1969, they had made it to the Moon. The *Eagle* was intact, and they were alive. Above them, pilot Michael Collins oversaw the command module *Columbia*, the spacecraft from which the *Eagle* had launched and to which, everyone hoped, it would soon return. While Aldrin and Armstrong took stock of their landing site, Collins guided the *Columbia* into a series of lunar orbits. These would take him across the far side of the Moon, its much fabled 'dark side'. This is the section of the lunar surface that lies unobservable from the Earth, which looks out into deep space and which faces a tidal flow of incoming meteors. It would take Collins 47 minutes to pass through this territory and he would lose all radio contact with mission control in the interim. During these lacunae, he would be truly on his own, the furthest any human had ever been from the surface of the Earth.[3]

In Michael Moorcock's novel *The Final Programme* (1969), there is a secret text, a 'testament' written by 'G. Newman, Major, USAF, Astronaut'. Newman is described as having embarked on a space flight in 1968 during which he completed 'more orbits in his capsule than had been originally announced'. As Moorcock outlines the story, Newman is 'silenced' upon his return to Earth and commits suicide shortly after. His 'testament' thus becomes a much sought-after account of this mysterious mission but is ultimately revealed to be '203 neatly numbered pages' that contain nothing but madcap laughter: 'Ha ha ha ha ha ha ha [...]'. The clear implication is that Newman suffered a breakdown due to some 'encounter' during the mission or in response to the vast, open void of space he confronted while in orbit. Back in reality, Collins regarded his unprecedented isolation as a rare privilege. He did not succumb to the crushing pressure of his extreme position, but instead recalled it as a deeply solemn experience. As he passed over the far side he did not run into any of the UFOs or secret alien bases long rumoured to be hidden there. Instead, he saw a surface pockmarked by impact craters but which otherwise lay still.

None of this came as a disappointment or a surprise. Aldrin, Armstrong and Collins very much expected to find empty space and a quiet Moon. They did not believe in UFOs, aliens and That

Sort of Thing. They were taciturn, mission-focused All-American Boys who believed in flight trajectories, fuel levels and the physics of aeronautics. This is not to say that NASA's astronauts were unaffected by their missions – quite the opposite – but to the public eye the lunar trip appeared not to have made an impact on their interior lives. It seemed that the further out they went, the less important it became for them to turn inwards. As the British author J.G. Ballard later put it, astronauts 'aren't the type of guys who dream.'[4]

An estimated 600 million people – one fifth of the world's population – watched and listened to the coverage of the Moon landing. When he established contact with Neil Armstrong mid-Moonwalk, President Richard Nixon spoke of an even bigger audience. He claimed that with the success of *Apollo 11* 'for one priceless moment in the whole History of Man all the people of Earth are truly one.' Aside from the heavily-gendered nature of Nixon's language – 'it's the 1960s: women still count as men,' notes Andrew Smith in *Moondust* (2005) – the thrust of his statement is that the Moon landing was unprecedented. It was a once in a lifetime occurrence that generated hitherto unknown levels of global unity. Certainly, the Moon landing was a major media event, one that made headlines all over the world, but it was not an entirely unfamiliar spectacle. NASA's space programme rolled out at a time when rockets, space flights and trips to other planets were deeply embedded in popular culture.

In 1960 pioneering music producer Joe Meek released the EP *I Hear a New World*, a dizzying and imaginatively ambitious sonic portrait of life on other planets. Fresh from all-night stints at the appropriately named UFO club, Pink Floyd recorded a series of space-rock songs between *Piper at the Gates of Dawn* and *Saucerful of Secrets* (1968): 'Interstellar Overdrive' (1967),

'Astronomy Domine' (1967) and 'Set the Controls for the Heart of the Sun' (1968). In 1963 *Doctor Who* joined the likes of *Fireball XL5* and *Planet Patrol* on British television. *The Twilight Zone, The Outer Limits* and the soon to be phenomenal *Star Trek* had all appeared on American television by 1966 and would be seen by British audiences before the end of 1969. Nineteen sixty-six also saw the first Nebula Award for science fiction writing. With Frank Herbert and William Burroughs among the first nominees, from the outset the Nebulas attempted to bring an element of 'literary' judgement to a genre that had previously been considered the preserve of 'entertainment'.

Shadowed by this milieu, it's easy to see why the Moon landing attracted a global audience in the summer of 1969. The public had been primed for it. It was as if the *Apollo 11* crew and their strange mission had stepped right out of the pages of a science fiction adventure. 'You were a wonder to us, unattainable', wrote the poet Archibald MacLeish in 'Voyage to the Moon' (1969), where he gave voice to the sense that a figment of the imagination had suddenly been made manifest: 'Now / our hands have touched you in your depth of night'. Seen in this way, the Moon landing came to mean more than a technical or scientific victory. As a fantastic, almost surreal, voyage it spoke more to the ambiguous domain of inner space – the Jungian world of the dream and the psyche – than it did to a public interest in the mechanics of rocketry. This was particularly the case when writers and filmmakers of the Apollo-era imagined the return journey.[5]

Michael Crichton's novel *The Andromeda Strain*, published just before the Moon landing in May 1969, described a deadly bacterium finding its way to Earth in a returning NASA space probe. It was a microbiological take on 1950s films like *The Quatermass Experiment* (1955) and *The First Man into Space* (1959) which involved the return of astronauts who had mutated during their trips. What distinguished Crichton's scenario from this B-movie fare was the level of scientific detail he loaded into the narrative. At times *The Andromeda Strain* reads more like a report on an actual incident than a science fiction novel. Such veracity was appropriate given that the real NASA was just as anxious about space-born infections as were Crichton's heroic scientists. After splashing down on 24 July, Armstrong, Aldrin and Collins immediately entered three weeks of quarantine at the Manned Spacecraft Centre in Houston, Texas. With official celebrations timed to begin on 13 August, it was important for the astronauts to decompress, readjust to Earth's gravity and, most importantly, to submit to extensive medical examinations in case they had become irradiated or otherwise biohazardous in space. No one wanted a wildfire outbreak of a hitherto unknown contagion, nor would there have been – as in the novel – any appetite for wiping potentially infected towns off the map with targeted nuclear strikes. Armstrong, Aldrin and Collins thus had no choice but to sit out the time and stare at the walls of the Lunar Receiving Laboratory. In a weird repeat of the time the astronauts spent waiting in the *Eagle* before the Moonwalk, they were once again teasingly close to their destination but were at the same time cut off from it. It was as if Earth had now become the alien planet. In its strongest moments *The Andromeda Strain* conjures up a similar atmosphere. In the novel the town of Piedmont, Arizona is devastated by the cosmic disease. In twelve hours, a bustling community becomes a ghost town full of corpses, empty houses and overwhelming silence. Crichton's point is stark and bleak: the first human contact with an organism from outer space immediately renders a corner of the Earth as magnificently desolate as the surface of the Moon.[6]

Other works of late-1960s sci-fi similarly emphasised the terrestrial effects of space exploration. For the astronauts of these films, returning proves to be a far stranger journey than their flight into space because the Earth appears to have changed in their absence. In Robert Parrish's *Journey to the Far Side of the Sun* (1969) Roy Thinnes plays Colonel Glenn Ross, an astronaut who finds himself on a parallel world. Ross initially thinks he has arrived back 'home' before he notices a peculiar set of reversals: watches, clocks, electrical equipment and printed texts all run 'backwards'. This second Earth is a mirror image of the first, a *doppelgänger* beyond the sun. Unlike such interplanetary horror films as Kinji Fukasaku's *The Green Slime* (1968), there are no monsters or aliens on this double world to threaten Ross. Instead, the horror of the film comes from the deep uncanniness of his experience, the creeping realisation that what Ross thinks of as 'home' is in fact a different planet, one that is as far away from Earth as it is possible to travel. The classic example of this twist is, of course, *Planet of the Apes* (1968) in which the American astronaut Taylor, played by Charlton Heston, crash lands on a seemingly distant planet, a savage, inverted world in which apes rule over passive humans. After fighting his way through such a bizarre situation, desperate to find some way home, he discovers that he needn't travel far. Deep in the wasteland of the planet's 'Forbidden Zone', Taylor encounters a desolate coastline and the ruins of an ancient civilisation: late 20th-century Earth.

These fantasies have little interest in the technicalities of space travel. They're more concerned with the existential challenges faced by those who undertake voyages into the unknown. Are humans psychologically robust enough to head off into infinite space, they ask? For all intents and purposes, Armstrong, Aldrin and Collins were indeed robust enough. When they finally emerged from the Lunar Receiving Laboratory they were in good health and the world was just as they had left it. However, not everyone could share this sense of security. For a small group of people over in Los Angeles things had become very different during the mission time of *Apollo 11*. Between the take-off and the splashdown, the quarantine and the parades, their world had changed beyond all recognition.

On 25 July, Bobby Beausoleil made his way over to Topanga Canyon to see his friend, the music teacher Gary Hinman. During 1968 and into 1969 Hinman had been one of the Family's frequent ports of call. He was easy to tap for a place to crash and sometimes had drugs to sell. Manson had also come to believe that Hinman was rich. He was convinced that Hinman had a large amount of money stashed away somewhere and was eager to have it added to the Family's coffers. If he couldn't convince Hinman to join the group and hand everything over 'voluntarily', Manson would get it another way. Hence Beausoleil's visit on 25 July in the company of Mary Brunner and Susan Atkins. They had been dispatched by Manson to take what they could by force.

Since drifting in and out of *The Ramrodder*, Beausoleil had become part of the scene surrounding Charles Manson at Spahn Ranch, and his loyalties had changed accordingly. Hinman initially thought he was being paid a social call until Beausoleil pulled out a handgun and demanded the cash. After protesting that he had nothing to give, Beausoleil started to beat Hinman with the gun. The money still didn't appear. Manson then came down to the house armed with a sword and proceeded to cut Hinman's left ear in half before leaving Beausoleil, Brunner and Atkins to it. For the next two days Hinman went in and out of consciousness as he was beaten and berated, the constant demand being for the money that clearly only existed in Manson's head. Hinman finally died after Beausoleil stabbed him on 27 July. Brunner, Atkins and Beausoleil left the scene, taking with them Hinman's bagpipes and his two cars. Before he left, Beausoleil dipped his hand into Hinman's blood and wrote a series of 'piggy' messages on the wall along with a paw print. Apparently, the police were meant to see this and immediately think the chaotic scene was the work of Huey Newton and Bobby Searle's urban protection group, the Black Panther Party.

In the days that followed Beausoleil virtually lived in Hinman's car. He drove it around the LA hills and slept in it on the roadside, all the while carrying the murder weapon and a set of ownership and insurance documents which led directly back to Hinman. Meanwhile, back in Topanga Canyon it was not long before the murder scene was discovered, and the police began their search for the missing cars and likely suspects. Beausoleil was picked up on 6 August. He was found in Hinman's car and soon after was charged with the murder. When news of the arrest reached Manson, it sent him into a fit of paranoia. While he had encouraged violence towards Hinman, Manson was incensed at just how easily Beausoleil had let himself get tied to the crime. He thought it only a matter of time before the police dug further, made the link to the Family and arrived at Spahn Ranch. He considered making a break for it, escaping on his own and leaving the Family behind. Such a move, though, would have seriously undermined the group ideology upon which Manson relied for much of his authority. Faced with a need, then, to take control of a quickly deteriorating situation, Manson fell back on the galvanising idea that had previously bound the Family together and given them purpose. He announced that it was 'time for Helter Skelter' and the plan, such as it was, rumbled into action. By 10 August, Sharon Tate and her friends were dead, as were Leno and Rosemary LaBianca. For Manson, this was the beginning of the end. The race war was imminent, and he and his followers now had to travel into the desert in search of 'the bottomless pit' where they could wait out the apocalypse in peace.[7]

*

Whether acting through politics, chemicals or criticism, the varied projects that characterised the sixties counterculture shared a common goal. From the small businesses and artistic enterprises that converged on Haight-Ashbury to the outer reaches of psychedelic experimentation and New Left activism, 'counterculture' could be taken to describe the collective attempt in the post-war period to imagine another world into existence. In the final analysis though, beyond all of the day-glo colours, the drug-induced mysticism and the overwhelming *passion* to change the order of things, the only ones to fully realise this goal during the 1960s were NASA's astronauts. They were the ones who had, by 1969, gone all the way and set foot on some place *other*.

By contrast, 1969 found the likes of Timothy Leary broke and exhausted. Thanks to a series of marijuana convictions he was facing a long stretch in jail. Financial support for the enterprises he had operated, like the International Foundation for Internal Freedom (IFIF) and its successor the League for Spiritual Discovery (LSD), had dwindled. A buoyant black market still existed for LSD but, as Sidney Cohen had predicted on the *LSD* album back in 1966, users were less and less interested in spiritual discovery and keener to use acid to supplement to the effects of heroin and amphetamines. As such, hospitals were increasingly turning to antipsychotics like Thorazine as the standard treatment for the use of LSD. Bad trips were becoming the norm.[8]

The culture of protest was experiencing a similar decline. By the time Whitehead came to screen *The Fall* at the Edinburgh International Film Festival, it was clear that non-violent activism was losing ground to a harder, more aggressive mode. Indeed, between the completion of the film and its release the collective which had organised the Columbia occupation, the Students for a Democratic Society, had given rise to a radical splinter group, the Weather Underground, also known as the Weathermen. Headed by Bill Ayers, Bernardine Dohrn and Mark Rudd, the Weather Underground combined the militancy of the Black Panther Party and the social agenda of the wider Black Power movement with the anti-Vietnam ethos of their campus origins. As they outlined in their mission statement, 'You Don't Need a Weatherman to Know Which Way the Wind Blows' (1969), they directed their critique against 'US imperialism' and advocated the use of 'violent and illegal struggle' – public disorder and an extensive bombing campaign – to enact a revolutionary change at the level of government. 'The goal', according to their statement was 'the achievement of a classless world: world communism'.

The Weather Underground first came to public attention on 8 October 1969, with the so-called 'Days of Rage', a demonstration-cum-riot in Chicago. The city had played host to a series of anti-war protests in August 1968 timed to coincide with the Democratic National Convention. Mayor Richard Daley had organised a heavy police presence, had brought in the National Guard and had authorised the use of force to quell the demonstrations. The inevitable result was a large amount of disruption and violence as the two sides, protestors and guardsmen, clashed on the streets. Some of the main participants in the protest, left-wing youth leaders like Abbie Hoffman and Tom Hayden, were also arrested and charged with conspiracy to incite a riot. The Days of Rage were intended as a protest against these arrests as well as a destructive raising of the stakes as regards the idea of direct action. As several hundred members of the Weather Underground clashed with heavily armed police and damaged property in some of Chicago's most affluent areas, the aim was to show the city what a riot really was.[9]

Two days later, on 10 October, *International Times* published 'Open Letter to the Underground', a text attributed to Dave Williams and Ron Bailey of the London Street Commune. The commune was a loose group of squatters who were occupying 144 Piccadilly, a large central London house. Having been served with an eviction notice and with action from the Metropolitan Police becoming increasingly likely, the commune members approached the underground press for exposure and support. Reports about the operation of the commune had previously appeared in *International Times* but little concrete help had emerged. The 'Open Letter to the Underground' thus sounded a note of angry frustration. Williams and Bailey castigated 'the so-called Flower Children and their ideology of love' as harmfully narcissistic. There was too much navel-gazing and self-love for any real action to take place. While the London Street Commune were in no way as militant as the Weathermen, they too had little time for so-called 'activism' that did not take the form of direct action. Dancing to poetry in the Albert Hall was simply not enough. Bailey and Williams would have seen such spectacles as self-indulgent, lacking in social consciousness and basically *violent* in their 'total non-recognition of the otherness of the other person'. The 'Open Letter' thus concluded with a call for the editorial reins of *International Times* to be turned over to the commune. They argued that any group – however informal – which lays claim to the term 'underground' should act as a force of resistance, not pacificism. If the *International Times* crew were not going to live up to the term, the London Street Commune would.[10]

Late 1969 was thus a period of extremes. Rife with factionalism, saturated with violence and full of the flotsam of personal and political burnout, the counterculture – despite its early promise – appeared to be tearing itself apart. Meanwhile, the white heat of science and industry had completed the almost visionary task of putting a man on the Moon. Although far removed from Leary's legal troubles or the decline of the protest movement, the Manson case, with its proximity to the Moon landing, offers the perfect dark glass in which to bring this difference into sharper focus. Just as the first *Apollo* celebrations were gearing up, ready to welcome in a new age of outer space exploration, Manson was revving up his dune buggies ready to retreat further into the interior. The great scientific narrative of the West was continuing into the final frontier, while those who had chosen to go another way, to step away from the conventions and aspirations of the dominant culture, were falling ever deeper into a rabbit hole.

For writers like J.G. Ballard though, this division was not merely a case of scientific success on the one hand and cultural failure on the other. Rather, it pointed to a stark difference in priorities between different sectors of society at the decade's end. Ballard claimed that, despite all the political and scientific fireworks that surrounded the space programme, 'outer space' held little real interest for those who lived through the 1960s in 'Western Europe and the USA.' 'What people wanted to gratify,' he explained in a 1979 interview with the computer scientist Dr Chris Evans, 'were psychological rather than material needs':

> They wanted to get their sex lives right, their depressions sorted out, they wanted to come to terms with psychological weaknesses they had. And these were things that a materialistic society was unable to supply – it couldn't wrap them up and sell them for a pound down and ten pence a week.

Continuing, Ballard added that this 'rejection of external in favour of internal values was mirrored in the great popular movements of the time'. He mentions the Beatles, 'who began in the traditional materialistic mould of young Rock 'n' Roll stars' before they moved away from their 'flashy cars, expensive clothes, big stadium concerts and all that' towards 'meditation, mysticism, the pseudo-philosophical drug culture of the psychedelics, and so on'. Nixon may have claimed that *Apollo 11* had unified the world, but for Ballard the focus on 'internal values' suggested a different attitude among the public: 'by the time Armstrong had put his foot on the Moon no one was really interested'. Even allowing for Ballard's characteristic tone of polite provocation, it's difficult to see how this could have been the case. The science fiction of the period clearly points to a great deal of interest. This may have peaked in 1969 but it certainly did not dissipate. What Ballard had in mind, however, was not boredom exactly, but the sense that the 1960s were marked by a series of currents that moved in 'a direction completely opposite to that emanating from the Kennedy Space Center'. As he puts it, by 1969, 'The stars and the planets were out, the bloodstream and the central nervous system were in.'

Ballard is right to suggest that the space programme was not the defining feature of 1960s culture. That said, it was not entirely separate from 'the pseudo-philosophical drug culture' either. As the decade progressed the two often overlapped, with spaceships and astronauts finding their way into the psychedelic cosmos opened by LSD.[11] Case in point, Stanley Kubrick's science fiction masterpiece, *2001: A Space Odyssey* (1968). When first released in April 1968 it carried the tag line 'an epic drama of space and exploration' and its posters appropriately depicted industrious astronauts and orbiting space stations. This was the visual language of the film's first half and it clearly evoked the technological optimism, triumphant rationalism and neo-colonialism of 1950s science fiction films like *Conquest of Space* (1955). By 1969, however, the tone of the campaign had changed. Drawing on the film's mystery, ambiguity and loudly spoken silences – basically, its second half – as well as the cortex-frying intensity of its final 'Star Gate' sequence, *2001* was now dubbed 'The Ultimate Trip'.[12] As the artist and writer Yvonne Salmon has noted, this was very much a knowing pun: there could be no better image of 'getting high' than that of a spacewalk, a man on the Moon or, as in the case of *2001*'s Dr David Bowman, a process of transformation into a highly evolved Star Child. With this figure now staring out from the film's posters in place of the astronauts, surveyors and pilots of the first campaign, *2001* no longer stood as a hymn to scientific progress. With MGM showing a keen awareness of the film's core audience as well as the ambience of the culture at large, it was now presented as a gateway to the vast, star-filled cosmos of the mind.[13]

The flipside of this ecstatic image was the idea of space travel as an isolating and possibly fatal experience. One that, at best, causes the astronaut to become lost or otherwise adrift. Despite Bowman's sublime transformation, *2001* has its fair share of these more forsaken figures. On board the *Discovery One*, Bowman travels with Dr Frank Poole and a team of scientists in suspended animation. When HAL 9000, the supercomputer that controls the *Discovery One*, suffers an acute emotional crisis, it terminates the life-support systems of the hibernating crew and kills Poole during a spacewalk. His airline is severed, and he floats out into deep space, despite Bowman's attempts to retrieve him. A similar, and possibly more famous, fate befalls Major Tom in David Bowie's 'Space Oddity' (1969), who loses radio contact and floats out of the song with no hope of return. Another lost in space narrative, Michael Moorcock's *The Black Corridor* (1969), explored much of the same existential territory. The novella describes the journey of Ryan, a man who travels as part of an interstellar voyage away from an exhausted and discordant Earth. As with the *Discovery One*, his enormous space ship the *Hope Dempsey* contains a handful of passengers in suspension over whom he keeps watch. They are the seeds of Earth's future among the stars. Various rock bands of the time including Ramases, Magma and Hawkwind (with whom Moorcock would go on to collaborate on the 1973 album *Space Ritual*) extended this theme of planetary escape, but in contrast to their optimistic hopes for an eventual arrival at a better world, *The Black Corridor* focuses on the transit of Ryan alone. Wandering among his ghosts with only the ship's computer for company Ryan's mind slowly collapses into hallucination, psychosis and delusion.

Pink Floyd's mega-hit *The Dark Side of the Moon* (1973) would become one of the most enduring documents of this motif: the Icaran drama of the internal explorer who goes too far. Although clear in its references to grand social obsessions like time and money, the album was, in part, inspired by the life and problems of the band's former guitarist and songwriter, Syd Barrett. Barrett had been removed from Pink Floyd, the band he helped to form, in 1968 due to his erratic and increasingly insular behaviour; a depressive state that has generally been attributed to his excessive drug use. Two solo albums followed, *The Madcap Laughs* (1970) and *Barrett* (1970) before he effectively withdrew from public life, an absence that quickly attracted stories of madness and nervous breakdowns. 'He became the perfect icon for the 60s drug scene,' Peter Whitehead would later remark of his former friend, 'the perfect recluse. The suicide who is still alive.' It is this version of Barrett that looks out from the photographs taken of him in 1969 by Storm Thorgerson. From the bare floor of his apartment in London's Wetherby Mansions, Barrett gazes into the camera looking like an Earth-bound Major Tom; lost somewhere in his own mind, spaced-out on too much Mandrax and LSD.[14]

For Ballard, these captains of inner space – doomed space pilots, obsessive explorers and psychological pioneers – were the perfect protagonists. Little interested in the heroism of space opera, Ballard used his fiction to plot out a distinctive 'zone,' a borderland between the mind and the wider world, in which memory, buried history and intense sensory experience could freely mix. As he argued in his essay-manifesto 'Which Way to Inner Space?' (1962), 'The only truly alien planet is Earth.' Ballard's point was that the massive social and cultural changes that occurred in the first half of the 20th century – advances in fields ranging from psychology to warfare, communications media to industrial technologies (not least the emergence of the advanced technologies that made the space programme possible) – had an impact on the human mind, one that was yet to be fully mapped out in terms of its implications and potentialities. As such, he argued that it was 'inner space, not outer space' that science fiction needs to explore.

The answer as to why this type of writing should be so important in what Ballard labels 'an age of Hiroshima and Cape Canaveral' lies in two short stories he published at opposite ends of the 1960s, 'A Question of Re-Entry' (1962) and 'The Dead Astronaut' (1968). 'The Dead Astronaut' imagines the space programme in ruins.

NASA has closed down its operations and has left Cape Canaveral as a wasteland of technical detritus and mission debris, strewn with the wreckage of capsules (and pilots) abandoned in orbit and left to 'burn-out on re-entry'. For the scavengers who converge on the site looking for relics, the most valuable of all are the remains of these men who fell to Earth, 'the mummified corpses of dead astronauts'. There's a similar search in 'A Question of Re-Entry' in which a recovery team headed by the inquisitive Connolly and the belligerent Ryker set off into South America to locate *Goliath 7*, a spacecraft which had crashed there five years previously. Hoping to find some trace of the pilot Colonel Francis Spender, Connolly and Ryker find that his remains and the wreckage of the craft have become objects of worship by the 'Amazonas', a cargo cult who 'eat their gods'.

'Why did they really send a man to the Moon?', asks Ryker part way through the search, more out of provocation than curiosity. He adds that the '*real* reasons' have little to do with military matters, political matters or the spirit of exploration. Connolly finds himself agreeing and reflects that 'the entire space programme was a symptom of some inner unconscious malaise affecting mankind and in particular the western technocracies'. In response to this malady, spacecraft had been launched to try and satisfy 'certain buried compulsions and desires'. Ballard offers no detail regarding the nature of this 'malaise' but one could assume the 'buried compulsions' relate to escapist concerns, the wish to fly: a desire to move beyond the 'barbed wire fences and regimentation of twentieth century life'. According to Ballard, these projections mean nothing in 'the jungle' where 'the unconscious was manifest and exposed'. There's a clear primitivism at play in such a massively generalised view of 'the jungle', but this questionable framing aside, Ballard's basic point is this: 20th-century life, particularly in the 'advanced' West, cuts the individual off from the power of their imagination. Starved, the imagination exercises itself through an attachment to huge public spectacles like the space programme. These displays of technological victory over gravity and the confines of the planet as well as their attendant stories of courage, fortitude and exploration fulfil a broad collective wish for some form of ecstasy. However, for Ballard, they also have the effect of obscuring the strangeness and potency of the interior world, of inner space. In much of his writing Ballard sets out to chart this territory, particularly through stories in which the inner world encroaches on and intermingles with the outer. In 'A Question of Re-Entry' and 'The Dead Astronaut' the focus shifts. In presenting failed missions, crashed spacecraft and abandoned launch sites, Ballard points to the poverty of space flight as a vehicle for the unconscious. As a response, Ballard does not recommend sifting through the detritus in the hope of satisfying compelling psychological desires. The consumerist accumulation of *stuff* is never the answer. Instead, he suggests turning the search elsewhere, towards inner space, a zone in which the need for transcendence and the need to experience an elsewhere can be confronted head-on. Faced with the imaginative wreckage of space flight and the failure of its psychological mission, Ballard tries to tell another kind of story.[15]

'We tell ourselves stories in order to live,' writes Joan Didion at the start of her essay 'The White Album'. For Didion, this storytelling has less to do with the enduring popularity of the sixties than with the peculiar conditions that characterised life during the decade itself. To put this another way, as the 1960s wore on, the old stories simply started to wear out. The feelings of vertigo and nausea

Didion describes in 'The White Album' come from her sense that as a journalist and a professional writer she had previously relied on a 'script', a set of narratives with which to make sense of her experiences. When faced with the essay's dizzying parade of violence, murder, assassinations and intolerance that cover the years 1966–71, Didion finds these trusty devices sorely lacking. The world of Charles Manson, My Lai and children left to die on the interstate is all but unintelligible, a 'story without a narrative'. It is also a world in which the institutions that one might look to for stability (law enforcement, the military, government, the culture at large), are unable to offer clarity or anchorage. Reading 'The White Album', it is difficult not to think of William Butler Yeats' poem 'The Second Coming' (1919). Didion had drawn on this for her earlier essay on Haight-Ashbury, 'Slouching towards Bethlehem' (1967), but its ominous imagery seems better suited to the world she unveils in 'The White Album', one in which 'Mere anarchy is loosed', where 'The best lack all conviction, while the worst / Are full of passionate intensity.'[16]

Ballard does not share Didion's dread, but in his fiction there's an equal sense that in the 'ad-saturated, Bomb-dominated, power-corrupted' era of the 1960s the standard narratives just won't do. Ballard often published in *New Worlds*, a science fiction magazine edited by Michael Moorcock. In 1964 Moorcock used an editorial in the magazine to call for 'a new literature of the space age', a movement away from 'the fast-stagnating pool of the conventional novel' towards a kind of writing that could reflect the state of the world as he saw it. According to Moorcock, science fiction was the genre best suited to this task given that it typically imagined tomorrow based on the technology of today. To comment on what was going on in the 1960s, though, would require a version of science fiction that did not rely on Buck Rogers-style space opera. Flash Gordon may have conquered the universe in the Republic film-serials of the 1930s and 1940s, but to reflect the advances and discords of the 1960s would require a different kind of mirror.

Ballard's hymns to inner space captured this mood, but so did his aggressively experimental novels like *The Atrocity Exhibition* (1970). Full of the urban sprawls and deserted car parks of modern life and suffused with pseudo-technical language drawn from obscure fields of scientific research, it's initially difficult to call *The Atrocity Exhibition* a 'novel'. It has a lot to say but it doesn't really *go* anywhere because there's no through-line in place to hold all the weird images together. Ballard, however, would disagree: it certainly was a novel, just not as you knew it. In the 'Author's Note' he advises the reader to 'simply turn the pages until something catches [the] eye', an associative approach that according to Ballard would permit the 'underlying narrative' of *The Atrocity Exhibition* to 'reveal itself'. This invitation to follow not a linear narrative but a series of juxtapositions meant that *The Atrocity Exhibition*, with its archive of extreme experiences, disturbing medical evidence and obsessive documentation, became the ultimate inner space novel. It not only dealt with the life of the mind via its focus on psychopathology, but its dream logic was also intended to work away at the unconscious of the reader. At the same time, *The Atrocity Exhibition* exemplified Moorcock's concept of 'space age' literature. The world of the novel is one swamped by technology and transformed by violence in which the human subject falls out of view. Just as NASA's astronauts were encased in their suits, welded into their spacecraft and entangled into mission control's web of communication systems, so too are Ballard's 'characters' wrapped up in the novel's flow of information. *The Atrocity Exhibition* riffs on the psychological and creative implications of this position. Where 'conventional' novels may have had a main protagonist to guide the reader through the narrative, Ballard removes this fixed centre.[17]

For Didion, the difficulty she had in telling a comprehensible story of the sixties was a source of great anxiety. For Ballard, the same problem was an opportunity to develop 'advanced literary techniques'. Elsewhere in the intellectual ether, other thinkers like the semiotician Roland Barthes and the philosopher Michel Foucault were working through similar ideas via an intense, extended study of language. In essays like Barthes' 'The Death of the Author' (1967) and Foucault's 'What is an Author?' (1969) they each questioned the traditional reliance on the idea of an 'author' when engaging with a piece of writing. As they put it, to presume that everything on the page is an outgrowth of a single author's mind means to put an enormous amount of faith in the ability of language to clearly communicate a given intention. For Barthes and Foucault this is a futile belief. Language is an ambiguous, fluid, allusive and elusive system. What an author chooses to set down is never *exactly* that which emerges in the mind of the reader at the other end. In the grey area between the two, language is busy doing its own work. Although the reliance on the figure of the author is a convenient way to give anchorage to a piece of writing, the 'text' will always be drifting away into the free play of language. Complex and theoretically dense, these essays nonetheless reflected the spirit of their times. By stepping into the critical, cultural and artistic area to question the role of the author, Barthes and Foucault were challenging a key source of authority.[18]

Whether looked upon with incomprehension or delight these intellectual manoeuvres pointed to a wider sense of paradigm shift. Work produced in parallel by writers as diverse as Didion, Ballard, Barthes and Foucault registered the feeling that in the late 1960s the old ways of thinking had become redundant; that the *centre*, as Yeats would again put it, was not holding. In different ways and in different times their ideas fed into the field of thought that became known as *postmodernism*. The subject of academic debates, dinner-party chatter and artistic endeavour across the latter half of the 20th century, postmodernism is generally understood as a 'populist attack on the elitism of modernism'. As John Storey explains, one source of this attack in the 1960s came from pop art. Work produced by the likes of Pauline Boty, Andy Warhol, Jim Dine and Roy Lichtenstein shone the light of artistic seriousness onto popular culture via a celebration of comic books, soup tins and film stars – material so often disregarded by once-shocking but now canonised modernist artists of the early 20th century like 'Bertolt Brecht, T.S. Eliot, James Joyce, Virginia Woolf, Pablo Picasso, Igor Stravinsky and others'. Picking up where the modernist project left off while railing against its embrace of the establishment, postmodernism was another version of the 'generational refusal evident in the cultural politics of both the American counterculture and the British Underground'. Its impulse was not just limited to visual art. From the late 1960s onwards the trend quickly made the leap from artistic practice to 'cultural condition'. Suddenly we were all 'postmodern', all part of a society that seemed to define itself either through a wholesale rejection of the past or through a restless process of recycling these traditions into 'new' identities in a vague attempt to cultivate something innovative.[19]

As with 'Swinging London' it seemed that everyone was talking about postmodernism, but no one really knew exactly what it meant. The philosopher Jean-François Lyotard took a crack at it in his book *The Postmodern Condition* (1986) in which he defined postmodernity as a period characterised by an 'incredulity towards metanarratives'. Granted, this is not the clearest definition, but it's a working definition nonetheless: that rare thing in postmodern theory. A metanarrative is a 'big' story: a myth, a belief or some other kind of universal pattern that's used to explain history, society and culture. 'Christianity' is a metanarrative as is the history of 'man' and so too is the 'human condition', an idea that so many great works of literature allegedly meditate upon. To this list we could add the concept of the 'Author' as singular creative genius, as well as the trope of the quester or explorer, which finds its fullest definition in the 1960s with Neil Armstrong setting foot on the Moon. To use Didion's phrase, metanarratives are the stories we tell each other 'in order to live.' They are the stories which are told and re-told that help give shape and form to the chaos of the world. They help us understand who we are, where we've come from and where we're going. The problem is, they typically do this by separating 'our' story from 'their' story. The world is far too complex and varied to be defined by a small set of stories. And, although often useful and attractive, metanarratives tend to perform vast acts of simplification to make things understandable. As Storey puts it, they 'silence other voices, other discourses, in the name of universal principles and general goals'. Thus, Christianity marginalises the 'pagan' experience, the history of 'mankind' excludes the history of 'womankind', and 'history' itself so often only tells the story of the victor. In response, to express 'incredulity towards metanarratives' means to criticise, to interrogate and to re-write these stories to bring voices back from the margins and let them speak from the silence.[20]

Peter Whitehead's *Tonite Let's All Make Love in London* provides another view of this shift in the fabric of the sixties. One of the talking heads who appears throughout the film is the actor Michael Caine, then a rising star on the back of *Zulu*

(1964), *The Ipcress File* (1965) and *Alfie* (1966). Where other voices in the film like the author Edna O'Brien and the painter David Hockney celebrate the liberalism of the period – the changing attitudes to marriage, sex, social expectations and the gradual erosion of English provincialism – Caine is rather more reserved. Appearing at intervals like a disapproving parent or older brother, he's clearly not averse to reaping the benefits of being a young, famous white man in the sixties, but Caine nevertheless appears perturbed to witness the country's loss of 'moral fibre'. In a nod to the Conservative political stance he would increasingly adopt later in his career, Caine attributes this state of affairs to 'the loss of the British Empire'.

By 1900 Britain had gained legal, economic and cultural control over nearly a quarter of the world's population. Colonies had been established on the back of exploration campaigns to the Americas across the 17th and 18th centuries and were maintained through the British control of trade which, in the 19th century, was bolstered by the country's rapid development as a capitalist nation. Sea power was an essential factor in the success of these enterprises and with its modern navy and fleet of commercial steamships Britain was also dominant in this regard. Indeed, Britain's 'imperial century' of 1815 to 1914 came to be known as *Pax Britannica*, an era of 'British Peace' during which Britain used its maritime expertise to govern multiple territories at once. Of course, 'peace' does not equate to a lack of violence. Violence, aggression and warfare were just as much a tool of empire as trade was. Hence, in Thomas Arne's setting of the enduring hymn to imperialism 'Rule Britannia' (1740), the nation stands steadfast in the face of 'each foreign stroke' because of its naval supremacy: it 'rules the waves' and thus can strike back with military force. In reality, this position was just as much offensive as it was defensive.

While the lyrics have Britain virtuously standing apart from 'haughty tyrants', much of the empire was won by the sword and controlled thanks to the deployment of colonial troop garrisons. To put it another way, Britons would never be 'slaves' precisely because up until the start of the 19th century the empire owned, used and abused so many of them elsewhere.[21]

It was in the aftermath of the Second World War that this dominance began to dissolve. Large swathes of Europe had been destroyed and its political map was in need of a radical redesign. Within this political uncertainty, colonies of the European powers petitioned for independence amid what Harold Macmillan would refer to in 1960 as a 'wind of change' and a 'growth of national consciousness'. By then, Clement Attlee's Labour government of 1945–51 had responded to this new, post-war situation via a process of decolonisation directed mainly at India and Palestine. Imperial tensions re-ignited though during the Suez Crisis of 1956 in which Conservative Prime Minister Anthony Eden attempted to orchestrate military action on the Suez Canal, then operated by the Egyptian government under Gamal Abdel Nasser. Britain was manoeuvring to gain control of the area in order to retain influence in the Middle East. Such were the international repercussions of this reckless move, that under considerable pressure from America and facing the possibility of Russian support for Egypt, Britain pulled out of the Suez zone. This was a sensible political move given the stakes involved, but the overarching public feeling was that of 'crushing humiliation'. Britain, formerly ruler of the waves, now stood as a diminished power with its territory greatly reduced and beholden to the orders of the Americans.[22]

It's the impact of this change on the British psyche rather than the reality of the political situation that Caine reflects on in *Tonite*. Economically Britain benefitted from decolonisation because, as

Graham K. Riach describes, large numbers of Caribbean and South Asian migrants filled vacancies in key industries like 'British Rail, the London Underground and the NHS'. Caine however, laments 'the loss of the British Empire' as if it marks the collapse of a supreme metanarrative: the *idea* of British confidence and global authority, the fantasy that the country held sway as a single governing power and moral compass over the citizens of the world. The forces that changed social attitudes to such hallowed British traditions as marriage, and which led Whitehead's 'Dolly Girl' interviewees to say things like 'sex? [...] it's sort of free, isn't it?', had more to do with post-war domestic policies regarding education, contraception and divorce than they did post-war foreign policies regarding decolonisation. For Caine, though, his comments imply that the root cause of this spiritual shift was the loss of a guiding principle; that with the changing of the guard, the lid came off and, for good or for ill, new social mores emerged as a result.[23]

This view was not by any means exceptional. Reflections on the evaporation of *Pax Britannica* and the 'demise' of the Empire found their way into various aspects of British popular culture during the 1960s, explicitly in the case of films like John Guillermin's film *Guns at Batasi* (1964) and rather more implicitly in the case of the Beatles' 'Helter Skelter'. Discussing the origins of the track with his biographer Barry Miles, Paul McCartney said that for him all the ascents, descents and return trips 'back to the top of the slide' were meant to evoke the 'rise and fall of the Roman Empire'. Such a lofty theme may seem at odds with lyrics about English fairground rides and have little to say about the British Empire, but in offering his interpretation, McCartney was using a common code that reflected a prevalent mood. Anthony Mann's film *The Fall of the Roman Empire* had made the rounds in 1964 and this, combined with the continued availability of its source text, Edward Gibbon's *Decline and Fall* (1776–89), had helped to establish 'the ruins of Rome' as a tool for understanding the increasingly decolonised, post-Suez state of the British Empire.[24]

*

Postcolonialism, the death of the author, the mysterious expanse of inner space, the poverty of the 'old' stories: in the helter skelter world of postmodernity, a series of gaps appeared across the once familiar map of contemporary Western culture. Out of these fissures came the marginalised, the hitherto unacknowledged and those with radically different ways of doing things. The cultural stage was now filled with new players challenging the legitimacy and entitlement of the old. Across the political and social spectrum dominant attitudes, ideologies and institutions were being made aware of their contingency: in their own fields they were now one voice among many rather than *the* voice which spoke to, spoke for or spoke over the many. As unpalatable as it may at first seem, Charles Manson was a symptom of this cultural shift. In taking his pick of L. Ron Hubbard, Robert Heinlein, the Beatles and the Bible he was developing his own semi-religious outlook from the ground up. The problem, of course, was that in offering 'Helter Skelter' as a roadmap to the 'bottomless pit' he was clearly writing a story that was aggressive and misanthropic. As well as the obvious human cost of his project, there was also the fact that Manson intended to be a voice of authority. However anti-authoritarian or populist it may have appeared to establish his own microcosm within society at large, Manson expected the Family to adopt his apocalyptic worldview as gospel.

Rosemary's Baby plays out to a similar backdrop. The film takes place very specifically between 1965 and 66, and Polanski takes care to have the plot bookended by two actual events: the visit of Pope Paul VI to New York on 4 October 1965 and the publication of the *Time* cover featuring the question 'Is God Dead?' on 8 April 1966. The impending arrival of Pope Paul VI forms part of an early conversation between Rosemary, Guy and the Castevets, while later in the film a copy of the *Time* issue is visible as Rosemary sits in her doctor's waiting room. Her pregnancy and the eventual birth of Satan's son on Earth thus takes place between the first papal visit to America and the widespread circulation of an article detailing the struggle of theologians to keep religious worship relevant in the modern world. It is as if religious authority weakens as the birth approaches.[25]

One could say that in depicting the apparent victory of Satanic forces, Polanski's film (and before it Ira Levin's novel) presents the shift of modern American society towards the dark side: occult knowledge, esoteric practices and devil worship. Those observing, with horror, the parallel rise of the Church of Satan in San Francisco would readily agree. In the context of the political and philosophical shifts in the period, one could liken this dark side not to ghoulish diabolism but to the *terra incognita* – the uncharted territory – best symbolised in the late 1960s by the dark side of the Moon. Although the success of the *Apollo 11* Moon landing suggested that America – and the West – were pursuing their scientific manifest destiny beyond the end of the sixties and into the seventies, the focus of the social mood was much more wide-ranging. Scientific progress and the exploration of the final frontier was not the only issue on the cultural agenda during the decade. It was one guiding story among many, a number of which were being told for the first time.

Carl Jung died in 1961 and did not witness Neil Armstrong's giant leap, but towards the end of his life he had been directing his attention to the reports of other things seen in the sky: flying saucers, UFOs, aerial lights and various cigar-shaped vessels. For Jung, these strange phenomena were the real barometers of the cultural climate. As he outlined in 1959 in his book *Flying Saucers: A Modern Myth of Things Seen in the Sky*, reports of 'such objects' tend to herald 'the end of an era [...] or accompany long lasting transformations of the collective psyche'. This was Jung's take on the Age of Aquarius. Writing at the cusp of the 1960s as the Aquarian, post-Christian age was coming into being, these weird portents spoke of changes so momentous that Jung expressed concern 'for all those caught unawares by the events in question.' The various transitions – social, cultural and political – that took place up to 1969 seemed to bear out Jung's predictions. By the end of the decade no revelation had occurred regarding flying saucers, but various parties had undertaken hazardous and unprecedented expeditions to inner and outer space and a definite map of these territories was yet to be drawn. The *Eagle* may have landed in 1969 but the 'odyssey in search of wholeness' was still ongoing. Whether the pursuit of these 'spiritual aspirations' would turn out to be harmonious or apocalyptic remained to be seen.[26]

Interlude: *Island of Death*

In November 1969 Yoko Ono and John Lennon took a holiday to Greece and spent time with their friend, the broadcaster and DJ Nico Mastorakis. Mastorakis had been influential in introducing the music of the Beatles to Greek audiences, and in 1967 had organised concerts in Greece by the Rolling Stones. During the trip Lennon and Ono stayed at the Athens Hilton and were planning to take a cruise to some of the nearby islands on a yacht owned by the singer Donovan. The day before, they met up with Mastorakis and asked him to take them around town. They wanted to see some astrologers and have their fortunes told, 'just for the fun of it'. Having just left the Beatles after the creative tensions of what became the band's final days, Lennon was trying to decompress. He was also upbeat about his future creative life with Ono. Making *Apotheosis* in Hampshire a couple of months before had been a key part of this new phase. Consulting the astrologers in Athens may also have been part of it too. A bit of fun, maybe, but also a good way of setting a new direction or, better still, having an intention confirmed by the stars themselves.

Mastorakis was happy to oblige and, as he recalls, they spent the day visiting astrologers, palm readers and psychics, all of whom immediately recognised Lennon and Ono. Towards the end of the day, however, there was one woman who did not. The woman took Lennon's hand and studied it carefully. She knew nothing about him, his life with the Beatles nor his plans with Ono, but as she considered his horoscope a sense of tension descended on the room and she became unnerved. The stars had some bad news. Lennon's death was very near; it would be sudden, it would be violent, and it would take a particular form. As Mastorakis recalls she told Lennon to take care because he was 'going to be shot on an island'. Assuming the prediction related to one of the islands they were intending to visit the following day, Lennon and Ono cancelled the rest of their trip and returned to London.

Cutting short their holiday and immediately flying back home due to an ominous palm-reading might seem like drastic action. In the immediate post-Manson period of November 1969, though, with America's recent history of public assassinations in mind, Lennon and Ono might be forgiven for being cautious. Since September, there had also been a spike in the 'Paul is Dead' conspiracy theories coming into the Beatles' press office. These had first surfaced in 1967 when the band's fan magazine *The Beatles Book* responded to rumours that Paul McCartney had been killed in a car crash. In September 1969 a student newspaper in Iowa returned to the rumour before Russ Gibb, a Detroit DJ, gave it further publicity. This time the story spread like a virus into a full-blown conspiracy theory, eventually involving codes in reversed recordings, claims that lookalikes were impersonating McCartney, and McCartney himself having to give a series of interviews throughout October and November to assure the public he was indeed alive. With Lennon and Ono now receiving news of a death yet to come, it's not surprising that they chose, in Mastorakis' words, to 'fly away from it'. The morbid paranoia appeared to be catching.[1]

In 2000, Ono sat down for an interview with her old friend Mastorakis. By then he had gained some notoriety as a filmmaker because of his first feature *Island of Death* (1976), a savage tale of murder on the Greek island of Mykonos. In the interview, it's not long before talk turns to the details of Lennon's death on 8 December 1980. He was shot by Mark Chapman outside the apartment he shared with Ono at the Dakota Building on New York's Upper West Side. Ono bristles at the painful memory before Mastorakis adds the clincher. He reminds Ono that Manhattan is an island and thus the prediction of the astrologer seems to have come true. Ono is taken aback by this, as if the pieces of a long, drawn-out puzzle have finally slotted into place.[2]

Beatles conspiracy theories generally tend to focus on the connection between the Dakota Building and *Rosemary's Baby*. Roman Polanski used its imposing frontage as the exterior for the film's Bramford apartment building. That Lennon was shot on the site of Polanski's fictional Satanic cult is a tempting synchronicity that has led some to view his death as proof of the film's alleged 'curse'.[3] Coincidental speculations are of little interest to Ono, but in the interview she comes to agree with Mastorakis that they 'cannot disregard the prediction'. It offered no real foreknowledge, nor did it allow Lennon to avoid being killed by Chapman. Instead, reflecting in retrospect on the words of the astrologer gives Lennon's untimely death a sense of inevitability. Ono and Mastorakis bring their conversation to a close reflecting on that day in late 1969 when they tried to look into the future and got in return a glimpse of disaster.

PART II

Lucifer Rising

CHAPTER VI

The Rebirth of Dionysus

London, 13 April 1969. Alexander Trocchi is in the basement of the Arts Lab, preparing. An audience has filed in and, because the room is no bigger than a decent sized church hall, it doesn't take much to fill it. Everyone lights up – tobacco, weed, whatever – and it's not long before a cloud of smog hangs heavy in the air. At the far end of the room Trocchi, Jeff Nuttall and William Burroughs sit awkwardly on a haphazard arrangement of chairs. The assembly has gathered for 'Alexander Trocchi's State of Revolt', an event billed as a day of music, performance and lectures all dealing with the theme of social revolution.

Despite its title, 'State of Revolt' was a rather languid affair. Filmmaker Jamie Wadhawan recorded the proceedings, as part of a short cinematic study he was making of Trocchi's life and work called *Cain's Film* (1969). In the grainy footage Trocchi can be seen looming out of the smoke to read some of his poetry before Nuttall and Burroughs take turns to address a hazily defined idea of 'insurrection'. Burroughs, looking immaculate in a double-breasted suit and waistcoat, tells the crowd they should cut their hair and smarten up. Real revolutionaries, he argues, should not draw attention to themselves, they should look and act like bank managers and trouble the system from within. Trocchi and Nuttall nod and smoke.

Four years earlier, Trocchi had been on stage at the Albert Hall, acting as compere at the International Poetry Incarnation. He read from his existential novel *Cain's Book* (1960) and, in doing so, addressed the 7,000-strong audience on the mysterious power of literature. By 1969 much of Trocchi's promise as a bold, experimental author had evaporated into a morass of incomplete projects and chronic heroin addiction. Trocchi had once claimed that the 'traditional' novel had no future and that his writing would take things in a dynamic new direction. As his drug use intensified, his personal problems mounted up and his literary career stalled, it seemed to many eyes that it was Trocchi himself who had no future.

Whether by accident or design, it is this negative aura that Wadhawan captures in his footage of 'State of Revolt'. Trocchi is framed holding court, but gone are the large crowds and the powerful, electrifying statements. Instead, Trocchi sits drawn and gaunt in a dark, cramped hall talking about violent action and ways of attacking 'the system'. There's no shortage of ideas, but they all get lost in the smoke. Action of any kind also seems unlikely. It is as if the icy paralysis of heroin has somehow pervaded the whole room. The overriding feeling is not that of failure exactly, but more a sense of decline. As if a promise made at some point in the past has ultimately, disappointingly, come to *this*: a small group of tired-looking hippies making vague plans for a future that will never arrive.

The writer Stewart Home perfectly encapsulated this atmosphere in his essay about the event and *Cain's Film*, 'A Walk on Gilded Splinters' (2007). Home's mother, Julia Callan-Thompson was in the audience on the evening and his interest in *Cain's Film* lies in its fleeting shots of her. A *habitué* of Trocchi's circle, Callan-Thompson died in 1979 in circumstances strongly suspected to have been drug-related. For Home, *Cain's Film* is an appropriately mournful setting in which to see his late mother because it's a scene suffused with death, not just because of the glimpses it offers of the sadly departed, but because watching the film is not unlike watching the death throes of the British counterculture. As Home puts it in the essay, Wadhawan's footage makes it 'glaringly obvious that this is the first and best in an endless series of somnambulistic wakes for full-on long haired freakdom.' It's as if 'State of Revolt' bids farewell to the counterculture's revolutionary intentions even as it gives voice to them.

If the sixties emerged part way through the 1960s as a sexy, fashionable product of the media, Home argues that by 1969 this image had started to darken. The sixties stopped swinging. They became slow, heavy and started to fall apart. 'Zombiefication' is the word Home uses. Reflecting on the spectacle of *Cain's Film*, he suggests there's no life in the Arts Lab, just the shuffling of the undead. Trocchi and friends might be going through the motions of insurrection and speaking its language, but they've all lost the vital spark. The wider implication is that even before the decade was out, the big figures of the sixties were commemorating the end of an era.[1]

*

In May 1969, a month after the State of Revolt event, Dennis Hopper and Peter Fonda arrived at the Cannes Film Festival with their film, *Easy Rider* (1969). The film follows Wyatt (Fonda) and Billy (Hopper), two bikers who, with the proceeds of a drug deal, leave Los Angeles and head out for New Orleans, a journey of nearly 2,000 miles. Their interior journey however is much more ambitious: they are 'looking for America.' Featuring fabulous images of the modern American landscape courtesy of cinematographer László Kovács, *Easy Rider* combines the frontier myths of the classic Western with the automotive delight of Jack Kerouac's novel *On the Road* (1957). The result, when filtered through a soundtrack featuring Steppenwolf, Jimi Hendrix and the Byrds, is a film that connects freedom with travel and carefully presents its nomads as members of America's post-war youth culture.

Fonda, Hopper and their co-star Jack Nicholson had all previously starred in biker movies like Roger Corman's *The Wild Angels* (1966) and Richard Rush's *Hells Angels on Wheels* (1967). Where these and other films like Al Adamson's *Satan's Sadists* (1969) had tried to tap into certain sectors of the youth market, *Easy Rider* was not intended as an exploitation movie. It was a statement made by and for its core audience: the bikers, the longhairs, the misfits. As Fonda, Hopper and company lounged on the beach at Cannes contemplating the coveted *Grand Prix du Festival International du Film*, they were aware that in making *their* film *their* way, *Easy Rider*'s rebellious spirit was also filtering into the film industry. Along with the developing talents of George Lucas, Francis Ford Coppola and William Friedkin, Fonda and Hopper represented the influx of America's 'youthquake' into yet another long-standing cultural establishment: the once all-powerful, paternalistic territory of the wealthy elders, the Hollywood studio system.

That said, for all the energy of the film and the dynamism of its makers, *Easy Rider* carries an ominous, melancholic tone throughout. Although they reach New Orleans, Billy and Wyatt's *quest* remains unfulfilled. As the film's tag line puts it, the bikers 'couldn't find [America] anywhere'. Instead they find intolerance, violence and a final, terminal end on a lonely road outside New Orleans. In between, they experience a nightmarish bad trip in a graveyard during Mardi Gras. Soon after, when sitting round a campfire with Billy and Jack Nicholson's drop-out lawyer George Hanson, Wyatt looks off into the middle distance and mutters, 'We blew it.' Although brief, this now famous line finds Wyatt lamenting more than just money wasted on a pointless trip. It speaks of an opportunity lost somewhere along the way.

'We' could mean Wyatt and his two friends, but it could equally mean young America, the demographic who, according to Peter Biskind, would have watched the film 'stunned [...] with a shock of recognition'. *They* have 'blown it' because despite all their talk of changing the world, the hostility encountered by Billy and Wyatt shows that any such attempt has been an abject failure. Nothing's changed.[2]

Easy Rider was given general release in July 1969. A month later a dairy farm in upper New York State played host to the Woodstock Music and Arts Fair, an event that's come to be known more generally as the Woodstock Festival. Organised by a quartet of hippie-ish entrepreneurs, Michael Lang, Artie Kornfeld, Joel Rosenman and John Roberts, Woodstock was, on paper, the ultimate riposte to Wyatt's pessimism. Bringing together nearly half a million people who lived, ate, danced, slept (a bit) and did everything else together across three, eventually four, days the festival was the ideal bubble of possibility. As an *event* it was built on the success of previous large-scale concerts like the Monterey Pop Festival of June 1967. But as a *symbol,* Woodstock presented itself as something more ambitious: not just 'three days of music' but also three days of 'peace'.

Although it was primarily a business venture, in spirit Woodstock mirrored other public acts like the 'Bed-Ins for Peace' staged by Yoko Ono and John Lennon in March and June that year. Equal parts press conference and anti-war demonstration, Ono and Lennon invited the world's media to visit them in hotel rooms, first at the Amsterdam Hilton and then at the Queen Elizabeth Hotel in Montreal. On both occasions they received the press from their bed and held court on the need to achieve the modest aim of world peace. It was during the Montreal Bed-In that Lennon, Ono and a gaggle of friends including Allen Ginsberg and Timothy Leary recorded the now-classic protest anthem, 'Give Peace a Chance.' Whether seen as committed or naïve, the Bed-Ins were intended to be exemplary acts of non-violent protest: calm pockets of time that focused as much energy as possible on the issue at hand. Likewise, Woodstock with its heavy use of doves and CND signs as part of its promotion offered itself to an uncertain world as a spectacular and harmonious tribal gathering.

In practice, however, things were rather different. From the start, the festival was beset by serious organisational problems. As Woodstock Ventures Incorporated, Lang and company had approached various sites in and around the town of Woodstock, but permission to stage the concert had been repeatedly refused. By 1969 there had been enough events mounted around the country for the phrase 'rock festival' to instantly cause concern for local councils. A rock festival meant loud music, bad attitudes, pot smokers, loads of traffic and dirty hippies clogging up the streets. Woodstock may have been a thriving musical and artistic community, but it was also a *quiet* musical and artistic community, one that had no appetite for hippie rock 'n' roll, no matter how much Woodstock Ventures tried to sell the event as a folky arts fair. Widening the search Lang eventually made a deal to use Yasgur's farm in Bethel, a town some 70 miles away from Woodstock. By this point it was mid-July and 50,000 tickets for the festival, set to run from Friday 15 August through Sunday 17 August, had already been sold. While all agreed that the massive, 600-acre site was perfect, the time taken to finalise the location had left little time for it to be adequately prepared.

When the date came around and numbers had swelled beyond expectation, the site had no ticket booths, no fencing nor any proper security controlling access. Of the estimated 400,000 who flocked there, most had no tickets and simply walked on site unchallenged. Getting in was easy, that is, if you could actually reach Yasgur's farm in the first place. As predicted, a mass of cars had turned Bethel's roads into a single choking tailback some fifteen miles long. Before a note had even been played, Woodstock Ventures had generated 'the worst [traffic] jam in the history of upper New York state' and had immediately sent their money-making enterprise spiralling into debt when, faced with no other option as the crowd surged in, they declared Woodstock a free festival. With bands also caught in the tailback, last minute changes were made to the schedule and there were lengthy delays in getting acts to the stage. In another money-sapping decision, helicopters were brought in to try to get performers on and off site as quickly as possible. If all this wasn't bad enough, there was also the weather to contend with. Rainfall, from light showers to torrential downpours, covered the site at regular intervals during the weekend, and with so many bodies churning up the ground Yasgur's farm quickly became an epic mudbath. 'Thousands flee Woodstock chaos, mud', said a report from United Press International issued on 16 August, succinctly capturing the atmosphere on the ground. It also announced the death of 'an unidentified youth' (later revealed as seventeen-year-old Raymond Mizak) who was killed when a tractor drove over him. Mizak was under a blanket among a pile of water-logged garbage having bunkered down on the Saturday morning to sleep. According to the report the driver of the tractor, who was hauling away sewage, 'was unable to distinguish [him] from the surrounding marsh'. There would be two further deaths, both drugs related, and a host of hospitalisations before the end of the festival.[3]

Filmmaker Michael Wadleigh caught all this and more as he and his crew wandered the length of the site filming bands and audience members alike. Wadleigh was there because in the weeks leading up to the festival Lang had made a deal with Warner Brothers to produce and distribute a documentary. The finished film, *Woodstock: 3 Days of Peace and Music* (1970) clearly captures the excitement of the event but also does a good job of showing its discomforts. Footage of the crowds flowing onto the festival site initially shows lines of delighted faces, but as the weather takes a turn for the worse and the heavy rain sets in, the carnival atmosphere starts to dissolve. New arrivals are seen shuffling onto the grounds. They're all drenched, and as they walk by clutching a few belongings they turn to the camera with faces of bewildered exhaustion. In these moments, *Woodstock* shows not a mass gathering but a festival straining under the weight of massive overcrowding. In general, though, the film sticks close to the spirit of its subtitle. With its shots of mud-covered revellers and skinny-dipping hippies alongside footage of celebratory performances by the likes of Richie Havens, John Sebastian, Joan Baez and Jefferson Airplane, *Woodstock* is shot through with a sense of bucolic ecstasy. No one is washing in the pond because of the site's inadequate facilities and sanitation; they're shedding their inhibitions in a delightful encounter with the natural world.

Ultimately, *Woodstock* offered a glimpse of what the festival *could* have been. It doesn't show, for example, the ugly scenes that unfolded on Saturday afternoon when rising anger among those queuing for overpriced, trashy hot dogs led to some food carts being smashed and set alight. As Barry Melton, guitarist for the band Country Joe and the Fish would later put it, 'I can always tell who was really there [...] When they tell me it was great I know they saw the movie and they weren't at the gig.' The Grateful Dead were there, and for them, Woodstock was certainly not 'great'. When they finally started to play on the evening of 16 August, they found a scene of disarray: broken equipment, a sinking, waterlogged stage and a sodden, exhausted and sleep deprived crowd. As they meandered through a shambolic gig and a twenty-minute version of their song 'Dark Star', Robert Hunter's lyrics of cosmic collapse could not have been more appropriate. Thanks to its freewheeling (mis)management Woodstock was clearly 'pouring its light / into ashes'. It had descended, within a matter of days, into a filthy ocean awash with bad acid and bad trips.

Hunter's description of a dark star crashing also mirrored the wider sociopolitical climate that overshadowed the festival. In January 1969 Richard Nixon had succeeded Lyndon Baines Johnson as President. Johnson had been the public face of America's growing involvement in Vietnam and as such had been the target of vociferous anti-war protest and political pressure from both sides. His administration was bookended by the Gulf of Tonkin incident of 1964, in which the USS *Maddox* allegedly came under fire from North Vietnamese Navy vessels, and the 1968 Tet Offensive, a series of North Vietnamese surprise attacks on South Vietnamese and American forces. The first allowed America to push its troops further into the conflict, the second was a major defeat that shook public confidence in the country's ability to win the war. Faced with this serious decline in domestic support, as well as an apparent lack of progress in the actual conflict despite increased troop deployment, Johnson announced that he would not run for re-election in 1968. Responding to these issues, Nixon came into office on promises of troop withdrawal and an end to the automatic draft. However, during the first six months of his administration the fighting in Vietnam seemed to get worse, with American forces suffering up to 8,000 fatalities. In early May *The New York Times* disclosed details of 'Operation Menu', a secret American bombing campaign initiated in March 1969 that targeted suspected communist supply sites in Cambodia. At the same time, reports also began to emerge of fierce fighting at Ap Bia Mountain, close to the border of Laos. 'Hamburger Hill', as it came to be known, was a meat-grinder of a battle: a bloody attack on North Vietnamese fighters which brought little in the way of lasting strategic advantage. Appearing to have learnt nothing from the virtual impasse Johnson had arrived at after five years of American involvement in Vietnam, 1969 thus found Nixon presiding over peak numbers of troops on the ground, heavy casualties and an escalation of the conflict via combat-led border crossings into supposedly neutral territories.[4]

This ongoing chaos was at the forefront of Jimi Hendrix's mind when he took to the stage with his band Gypsy Sun and Rainbows, nearly a day late, on Monday 18 August. Rattling a much smaller, bleary-eyed crowd back into life, Hendrix rolled through songs like 'Foxy Lady', 'Fire' and 'Voodoo Chile (Slight Return)' before letting rip with an exhilarating, excoriating version of America's national anthem, 'The Star-Spangled Banner'. It was a superb act of musical protest in which the song that was supposed to bind the nation together in patriotic unity was interrupted by Hendrix's expert control of distortion. After playing a few familiar bars, he unleashed a howl of feedback that made it sound as if a wounded wolf was lurking just under the surface of the tune. Dragging the tremolo bar further, Hendrix then pushed the howl into a thrashing squall of guitar noise, a potent brew that sounded like the clamour of combat: gunfire, screams and rockets flying overhead. For all its discord though, this was not the sonic equivalent of a flag-burning. Hendrix was not acting out of petulant disrespect. Instead, his electric rendition was a scream of outrage: a protest against the acts of violence committed at home and abroad under the banner of the flag. Sending Americans to kill or be killed in Vietnam and pitting American police against the American public on domestic frontlines like Columbia and Chicago, these were acts that took the values emblematised by the Stars and Stripes – liberty, freedom, democracy – and bent them all out of shape.

Hendrix poured all of this disgust and sadness into the performance and from it got a guitar piece that was duly tragic but also galvanising. It said what many others at Woodstock and around the country were thinking: somewhere down the line America's gone wrong; it's now up to us to set it right. Coming near the end of Hendrix's set, in the last moments of the festival, and thus towards the end of Wadleigh's film, 'The Star-Spangled Banner' came to exemplify Woodstock's political charge. Although it was a spectacle that took place when the festival grounds were emptying and when food and fresh water had long run out, Hendrix's performance floated above these material difficulties. Thanks to the festival's heavy media exposure, it came to symbolise the idea that Woodstock brought together and gave voice to an alternative America, one that, to use Al Aronowitz's words, loved the country but hated the government.[5]

For activists and writers like Abbie Hoffman, however, powerful symbolism was not enough. Hoffman had been involved in the protests at the Chicago Democratic Convention and along with Tom Hayden had been charged with inciting a riot. In July 1969 when he attended Woodstock, he was awaiting trial. Hoffman famously barged on stage while the Who were playing and launched into a speech in support of the recently imprisoned activist and Chicago veteran, John Sinclair. The impromptu address was cut short when Pete Townsend hit Hoffman with his guitar and booted him offstage. Undaunted, Hoffman dusted himself off and proceeded to spend the five days following the festival writing his response, what became *Woodstock Nation* (1969). With the recent Moon landing in mind, he cryptically described the

'Woodstock experience' as 'the first attempt to land a man on the Earth'. Hoffman's point was that the size and scale of Woodstock demonstrated the presence of a 'youth colony' within American culture. Previous festivals and large-scale demonstrations on the part of various New Left interests had pointed to a rising tide of radicalism across the 1960s, but at Woodstock these islands of activism came together to form a vibrant temporary community. If this energy could be funnelled into long-term collective action, Hoffman argued, the Woodstock nation could be a potent political force.

The book, *Woodstock Nation*, was thus not a celebratory paean to the festival itself, but a clarion call to the hippies who attended 'to grow thorns and defend themselves and their lifestyle'. As Lee and Shlain note, the idea of a 'Woodstock People's Party' was mooted 'which would serve as the militant vanguard of the psychedelic liberation front'. Great ideas but none of them came to pass. Despite its successes the momentum of the festival dissipated. Woodstock inspired more festivals, but nothing like the autonomous action Hoffman hoped for. It had instead blossomed into a popular film that showed a large group of people having a wonderful time. *Woodstock* made money for Warner Brothers but in Hoffman's view did little to extend or amplify the festival's political potential. It didn't even include footage of Hoffman's encounter with Townsend. 'Woodstock without any politics, without a commitment to self-defence of the nation is a shuck', he argued in the epilogue to the 1971 edition of *Woodstock Nation*. And this, he speculated, was the actual *purpose* of the Woodstock film; it rendered the Woodstock nation 'impotent' by distilling its collective power into nothing more than an entertaining record of a single weekend in the country. Seen through the film, Woodstock is collection of performances that point to a revolution but do not bring it about: it becomes another zombie to join the state of revolt.[6]

Although full of firebrand energy, *Woodstock Nation* carries a tone of melancholy that's not unlike the mood of *Easy Rider*. Writing two years after the Human Be-In and the critical mass of Haight-Ashbury, and one year after the Chicago protests, Hoffman comes to see Woodstock as significant only in terms of what it promised and, by 1971, that promise seemed to have faded. Considered on its own terms Woodstock demonstrated that, despite its best efforts, the countercultural impetus remained largely ineffectual. Faced with a world in crisis the best it could come up with was a massive party, one that generated a pile of garbage and an even bigger pile of debt for Woodstock Ventures. A gathering of the tribes? *We blew it.*[7]

It was not just *Woodstock* that diluted the festival's radical potential. As the posters made clear, Woodstock was billed as 'An Aquarian Exposition', a phrase that clearly evoked Gavin Arthur's astrological speculations made in the pages of the *San Francisco Oracle* throughout 1967. By 1969 though, the Age of Aquarius more readily recalled 'Medley: Aquarius / Let the Sunshine In', a number one single by the R&B vocal group the 5th Dimension, released in March 1969. 'Medley', or as it's more generally known, 'Let the Sunshine In', drew on two songs written for *Hair* (1967), an off-Broadway musical by Gerome Ragni, James Rado and Galt MacDermot based on the countercultural communities of New York and San Francisco. The single was a rousing anthem which preached a message of unity and the imminent arrival of harmony of Earth. Although it was enthusiastically sung by the massive Woodstock crowd during the weekend, what the Age of Aquarius meant to the 5th Dimension was not the same as what it meant to certain sectors of the countercultural underground.

As astrologers, members of the Process and readers of Aleister Crowley would point out, the Age of Aquarius refers to a period of great cosmic realignment, the coming of a new age but one that follows on from the turbulent, if not destructive eclipse of the old. While this new age may well be full of sunshine, its rays will likely fall on ruins and the remnants of whatever struggles preceded it. Seen in this way, the dawning of the Age of Aquarius equates to the coming of the end times. To invite it with calls of 'Let the sunshine in' means not to avoid the threat of an apocalypse by moving into an era of peace, but in some ways to bring it about, to inaugurate a time of tribulation: a period which, one might argue, was already in full flow in the war-dominated, nuclear-fixated, civilly disobedient climate of the late 1960s.[8]

More so than 'Let the Sunshine In' then, it's probably grim songs like Jefferson Airplane's 'Wooden Ships', released in February 1969, that better define the underlying implication of the Age of Aquarius. Taken from the band's sixth album *Volunteers* (1969) and performed as part of their Woodstock set, 'Wooden Ships' is a post-apocalyptic fable: the perfect anthem for the Woodstock nation. It describes the survivors of a nuclear conflict – the causes of which are long forgotten – setting sail away from a devastated coastline. In this landscape, they must revert to ships made of wood to avoid travelling in irradiated vessels of metal. Having left the dead and dying behind, the passengers now face an uncertain future. It's a bleak, cautionary scenario but one that, at the very least, speaks of a transition, a journey elsewhere and the need, as a matter of survival, to establish a new society.

In contrast, although it's a wonderful, utterly joyous pop song, 'Let the Sunshine In', is the mainstream chart hit which then, as now, conjures up tie-dye shirts and the distinct whiff of patchouli. There is much pleasure to be had from such inoffensive fantasies, but the sugar coating of 'Let the Sunshine In' starts to do harm once it so persistently becomes associated with the Woodstock milieu. It erases the apocalyptic undertow and political urgency of the countercultural worldview that fed into the festival and its performances. As a result, rather than exemplifying the type of autonomous gathering Hoffman described in *Woodstock Nation*, the festival becomes something akin to *Hair*, a cultural artefact that's easily interpreted, digested and thus contained within the wider public imagination. Radical acts lose their potency as soon as they come to occupy this type of position and this, according to the writer Robert Anton Wilson, was very much the fate of Woodstock. Because of its hedonism and excess, he argued, Woodstock marked 'the rebirth of Dionysus' in the modern era. However, in moving out of the underground to reach this glorious apex, its power was quickly neutralised and made safe. As Wilson, co-author of the conspiracy classic *Illuminatus!* (1975), put it, 'right away the lid came down.'[9]

There's a glimpse of this 'lid' coming down part way through *Woodstock*. Alongside shots of festival-goers gleefully hurling themselves into pools of mud, there's a short scene in which two young men break off from the crowd and approach the camera. Agitated and soaked to the skin they excitedly talk over each other and point to the sky. According to the pair, it's not just bad luck that a torrential downpour should have occurred during the weekend:

> FIRST MAN: I got something to say. I wanna know how come the fascist pigs have been seeding the clouds?

SECOND MAN: Right, the past hour and a half.

FIRST MAN: We could see the airplanes going over twice with all the smoke coming out of them, seeding the clouds. And I wanna know why all that stuff is going down, man. And why doesn't the media report all that stuff to the people, man?

'Cloud seeding' was a way of making it rain. Two projects sponsored by the American government, Project Cirrus (1946–7) and Project Stormfury (1962–83), attempted to develop cloud seeding as a preventative measure against the destructive power of hurricanes. By using planes to drop large amounts of silver iodide into the centre of a storm system it was hoped that the inner clouds would freeze, the hurricane's structure would become unstable and the storm would dissolve into rainfall.

Project Cirrus put this technique into practice in October 1947, when a Boeing B-17 dropped 180 pounds of dry ice onto Hurricane King some 350 miles off the coast of Florida. The behaviour of the hurricane changed, but instead of dissolving it changed course and made landfall in Savannah, Georgia causing considerable damage and loss of life. 'Pretty soon', notes Sam Kean, 'reports about the B-17 began circulating in southern newspapers' prompting the military to deny 'that the experiment had diverted the storm'. Project Stormfury met with a similar response in 1965 when, after an attempt to modify the structure of Hurricane Betsy over the Atlantic, it began to head towards land. The seeding was cancelled but no information about this change to the plan was offered to the press. As a result, it was widely assumed that the hurricane landed because of the project. Although the full details of projects Cirrus and Stormfury were not disclosed at the time, there was enough in their official denials and press releases to push public knowledge of cloud seeding towards the realms of conspiracy theory. Stories of targeted storms and weaponised hurricanes provided the ideal backdrop against which to accuse 'them', the American government, of acting under the auspices of a shadowy meteorological project to control and disturb 'us', the public.[10]

Project Stormfury continued throughout the 1960s with a major cloud-seeding operation launched against Hurricane Debbie between 18 August and 20 August 1969, the days immediately following the Woodstock festival. Maybe the two young men had got it absolutely right. Maybe upper New York State was used as a last-minute test bed before the B-17s refuelled their ice-bombs and headed out over the Atlantic. Or, maybe not. No matter: as with most conspiracy theories the real interest lies not with the alleged truth of the issue at hand but in what the details of the theory reveals about those making the claims. In saying that 'fascist pigs', parties of 'unknown origin', were 'seeding the clouds over the area' to create rainfall, Wadleigh's impromptu conspiracy theorists were, like the hurricane-struck inhabitants of Savannah, Georgia, attributing their difficult conditions to the intervention of 'higher' establishmentarian powers. Paranoid or not, this type of claim is a way of amplifying the significance of an event like Woodstock. In the view of the two ranting men, Woodstock's quite literal failure to let the sunshine in and its descent into a waterlogged mess had nothing to do with the vagaries of the weather but with the machinations of the enemy. In their view 'They', 'The Man', the undefined, ever-powerful masters of control, recognised the seismic challenge the festival issued to the 'straight' world and took immediate, large-scale action to bring the lid down.[11]

⁂

Robert Anton Wilson became well acquainted with this type of conspiratorial logic while working for that bastion of American culture, *Playboy*. Between 1965 and 1971 he and fellow writer Robert Shea edited the magazine's 'Forum' pages and handled much of its correspondence. Launched by Hugh Hefner in 1953, *Playboy* was first marketed as a lifestyle magazine for the wealthy young man about town. Laying out his stall in the first issue Hefner, with no hint of irony, defined his ideal reader as the type of sophisticated chap who would invite young ladies to his apartment for dinner followed by a discussion of 'Nietzsche, jazz, sex'. By 1969, *Playboy* had distilled this formula down to its most profitable essence: a combination of sexist pretentiousness and sexist centrefold spreads. By some strange magic, Hefner had also managed to cultivate a popular and equally profitable public persona, that of a bizarre, calcified sex-vampire with a penchant for women dressed as rabbits.[12]

Meanwhile Wilson and Shea found that many of the letters written to *Playboy* in the late 1960s and early 1970s still talked about Nietzsche, jazz and sex; although in the space between these topics, where the borderlines of philosophy, popular culture and human desire started to overlap, there appeared an insistent, obsessive type of letter-writing. More and more, much to their growing fascination and delight, Wilson and Shea were reading letters that drew on all manner of conspiracy theories to set the world to rights. These missives were expressive of views across the political spectrum. Variously libertarian, conservative, socialist and anarchistic, they railed against the erasure of civil liberties as well as the spread of the civil rights movement; they declared the singular guilt of Lee Harvey Oswald while others named the assassination team that fired from the grassy knoll; some decried the student-led peace movement, and some called for a change in government in response to the conflict in Vietnam. UFOs got a fair amount of coverage as did the Moon landing, the Freemasons and the 18th-century group of super-conspirators, the Bavarian Order of the Illuminati. Similar material could be found in *The Skeleton Key to the Gemstone File*, a xeroxed missive written and circulated in 1975 by the journalist Stephanie Caruana. It outlined decades of alleged collusion between the American government, the Mafia, Howard Hughes and Aristotle Onassis. Writing in the mid 1970s, Caruana offered *The Gemstone File* as the Rosetta Stone of conspiracy theory, the secret key to the *real* history of the 20th century. For Wilson and Shea, though, the 'Forum' letters got there first. There was no need for them to seek out obscure, underground texts, as Caruana had allegedly done, because the *Playboy* mailbags were the primary repository of post-JFK, post-MLK, post-RFK 'classic conspiracy theory – fact mixed with conjecture, blended with error and expressed with conviction.'[13]

Where Caruana repeatedly stressed the truth of the *Gemstone* texts, Wilson and Shea had little concern for the veracity of the material they encountered. In its absurdity and paranoid excesses, they saw a fictional complexity equal to the work of such subversive fantasists as Mervyn Peake or William Burroughs. Following this line of thought to its logical conclusion they spent the years 1969 to 1971 writing what became *Illuminatus!*, an epic trilogy in which the Illuminati are cast as the secret puppet masters of history. Published in 1975 and again in 1976, exactly (and by mere coincidence, of course) 200 years after the founding of Illuminism in 1776, the novel consists of three volumes, *The Eye in the Pyramid*, *The Golden Apple* and *Leviathan*. Together they tell a massively convoluted story of information, misinformation and contemporary activism, all shot through the head-spinning lens of an endlessly intersecting web of conspiracy and counter-conspiracy.

Beaming with pride at the achievement of its alumni, *Playboy* declared it 'a literary acid-trip'. This was not just a throwaway remark. *Illuminatus!* was firmly rooted in the counterculture of the late 1960s with the 'story', such as it is, starting in 1968 and unfolding in the early to mid 1970s. It focuses on the plight of Joe Malik, editor of the 'left-of-centre' magazine *Confrontation* whose offices are bombed after he begins to investigate the Illuminati, which the novel initially defines as 'a short-lived movement of republican free-thought [...] ultimately banned by an edict of the Bavarian government in 1785'.

Malik finds that the history of the group is much more extensive, beginning in the 11th century as a Christian sect that 'plundered the rich and announced the imminent reign of the Spirit'. Crucially for the events of the novel, the contention is that the Illuminati moved beyond these heretical origins and remain active in the present day as 'a secret society that keeps screwing up international politics'. Here, the *Playboy* material kicks in with Wilson and Shea providing fictionalised versions of the material they encountered. Malik quotes from a letter sent to 'The Playboy Advisor' dated April 1969:

> I recently heard an old man of right-wing views – a friend of my grandparents – assert that the current wave of assassinations in America is the work of a secret society called the Illuminati. He said that the Illuminati have existed throughout history, own the international banking cartels, have all been 32nd-degree Masons and were known to Ian Fleming, who portrayed them as *Spectre* in his James Bond books – for which the Illuminati did away with Mr. Fleming. At first all this seemed like a paranoid delusion to me. Then I read in *The New Yorker* that Alan

> Chapman, one of Jim Garrison's investigators in the New Orleans probe of the John Kennedy assassination believes that the Illuminati really exist …

The 'actual' Illuminati of the 18th century were the product of enlightenment thinking and worked to oppose the dominance of religious authority in society. In Wilson and Shea's hands this project is amplified, not just in terms of its historical range but also in the scope of its ambition. Their version of the Illuminati stands neither wholly to the left nor fully to the right of the political spectrum, nor is it concerned with the power of the clergy. Instead, it is described as pursuing an absolute and overwhelming will to power. This is made manifest through the continual manipulation of world events in ways that benefit the group and shore up their covert role as the true power behind multiple thrones.[14]

In this blurring of ambiguous fact and incredible fiction as well as Wilson and Shea's playful weaving together of complex links between conspirators and conspiracies, *Illuminatus!* exemplifies what the historian Richard Hofstadter called 'the paranoid style'. In his essay 'The Paranoid Style in American Politics' (1964) Hofstadter analyses what he sees as the main characteristics of right-wing political debate in the post-war period: a 'sense of heated exaggeration, suspiciousness and conspiratorial fantasy'. This stance, he argues, comes from a feeling of dispossession on the part of the right, the belief that 'America has been largely taken away from them and their kind' via projects like 'Roosevelt's New Deal' which undermined 'free capitalism', brought the economy 'under the direction of the federal government' and paved the way for 'socialism and communism'.

Hofstadter was writing during a period of democratic rule shortly after Lyndon Baines Johnson took office following the death of John F. Kennedy in November 1963. When he speaks of right-wing politics and the modern discovery of conspiracies, he has the communist witch-hunts of the McCarthy-era in mind as a primary example. *Illuminatus!* mirrors aspects of this worldview, particularly the apocalyptic and personal view of history held by what Hofstadter calls the 'paranoid spokesman.' This is the idea that the enemy is a force of singular malice – 'sinister, ubiquitous, powerful, cruel' – and that the achievement of their aims is imminent, it will be total, and unless action is taken it will involve 'the death of whole worlds, whole political orders, whole systems of human values.' What Wilson and Shea add to this model is a set of counter-conspirators, the Discordians, a group who oppose the Illuminati's desire for order with magic, confusion and – their guiding principle – chaos. As a result, the main conflict of the novel is not that of 'good vs evil' as in Hofstadter's model but the fuzzy, guerrilla warfare of one secret society trying to subvert and outflank the work of another. The 'values' under threat in *Illuminatus!* are also not those of the American right but are instead linked to the progressive social mission of the New Left and the counterculture.[15]

As described in *The Eye of the Pyramid*, as well as bombing the offices of *Confrontation*, the Illuminati had their hand in the 1968 riots at the Chicago Democratic Convention. True to form, the infiltration of the Illuminati also extends the other way, with the counterculture operating as a 'front' for recruiting young people to their cause:

> The theory in essence was that the Illuminati [...] turned them on to some sort of *illuminizing* experience through marijuana (or some special extract of marijuana) and converted them into fanatics willing to use any means necessary to 'illuminize' the rest of the world.

Although the visionary implications of this 'conversion' recall Timothy Leary's acid evangelism, the willingness of the Illuminati to 'systematically' assassinate along the way 'every popular political figure who might interfere with their plan' simultaneously aligns them with authoritarian violence at its most despotic. For the character Saul Goodman, the jaded and increasingly bewildered detective assigned to the Malik case, realising the extent of the Illuminati's hold over the youth culture brings with it disturbing implications. He thinks 'suddenly, of Charlie Manson', the Weathermen, 'the popularity of pot smoking' and the popularity of the slogan 'by any means necessary' among contemporary radicals. The effect of this anxiety on Saul, 'a lifelong liberal', is that he suddenly feels 'a pang of typically right-wing terror towards modern youth'. That is exactly what the Illuminati would *want* him to feel. Controlling culture and fostering its counterculture; propping up the establishment and sowing the seeds of its collapse; causing liberals to become reactionaries, hippies to become murderers and protesters to become violent revolutionaries: according to Wilson and Shea, this constant shadowplay is how the Illuminati seize power and stay in power. Standing behind the glass, working only to their own plan, they silently and determinedly guide society through the hall of mirrors that is modern history.[16]

Illuminatus! is, on the surface, a satire of conspiracy theory. At the same time, it wilfully encourages the paranoid worldview, or at least reminds the reader that things – received historical narratives, established institutions, sources of control and rebellion – are not always what they seem. For the two men ranting about cloud seeding at Woodstock, *Illuminatus!* would have offered something of a validation. For everyone else there that day, its message could potentially have been more disturbing. It's often said that the unofficial motto of the counterculture was 'never trust anyone over 30'. *Illuminatus!* utterly explodes this neat division between the solidarity, dynamism and sincerity of the 'young', and the compromises, conservatism and authority of the 'old'. Instead it suggests that the battlefield is wider and much more complex, with multiple theatres and multiple combatants in play at any one time. Within this scenario, Wilson and Shea suggest that the counterculture itself may well have been 'seeded'. Rather than emerging as a form of post-war opposition to the status quo, they imply that the Illuminati, the hidden establishment of the novel, fostered the alternative and protest cultures of the 1960s as one part of a wider, orchestrated conflict between different sectors of society. And it is Woodstock, or at least a version of it, that forms the locus of this orchestration in the novel.

Throughout *Illuminatus!* frequent reference is made to 'Woodstock Europa', the 'largest rock festival in the history of mankind'. Organised by the Illuminati after having gained 'control of the rock music business', Woodstock Europa is intended to take place at the group's spiritual home, Ingolstadt in Bavaria. In what is, even by the standards of the novel, one of Wilson and Shea's more outrageous claims, they describe the festival as an energy conduit. The Illuminati attempt to use the 'biomystical waves' of this mass gathering to incite a nuclear war. This will mark the completion of their great project. They will have achieved 'transcendental illumination' by having finally 'immanentized' the 'Eschaton', quite literally the 'end times'.

This is conspiratorial fantasy taken to the extreme, but within such an elaborate, absurd fiction as *Illuminatus!* it makes a certain degree of sense. Wilson and Shea use the scenario to pointedly reimagine countercultural spectacles like Woodstock as flimsy facades. In their view, whatever the sincerity of the long-haired kids who attend the festival, their sentiments mean nothing when compared to the intentions of the Illuminati, the group who are *really* in charge. This is an image of the counterculture as a tool, the product of a huge confidence trick that has spanned the centuries, one that has drawn its unwitting participants into a trajectory totally at odds with their own intentions. For all their claims of independence and autonomy, in the world of *Illuminatus!* New Left activists, anti-war protestors and hippies alike are presented as pawns. As with their supposed antagonists, the pillars of the establishment, they're all locked in a game so big no one can see the chessboard.[17]

When *Illuminatus!* was published in 1975, the 1960s were beginning to recede into history and the novel stood far enough away from its decade of inspiration to offer something of a vantage point, from where the sixties could be mapped and tentatively called to account. Despite the novel unravelling a long history of the Illuminati, its plot sets forth from the events of 1968, primarily the Chicago Democratic Convention. Alongside the disturbances at Columbia and those of Paris in May, the events in Chicago added to the sense that in 1968 the political left were standing on the cusp of great social change. *Illuminatus!* emerges out of this context of possibility, but by the time it was widely read the prevailing view of 1968 had altered. Rather than being a year that changed the world, it was seen as period of unfulfilled potential, a year defined by a sense of *almost but not quite*. Despite the lasting cultural significance carried by the events of the year, by 1975 it was clear that its revolutionary push had been short-lived. Indeed, writing in *French Revolution 1968* (1968), a book published mere months after the events it describes, Patrick Seale and Maureen McConville conclude that the 'May Revolution' yielded little in terms of an actual 'bid for political power'. It was a 'revolt against ruling bureaucracies, administrative machines, professional apparatuses', but the factionalism of 'the young revolutionaries, the undisciplined students, the rebellious professional men and the sullen strikers' caused the revolutionary drive to 'collapse under the weight of personal and doctrinal rivalries'. Overall, they surmise, the 'May Revolution' was a mass statement of discontent rather than a *coup d'état* in which 'Nobody set out determinedly to topple [de Gaulle] because no one believed it could be done'.

In addition to their internal instabilities, these events were also pockets of left-wing activity within a wider political climate largely dominated by the thinking of the right. As such, they inspired not lasting change, but reactive, knee-jerk conservatism. As Seale and McConville put it, 'every fire lit in the streets is a vote cast for the Right at the next election'. And so, by 1970 not only was Richard Nixon in the White House, but Conservative Edward Heath was in Downing Street and loyal Gaullist Georges Pompidou was in the Élysée Palace. Whatever challenges had been issued by these radical, student-led movements, they were gradually smoothed over during the decade that followed. Everyone back to work. During the Nixon administration, for example, the President's promise to restore order blossomed into a domestic policy of heavy-handed confrontation. This was felt most by those who continued to protest the business of war as the conflict in Vietnam spilled over into Cambodia and Laos. The most infamous example were the shootings at Kent State University in Ohio on 4 May 1970. After several days of increasingly tense demonstrations against American foreign policy, Ohio's National Guardsmen entered the campus and attempted to disperse the crowd. Possibly acting out of fear, possibly acting out of pure hostility, the Guardsmen decided to open fire on the protestors.

The result was not a pacification but something akin to a massacre: four students were killed and nine more were left with life-changing injuries.[18]

The net effect of this show of force was a corresponding push the other way. Student-led and non-violent groups gave way to and, in some cases, recalibrated themselves as aggressive, terroristic units. The Weather Underground continued with their domestic bombing campaign that lasted until 1975 (with sporadic actions thereafter), and during the same period an international range of other left-wing splinter groups carried out similar actions. Their motivations were varied but, from an American perspective at least, it appeared as if Kent State coincided with and ignited a widespread rise in far-left militancy. In England, a group of anarchists promoted proletarian revolution in the name of 'King Mob', a reference to graffiti left on the walls of London's Newgate Prison during the Gordon Riots of 1780. Between 1970 and 1972 the anarchist communist group the Angry Brigade took the often surreal provocations of King Mob one step further. Convening on the back of the 1968 anti-war demonstrations in London's Grosvenor Square, the Angry Brigade bombed public buildings, large-scale media events like Miss World and the homes of Conservative politicians. An explosion at New Scotland Yard in May 1971 was attributed to the group, and later in the year on Halloween, they launched a much higher-profile attack when they fire-bombed the key symbol of Harold Wilson's modernising project, London's Post Office Tower. In December 1969, in Dublin, the paramilitary group the Provisional Irish Republican Army announced their separation from the 'old IRA', a group that had been attempting to achieve its republican aims, the withdrawal of British rule from Northern Ireland, via increasingly parliamentary means. In the fraught, sectarian atmosphere of late-1960s Belfast where calls for civil rights for Catholics were met 'by the violence of Protestant loyalists', the Provisional IRA argued for a return to the 'basic military role of the IRA'. They resolved to protect the Catholic community and continue a campaign of guerrilla warfare against the colonial power: the British.

While Britain's militant groups would be short-lived, lasting in the main until the mid 1970s, the Provisional IRA remained active throughout the 'Long War' of the 1970s, into the 1980s and up to the peace process of the 1990s. Another extended campaign was staged in Germany by the Red Army Faction, also known as the Baader-Meinhof Group, who in 1970 instigated a wave of bombings, shootings and robberies that resulted in 34 deaths by 1977. At the same time, Italy's far-left paramilitary faction, the Red Brigades, started a similar action. In what has become known as the 'Years of Lead', the group attempted to use armed struggle to put in place a 'revolutionary state' that would lead to Italy's removal from the North Atlantic Treaty Organization (NATO). This culminated in 1978 when the group kidnapped and murdered the Christian Democratic politician and former Prime Minister of Italy, Aldo Moro.[19]

All this was a far cry from the doves that adorned the posters used to promote Woodstock and the calls for peace that John Lennon and Yoko Ono had issued from their Bed-In. For some, like Jeff Nuttall, this shift marked a detour in the progress of the countercultural project which he explored in his novel *Snipe's Spinster* (1975). Something of a follow-up to *Bomb Culture*, *Snipe's Spinster* describes the fortunes of a disorganised group of would-be conspirators who plan to assassinate 'the Man', a symbolic figure most likely modelled, according to Douglas Field and Jay Jeff Jones, on Richard Nixon. From a decade of revolutionary potential to a vague desire for violence wrapped up in a chaotic assassination plot, Nuttall uses the events of *Snipe's Spinster* to show the wholesale dilution of the political energy that characterised the 1960s. Other parties, by contrast, came to see the radical violence of the 1970s as the energy of the 1960s finding its apogee. As Richard English argues when discussing the Provisional IRA and 'the youthful radicals who would emerge as leaders of the next generation of Irish republicanism,' they were 'greatly influenced' by the 'political and social zeitgeist' of the 1960s: the sense that, as Gerry Adams put it 'one *could* change the world.' Danny Morrison who joined the Provisional IRA in 1969, put it more succinctly, as cited by English: 'people of my age, my generation, we watched the civil rights movement in the States, we watched the Vietnam war and the anti-war protests.'[20]

Read in the light of this fraught context, the conspiracies that make up *Illuminatus!* give shape and form – however absurd – to the period's political and social complexity. The 'paranoid style' of conspiracy theory with its shadows and puppet masters is all about connecting dots that would otherwise not join up. Conspiracy theories are metanarratives that allow the chaos and dysfunctionality of the world to make sense. They provide a veil of security in the face of great insecurity. This is a view of the world in which there are no coincidences and there are no accidents. Hurricanes making landfall, concerts disrupted by terrible weather and the shift of protest groups into tailspins of violence: everything happens for a reason in the conspirasphere because groups behind the scenes, whether they be the Illuminati, the Priory of Sion, the Freemasons or the CIA, have made it happen for their own purposes. If presented with Wyatt's downcast claim in *Easy Rider* that 'We blew it,' the conspiracy theorist would say the fault lay elsewhere. The problem was not that the counterculture failed to realise its potential or was derailed by violence or, worse still, merely withered into inconsequence. Rather, it was doomed from the beginning because, despite its loudly stated aims, its 'real' agenda was dictated by the strategic needs of those fighting a much bigger, invisible war.

Illuminatus! appeared after the revelations of the Watergate scandal and after the publication of Carl Bernstein and Bob Woodward's account of the investigation, *All the President's Men* (1974). Now a byword for political conspiracy, 'Watergate' describes the investigation, attempted cover-up and political fall-out relating to a break-in at the Democratic National Committee headquarters (part of the Watergate office complex in Washington D.C.) on 17 June 1972. The revelation that the incident was part of the illegal tactics employed by Nixon as part of his re-election campaign eventually led to his resignation as President in August 1974, just shy of an impeachment. Soon after, in December 1974, *The New York Times* journalist Seymour Hersh lifted the lid on more of Nixon's dubious activities. In a front-page story, he revealed that the CIA, in a 'direct' violation of its charter, had 'conducted a massive, illegal domestic intelligence operation during the Nixon Administration against the anti-war movement and other dissident groups in the United States'. The 'Nixon years', as Hersh put it, were marked by 'anti-war hysteria' and the belief that left-wing protest groups and the Black Panthers were subject to both support and infiltration by foreign (i.e. Russian) governments. Hersh quotes various CIA officials who state that activities including 'break-ins, wiretapping and the surreptitious inspection of mail' were sanctioned as part of a counterintelligence procedure aimed at these 'foreign intelligence problems'. What emerges as the article progresses is that these actions were not so much intelligence gathering exercises as destabilising tactics aimed squarely at domestic parties. Hersh claims that in addition to grossly overstepping its jurisdictional boundaries, the CIA used 'plants, informers and doublers (double agents)' to combat 'anti-war activities and student turmoil that the White House believed was being "fermented" […] by black extremists'.

For *Illuminatus!* to then appear in this climate and for it to deal with far-reaching conspiracies is not surprising. It may have been presented by the *Village Voice* as 'the biggest SF cult novel since *Dune*', but just as Frank Herbert's novel was read as an astute reflection on psychedelic culture, Wilson and Shea's fiction came to emblematise a certain post-sixties disillusionment. Disillusionment not just because of what the counterculture seemed unable to achieve on its own accord but because the highest offices of government were increasingly revealed to be plotting against it. The Nixon administration did not contain, to recall historian Arthur Marwick's phrase, 'men and women of traditional and enlightened outlook who respond flexibly and tolerantly to counter-cultural demands'. Unlike Harold Wilson and Roy Jenkins, who rolled out a series of progressive policies in keeping with the reformist mood of the 1960s, the Nixon White House moved into the 1970s making no such concessions. It saw America's countercultures as a seditious fifth column and acted accordingly.[21]

In between Watergate, Hersh's story and *Illuminatus!*, Mae Brussell, a writer and conspiracy theorist, took this scenario one step further. From her home in Carmel, California Brussell published *Conspiracy Newsletter*, frequently contributed to Paul Krassner's magazine *The Realist* and held forth via her regular radio broadcasts on the Kennedy assassination(s), Watergate, 'Satanism, and so on'. In 1976 she wrote an essay titled 'From Monterey Pop to Altamont: Operation Chaos – The CIA's War

Against the Sixties Counter-Culture'. Written in parallel with the publication of *Illuminatus!* Brussell's essay was essentially the novel's flipside: not a fiction developed out of conspiratorial half-truths, but a missive that takes such material and presents it as 'FACT'. In her essay, Brussell catalogues the deaths, suicides and misfortunes that plagued the British and American music industry between 1968 and 1976 – a list that includes Cass Elliot, Jimi Hendrix, Otis Redding, Brian Jones and Janis Joplin – and claims that such high-profile losses were neither accidental nor coincidental. Brussell speculates upon government collusion, noting that those nine years 'were the same years that the FBI and the CIA waged a domestic war against any kind of dissent'.

Brussell names this 'domestic war' 'Operation Chaos', quoting the CIA code-name for the internal surveillance campaign in operation between 1967 and 1974 which extended across the Johnson and Nixon administrations. This is the same intelligence strategy described (but not named) by Hersh in *The New York Times*, but for Brussell it went far beyond illegal surveillance. She alleges that the CIA recognised the power of certain high-profile rock stars like John Lennon. Concerned about their ability to act as lightning rods for the youth movement, the CIA thus set out to 'kill or discredit' these 'leaders'. This sabotage was achieved through the clandestine use of drugs, particularly LSD to induce strange behaviour, psychological problems and then certain death. As proof of this theory, Brussell cites the case of Jimi Hendrix and an abortive show at Madison Square Garden in January 1970, in which it's alleged that acid caused him to act irrationally and stop playing after two songs:

> The result was that Hendrix was discredited. The effect of one LSD dose could cause permanent brain injury.

> Anything Hendrix did after this experience, up to and including the time of his death, could be attributed to that earlier event.

Brussell's elaborate take on Operation Chaos is bound up with what was known at the time about MK-ULTRA, another CIA project that investigated the intelligence and counter-intelligence potential of psychotropic chemicals. Officially running from 1953 to 1973, MK-ULTRA placed particular emphasis on LSD. The programme investigated the potential of the drug to work as a weapon, a mind-control device and truth serum.[22]

It would be 1977 before the project was subject to a Select Committee hearing and 1978 before its details would become widely known via books like John D. Marks' study *The Search for the Manchurian Candidate*. What Brussell offers in 1976 is the same type of speculation that forms the basis of *Illuminatus!* She works it into an all-encompassing theory of LSD-inspired subterfuge in which the misfortunes of the 1960s were all engineered by the CIA to defuse the revolutionary potential of the era's 'restless youth'. According to her account, Operation Chaos was responsible for both the Manson murders and the violence at Altamont, the two incidents fuelled by LSD and orchestrated as a joint programme between the CIA, the FBI and the US Army. Festivals and mass gatherings like Woodstock were also subject to a range of disruptive tactics: crowd manipulation, disinformation and the mass distribution of hallucinogens of dubious quality. It was a speculative, associative and, quite frankly, paranoid analysis but one that the men who spotted the cloud seeding at Woodstock would certainly have agreed with. Overall, Brussell's argument dovetailed exactly with the fiction of Shea and Wilson. In her view the forces of conspiracy did not just oppose the counterculture in its various forms, but also facilitated its growth. In the early 1960s Timothy Leary hoped to have 'turned on' 4 million people to the pleasures of LSD by 1969. According to Brussell, the CIA had the same idea but were much more direct about it: while Leary was in his pulpit extolling the virtues of the drug, the CIA were distributing acid, 'surreptitiously to large masses of the population.'[23]

Beyond the networks of conspiracy theorising, there is little evidence to substantiate the extent of the allegations Brussell makes. The FBI did collate an extensive file on John Lennon and, according to Jonathan Vankin and John Whalen, he was subject to CIA surveillance between 1969 and 1976. However, it is unlikely that this intelligence gathering operation included attempts at spiking him with LSD. That said, the wider implications of Brussell's and Wilson and Shea's writing – the sense that the counterculture was compromised and essentially redundant – was a view not lost on the its key players.

True to their name, the Weather Underground were able to sense this change in the climate and as 1969 became 1970 their guerrilla war began. If *Illuminatus!* brought to the fore the idea that conspiracies were afoot against the countercultural world, the Weathermen pre-empted this revelation and adopted the same techniques as the 'enemy'. They went from protestors to active conspirators, planning not demonstrations but the 'terrorist actions' that would dominate the first half of the 1970s. Their sign-off to non-violent protest came in late December 1969 at their National War Council in Flint, Michigan, an event that has also become known as the Wargasm Conference. There they officially adopted the stance of armed struggle and discussed a range of possible targets. Writing in *Acid Dreams*, Martin A. Lee and

Bruce Shlain note that soon after this event 'approximately one hundred of the Weather cadre were living clandestinely with the avowed objective of making war on the state'.

Back in London, in April, Alexander Trocchi and the smoking crowd at the State of Revolt had none of this energy. Trocchi talked about 'insurrection' but nothing came of it, precisely because there was no real sense of a conspiracy at hand, just a vacant desire for something that sounded like revolution. This is why it seemed so deathly. For the Weather Underground, the idea they were *at war* gave them a drive, a sense of purpose. The path they embarked on was deeply problematic, but it was one born of their belief that a gathering of the tribes was not enough, however Dionysian such a meeting may have been. For Bernardine Dohrn, Bill Ayers, Mark Rudd and the other members of the Weather Underground, the sixties had come to an end because the decade's progressive project had run its course. The energy was still there but it had to be channelled in a different direction and towards a different set of ends. To affirm this belief, towards the end of the War Council, the Weathermen joined together in a collective ritual of singing, dancing and yelling. They invoked a set of higher powers, first the spirit of the radical left, 'Women Power!', 'Struggling Power!', 'Red Army Power!' and then they called upon the new gods of violence and conspiracy: 'Sirhan Sirhan Power!', 'Charlie Manson Power!'. For the Weathermen, the future would prove to be full of flames. Within a year of the War Council three members would be dead, killed in an explosion in Greenwich Village in March 1970 thanks to a bomb-making session gone wrong. On this night in late 1969 though, calling on these powers put a spark back into the zombie. In a gesture of terrible beauty, it rose up and slouched forward.[24]

CHAPTER VII

Pandemonium '69

The problem with invocations is that they have a habit of working. They are particularly effective when made at points of critical mass, when other parties are calling similar forces from the ether. Throughout December 1969 the air was crackling with heavy anticipation. On 6 December, some weeks before the Flint War Council, the Moon moved into the house of Scorpio, the point in the month 'when the Universal Vibration is at its most unstable.' At the same time the Rolling Stones took to the stage at the Altamont Speedway in Northern California. This was to be the last date of their 1969 North American tour – a month-long junket to support their tenth American album *Let It Bleed* – and the West Coast astrologers started to get nervous. Since the release of their eighth LP, *Their Satanic Majesties Request* in December 1967, the Stones had been flirting with darkness. The violence of their songs seemed more and more to mirror the tribulation of the late 1960s: street riots, assassinations and the grinding continuation of the war in Vietnam. Stanley Booth, a writer travelling with the band, was taken with their song 'Midnight Rambler', a queasy homage to Albert DeSalvo, the Boston Strangler. It made him think of George Howard Putt, the recently arrested 'sex-slayer' of Memphis, as well as the Zodiac Killer who was at that point rambling free throughout the San Francisco Bay Area. A mere three months had passed since the Tate–LaBianca murders. As the concert crowds amassed at Altamont, reports of Manson's arrest were just beginning to circulate. Seeing the landowners of Livermore shut their doors fearing more of the same violence,

Booth wrote in his notebook that 'murder seemed to be in the air these days, like the scent of flowers in the spring.' And now, singing about death and the devil while wearing a shirt emblazoned with the sign of omega, and flanked by Hells Angels, Mick Jagger seemed to be deliberately playing with the date's astrological fire. Only misfortune could come of this.[1]

Earlier in the tour, a show at the Inglewood Forum in Los Angeles started late. By 4am the audience had had enough and, according to Tony Sanchez, 'pandemonium' ensued. 'Who do you think you are?' they shouted at the empty stage as bottles flew through the air. Pandemonium? This was *nothing* compared to Altamont. Part way through the day-long festival, members of the Hells Angels Motorcycle Club arrived to provide 'security.' They were armed with bike chains and weighted, sawn-off pool cues. A single, thin rope separated the swelling crowd from the three-foot high stage and the Angels, one of whom wore the remains of a fox as a hat, surrounded this platform with their bikes before digging in for the duration. In such tense, close confines the tidal movements of the crowd resulted in frequent fights as the Angels squared up to anyone who came near.

Chain-smoking, haggard and paranoid, tour manager and MC Sam Cutler took stock of the situation. 'We're in chaos backstage, man,' he confided to a friend. All these hassles caused problems getting equipment on and off the platform. Cutler, a no-nonsense Londoner, picked up a microphone and spoke eyeball-to-eyeball with the Angels and the crowd. Curt, straight to the point and with no hint of hippie rhetoric, Cutler called for people to be reasonable, to calm down and to move back from the stage. He needn't have bothered: no one really took any notice, least of all the Angels. They stayed put and defended the stage as if it were a Viking fortress.

As the Stones waited in their caravan, all the other bands were bearing the brunt of this bad atmosphere. Marty Balin from Jefferson Airplane was knocked out when he tried to stop the Angels stomping on some poor unfortunate who'd looked at them the wrong way. Backstage the Grateful Dead heard about the violence and said 'Oh bummer' before deciding not to play. Meanwhile, as the night drew in and the temperature dropped, swathes of bad acid moved through the field. Bodies flailed in the darkness far from the help of the skeleton crew first aid team. Amid all the concussions, bruisings and fist fights, a man drowned in a drainage pit, two more were killed in an on-site hit and run and later, as the Stones played 'Under My Thumb', a young black man, Meredith Hunter, was stabbed, beaten and stomped to death by Alan Passaro, one of the Hells Angels, in full view of the stage. All this in the middle of an isolated dragstrip strewn with the wreckage of stock cars, the air thick with smoke from makeshift garbage fires.[2]

Altamont means 'high mountain'. There are places named Altamont all over the US but the one in Northern California is a strange ghost of a town. In 1869 the Central Pacific Railroad cut a line through the Diablo Range near to the Livermore Pass, a small way station and trading post. With the railway came business and prosperity. The trading post, originally named the Summit, quickly began to grow. It gained a post office. More and more people wanted to settle there and open their own storefronts. By 1872 the settlement, seated at an elevation of some 741 feet, established itself as the town of Altamont. Soon after the Livermore Pass became the Altamont Pass, a name that's survived despite the almost complete disappearance of the town.

Like most of the communities set up in the wake of California's Gold Rush, Altamont lasted little more than a generation. When the Speedway opened in July 1966 it was one of the few discernible landmarks in a barren, twenty-mile stretch of land between Livermore and Tracy. To most people in the Tri-Valley area, including photographer Bill Owens, Altamont was an unlikely location for a festival, mainly because it was barely a location at all: just a name on a map and beyond that nothing but a dirt track, hills and cows. Who would want to hike all the way out there just to watch a few rock bands? Owens soon found out when he got stuck in a huge tailback on the Patterson Pass Road, one of the main routes out of Livermore that led to the Speedway. Abandoning his motorbike alongside the other gridlocked cars, he joined the crowds of young people dressed in ponchos and faded jeans. Carrying provisions and supplies they marched into the hills like prospectors seeking the hope of gold.

Owens worked for the *Livermore Independent*. In December 1969, he was hired as a freelancer to cover the event for the Associated Press Agency along with his friend and fellow AP photographer Beth Bagby. Because their images were likely to be the first to emerge from the festival, Owens was hoping for national press coverage. Passing makeshift tents, improvised toilets and stalls selling acid, Owens was taken aback by the size of the crowd and the level of confusion. It was hard to tell who was in charge. People were heaving round this tiny platform, and the atmosphere was distinctly unfriendly. Owens took shots of a naked Mexican guy being thrown off the stage. He got pictures of the Angels lashing out with their pool cues. He saw bad trips, freak-outs and one beating after another. Thirteen rolls of film later, and with a big sigh of relief, he trekked back out to the roadside. Bagby however stayed for the duration so she could get some shots of the Stones. Framed in her lens they look like a gang of teenage devils flanked by a group of menacing archangels. Her pictures captured the onstage tensions, the band's increasing anxiety and one scuffle in the crowd that turned out to be the last moments of Meredith Hunter's life.[3]

There were deaths at festivals before Altamont. Woodstock had its share of casualties and, unfortunately, in the years that have followed there have been fatal incidents at many more events. In this regard Altamont is far from America's worst concert tragedy. In terms of actual lives lost, the worst was the 1979 Riverfront Coliseum disaster in Cincinnati, Ohio at which a crush at the entrance gates in the moments before a sold-out show by the Who led to the death of eleven people. Nevertheless, Altamont is known as 'Rock's darkest day' due to the violent, very much non-accidental death of Hunter, to say nothing of the event's ominous symbolism. Altamont started to tighten its grip on the American imagination as soon as Owens and Bagby developed and transmitted their photographs. There can be no clearer signpost for the evaporation of 1967's Summer of Love than a concert in the decade's dying days performed by one of its most iconic bands, who play in the middle of a dark, overcrowded wasteland. As the counterculture's disastrous last waltz, Altamont has come to mark the point where everything started to come apart.[4]

The enduring aura has much to do with the visibility of *Gimme Shelter* (1970), the documentary co-directed by Albert Maysles, David Maysles and Charlotte Zwerin that covers the last ten days of the Stones' 1969 tour. The film features footage of the band playing at New York's Madison Square Garden intercut with preparations towards the concert at Altamont. On the day, the Maysles worked with an extensive crew – including one George Lucas – and it was cameraman Eric Saarinen who, like Bagby, caught the killing of Meredith Hunter. Zwerin, who edited the film, gives the footage an appropriately catastrophic narrative. She weights its latter parts with the worst of the violence and ends with the killing. The net effect of this built-in downturn is an overwhelming sense of vertigo. As the band rumble on and the administrators struggle to keep up, things very quickly get out of control. As well as Hunter's death, the beatings, scuffles and acid casualties seem to exponentially increase as the film progresses. As writer Michael Sragow puts it when describing the film's framing of Hunter's death, 'the harrowing context gives the deadly scene an apocalyptic stature [...] it's part of a colossal, mass bad trip.'[5]

The film was released in December 1970. By this point, the events at Altamont were well known with all manner of news outlets and magazines, among them *Rolling Stone*, having given it detailed coverage. At the same time, memories of the Woodstock festival also loomed large in the public imagination. Michael Wadleigh's film of the event had arrived in theatres in March 1970 to great critical acclaim and critical success. Although both events were chaotic and badly organised, the gravity of the violence at Altamont made it stand apart from Woodstock's harmonious on-screen image. Within months of December 1969, Altamont became Woodstock's dark mirror, an event that seemed so utterly opposed what the earlier festival had come to symbolise. As Ralph J. Gleason put it in 'Aquarius Wept' (1970), his August 1970 article for *Esquire* magazine, 'If the name Woodstock has come to denote the flowering of one phase of the youth culture, "Altamont" has come to mean the end of it.' When *Gimme Shelter* appeared, then, with its emphasis on the death of Hunter, it served only to further crystallise this view.

For film critics Pauline Kael and Vincent Canby, the film was just as problematic as the events it depicted. They seriously questioned its ethics and saw it as little more than a snuff movie. To them, the Rolling Stones seemed to have staged a badly organised event solely for the benefit of the cameras with little regard for the welfare of the audience involved. True, *Gimme Shelter* is not easy to watch. But neither is it a work of pure exploitation. If anything, the film drives a wedge between reality and representation. As well as cutting between on and off-stage action, the film focuses on members of the band – Mick Jagger and Charlie Watts in particular – as they view the footage on a Steenbeck editing machine. All the flamboyance, arrogance and mismanagement of the tour is seen here in the light of day. It's the worst hangover you can imagine. When finally presented with sketchy frames of what appears to be Hunter drawing a gun, Jagger stares at the screen, Sphinx-like. There's no apology or anything, but it's hardly the whitewash that Canby claimed it to be. In these moments of reflection, the film pushes its awful violence and the issue of responsibility right to the centre of the frame. Whose fault *was* this?[6]

Seen now, these scenes also remind us that most of our knowledge of the 1960s comes from films of one sort or another. The decade is so readily available via pre-digested clips that its complex history has been boiled down to a few iconic images. Helicopters in flight mean Vietnam, teenagers in the street mean protest, day-glo colours mean psychedelia, and clips from the likes of *Woodstock* that show naked people dancing in the open air conjure up the counterculture as a whole. *Gimme Shelter* contains all these icons and more. The resonance of Altamont comes not just from the particularities of time, place and action that marked the event, but from its gradual merger with this film. Whereas *Woodstock* filtered out some of the festival's difficult moments and presented a joyous image of the sixties in full swing, *Gimme Shelter* scrutinises the discord of Altamont and in doing so announces the decade's terminal end. When we finally see Hunter's death it arrives like a full stop. It's both a terrible human tragedy and a potent symbol for the sudden overturning of the values the 1960s held high: pacifism, idealism, peaceful revolution. Whatever future this thinking may have promised suddenly appears to have been 'cancelled' by the time the credits roll. *Gimme Shelter* is by no means the only documentary of the era to depict the 1960s as a strange and difficult time, full of discomfort and pessimism. There's *Harvest of Shame* (1960), an account of poverty amongst migrant workers, *Fields of Sacrifice* (1964) about battlefield experiences, and *Army Medicine in Vietnam* (1970) which speaks for itself. None of these other documentaries, however, have the profile and the fame of *Gimme Shelter*. Thanks to numerous anniversary re-releases and special editions, it has become the go-to film for utopia soured. As a result, 1969 and Altamont have become equally cryogenic as *the* time and *the* place where it all went wrong.[7]

This is not just a matter of *Woodstock* and *Gimme Shelter* offering opposing views of the late 1960s. Watch *Gimme Shelter* alongside pop and concert films made across the 1960s like *Pop Gear* (1965), *The Beatles at Shea Stadium* (1966), *Cream's Farewell Concert at the Albert Hall* (1969) and particularly D.A. Pennebaker's *Monterey Pop* (1968), and the events of Altamont look like a tragic anomaly. Held in June 1967, the Monterey International Pop Music Festival has become famous for the epic, meditative performance of Ravi Shankar; but it also played host to the Who and the Jimi Hendrix Experience, both of whom destroyed their equipment at the end of their sets. Spectacular, intense and – to the West Coast audience – largely unprecedented, these wilful acts were nonetheless extremely performative. Whether read as gestures of protest or attempts at showboating, sonic experimentation or auto-destructive art, guitar smashing worked as part of the safety valve experience that a festival provides. By contrast Altamont, as depicted in *Gimme Shelter*, shows rock's negative energy in full force. All its pantomimic diabolism and pent-up libido seems to spill off the stage, free to generate tension, aggression and finally, death. When filming the audience for *Monterey Pop*, Pennebaker focused on people who watch the entertainment open-mouthed, entranced. There's none of this wonder in *Gimme Shelter*, just shock and disbelief as audience members turn from the violence to the stage and back again, helpless and dumbfounded. We recognise the setting. It has all the trappings of a sixties rock concert but this, surely, is not the way it should be. With its bikers and its devilish atmosphere, *Gimme Shelter* seems more like Al Adamson's *Satan's Sadists* (1969), David Durston's *I Drink Your Blood* (1970) and any number of other hippy exploitation movies that filled grindhouses in the late 1960s and early 1970s. It also carries striking similarities to Kenneth Anger's short film *Invocation of My Demon Brother* (1969). If watched with these films rather than other concert films of the 1960s, the events of Altamont start to take on a very different significance. Suddenly, in *Gimme Shelter* the Maysles appear to have made a real-life horror movie. When viewed with Anger's film, they seem not to have recorded an unpredictable trauma, but something much more intentional: the activation of a magical spell.[8]

Invocation of My Demon Brother grew out of Anger's attempt to make *Lucifer Rising* in 1967. That project ended with mutual recriminations between Anger and Bobby Beausoleil. Beausoleil said Anger had nothing to show because he'd gone through the budget before properly finishing the film. Anger said Beausoleil had stolen the film and so put the toad curse on him as an act of revenge. Then, possibly as an attempt to escape his creditors, possibly as an attempt to express how the loss of the film was a mortal wound, Anger took out a full-page ad in the *Village Voice*. Appearing on 26 October 1967, it read: 'In Memoriam. Kenneth Anger. Filmmaker 1947–1967.' Having announced his 'death' Anger burnt a pile of his older work. Thankfully for cinema, Anger re-entered public view in 1968 and, with the patronage of John Paul Getty Jr., he de-camped to London with some of the *Lucifer Rising* fragments. With his charm working at full force, Anger ingratiated himself into the Mayfair *demi-monde* that circulated around art dealer Robert Fraser. He met the Beatles, the Rolling Stones, and in Mick Jagger he saw the spark of Lucifer he'd previously sought in Beausoleil.

Sitting down at the editing desk in mid 1969 Anger knew he needed more footage if he was going to complete the *Lucifer* project. But he did have enough to do something else. Using some of the material he had shot during his English sojourn, Anger put together *Invocation of My Demon Brother* as 'a fragment made in fury ... the last blast of Haight consciousness.' It's an eleven-minute film that combines footage from Haight-Ashbury with brief images of Jagger performing in Hyde Park on 5 July 1969, following the death of Brian Jones. As Deborah Allison puts it, the 'demon brother' of the title is Anger's description of the secret 'inner self', the site of one's own 'true' will. The film suggests that making manifest this higher, metaphysical self will act as a kind of psychic catapult, propelling the now-enlightened individual into the coming Aeon of Horus. It's an ambitious claim for what is, in effect, a ten-minute home movie. Anger just about pulls it off though due to his hyperactive editing style. The film draws together all kinds of juxtapositions, semi-subliminal images and, as with *The Inauguration of the Pleasuredome*, moments of hypnotic superimposition.[9]

Working with two parallel film strips allowed Anger to imbue *Invocation* with the visual density of a sigil: an inscribed, typically multi-layered symbol saturated with magical potency. This was not just a stylistic choice. Film, for Anger, was a magical tool. It was a format that allowed him to cast a spell, to make manifest figments of his imagination in 'trapped light'. Ideas, thoughts and concepts could cross over from the mind to the projection screen and once there take on a life of their own. As Anger put it, film, had:

> the potential, when properly used, to invoke primal forces, perhaps even demons. Once released, these demons can affect not only those involved in the film's production, but also, through a series of occult circuits connecting physical with spiritual dimensions of existence, the film's audience.

It is difficult to see exactly how filmmaking *could* result in 'demons', but beyond the intensity of his language Anger's point could apply to multiple art forms. He is, in essence, talking about the power of artistic creation. That said, as regards film, he has in mind something more than the entertaining 'magic' of Hollywood, the way an audience is invited to suspend their disbelief and immerse themselves in a flickering on-screen fantasy. When Anger speaks of 'magic' he means 'magick': Aleister Crowley's use of the word. For Crowley, 'magick' is not a matter of illusions or trickery but describes instead 'the Science and Art of causing Change to occur in conformity with Will'. Performing magick is a deeply intentional process, and it was with this level of intense concentration that

Anger constructed *Invocation*. He intended it as the manifestation of his own 'will', a film designed to flick a switch in the mind of the viewer to make them aware of, and gravitate towards, the coming Aeon.

During *Invocation*, spectral images of Anton LaVey of the Church of Satan float over the faces of leering bikers; occult symbols flicker on and off as Jagger makes a brief appearance; and, in amongst it all, Anger can be seen in full flight during the performance he filmed in San Francisco back in 1967, the 'Equinox of the Gods'. These images, coupled with opening vignettes of a 'Wand-Bearer' presiding over a group of naked acolytes, are used by Anger to suggest that within America's post-war demographic, ancient knowledge becomes indigenous to the new culture of the young. At the same time, looped images of helicopters in Vietnam point to the flipside of this magickal zeitgeist. The Aeon of Horus is approaching, and the planet's state of perpetual war proves it. By superimposing images of his dynamic new tribe over those of combat, Anger was attempting to banish the 'forces of war' so as to announce the coming of a 'much more joyful, life-affirming time'.

Invocation could be tagged as a work of avant-garde cinema, far removed from the public documentations of *Monterey Pop* and *Gimme Shelter*. But despite its highly specific and idiosyncratic symbolism, a dialogue nevertheless opens up with the Maysles' film when we think of the specificity of Anger's motifs: bikers, Satanism, Mick Jagger. As well as waving the flag for the Aeon of Horus, these details spookily foreshadow all the images that would come to define Altamont. Premiered in Denmark in October 1969, a matter of weeks before the concert, *Invocation* seems weirdly prescient: a film that managed to predict – if not conjure – the events of December.[10]

There's a lot of coincidence here. Anger had dabbled in this imagery before meeting the Stones in London, and he took most of the biker footage from *Scorpio Rising*. You also don't have to look too far to find horror films of the period like *Curse of the Crimson Alter* (1968) and *The Dunwich Horror* (1970) containing visuals just as weird and intense as Anger's. His talk of 'demons' and 'occult circuits' is intoxicating, but it's clearly going too far to make the leap from the production of a film to the eruption of violence at a concert.

That said, contemporary novelists like Zachary Lazar have played with the fictional implications of a magickal overlap between *Invocation*, Altamont and *Gimme Shelter*. In his novel *Sway* (2008), an exploration of the grey area between fact, fiction and myth, Lazar weaves the biographies of Anger, the Rolling Stones and Charles Manson into a spider's web of inference and coincidence. Within this mix, *Invocation* is recast as an active magickal document, one capable of producing long-lasting effects. Lazar puts it to the reader that 'an invocation draws forces in', but it can also lead to an 'evocation which spits the forces back out'. In *Sway*'s take on the sixties, the events of Altamont are the result of one such evocation: its disastrous circumstances lead on from the premiere of Anger's film.[11]

Some of this does recall the way the events at Altamont were originally reported. The *Rolling Stone* writers were quick to pick up on the inauspicious setting, the teeming crowd and the generally devilish appearance of the Stones before comparing the concert site to a painting of 'tortured souls in the Dance of Death'. They remarked that when Jagger sang 'Sympathy for the Devil', his song 'about how groovy it is to be Satan', it had never 'been sung in a more appropriate setting'. But *Sway* contains more than occasional moments of embellishment. Lazar casts Altamont as

Pandemonium itself: the 'proud seate of Lucifer', the place of all demons, the high capital of hell. The concert becomes a weird ritual that's umbilically linked to Anger's spell, one that not only closes the decade but also causes the era to implode.[12]

Sway shares a lot of common ground with Chris Petit's *Back from the Dead* (1999), a modern-day detective story that features McMahon, an ageing Mick Jagger-esque rock star and Alexander Blackledge, a fictionalised mixture of Anger and Peter Whitehead. Throughout the book Petit speaks of 'the malfate', a projected sense of deep misfortune that emanates from Blackledge's films. The malfate, Petit explains, is 'a kind of negative version of our lives which is played out in some shadow world'. Although fantastical, both of these novels draw on the rich symbolism that has covered Altamont in the years following 1969. The events of the concert have gradually blurred into *Gimme Shelter*, and *Gimme Shelter* has increasingly been used as a dark counterpoint to the likes of Woodstock. When linked to Anger's sorcerous work and further fictionalised as a carnival of bad magick, these transformations have the effect of distorting a concert which holds a place in the cultural history of the 1960s, and a very real human tragedy, while at the same time crystallising what 'Altamont' has come to mean in the imaginative history of the sixties. 'Altamont' has entered something akin to Petit's 'shadow world'. And there, it has proceeded to develop a peculiar aura.[13]

Given the human cost involved, it's tempting to demythologise the whole sordid enterprise. As you'd expect, the Stones don't like to talk about it. In 1999 Rick McDonald, Tracy resident and former barbecue pedlar at the Altamont Speedway, tried to lobby the band to return to the site for a 30-year 'reunion' concert. Unsurprisingly, nothing ever came of the idea to stage a lucrative pay-per-view festival. As well as being grossly disrespectful to the memory of Meredith Hunter, what would there have been to celebrate on such an anniversary? But the very fact that the spectre of Altamont is still able to rise from its own ashes decades later, speaks volumes about the fascination it generates. Altamont is a cultural phenomenon, one that combines cinema, occultism and rock 'n' roll. These are the energies that surround the event, and which continue to preserve it as a symbol that far exceeds its role as a name for a now-abandoned raceway.[14]

When the Rolling Stones toured America for the second time in October 1966 they were promoting their fourth album *Aftermath* (1966). This was the version of the band cultivated by manager Andrew Loog Oldham, as the aggressively modish anti-Beatles. They were not the boys next door: you wouldn't let your sister 'go with' them. But the band who arrived in November 1969 had been significantly recalibrated. Privately they were exhausted, riven with drugs and internal tensions, but publicly they had morphed from possibly smelly public urinators into anti-establishment Lucifereans, if not out and out left-wing heroes.

This shift began in 1967 when the band became embroiled in an escalating series of high-profile controversies. They ruffled feathers in January when they refused to participate in the traditional goodbye wave on the family favourite *London Palladium* TV show. Soon after, the *News of the World* broke a story claiming Jagger was an avid user of LSD, an 'exclusive' that was swiftly followed by a writ from the singer's lawyers. In a possible act of retaliation on the part of the newspaper, 12 February (some five days after Jagger's legal action) saw a drug bust at Redlands, Keith Richards' country house. This resulted in the arrest of Jagger, Richards and Robert Fraser, all of whom were given custodial sentences. The young were being set an example. By the end of July, a successful appeal had been mounted, spurred on by a wave of public support and heavy criticism of the legal decision. Most notably William Rees-Mogg, editor of *The Times*, wrote an editorial entitled 'Who breaks a butterfly upon a wheel?' which lambasted the prison sentences as massively disproportionate to the original offences of drug possession. What was intended as a show of punitive authority became an embarrassing climb-down, when the Lord Chief Justice overturned Jagger and Richards' convictions. (Fraser, however, went to jail for six months after pleading guilty to possession.) In August, Jagger and Richards offered their own comment on the case, by way of Peter Whitehead's promo film for their top ten single 'We Love You'. Working closely with Whitehead they created a dressing-up box homage to Oscar Wilde and his friend and lover Lord Alfred Bruce 'Bosie' Douglas that featured a grinning Jagger in front of Richards playing the judge.[15]

In the middle of all this, the Beatles released *Sgt. Pepper's Lonely Hearts Club Band* in June 1967, an album that far surpassed the ambition and sophistication of the Rolling Stones' *Their Satanic Majesties Request*, released that December. But whereas the Beatles had produced a key work of psychedelia, it seemed that by the end of the year, the Stones had gone beyond 'merely' making music into a head-on entanglement with the British establishment. True, the Beatles had signed a petition calling for the legalisation of marijuana in July 1967, but, like the imprisoned John 'Hoppy' Hopkins who inspired the petition, Jagger and Richards had actually faced jail. This, coupled with the explicit 'we don't care' stance of 'We Love You' – as opposed to the harmony of the Beatles' 'All You Need is Love' (released that July) – further polarised the groups, despite their collaboration on aspects of each song.

By the time the Stones released 'Street Fighting Man' in August 1968, their status as agitators had been cemented. Jagger had been inspired to write this, his most political song, after taking part in the March 1968 anti-war demonstration in Grosvenor Square in London. Here, the police had violently clashed with protestors who had in turn vandalised the American Embassy. The energy and commitment of the crowd impressed Jagger, as did the fiery left-wing rhetoric of the writer and activist Tariq Ali. In 'Street Fighting Man' the scene is vividly recreated with the added caveat of rock 'n' roll offering the ideal conduit for every protesting, discontented 'poor boy'. It was this mix of violence and class consciousness that piqued the interest of filmmaker Jean-Luc Godard who travelled to London in August to film the band in the studio. He caught them during the *Beggars Banquet* (1968) sessions recording 'Sympathy for the Devil'. The resultant film, *One+One* (1968), also released as *Sympathy for the Devil*, intercuts between the recording and scenes mixing celebrity culture with revolutionary activism.[16]

It was with this level of cultural kudos and revolutionary expectation that the band returned to America. On the face of it they seemed totally in tune with the counterculture's radical politics and burgeoning festival scene. Despite all the problems at Woodstock, bands like Jefferson Airplane and the Grateful Dead believed that if anything like a youth 'nation' was to establish itself, it was important to keep organising mass gatherings. And so, it was decided that the West Coast needed a monumental event without delay. The high-profile arrival of the Rolling Stones offered the perfect opportunity. When Jagger finally announced the event at a press conference in Los Angeles on 25 November, he certainly seemed to be talking in countercultural terms. On camera he spoke about how the 'free festival' aimed to create 'a microcosmic society which sets an example to the rest of America as to how one can behave in large gatherings'. There's that sense of positivity, harmony, innovation but with the clear hint that all the other squares – 'the rest of America' – have not previously been able to achieve it.

Despite Jagger's outward confidence, things were already starting to go wrong. The tour was well underway by 25 November and, since kicking off in Colorado just over two weeks earlier (on the seventh), the Stones camp had been dogged by complaints about delays, extortionate ticket prices and unreasonable demands made of promoters. Fans and journalists were beginning to agree that the reality of the Stones didn't quite live up to their 'Street Fighting' image. For all the claims made in their songs, they were neither 'poor boys', nor did they care about their audience. Such criticisms mattered in America, particularly on the West Coast. The Grateful Dead, at that point the main American rival to the Stones in terms of popularity, were plugged in to the social activism that characterised the San Franciscan counterculture. The Dead did free concerts; the Dead did benefit shows; the Dead encouraged bootleggers; the Dead funnelled their money into food and housing projects; the Dead worked with the Diggers to maintain the amenities of Haight-Ashbury. Sustainable or not, this type of activity was the lifeblood of the American counterculture and the Stones offered only lip service towards it.[17]

The Stones were never the most charitable of bands. Whereas the Beatles covertly funded the Indica Gallery and *International Times*, Jagger – a former student at the London School of Economics – was a young man on the make who very much followed the entrepreneurial lead of manager Andrew Loog Oldham. It's true that by 1969 the band were experiencing serious financial difficulties, partly due to their legal wrangles with Allen Klein who had come into the Stones' camp as business manager in 1965 at the request of Oldham. Following Oldham's resignation as band manager in 1967, Klein took over the role. He increased their income from record contracts and publishing deals, but at the same time the band accused him of withholding advances and royalty payments. In these circumstances, the band had little in the way of ready money to play with. When approaching the 1969 American tour, the demand of pre-payment from promoters was a means of funding the shows in the first place.

But beyond this harsh pragmatism, the band were pursuing a set of priorities different to those of social revolution. Following on from their work with Godard, the Stones were keen to secure a document of their American performances, but one that conveyed magnitude as well as spectacle. Jagger wanted to attract the biggest crowds and to mount the biggest events. It was on this tour that the Stones gained their soubriquet 'The Greatest Rock 'n' Roll Band in the World' courtesy of MC Sam Cutler. There's no point having a label like that if you're not going to live up to it. But surely no stadium, however cavernous, could compete with the oceanic scale of Woodstock just four months before. It didn't matter that the Stones had, pretty much in parallel, played to 500,000 at Hyde Park. Their television film of this event, *The Stones in the Park* (1969) was set for broadcast on 2 September 1969, but it would be no match for Michael Wadleigh's *Woodstock* that was expected to land in 1970. That was the bar as far as Jagger was concerned. Playing 24 shows to packed houses and vast profits was not enough. If the Stones were to cement their reputation in America and assume the status of bona fide superstars, the North American tour had to be a display of raw ego; it had to produce something historic. This explains the appointment of the Maysles as court filmmakers. The Stones had previously approached Pennebaker and the cinematographer Haskell Wexler, but the attraction of the Maysles was their speed and efficiency. The brothers felt confident they could have the film shot, edited and released before the overburdened *Woodstock* hit the screen. They were brought on board on 25 November and invited to shoot the Madison Square Garden shows on the 27 and 28. At the same time Jagger was in Los Angeles announcing the free festival on 'December – er – sixth in San Francisco.'[18]

Whether he was conscious of it or not, Jagger's hesitation, accurately recorded by Philip Norman in *The Stones* (1984), deftly sums up the fragility of the whole enterprise. It had taken eight months and a significant cash injection to organise Woodstock. Now the Stones and a loose collective of scenesters were trying to do something similar in just under two weeks. Part way through the tour Sam Cutler took a reconnoitre to San Francisco with an eye to booking the Fillmore Ballroom or Golden Gate Park. When neither of these worked out, the search went further afield, and a deal was struck with the Sears Point Raceway in Sonoma County, Northern California. Sears Point had space, the right kind of infrastructure and a track record of successful concerts. They offered good terms, negotiations moved fast, and it wasn't long before Chip Monck, the Stones' stage manager and Woodstock veteran got his crew together and began setting up on site.

It was all going great before a series of last-minute contractual wrangles threw the whole thing up in the air. By this point the proposed free festival was 24 hours away. The stage had been built and people were starting to arrive at Sears Point. To sort things out the Stones had appointed the attorney Mel Belli, who can be seen in *Gimme Shelter* holding court in his palatial office. He's concerned that the *San Francisco Chronicle* are about to put out a story saying the whole thing's off. Just then word comes in of an alternative site. Enter Dick Carter, owner operator of the Altamont Speedway: previous record attendance 6,000 and no prior experience of hosting rock concerts. Belli wants a venue and Carter wants the publicity: deal? Deal. The only issue now is the matter of transporting the stage, equipment, all the bands and everyone else 65 miles from Sonoma to Livermore and then to the dustbowl of Altamont. Overnight.

Belli and his team finally start to look nervous at this point, like they were all secretly hoping it would be called off and they could forget the daft tasks their bosses, the Stones, had set them. They talk numbers. There could be anything between five and 25 thousand kids turning up in the next 24 hours. 'It's like lemmings to the sea', says one guy in the corner who looks like he's just managing to hold off a full-scale meltdown. Meanwhile back at Altamont, Carter is in his office making more calls. By Saturday 6 December he's secured 1,000 portable toilets, 2,000 garbage cans and sixteen helicopters. There's parking for 12,000 cars. Later, Carter will claim he was told to expect 50,000. By midday on the sixth an estimated *300,000* had trekked overland to his barely functional site. The parking places were already filled, and Associated Press photographer Bill Owens had abandoned his motorcycle among the gridlock on the Patterson Pass Road.[19]

Once he got on site, Owens tried to take a sequence of shots from the scaffolding next to the stage. He was part way through a roll when one of the Angels lumbered over brandishing a tire iron. If Owens didn't get down, the Angel explained in no uncertain terms, he would 'smash his skull in'. Stewards, bodyguards, ceremonial cortege: it's hard to tell what the precise job description of the Angels was during the concert. They were given $500 worth of beer in exchange for their services. Cutler paid for the beer, but it may have been (Grateful Dead manager) Rock Scully's idea to get them involved. Both had some prior experience with the organisation. The Oakland chapter headed by Ralph 'Sonny' Barger were long-standing fixtures of the Berkeley scene during the 1960s. The Dead, along with Ken Kesey and the Diggers, had been keen to involve them in the area's countercultural community. Cutler had had a good experience using the British Hells Angels as stewards at Hyde Park, despite the view of the Metropolitan Police that they were 'totally ineffective' as security. They were also, of course, the *British* Hells Angels: boisterous but generally polite ex-rockers who collected military badges and were happy to work for a cup of tea and a bacon sandwich. The Oakland Hells Angels were more 'professional'; they were an ultra-aggressive contingent of self-identifying 'one percent-ers', viewed by the American authorities as an active organised crime syndicate. This was Owens' concern. He thought the Angels didn't want to be identified and would try to take his camera away. Worse, he started to think they might try to find him after his pictures appeared. Leaving the site, feeling as if he was smuggling information to the outside world, Owens began to think of his family. It crossed his mind to have the pictures printed anonymously.[20]

Fear, intimidation, anxiety. In the chaos of its organisation and with its multiple deaths, injuries and who knows how many bad trips, Altamont succeeded only in replicating the worst aspects of the world it was attempting to stand apart from. One of the stand-out quotes from 'Aquarius Wept', Ralph J. Gleason's report on the event for *Esquire*, is the damning summation by an unnamed audience member: 'In twenty-four hours we created all the problems of society in one place: congestion, violence, dehumanization.' And this was based, according to *Rolling Stone*, on 'diabolical egotism, hype, ineptitude, money manipulation, and, at base, a fundamental lack of concern for humanity.' If the idea behind Altamont was to create an exemplary mass gathering then, more so than Woodstock Ventures, they *really* blew it.

Not that any of this really deterred the success of the Rolling Stones. They went into the enterprise for promotional rather than social reasons and would return to America in 1972 for an even bigger tour involving more money, more hype and more security. A few months after the events at Altamont, the MC5 played at Phun City in the UK and the British Hells Angels were once again enlisted to guard the stage. To many eyes though, Altamont signalled the *symbolic* end of the counterculture because, beyond its tragic human cost, it showed up the fragility of its revolutionary, utopian designs. The event was quite literary apocalyptic: it revealed the futility of the attempt to create a new world of the young, however temporary. Put them in a field together and what happens? They start to fight and kill each other.[21]

'If people didn't dig it, I'm sorry'. It's 7 December 1969, the morning after the night before and Sam Cutler is speaking on KSAN radio's post-Altamont broadcast. Hosted by the station's DJ Stefan Ponek, the four-hour show tried to piece together exactly what had happened. Emmett Grogan, leader of the Diggers, had his say, as did Sonny Barger, leader of the Hells Angels. Barger's take was that they merely did what they were asked to do. He also claimed that the worst of the violence came from 'pledges', associates of the Angels who were being considered for full membership. All the stuff with the pool cues, it seems, was an overeager attempt to out-Angel the Angels. As Cutler offered his side of the story, the rest of the Stones party were heading back to New York. He had been left to deal with the fall-out on his own. Altamont would be the last time he saw the band.

Endings invariably invite attempts to make sense of them, and this is one of the jobs of art. Faced with the chaos of history, art can pick up the pieces and make something out of the mess. The result is never the holy grail of 'truth' but something a lot more interesting: commentary, speculation and the strange edifice of cultural memory we choose to call 'legacy'. Altamont's legacy of disaster was quickly established by *Gimme Shelter*, but other artists and other artworks have since embellished this image. Altamont has not by any means been rehabilitated, but its place within the cultural imagination has nevertheless been put to use in a variety of different ways. Of the original Altamont performers, it was the Grateful Dead, Cutler's next employers, who were among the quickest to offer an artistic response. 'New Speedway Boogie' from their album *Workingman's Dead* (1970) uses a countrified shuffle to take a typically oblique look at the day's events. It's low on detail but the song captures the rumours that KSAN tried to sift through: 'Now, I don't know, but I was told / In the heat of the sun a man died of cold'. 'New Speedway Boogie' is no protest song, but it's laden with a sense of doom and futility. Lyricist Robert Hunter creates a voice of vague optimism that repeats, 'One way or another, this darkness got to give'. But as the song fades out, the line begins to sound remarkably fragile, like the words of someone who's yet to hear the terrible news or is clinging to hope in the middle of an awful situation. Someone a bit like Cutler.

Fast forward to Sydney, 2004. Andrew Coates and James Lee of the Australian electronica duo Black Cab have included a cover of the song on their album *Altamont Diary*. Shifting from dreamy soundscapes to funereal dirges, *Altamont Diary* documents the mood swings of the event. It's a sonic narrative that goes from joy to horror. The inclusion of the Dead cover is the album's most tuneful offering, retaining all the original's regretful past-tense.

With the album dedicated to 'Jerry Garcia and those who were there' there's a definite sense of lament, if not eulogy, for the 'flowers that wither then die'. Cutler loved the album. He'd moved to Queensland just before its release and a journalist had sent him a copy asking for his opinion. He thought it uncannily evocative, frightening and invigorating in equal measure. Not only did he relive the anxiety of Altamont, he heard his own words bubbling out of the mix like a long-lost ghost: 'If people didn't dig it, I'm sorry.' Coates and Lee had sampled the KSAN interview. *Altamont Diary* stands alongside Zachary Lazar's novel *Sway* as part of the concert's contemporary afterlife. As with bands like the Lords of Altamont who describe themselves as 'bring[ing] forth a raw rock and roll fury birthed from the ultimate end of the era of peace and love', the name 'Altamont' is used to conjure up a dark, disastrous image of the sixties.[22]

But within this range of work, Altamont's symbolic role is a lot more flexible and ambivalent than it might first appear. When New Order played Glastonbury in 1981 they shared a bill with Hawkwind. Bassist Peter Hook calls that gig 'our Altamont', not because anyone died (thankfully) and not just because singer Bernard Sumner was drunk out of his mind, but mainly because the billing was hopelessly inappropriate. None of the bikers in the audience were there to hear New Order plough through the cool, post-punk angst of their first album *Movement* (1981). They wanted Hawkwind with their massive, space-rock riffs, laser shows and songs like 'Masters of the Universe'. In Hook's recall, 'Altamont' simply translates as 'terrible gig'. When Primal Scream appeared at Glastonbury in 2005 they used Altamont to describe their hopes for a *great* gig. Interviewed by Edith Bowman before their show, singer Bobby Gillespie goes on about having just arrived in a helicopter, adding that the band was 'trying to relive the Rolling Stones at Altamont.' Next to him, bassist Mani chips in with: 'We're just going to go and stab some hippies to death at the end of the night.' What Gillespie calls 'rock 'n' roll fantasies' are then compared to another of that year's performers, Brian Wilson of the Beach Boys. 'Bad vibrations,' states Gillespie by way of response, 'that's what Primal Scream is, bad vibrations.' Whether this is cultish appreciation or adolescent provocation, it clearly begs the question: if Altamont was so terrible, and if it has since become a means of labelling terrible events, why would you want to celebrate it in this way? Isn't invoking Altamont before a massive gig not unlike shouting the name of *that* Scottish play just before the curtain rises?[23]

The secret of this talismanic status lies in one of the out-takes from *Gimme Shelter*. Shooting backstage at Madison Square Garden, the Maysles picture Jagger sat with his support act, Ike and Tina Turner. Jagger and Tina Turner leaf through what looks like a concert programme as Ike Turner tunes up beside them. It's filled to the brim with pictures of the Rolling Stones, sporting what Tina Turner refers to as 'short' hair. Short, that is, in comparison to the 1969 version of the band whose hair, demeanour and music has moved beyond the sharp precision of early-1960s British R&B. Turner then points to another picture of Jagger and shows it to the camera. It's a portrait shot in which he appears to be wearing a suit. His hair is jet black and combed back, close to the skull. He looks like a businessman or a gangster. The lost Kray twin.

'You look pretty bad with that hair,' she tells him.

'It's from a film,' Jagger replies.

'What's the name of the movie?'

Jagger doesn't say, or at least the sound doesn't pick it up. The film then cuts to the continued awkwardness of Jagger playing one of his own songs on Ike Turner's guitar. Turner looks on ambivalently. For the record, the name of the movie is *Performance*.

Performance (1970) could best be described as a shamanic gangster film. Fleeing the wrath of his boss, Harry Flowers, the violent underworld enforcer Chas (played by James Fox) takes refuge in 81 Powis Square. This is the Notting Hill home of one Turner Purple (Jagger), a reclusive rock star who has, in the words of his paramour Pherber, 'lost his demon.' What follows is a radical departure from the crime genre trappings of the film's first half. Chas is drawn into a hermetic world of psychedelics and identity confusion. It's a ritualistic process in which each man begins to desire what the other has. For Turner, Chas' animal violence is the key to recovering his mojo. Meanwhile Chas sees his absorption into Turner's life as an escape route, a means of abandoning not just the forces that pursue him, but also the rigid barriers of sexuality and psychology that limit him. At the explosive end of the film, this exchange seems to take place.[24]

Performance was written by Donald Cammell, a hip Chelsea habitué and former society portrait painter. He had worked on earlier films and screenplays that featured cool criminals like *Duffy* (1967) with James Coburn and the future Chas, James Fox. But with *Performance*, which he co-directed for Warner Brothers with Nicolas Roeg, Cammell synthesised two key zones of 1960s London: the rock aristocracy of the Rolling Stones and the gangster radiance of the Krays. Both were symptomatic of the celebrity culture that blossomed during the decade. With the decline of its imperial structure, Britain's global dominance had to be maintained by other means. And so, the country started to realise its cultural assets. The strange creature that was the celebrity – actor, model, public figure, whatever – emerged fully formed as the ideal export. Celebrities could sell things, and if there was nothing specific to sell, they could be used to sell an idea or an image, hence the parallel emergence of the celebrity photographer. Brian Duffy, Terence Donovan and David Bailey specialised in shots of the famous, and became famous for doing so. Bailey's collection *Box of Pin-Ups* (1965) is the ultimate commodity catalogue from this era. Designed intentionally as a highly desirable object, it fetishised the personality in place of the product. Buy this, it said, and you can have all the glamour, confidence and success that these faces possess so effortlessly.

Although international in scope with appearances by Andy Warhol and Rudolf Nureyev, *Box of Pin-Ups* was a cultural manifesto for sixties Britain. The Beatles, Jean Shrimpton, Terence Stamp and Mick Jagger exemplified the nation's (i.e. London's) creative capital. What caused questions though was Bailey's decision to include portraits of the well-known East End 'entrepreneurs' Ronald and Reginald Kray. Until their conviction for double murder in 1969, the Kray twins controlled an empire of protection rackets and a series of gambling clubs. Where other gangsters would seek the anonymity of the underworld, the Krays actively sought the limelight. This was not so much an attempt at hiding in plain sight as a desire to cultivate a celebrity aura from their status as professional criminals. Their use of violence, intimidation and extortion was well known, and it was something of an open secret that they had links to the upper echelons of British society. Whatever provocation was at play on Bailey's part by aligning the Krays with celebrities from the arts, it was certainly a move the twins approved of. It was also a connection that made perfect sense to Cammell. He saw no difference between the artist and the gangster, especially when the artist was a singer in a rock 'n' roll band. Art is violence and violence is art. Vice and versa. For

Cammell the impulses are inextricably linked because they are each so utterly ego-driven.[25]

This is the nucleus of *Performance*. What Cammell shows in the film is the convergence of these spheres until they become, quite literally, interchangeable. It's a bold theory that clearly bears the traces of Cammell's exposure to avant-garde writers like Antonin Artaud and Georges Bataille, as well as to David Litvinoff, the 'chat-artist' and erstwhile Kray associate who acted as a 'dialogue coach' on the film. It's the absorption of Litvinoff's experience that gives the film its uncanny sense of authenticity. All the punishment and humiliation that Chas doles out on the orders of his boss – the beatings, the head-shavings, the acid on car bonnets – Litvinoff had witnessed it all. He also helped to recruit the likes of John Bindon, an 'actual' criminal with a history of gangland violence, into the cast. This authenticity extended to the principal players. You could say that very few were *performing*. Mick Jagger played Turner, the inscrutable rock star, and model Anita Pallenberg, then best known for being the girlfriend of Keith Richards and ex-girlfriend of Brian Jones, played girlfriend Pherber. The third in the film's central *ménage à trois*, the adrift and waif-like Lucy, was played by the adrift and waif-like Michèle Breton whom Cammell reportedly met on a beach in St Tropez shortly before filming began.[26]

Shot in 1968 and released in America in August 1970, four months before *Gimme Shelter*, *Performance* effectively bookends the tumult that the Maysles would depict. Critics were quick to pick up on the curious overlaps. Writing in *Rolling Stone* Michael Goodwin found *Performance* 'weird' not because it reflected *Gimme Shelter* but because the casting of Mick Jagger as a figure of violence seemed to foreshadow the events of Altamont. 'If *Woodstock* presented one sort of reality,' he offers, '*Performance* presents another sort, a dark yin to *Woodstock*'s yang.' Goodwin's evidence for this prophetic quality is tenuous at best. His cites 'Memo from Turner', the Jagger song featured in the film that speaks of a moment 'when the black man drew his knife'. Although this line carries practically no similarities to the death of Meredith Hunter, the black man who drew a gun at Altamont, it seems proof enough for Goodwin: '*This* is the Altamont movie'.[27]

Cammell, possibly with the encouragement of Warner Brothers, was not shy about flagging up and amplifying these intersections. In an interview just prior to the UK release in January 1971, Cammell spoke at length about the film's preoccupation with violence. His track, as ever, was towards violence as an inherent state of mind, particularly amongst the young. 'You have to understand that youth is still attracted to violence,' he says before clarifying: 'The Woodstock Nation is attracted to violence'. Then he adds: 'This movie was finished before Altamont and Altamont actualised it.' The implication here is that *Performance* is not just 'weirdly' – unexpectedly – predictive, but that the dynamic of prediction is intentional. Cammell teasingly suggests that his film has the power of a magickal spell: he's not just reflected the events of Altamont but has in some way caused them as a direct result of making *Performance*.[28]

The writer Iain Sinclair took this one step further in 'Who Cares for the Caretaker?' (1999), an essay that dealt, in part, with the life and career of David Litvinoff. When commenting on the later lives of those who participated in the film he tells us that:

> So many of the cast and crew of *Performance* had already stumbled into madness, messianic seizure, violence, obscurity and death that the film had the reputation of being a psychic vortex. It fed so successfully on the demonic

energies of the period that it heated time, sending a portion of London into a terminal tailspin.

Sinclair is not describing the on-screen chaos of *Performance* but the alleged after-effects of its production. In this he's fairly accurate: after the shoot Pallenberg and Breton both fell into serious drug addiction, and James Fox left acting to join a religious group (although Fox did not see this as a negative decision and maintains it had nothing to with *Performance*). Biographical fidelity, though, is not Sinclair's main concern in writing his essay. He's trying to convey a certain aura that's come to surround the film, one that mixes fact with half-truths and the heady language of magick. In Sinclair's terms the film is an inverted talisman: an object which confers misfortune upon those connected to it. Of course, this is not to say that *Performance* actually does possess occult powers. Instead, the point is that, as with Zachary Lazar's depiction of *Invocation* in *Sway*, *Performance* is routinely spoken of – by writers, filmmakers and its own creators – as if it carries supernatural potency. It's this seductive language that lies at the heart of its enduring cult appeal.[29]

'Altamont', meanwhile certainly does have its double in the 'shadow world' of music and literature, but the energy of this work has also produced an evocation, just as Lazar hinted at. Something has come back the other way. 'Altamont' is now a magic word because it allows you to speak about so many things at once: a band, an event, a period. It still names an actual place, but that place has been irrevocably changed by the word's transformation. When the *San Francisco Chronicle* reported on Rick McDonald's 'return to Altamont campaign', they took a photo of him standing at the site with a large hand-painted banner. Buffeted by the wind, it looked more like the work of a Stones-worshipping cargo cult than a PR exercise. The late Paul Kantner, formerly of Jefferson Airplane, was asked for his thoughts on this second 'Altamont'. 'Yeah right,' he replied. 'Bring your switchblade. Come to hell.'[30]

CHAPTER VIII

The Cataclysm

Hell had never seemed so inviting. Or so informal.

Dawn and Nicki are lounging on a double bed in their New York apartment trying to convince their new roommate Cindy, to join their Satanic cult: 'Worshipping the devil, it's the in-thing to do.' Cindy is shocked. 'It used to seem very spooky to me too,' says Nicki who languidly brushes her hair while dressed in nothing but a towel, 'but actually if you think about it its quite logical. And very stimulating.' Cindy remains unconvinced so Dawn, dressed from head to toe in black, gives her the hard sell: 'The cult believes that the evil in this world far outweighs the good. And so, we believe that Satan is our true saviour.' With perfect timing and a wide smile, she adds, 'Why don't you come to our next meeting?' Fade to black then cut to shots of a deep, dark stairway. Drone music and weird rituals on cracking, sulphurous film. Suddenly a shot of the horizon appears and a dark figure walks towards the sunlight. It is not clear what has become of Cindy.

This is the plot of *The Virgin Sacrifice*, a short film allegedly made in 1969 by the mysterious, reclusive and pseudonymous director J.X. Williams. Intended as part of a longer, three-hour film funded by a member of the Church of Satan, the production was beset by problems: cast members overdosed, Williams was the victim of a car-bombing, the film negative disappeared, and the processing lab burnt down. Writing in his (as yet unpublished) autobiography *The Big Footnote*, Williams claims that his previous film *Incubus* was made in equally ominous circumstances. Amongst other mishaps 'the production company went belly-up' and, in a sign of bad things to come, 'Roman Polanski and Sharon Tate attended the premiere'. Only nine minutes of *The Virgin Sacrifice* are known to have survived and Williams has little good to say about it. According to his archivist, the curator and video artist Noel Lawrence, Williams came to regard *The Virgin Sacrifice* as cursed. Where *Incubus* was shadowed by coincidental mishaps, the chaos of *The Virgin Sacrifice* was, according to Williams, of a wholly different order: 'You could just smell the vapor of evil clouding the set'. At least, that's the story.

The Virgin Sacrifice is about the length of *Invocation of My Demon Brother* and, as with Anger's film, its intense, hypnotic images give the impression that a spell is being cast as symbols move across the screen. *Invocation*, though, is utterly distinctive, with the film's colour scheme, imagery and editing style bearing Anger's artistic signature throughout. By contrast, a closer look at *The Virgin Sacrifice* reveals that it consists entirely of clips taken from other films, David Durston's *I Drink Your Blood* (1970) and Lucio Fulci's *A Lizard in a Woman's Skin* (1971) among them. The meeting between Nicki, Dawn and Cindy comes from *Devil's Due* (1973) a pornographic film directed by 'Ernest Danna'. *The Virgin Sacrifice* came into public view via the DVD *Experiments in Terror* (2003), a collection of 'found' and repurposed short films curated by Noel Lawrence, which offers a further wink that this reliquary of the late 1960s might not be all it seems. As a fragment of a vanished film, one that might never have existed at all, there is nothing certain about *The Virgin Sacrifice*, least of all its director, J.X. Williams, who may well be an invention of Lawrence (or vice versa). Within the smoke and mirrors that surrounds the film, the best that we can say is that *The Virgin Sacrifice* is a contemporary short designed to look as if it was made in 1969.[1]

That Williams (or Lawrence, or whoever), refers to Roman Polanski and Sharon Tate when sketching out the film's 'history' suggests that he's keen to weave *The Virgin Sacrifice* into the complex web of associations that have come to surround their names since 1969. As with the likes of 'Altamont' and 'Charles Manson', 'Roman Polanski' and 'Sharon Tate' have become magic words, talismans which when uttered or written call to mind an enduring set of ideas. In their case the associations relate not just to death and murder but to a wider 'mythology' of Hollywood, celebrity and occult conspiracy.

Such ideas started to circulate immediately after the murders, thanks to rumours of a collection of film reels found at Cielo Drive during the initial police investigation. Stories of these 'home movies' – works, allegedly, of DIY pornography featuring Tate, Polanski and members of their Hollywood circle – parallel the equally persistent rumours of 'snuff' movies made by the Manson Family in the years leading up to 1969. Tony O'Neill wrote about this material in his novel *Sick City* (2010), while John Aes-Nihil's film *The Manson Family Movies* (1984) was intended as a gory (re)creation of the much-whispered footage. Similar stories about Bobby Beausoleil and the alleged theft of Kenneth Anger's original *Lucifer Rising* rushes have frequently overlapped with these speculations. Mainly propagated by Anger himself as part of his 'split' with Beausoleil, he claimed that the musician buried a carload of ritualistic film somewhere in the desert just before joining Manson's group. It's an assertion that brings a tenuous magickal potency into the orbit of the Family's 'hidden' filmography.[2]

Set against this backdrop, *The Virgin Sacrifice* takes the place of these 'lost' films, one imaginary movie that stands in for the countless others which pepper Manson biographies, fictions and conspiracy theories. As for its 'vapor of evil', there's an additional hidden point of reference that guides the film, one implied by the images and hinted at in the commentary of its makers but which the film never invokes directly. As a knowing attempt to evoke a certain atmosphere, mood or *sensibility* of the late sixties, *The Virgin Sacrifice* draws heavily on the resonant energies of *Rosemary's Baby*, another 'cursed' film that stands between Roman Polanski, Sharon Tate and Charles Manson.

*

According to Nikolas Schreck, the 'curse' of *Rosemary's Baby* is a 'stubborn legend', one that has grown out of the personal tragedies which befell some of those involved in the film shortly after its release. In April 1969 composer Krzysztof Komeda succumbed to a 'fatal brain aneurysm' that stemmed from a head injury he received in late 1968. At the same time the film's producer William Castle was hospitalised after suffering kidney failure. It was when Castle was recuperating in San Francisco that he heard about the murder of Sharon Tate, at which point he drove down to Los Angeles to see Polanski and promptly 'fell apart'. Meanwhile, when interviewed about the murders by the LAPD, Polanski allegedly claimed that 'witchcraft' may have been a factor in the death of his wife: he thought he might have been the target of a group fixated on the occult ideas in the film. Where Castle would go on to claim that the entire production of *Rosemary's Baby* and its aftermath was 'controlled by some unexplainable force', Polanski was more sceptical. Witchcraft (in some form) may have been a factor, but he did not admit to a belief in it. Either way, both Castle and Polanski connect the making of the film with a deep sense of misfortune: it could easily be another version of the *malfate* from Chris Petit's *Back from the Dead*. As with the 'Curse of the Pharaohs' that was said to have descended on Howard Carter and his team after they opened the tomb of Tutankhamun in 1922, bad things seemed to follow the completion of *Rosemary's Baby*. Whether such events were seen as part of a Faustian pact, or divine retribution for dabbling in infernal matters, the film's enduring legend carries a clear, cautionary message. As Schreck puts it, 'Anyone who dares to make a film about the Devil is asking for trouble.'[3]

Writing in *The Satanic Screen* (2001), Schreck is keen to point out that the 'curse' of *Rosemary's Baby* was mainly talked up by William Castle, who was well known in Hollywood as a 'master of contriving the most outlandish publicity for his films.' With all the hype of a 'spook-show barker at the carnival' he had few qualms about 'exploiting the unrelated deaths of others to garner more attention.' Castle, it's worth remembering, directed *The Tingler* (1959), a horror film that featured LSD and spinal parasites which feed on fear, and which was intended to be screened using seats wired to give audience members electric shocks whenever the titular monster appeared. *The Tingler* exemplified Castle's raison d'être as a filmmaker and producer: he was interested in creating films which burst out from the screens to make their horrors physically manifest before the audience. With *Rosemary's Baby* he doesn't rely on inventive cinema gimmicks to achieve this, but instead gives the film a life of its own by conjuring a sinister reputation – cloaking the film, one might say, in a 'vapour of evil' – and claiming that it has had a terrifying, real-world effect on those involved. Like Donald Cammell's *Performance*, *Rosemary's Baby* emerges as another film that is not just concerned with the exercise of strange powers but seems to possess strange powers all of its own.

It's not all William Castle's fault, though. Anton LaVey, founder and High Priest of the Church of Satan merrily allowed the rumour to circulate that he had acted as a consultant to the production, at the personal request of Roman Polanski, to advise on the accuracy of its Satanic detail. Going further, much further – into the realms not just of bunkum but also of bad taste – LaVey also stated in numerous interviews that he appeared in *Rosemary's Baby* as the devil, no less. In the film's infamous dream/rape sequence in which Satan appears and impregnates Rosemary Woodhouse, the audience is given only a glimpse of an unearthly, beast-like figure. Rather than rely on the goat-headed spectacle of films like *The Devil Rides Out* (1968), Polanski's elliptical approach transforms the classic horror-movie monster suit into a dark, ominous presence. LaVey claims that he was the one wearing this costume, an assertion that Clay Tanner, the actor who actually wore the outfit on set and performed the scene with Mia Farrow, would very much dispute. Not one to be troubled by the inconvenience of facts, LaVey understood the power of a good story. With his goatee-beard, devil horns and gaggle of go-go dancers (which in 1966 included future Family member Susan Atkins) LaVey also aligned the Church of Satan with a camp, comic book aesthetic. As a former carnival organist, he knew that American popular culture appealed to the indulgent, pleasure-seeking instincts he placed at the heart of his church's teachings and would go on to celebrate in his book, *The Satanic Bible* (1969). As such, from both a philosophical and promotional viewpoint, it made sense for LaVey to try to associate himself with such a high-profile horror film as *Rosemary's Baby*.[4]

LaVey never went so far as to say that he had actually sired the Antichrist. Indeed, such a belief in the possibility of physical manifestation would have been very much at odds with the Church of Satan and its teachings. For LaVey, as for the members of the Process, Satan was not a deity who demanded worship so much as an aspect of one's personality that should be acknowledged and satisfied. 'Satan represents indulgence, instead of abstinence!', LaVey preached from the pages of *The Satanic Bible*, 'vital existence, instead of spiritual pipe dreams!', 'undefiled wisdom instead of hypocritical self-deceit!'. These and other maxims made up LaVey's 'Nine Satanic Statements', the commandments, as it were, of the Church of Satan. It was a creed that encouraged a focus on the self and the exercise of individual desires in the absence of a Christian morality that pushes the guilt-ridden worshipper towards humility, piety and subservience to a higher authority.

In the late 1960s and early 1970s, the weird aura of *Rosemary's Baby* fed into the popularity of the Church of Satan. Here was a horror film that gave the source of its 'evil' a certain mystique. Bad things happened but the perpetrators ultimately found success rather than punishment, divine, diabolic or otherwise. The film's Satanists were affluent, cultured practitioners who suggested that with the right exercise of the will one could achieve wealth, status and power. What LaVey offered was a ready-made belief system that reflected this worldview and, ever the opportunist, he pushed ahead with the publication of *The Satanic Bible* to capitalise on the film's success. Standing with his doctrinal text in hand, LaVey was ready and waiting to welcome those prepared to follow the path marked out by *Rosemary's Baby* and its mythology; a step across the line from the fiction of Satanism to its 'reality'.

Although it grew in the wake of Polanski's film, the Church of Satan was also born out of, and tapped into, a much wider field of public interest in witchcraft and the esoteric: what the writer Nat Freedland called America's late-1960s 'occult explosion'. Equally reflected in and fostered by the mainstream success of *Rosemary's Baby*, this revival of interest in tarot cards, astrology, paganism and other such topics was supported by the appearance of magazines like *Man, Myth and Magic* (1970–72) and *Coven 13* (1969–74). Books by and about Aleister Crowley, practical magick and folk-beliefs were easily available, and an increasing number of head shops were becoming occult dispensaries that supplied suburban witches with crystals, wands and black candles. At the same time, a slew of post-*Rosemary* occult thrillers like *The Deathmaster* (1972), *The Satanic Rites of Dracula* (1973) and William Friedkin's all-pervasive *The Exorcist* (1973) installed the devil as the ubiquitous face of horror in the early seventies. Meanwhile, records by bands like the Crazy World of Arthur Brown, Black Sabbath, Jacula and Coven ensured that ideas of the occult, however hazily defined, were no longer confined to the underground writing of Gavin Arthur nor to the avant-garde cinema of Kenneth Anger. It was Arthur Brown who declared himself 'the God of Hell-fire' at the start of his single 'Fire' (1968), before treating the British audience of *Top of the Pops* to the spectacle of him dancing with his head in flames. Brown would have been the perfect support-act for Coven, who included the track 'Satanic Mass' on their debut album, *Witchcraft Destroys Minds and Reaps Souls* (1969). Presented as 'the first Black Mass to be recorded, either in written words or in audio' the band claimed it was the real deal, 'as authentic as hundreds of hours of research in every known source can make it'. As such, it was potentially just as harmful to the health of the listener as *Rosemary's Baby* was to those within range of its 'curse'. The band 'did not recommend' 'Satanic Mass' to 'anyone who has not thoroughly studied Black Magic and is aware of the risks and dangers involved'.

This 'phenomenon', as Freedland puts it, invited the usual polarised responses. In his study *The Occult Explosion in America* (1972), Freedland cites the Harvard theologian Harvey Cox, who regarded the post-war popularity of astrology as a positive shift in the cultural landscape. It demonstrated how a 'tight, bureaucratic society' could still find itself 'fascinated with slipstream knowledge', that which 'doesn't fit'. On the other hand, the American clergyman William Sloane Coffin made a similar point about 'America's renewed interest in occultism' but came to a much more negative conclusion, offering it as a 'beautiful example of lobotomised passivity' that results from the 'alienating influence of modernity'. Summarising the debate, Freedland argued that whatever the assessment of public commentators, there was an overriding value connected to popular occultism: it had quickly proved to be 'fashionably commercial'. As *Time* magazine put it in their March 1969 cover story, 'The Cult of the Occult', by the late 1960s it was estimated that this 'niche' interest had grown into something approaching a million-dollar industry.[5]

For all its creaky amateurism, then, 'Ernest Danna's' *Devil's Due* was spot-on when Nicki offered devil worship as 'the in-thing to do'. Transformed into *The Virgin Sacrifice*, J.X. Williams' dreamlike fragment depicts in miniature the pleasures and temptations of this cultural shift. As a cinematic initiation it shows Cindy moving from the chintz of a late-1960s apartment into a kaleidoscopic world of weird images and even weirder sensations. Her journey is a hallucinatory trip through the type of ritualistic spaces that haunt the edges of *Rosemary's Baby*. There is a distinct atmosphere of evil running throughout the short film, but for all this sense of menace it's not all about impending doom. Certainly, if the final image is read as someone walking towards a sunrise, *The Virgin Sacrifice* ultimately shows something powerful entering the world. Although *Rosemary's Baby* and associated magic words like 'Polanski', 'Tate' and 'Manson' conjure up a sense of things coming to an end as the decade comes to a close, *The Virgin Sacrifice* shows the further progress of this Satanic culture beyond the 1960s. A new dawn approaches and, out of the cursed material of the sixties, a visionary figure boldly steps forward.

Not all new dawns are glorious. For some, the sunrise is wonderfully optimistic, but for others it brings with it the dreadful hangover of the morning after. This was the case for the writer and journalist Hunter S. Thompson for whom the New Year of 1970 came as quite a shock. On 9 January he received a letter from Jim Silberman, his editor at the publishing firm Random House. Silberman was enquiring as to the progress of Thompson's long-promised, still untitled book, a meditation on that perennial favourite 'the American Dream'. Four years earlier Random House had published Thompson's first book, *Hell's Angels* (1966), a 'Strange and Terrible' study of the 'Outlaw Motorcycle Gangs' and their place within American society. Growing out of Thompson's journalism, *Hell's Angels* combined reportage with fictional embellishment and a narrative drive that placed the author as the book's primary protagonist. When that formula proved successful, Thompson was sounded out for other ideas. He turned down an offer to do a similar book investigating surfing culture and instead pitched a much more ambitious project, telling Silberman that he would 'go out and write about The Death of the American Dream'. Silberman was interested. It sounded like it had the potential to be a Great American … *something*: maybe not a *novel*, exactly but another weighty tome of so-called 'New Journalism' to place alongside recently published doorstops by Tom Wolfe and Norman Mailer. Thompson and Silberman met to discuss the idea, they exchanged letters, everything appeared to be going well and then, silence. Other projects and other business seemed to take over. Thompson continued to write freewheeling articles for *Playboy*, *Rolling Stone* and others. He settled in Woody Creek, Colorado and got involved in local politics. Meanwhile, Mailer's *The Armies of the Night* (1968), a book covering the Chicago Democratic Convention, won the Pulitzer Prize for non-fiction. *Easy Rider* also burst onto the scene with its own take on the 'Death of the American Dream'. Suddenly, with the backdrop of Nixon's entry to the White House, Thompson's chosen theme was very much in the air and thus for Silberman it was high time that he delivered on the manuscript. And so, at the start of 'another year ... another decade', Silberman tried to light a fire under Thompson to get the book back on track, adding, with the tried and tested diplomacy of the very best editors, that 'it would be splendid to be publishing [him] once again.'[6]

Thompson, it turned out, had been expecting to hear from Silberman. Replying on 13 January Thompson explained that his letter had actually come 'as something of a relief'. Like a 'demand note on a long overdue mortgage' it had realised Thompson's own gnawing anxiety about the incomplete task at hand. In the long, drawn-out missive that followed, Thompson railed against writer's block, the difficulties of narrative structure and the tyranny of deadlines. He updated Silberman on how he had spent much of the previous year standing as the 'Freak Power candidate for the County Commissioner's Office', but most of all he talked about how he now sorely regretted 'getting locked into this nightmare assignment of explaining the Death of the American Dream'. The main problem was that he felt lost: 'Many words & no focus; that's my epitaph for the past three years'.

Despite this tone of defeat, Thompson's letter was not all procrastination and *mea culpa*. He was clearly trying get a hold on the project and work out, through writing the letter to Silberman, a suitable structure. To this end, in among his writers' complaints,

Thompson brings into focus a number of recent events as if trying out different hooks on which to hang the work in progress. As well as his political tussles in Colorado he also mentions the bad stuff that happened just a month earlier at the Altamont Speedway. 'Did you read the coverage in *Rolling Stone*?', he asks Silberman. 'That scene at the Altamont rock festival shames my worst fantasies', says Thompson, 'the sharks finally came home to roost'. By 'sharks', he means the Hells Angels. When he was writing about them for his book, Thompson gained the trust of key members in the group, but this relationship soured when an altercation at a Hells Angels gathering resulted in him receiving a severe beating at their hands. The incident provided Thompson with the conclusion for *Hell's Angels* and, alongside photos of him battered and bruised, the episode became a marker of Thompson's deeply immersive, participatory approach to getting the 'story'. The Angels however saw things differently. The incident, as well as other points in the book that revealed a healthy appetite for violence became a point of contention after its publication. Issuing (somewhat ironically) threats of extreme violence towards Thompson, the Angels claimed they had been misrepresented. As well as dealing with these missives, Thompson found himself on a gruelling book tour where he often had to defend his portrayal, sometimes in the presence of the Hells Angels themselves. For him to then hear, nearly four years after *Hell's Angels*, of their 'unspeakably savage' appearance at Altamont was horrifying given the level of violence involved, but it also served to vindicate his earlier judgements of the group.

As the letter continues, he laments the loss of John F. Kennedy, pours vitriol on Richard Nixon and considers using 'scenes like Chicago' (that is, the Chicago Democratic Convention) as a framework for the writing to come. Slowly, the impossibly open-ended notion of the 'Death of the American Dream' is chiselled into some sort of shape. Thompson puts it to Silberman that, 'Anything I write is going to be about the death of the American Dream', and thus there is no way of crystallising the theme in a single book. What he writes next will be a particular take on the idea, influenced by the 'personal brain-changes' he has experienced since 1960 and which brought him 'in the fall of '69' to an 'election-nite headquarters in a room above the Elks Club in Aspen, Colo[rado] ...' What Thompson was 'really trying to write about', then, was the decade he had just lived through, a period of bikers, beatings, political assassination and – to his eyes – political betrayal. His topic, as he put it, was the 'jangled chaos of what we now have to sift through and define or explain somehow as "the 1960s"'. The idea is still ambitious, still weighty, still vague, but knowing that he can write as an expert witness, Thompson no longer seems to be intimidated by its scope. By the end of the letter he has given himself a direction.[7]

Two years and a series of articles in *Rolling Stone* later, the project finally emerged as *Fear and Loathing in Las Vegas* (1972). A scorching masterpiece of 'gonzo journalism', *Fear and Loathing* follows Thompson's deranged alter-ego 'Raoul Duke' as he travels to Las Vegas with his attorney 'Doctor Gonzo' to report on a motor race in the desert, the 'fabulous Mint 400'. Thompson based Doctor Gonzo on his friend, the Chicano activist Oscar 'Zeta' Acosta, and the trip was modelled on two writing gigs that had taken Thompson to Las Vegas at either end of 1971. One was to report on the Mint 400 for *Sports Illustrated*, the other was an assignment to cover the National District Attorney's Association Conference on Narcotics and Dangerous Drugs for *Rolling Stone*. Combining them both for the book, Thompson counters the anti-drug agenda of the District Attorney's conference with an almost overwhelming emphasis on the personal use of 'extremely dangerous drugs'. Duke and Doctor Gonzo embark on their trip having made the trunk of their car, a 'huge red Chevy convertible' look like a 'mobile police narcotics lab'. As the novel opens they liberally sample these 'uppers, downers, screamers, laughers' and from there the 'narrative' gives way to a seemingly endless sequence of drug-related bad behaviour. This is told from Duke's delirious, intoxicated perspective, a narrative voice that repeatedly veers from insight to confusion, composure to paranoia. Doctor Gonzo, meanwhile descends into a haze of hotel room destruction and frequent threats of violence. That both characters are clearly seen to make 'beasts' of themselves is very much the point. Although *Fear and Loathing* is funny, quotable and has inspired any number of ill-advised trips to Las Vegas, it remains a work of intense self-disgust, a book best read in the cold light of a hungover morning.[8]

When he wrote to Silberman, Thompson had deferred to the heavyweight American author William Faulkner and his concept of 'seeing the world in a grain of sand'. Taking Faulkner's lead Thompson had suggested this approach as a way of giving form and purpose to his project:

> The job of a writer, it seems to me, is to focus very finely on a thing, a place, a person, act, phenomenon ... and then, when the focus is right, to *understand*, and then *render* the subject of that focus in such a way that it suddenly appears in context – the reader's context, regardless of who the reader happens to be, or where.[9]

In *Fear and Loathing*, Raoul Duke provides this point of focus. Although his story seems to get in the way of the book's apparent journalistic intentions, Thompson, like Joan Didion writing in

'The White Album', uses his central character to communicate a much bigger set of ideas, ones that in terms of *Fear and Loathing* go beyond the minutiae of the Mint 400.

Duke drives to Las Vegas from Los Angeles via 'the same lonely desert' that was 'the last known home of the Manson family'. In moving inland Duke is also moving away, more generally, from the West Coast and what, by 1971, it had come to represent. On a 'nervous night in Las Vegas', he feels himself filled with nostalgia for 'San Francisco in the middle sixties [...] a very special time and place to be a part of'. For Duke a mere five years, maybe six, have passed since he was part of 'the first rising curl' of the 'Acid Wave', but for him the difference between 'then' and 'now', San Francisco and Las Vegas, is undeniable. The gulf between them feels as long as a lifetime.

In what has become the most famous passage from *Fear and Loathing*, Thompson has Duke remember a sense of 'energy'; the confidence of a 'whole generation' that for some reason found itself concentrated on the West Coast. Duke wistfully describes a certain youthful dynamism, a period in which there was 'madness in any direction, at any hour'. This Dionysian state is not presented as hedonism for its own sake but represents the optimism of the counterculture at its most stereotypical, a propulsive drive towards cultural change for the better. As Duke puts it, there was 'a fantastic universal sense that whatever we were doing was *right*, that we were winning ...' Such overwhelming confidence forms the crux of what Duke tries to define and celebrate:

> And that, I think was the handle – that sense of inevitable victory over the forces of Old and Evil. Not in any mean or military sense; we didn't need that. Our energy would simply *prevail*. There was no point in fighting – on our side

> or theirs. We had all the momentum; we were riding the crest of a high and beautiful wave …

Five years later the self-belief of 1966–7 has evaporated. What Duke finds in Las Vegas is commerce, compromise and enterprise: political symbols reduced to tacky knick-knacks ('JFK half-dollar money clips for $5 each'), drug binges on expense accounts and an overall experience of 'freedom' that's chargeable by the hour. In Las Vegas, the heart of the 'American Dream', the pursuit of pleasure leads not to the expansion of consciousness but to the accumulation of debt.

According to Duke, American culture arrived at such a sorry state of affairs after having gone through 'a proper end to the sixties'. He reminds the reader that by the start of the 1970s many of the decade's guiding lights were out of the game. Bob Dylan was 'clipping coupons in Greenwich Village', both Kennedys had been 'murdered by mutants', Stanley Owsley the king of LSD was 'folding napkins on Terminal Island', and Mohammad Ali had been defeated by Joe Frazier, 'a man on the verge of death'. Duke does not go quite as far as the speculations found in *Illuminatus!* but his roll call indicates that at the turn of the decade there was an agenda, possibly formed by the undefined 'forces of Old and Evil', working against the popular, underground and progressive culture of the sixties.[10]

Given that Duke compares Frazier to Nixon because both had 'finally prevailed for reasons that people like me refused to understand', suggests that when Thompson refers to the 'forces of Old and Evil', he has in mind political conservatism and the shift to the right in American politics at the start of the 1970s. Equally, Duke's pessimism is linked to 'the brutish realities' of 1971, the sense, buried within the intensity of his nostalgia, that a lot has changed since the mid-sixties. The political climate has changed but, crucially, those who lived through the 1960s have also changed. They've grown up. When Thompson was writing about Duke and Las Vegas he was a fair way over the dreaded age of 30. He had a family, a house and a precarious freelance career. These responsibilities demanded he do more with his time than merely be 'there and alive' as part of San Francisco's historical greatness. Any counterculture built on an idealised notion of youth is inevitably doomed to fail precisely because it is so temporary. People age and their optimism, naïve or not, tends to harden with experience into something more like jaded cynicism. Before you know it, the task of establishing a utopian society is added to the never-ending to-do list that's stuck to the fridge and, every time this list gets too long and 'life gets complicated', you don't try to build the new world. You head off instead for a weekend bender in Las Vegas.

With Raoul Duke then, Thompson was applying Faulkner's method to his burnt-out narrator. Duke is a man out of phase with his time. He moves at speed into the 1970s but carries a head full of memories and chemicals that keep his mind entangled in the glorious simulation of the sixties. What the reader is meant to 'understand' through Duke's drug-addled anti-quest is that an era and a whole way of thinking has come to an end. It will not be revived, and America is now worse off in its absence. The role of Las Vegas in the novel is to help bring into relief this sense of an ending. The city, circa 1971, is the inverted mirror image of San Francisco circa 1967. It provides Duke with the ideal geographic and symbolic vantage point from where he can lament the end of the sixties and its 'beautiful wave'. Stuck in a hotel room in the middle of the Nevada desert, with the reality of the Nixon years looming in, he imagines looking back towards the West

Coast and *almost* seeing 'the high-water mark, that place where the wave finally broke and rolled back.'[11]

*

Thompson's wave was not the only one that ebbed and flowed through the sixties.

In June 1966, 30 members of the Process, including the leaders Mary Ann MacLean and Robert de Grimston, left England and travelled to Nassau in the Bahamas. They were seeking a place away from press scrutiny where they could practise their beliefs in peace and work on enhancing the 'group mind' of the community. From Nassau they went to Mexico City and then travelled on to the Yucatán Peninsula where they finally '[established] themselves on the deserted estate of a ruined salt factory called Xtul.' In October, a month after they arrived, Hurricane Inez made landfall on the Yucatán coast. The Processians decided to stay in their compound, and when the hurricane finally hit they were battered by torrential rain and huge crashing waves. By their own admission it was, quite literally, a miracle that the community survived. This was clearly a sign. They had been delivered for a reason. The hurricane at Xtul became the defining moment in the mythology and belief system of the Process. They returned to London emboldened, validated, flushed with a sense of mission and convinced that they were the 'chosen beings of God [...] come to announce and facilitate the ending of all humanity.' Moves were made to establish international chapterhouses, and in 1967 the Process rebranded themselves as the Process Church of the Final Judgement. By December that year they were operating in Haight-Ashbury. Like Raoul Duke, they too recognised that 'San Francisco in the middle sixties' was 'a very special time and place to be a part of.'[12]

In *Rosemary's Baby*, Roman Polanski leads the film into Rosemary's diabolical encounter via a dream-sequence set on board a storm-cast ship. In it, Rosemary dreams of her friend Hutch who earlier in the film had tried to warn her about the history of the Bramford Building. In the dream he stands at the ship's helm, struggling to keep the vessel on an even keel. Buffeted by strong waves, he calls to Rosemary to go down to the lower deck because a typhoon is rolling in. She complies and then finds herself in a very different situation. The space is dark, she's made to lie down and a strange presence with vivid yellow eyes forces itself upon her. In a clear foreshadowing of the invasions later in the film, there's no privacy for Rosemary, not even in her own subconscious. That this plays out against the backdrop of a typhoon recalls Jung's reflections on dreams of the sea which '[break] into the land, flooding everything'. According to Jung, such images announce a 'momentous alteration'; for Rosemary the waves that pummel the edges of her dream are similar harbingers of the auspicious events she will soon experience.[13]

If Thompson's wave of countercultural energy faltered when faced with the 'forces of Old and Evil', *Rosemary's Baby* and the extraordinary experiences of the Process show the tide flowing the other way. The waves they encountered *carried* the forces of 'Old and Evil': spiritual wisdom and the son of Satan born on Earth. All three are cataclysms of a sort: deluges, metaphorical downpours in which one set of ideas floods towards or washes over another. For Thompson though, the wave in *Fear and Loathing* signals a low ebb, in every sense of the word. By contrast, in Polanski's film and in the theology of the Process, they are moments which, for good or for ill, have a transformative, catalytic effect on those involved.

*

The 'wave-speech' of *Fear and Loathing* could be compared to the violent break-up of the Columbia occupation in Peter Whitehead's *The Fall*, as well as to the slow-motion, multi-angled shot of the exploding house that concludes Michelangelo Antonioni's *Zabriskie Point* (1970). Antonioni's film, his even more abstract follow-up to *Blow-Up*, essentially picks up where *The Fall* leaves off. Set in Los Angeles sometime in 1970, *Zabriskie Point* features Mark, a young student radical played by Mark Frechette, who at the start of the film storms out of a meeting about a campus strike. Like Mark Rudd leaving Students for a Democratic Society to join the Weathermen, Antonioni's Mark has little time for talk and is intent on taking direct action. He arms himself, gets mixed up in a violent encounter between students and the police, and then steals a small aircraft in which he flies from LA into Death Valley. There he meets Daria (Daria Halprin) a young woman en-route to a liaison in the palatial, modernist home of Lee, her property developer boss. After some oblique conversation they indulge in a session of hallucinatory sex on the desert floor. Mark then returns the plane and is shot by the police for his trouble. Daria meanwhile continues to her appointment with Lee but ends up fleeing his desert chateau soon after arriving. Driving away, she stops on the road and looks back to the building perched high on its outcrop. What follows is one of cinema's most elegant explosions. Beautifully choreographed to the music of Pink Floyd, the house is blown to pieces.

Viewers and critics generally agree that Daria is imagining this explosion, because for all its incendiary talk *Zabriskie Point*, more so than *The Fall*, is a film about ineffectual radicalism. Meetings are held, scuffles break out on the street, vehicles are stolen, but nothing gets *done*. Change only seems to occur in the realm of fantasy, as when the desert landscape bubbles into erotic life when

Mark and Daria get together. In the same way, when the building explodes, it is as if Daria has come to see the world through Mark's eyes and is projecting his rage onto a symbol of power, affluence and 'the Man'. It's a moment of intense self-assertion, but for Daria it remains an act of wish-fulfilment, a desire that's worked through in the imagination rather than performed in 'real' life. As with the foreshortened occupation of Columbia University in *The Fall* and the break of Thompson's progressive wave, the revolutionary sentiment is there in *Zabriskie Point*. The will of the New Left is present and correct on-screen, but as the film closes, the reality to match this political drive is yet to be made manifest.[14]

In his novel *Snipe's Spinster* Jeff Nuttall has Snipe, his narrator, deftly summarise this sense of unrealised potential. Describing the failure of the counterculture to realise its revolutionary aims, Snipe maps out a situation in which, come the turn of the decade, 'peaceniks', the 'Underground', 'flower children' and 'hippies' were in a

> [...] moral cul-de-sac in which we, left over from a revolution that went off half-cock, flounder, with our casual hallucinations, our cynically contrived schizophrenia, our habitual sado-masochism, our inability to expect anything but violence, betrayal, and yet more violence.

Snipe is not as intoxicated as Raoul Duke but, standing at the same crossroads between the end of the sixties and the start of the seventies, his voice is just as world-weary. Indeed, Nuttall has Snipe mention *Fear and Loathing in Las Vegas* in the novel's opening chapters. These are mainly given over to a wide-ranging survey of the post-war counterculture as it flourished in Britain and America. Where *Bomb Culture* placed the British counterculture as a clear outgrowth of the Aldermaston Marches and the Campaign for Nuclear Disarmament, before charting its parallel development in the avant-garde arts, *Snipe's Spinster* takes a much broader view. 'We were glad to entertain the Gods in 1964,' Snipe says, adding that in the post-war, post-nuclear period, 'Any old God would do.' The need was for 'bivouacs in the wilderness because in civilization we had just suffered a colossal defeat.' As a result, 'we had to move on away from the place of humiliation, which was society as we knew it.' And so, fed up with 'confronting the establishment on its own terms,' Snipe defines the countercultural tactic as an attempt to 'achieve, translate and present a quite new, and workable alternative.' This involved not just an enthusiasm for Bob Dylan, American Beat poetry and experimentation with LSD, but also the exploration of a wide range of spiritual and philosophical ideas. Nuttall, using Snipe as his mouthpiece, describes the establishment of alternative religions and an intense, visionary engagement with the English landscape and its history: 'we registered the ancient conical mounds and hummocks that punctuate England between the motorways.' Fantasy novels like J.R.R. Tolkien's *The Lord of the Rings* (1954) are cited as key influences on these ideas which collectively express the hope that 'the arrival of the Aquarian age would see true history restored and the economy of steel and plastic would be relegated to the earth.' The belief, according to Nuttall, was that such a shift would come 'not as a result of any political action [...] but as an evolutionary inevitability.'[15]

Scientology is mentioned as part of the novel's countercultural survey, as are the Process, as are the Manson Family. At one point Snipe discusses Charles Manson alongside Tolkien as a fellow mythologiser who adds to the fabric of countercultural thinking in the sixties. At first glance there's nothing to link the two, but Snipe alludes to Manson's stories about the 'bottomless pit' in the Nevada desert and connects these to the Tolkien-esque 'superstition' that 'the kindly and fanciful beings who had long ago inhabited the earth, were only hiding [...] under the ground'. In late 1969 some underground publications like *Tuesday's Child* were celebrating Manson as a hero of the far left. They saw him, as did the Weathermen at the Flint War Council, as someone who took the type of action in the war against the classes that everyone else merely thought about. With *Snipe's Spinster*, Nuttall was not engaging in the same type of provocation. But, by naming Manson as part of the countercultural worldview – not as its adversary – he has Snipe paint a picture of the 'Underground' as incorporating a wide range of influences into its frame of reference. This is the point Nuttall's trying to emphasise: it's an impossibly broad church.

Snipe, like Thompson's Duke, makes extensive use of 'we' when discussing the revolutionary potential of youth culture in the sixties. When speaking about a moment when, in Duke's case it seemed '*we* were winning', or in Snipe's case '*we* [tried to] expand and change society as *we* knew it', both Thompson and Nuttall emphasise the importance of a group identity and a set of common aims. But in placing Manson alongside Tolkien before going on to discuss the likes of Marc Bolan, Snipe maps out a counterculture that clearly lacks coherence. With such a mix of ideologies, practices and personalities at play, it comes as no surprise that the attempt to generate a 'new, and workable alternative' should result in 'a revolution that went off half-cock'. The cultural failure registered by Thompson and particularly Nuttall is not just the failure of a 'feeble attempt at revolution', but the failure to foster and maintain the necessary fuel for such an enterprise: a unified sense of collective ambition.[16]

*

In the second half of *Fear and Loathing*, when Duke and Doctor Gonzo attend the National District Attorney's Association Conference on Narcotics and Dangerous Drugs, they meet 'a man from Georgia', a 'sporty-looking cop about forty' in a casino bar. Over drinks they regale him with stories of crime and disorder in California. 'In L.A. it's out of control', they say, 'first it was drugs, now it's witchcraft'. Duke and Doctor Gonzo are clearly pressing the man's reactionary buttons. They tell him exactly what he wants to hear about the West Coast and in return they receive the expected response: '"Jesus God almighty", said the southerner. "What the hell's goin' on in this country?"' Beyond this conservative-baiting, Thompson has Duke use similar language elsewhere in the novel. 'Jesus freaks', the Process, Manson, 'goddamn Satan-worshippers': these are the parties Duke blames or invokes when he experiences a spike in paranoia or otherwise lets the 'bad craziness' of the early 1970s get to him. Such references are noticeably absent from Thompson's description of San Francisco in the middle sixties. Although Duke remembers there being 'madness in any direction, at any hour', there's no sign of occult or religious influences on the 'energy of a whole generation' that came 'to a head in a long fine flash'. For Duke, unlike Snipe, it is as if witchcraft and these seemingly new esoteric groups have no place among the counterculture.[17]

For the 'goddamn Satan-worshippers' of California the feeling was mutual. Anton LaVey castigated the hypocrisy of the stereotypical hippie counterculture, 'the ragtag, tie-dyed, egalitarian army who shouted, as one, that they were all individuals'. Such was his disdain that on 8 August 1969 he and other members of the Church of Satan gathered in the Black House, their San Francisco headquarters, and performed a ceremony they termed 'The Rising Forth'. According to the writer Gavin Baddeley this involved the placing of a 'venomous curse upon the hippie movement':

> Beware, you psychedelic vermin! Your smug pomposity with its thin disguise of tolerance will serve you no longer! We know your mark and recognise it well. We walk the night as the villains no longer! Our steeds await, and our eyes are ablaze with the fires of Hell!

LaVey later claimed this curse was catastrophically effective because, in his mind, it led to the events at Cielo Drive. Occult speculation aside, what 'The Rising Forth' ceremony made clear was the deep ideological differences between the Church of Satan and the inhabitants of Haight-Ashbury.[18]

For LaVey, one of the main tenets of Satanism is the need to recognise one's own desires and to accept the bestial nature of the human animal. Bound in with this view is an emphasis on strong individualism, a movement away from the subservience inherent to Christianity in which a single 'Father' dominates over the flock. Revelling in one's own fetishes and fantasies is part of the psychic process that allows the Satanist to become their own god, rather than remain beholden to another. This is an exceptional position, one afforded to those with the necessary strength of will to seize it. With echoes of Social Darwinism, it is a role that involves the Satanist elevating themselves above their perceived 'inferiors'. As LaVey emphasised in his 'Satanic Statements': 'Satan represents kindness to those who deserve it instead of love wasted on ingrates. [...] Satan represents responsibility to the responsible instead of concern for psychic vampires'. According to the Church of Satan then, not everyone was created equal. What LaVey observed in the rise of the San Franciscan counterculture was the utter opposite of this individualism: a herd that paraded under the banner of non-conformity. 'Suddenly,' LaVey reflected, 'the ingestion of lysergic acid made every man a king. It made nincompoops self-assured – created a culture of people who, no matter what they knew or had done, considered themselves your equal.' Satanism then, was not merely a case of inverting Christianity for its own sake. Rather, it involved the wilful rejection of the type of passive, group mentality that came with organised religion and which LaVey saw taking root in the so-called counterculture.[19]

The Process held a similar view, although their theology of 'The Three Great Gods of the Universe. JEHOVAH – LUCIFER – SATAN' was arguably more complex than the message of provocative (but essentially practical) self-improvement offered by *The Satanic Bible*. By encouraging their members to identify with either Jehovah the 'wrathful god of vengeance and rebirth,' Lucifer the light-bearer or Satan the god of chaos, the Process were placing three distinct personality types at the centre of their belief system. To be a Jehovian required purity and self-denial; Lucifereans were all about enjoying life, while Satanists were more ascetic, seeking to move beyond 'all human and physical needs and appetites.' Judging by this pantheon, the Process were keen to explore personality types *in extremis*. There was no place in their belief system for a neutral position. This was the source of the *real* evil in the world. Like the Church of Satan, the Process placed themselves in opposition to society's forces of mindless conformity. These they called the 'Grey Forces,' and 'John Grey' was their term for the man on the street, the anonymous figure of passive obedience who goes to work, does what he is told, consumes what he is told before going back to work to earn more money to buy more of the stuff he's told to consume. A living

John Doe, 'John Grey' symbolised everything the Process hoped adherence to their 'Great Gods' would allow them to escape: the horrifying apex of mediocrity.[20]

The Process and the Church of Satan both came into public view at a time when any hint of 'Devil-worship' would have immediately called up pseudo-medieval notions of blasphemy and other attempts to subvert the authority of the church. Despite claims that the post-war world was increasingly secular, the ominous spectre of the devil loomed large in the public imagination. It was certainly in evidence in March 1963 when St Mary's Church in the village of Clophill in Bedfordshire made headlines in the British media. The grave of one Jenny Humberstone, 'the young wife of an apothecary who died in 1770 at the age of 22', had been desecrated and her skeleton removed. Amid claims of black magic and necromancy, it was reported that her remains were 'discovered in the church arranged in a circle, with a cockerel's feathers scattered nearby'. The vandalism of St Mary's continued in this manner in fits and spurts throughout the 1960s with a second major spike of activity – grave destruction and the removal of bones – occurring around Midsummer, 1969. Coverage of these events featured comparisons to Dennis Wheatley's novel *The Devil Rides Out* (1934) and, with the recent success of Hammer Films' 1968 cinematic adaptation, the story gave rise to a vague image of Satanism; one connected with malevolent evil, wanton destruction and an inevitable wave of moral panic.[21]

This type of gothic ghoulishness was of little interest to the Process, long black cloaks notwithstanding. They would have been just as offended as anybody else by grave robbing and church desecration, seeing such actions as exemplifying the 'lower end' of Satan's 'nature', that which 'men fear'. This 'desire [...] to wallow in a morass of violence, lunacy and excessive physical indulgence' was the extreme end of the human instinct for destruction. Conventionally associated with the figure of Satan, such behaviour was the reason why he 'by whatever name' became 'the Adversary'. By contrast, what the Process focussed on in their exploration of the 'Satanic' personality was the opposite, the more positive side of this will to transgress: the urge to become 'all soul and no body, all spirit and no mind'. For the Process then, the pursuit of a Satanic 'pattern of reality' was a matter of trying to elevate oneself to a higher plane of existence. Their recruitment material made this point clear. In Françoise Strachan's *Aquarian Guide to Occult, Mystical, Religious, Magical, London and Around* (1970) the Process are listed alongside entries for the Pagan Movement, courses on 'Psychic Development and Healing' and the Ramakrishna Vedanta Centre. Their Mayfair address appears along with the statement:

> And at the judgement shall you show yourself a servant of the un-God, condemned to endless alienation from all truth or shall you show yourself a servant of the Gods, raised up and reborn in the New Age?

'Judgement', 'reborn' and 'New Age' all nod towards the apocalyptic leanings of the Process, but it's probably the emphasis on 'you' that really distils their message. There's no sign here of the 'we' that peppers the writing of Thompson and Nuttall. The Process may well be a group, but they are not a collective. As with the Church of Satan, the focus is resolutely individualistic.[22]

According to the journalist and writer Tom Wolfe, this shift from 'we' to 'I' described the predominant mood in American culture as the seventies took hold. Writing for *New York* magazine in 1976, Wolfe labelled it 'The Me Decade'. For Wolfe, the

'Me Decade' was marked by a widespread interest in 'changing one's personality – remaking, remodelling, elevating and polishing one's very *self*. In essence there was little difference between this language and the rhetoric of *The Psychedelic Experience*. Leary had offered the sensation of ego loss under acid as a tool of self-improvement, an experience the 'voyager' should reflect upon, post-trip, when defining the terms of their 'future personality'. In making the personal political, the New Left had also spent much of the 1960s trying to remodel the ideological make-up of 'the self'. That said, in writing 'The Me Decade', Wolfe was not providing a survey of the defining ideas of the sixties but was instead focusing on their presence in the seventies. Standing midway through the decade, what he found was a loss of political potency. Psychedelic experimentation and religious exploration had given way to a culture of pop-psychology, healing, couples' therapy, fad diets and cosmetic self-improvement, all of which came at a price.

This was an 'upward roll' which, like the wave in *Fear and Loathing* carried a sense of disappointment in its wake. None of these 'new' trends, Wolfe implied, had the ability to make good the promises of the sixties and change the world. Instead they gave rise to a cultural climate of atomised self-importance. Absorbed into the all-purpose, clarion call of 'Let's talk about me', the seventies focus on the self was deeply solipsistic, 'smacked so much of vanity' and emphasised personal concerns over and above political intentions. This indulgence, the desire to observe, study and dote on 'one's self' had previously been an 'aristocratic luxury [...] since only the very wealthiest classes had the free time and the surplus income to dwell upon this sweetest and vainest of pastimes'.

Throughout the essay Wolfe sounds incredulous and exasperated when describing the narcissism of the seventies. There's also an ugly undertow of misogyny. Wolfe directs much of his ire at suburban women who want to look after themselves, not just their husbands, and who wish to have an identity that goes beyond the gendered anonymity of 'woman, housewife'. Wolfe's pomposity aside, the essay's key point comes when he describes the 'Me Decade' as the 'Third Great Awakening'. What Wolfe references here are two prior periods of religious enthusiasm in American culture. The 'First' was the Evangelical revival of the early to mid 18th century, while the 'Second' refers to the growth of Methodism and the Baptist Church in the early 19th century. With Wolfe referencing charismatic Christianity and 'overtly religious' movements, it is clear that the 'Third Great Awakening' of the late 1960s and 70s does not lack a spiritual dimension. However, it's a climate of faith in which 'God' is peculiarly absent. 'Me', the self, has taken God's place and, although Wolfe is no advocate for the church, the thrust of his argument is that such a turnaround has ushered in a period of stupefying superficiality. Where the sixties might have called on you to 'do your own thing', the 'Me Decade' of the seventies puts its faith in the words of Burger King: 'have it your way'.[23]

When the 'Me Decade' was published, Kenneth Anger was in London trying, once again, to finish *Lucifer Rising*. The project had found a new direction in the early 1970s when, after filming a short section featuring himself as a Magus – a sequence he called *Lucifer Rising Part I* – Anger secured £15,000 worth of funding from the National Film Finance Corporation. A press conference and party in Anger's flat earlier in the year had also generated valuable publicity. It found him rubbing shoulders with the period's other cinematic adventurers, Dennis Hopper,

Alejandro Jodorowsky and Donald Cammell. Where Hopper and Jodorowsky were there to give their support to the project, Cammell went further and agreed to appear as the Egyptian god Osiris. His partner Myriam Gibril was to play the goddess Isis, Marianne Faithfull was enlisted as Lilith and after trying to work with Mick Jagger's brother Chris, Anger found a new Bobby Beausoleil in the form of Leslie Huggins, a young actor who took the role of Lucifer. With financial backing and this cabal of *Performance*-era Rolling Stones alumnae on board, Anger headed off for location shooting in Egypt and Germany. The project would get a further boost in 1972 when Anger struck up a friendship with Led Zeppelin guitarist Jimmy Page. Page was a fellow devotee of Aleister Crowley, and after Anger outlined the idea of *Lucifer Rising* he agreed to compose the soundtrack.

The first version of *Lucifer Rising* had eventually morphed into *Invocation of My Demon Brother* and where that film had mapped out a world in chaos, *Lucifer Rising* circa 1971 was a much more interior affair. Epic in scope and spanning centuries of magickal thinking, it depicts the coming of Lucifer the light-bearer and the arrival of the Aeon of Horus. Full of esoteric imagery and ritualistic detail, Anger begins the film with the appearance of Isis and Osiris. According to their respective myth-cycles, the union of Isis and Osiris results in one of the major deities of the Egyptian pantheon, Horus, the falcon-headed god of the sky and sun. In the film the elements stir in response to Isis and Osiris' conjurations. Lightning cracks the sky as they strive to bring Horus into being. From here Anger cuts to a sequence involving a magician who performs a set of intense rituals culminating in the shedding of blood. Then, in another cut across vast cultural and historical distance, Lilith the sorceress awakens and, in footage taken from the German leg of the shoot, she ascends to the 'ancient moon temple of Externsteine'. These powers activated, Anger then appears as the film's second Magus. He performs a working inside a 'Magick circle inscribed with the names of Crowley's pantheon: Lucifer, Nuit, Hadit, Ra Hoor Khuit, Chaos, Babalon and Lilith'. Following this, and amid more images of cosmic tumult, Lucifer appears. Returning to Isis and Osiris they gaze at a set of glowing flying saucers that appear over Egypt's sacred landscape. Hovering like Horus the falcon and glowing like Lucifer the morning-star, the flying saucers represent the result of the film's heavy magick: the dawn of the new aeon.[24]

Lucifer Rising combines the heady rush of popular occultism with the cosmic speculations of the counterculture. To a writer like Wolfe, the film could easily have stood as an exemplary artwork of the 'Me Decade': a comic-book epic of self-indulgence made by and for 'Flying Saucerites' that spoke loudly but said little. In response Anger would enthusiastically and vociferously argue that there was nothing superficial about the film nor did it advocate the almost misanthropic self-improvement of the Church of Satan. It certainly drew on the same 'vapor' that fed into *Rosemary's Baby* and would re-occur in *The Virgin Sacrifice*. What it really shared with these films, though, was not their giddy fascination with the diabolic but a focus on the emergence of someone or *something* powerful into the world.

For all its emphasis on magickal processes, *Lucifer Rising* was no Faustian drama; it was not about the acquisition of personal power. Instead, it showed a set of devotees giving themselves to a higher cause, that of bringing about the appearance of Lucifer. As Gary Lachman puts it, across the film 'the self is transcended'. It closes with a lingering shot of two colossi with a wisp of smoke between them and 'barely discernible figures crouching on the sand'.[25] There's no sense of a collective 'we' in this all but deserted scene, nor does one sense the victory of the Satanic 'I'. The hint of melancholy in the shot could easily be compared to the tone of lament expressed by Hunter S. Thompson and Jeff Nuttall as they reflect on the dissolution of the counterculture at the end of the sixties. For Anger, though, standing at the dawn of the 'Me Decade', *Lucifer Rising* was there to show that the old energy was still circulating. It was crackling in the air, within reach, but no mass movement was going to be able to channel it. Instead, the task now lay with the adepts and the magi, those prepared to tear the self apart in order to let Lucifer step of out the void.

CHAPTER IX

The Omega Men

It would be 1980 before *Lucifer Rising* really saw the light of day, when it was screened as a complete work at New York's Whitney Museum of American Art. This version did not include the promised soundtrack by Jimmy Page but carried instead a suite of extraordinary, hypnotic music composed by Anger's old partner and first Lucifer, Bobby Beausoleil. Beausoleil was in California's Tracy State Prison serving a life sentence for the murder of Gary Hinman. In October 1976 he heard that Anger had fallen out with Page, and with the superstar guitarist off the project Beausoleil wrote to his former friend and offered to complete their 'unfinished business.' With Anger's agreement, Beausoleil got on with the job and proceeded to spend the next three years locking horns with limited equipment, other incarcerated musicians, and the complexities of the prison system itself, to create a multi-layered, deeply personal, occult-orientated piece of experimental rock music. By the time Beausoleil sent off the final tape in 1979, *Lucifer Rising* – a film that finally clocked in at just over 28 minutes – had been in progress for nearly fourteen years. When the funding had come through in 1971 there had been a spike of publicity and activity, but after this attention dwindled *Lucifer Rising* had become something of a rumour, even when Page came on the scene. In the meantime, cinemagoers who entered the 1970s primed for Anger's purported masterpiece had to look to other screens for traces of that Luciferean spirit. In late 1971 they would have found it in the unlikely form of Boris Sagal's post-apocalyptic thriller *The Omega Man* and its star, the Moses of Hollywood, Charlton Heston.[1]

The Omega Man begins with Heston's character, Robert Neville, living out one of the ultimate dreams of Los Angeles: in a brand-new car and glorious sunshine he drives through streets that are completely devoid of traffic. With the city to himself Neville stops right outside a cinema, strolls in, fires up the projector and starts to watch Michael Wadleigh's *Woodstock* (1970). On-screen, Country Joe and the Fish start their set before a vox-pop with a stoned young man begins. The man is Artie Kornfeld, one of the four partners in Woodstock Ventures who organised the festival. The screen splits so that his interview plays out to a circle of happy people dancing in the crowd. Kornfeld has evidently had a life-changing experience at the festival and he tries his best to put it into words: 'This is really beautiful ... you have to realise the turnaround I've gone through in the last three days.' At this point *The Omega Man* cuts back to Neville who sits alone in the deserted cinema. Grimacing, fully-loaded machine gun by his side and with a familiarity that suggests he's screened *Woodstock* for himself many, many times before, Neville joins in with Kornfeld's speech:

> [...] just to see, just to really realize what's really important. What's really important is the fact that if we can't all live together and be happy, if you have to feel afraid of walking out on the street if you have to be afraid to smile at somebody, right [...]

Cutting back to *Woodstock*, Kornfeld has the last word: 'What kind of a way is that to go through this life?' After watching some more music Neville leaves the cinema and heads off into the twilight, gun in hand. 'No,' he muses to himself, 'they sure don't make pictures like that anymore.' Actually, in Neville's world – Los Angeles

1977 – nobody makes *anything* anymore. As the film's backstory unfolds we learn that sometime in 1975 war on the 'Sino-Russian border' escalated into a 'global conflict' and devastating germ warfare. The plague-like spread of this pandemic decimates human life across the world. Neville, a scientist, stumbles across a vaccine too late for it to be effective. He lives, but billions do not. It is this disaster that has made him the king of the city. Wandering amongst the streets of Los Angeles, empty but for corpses and wreckage, Neville comes to believe he's the only immune survivor: the last man on Earth.[2]

Showing the enormous crowd at Woodstock is a neat way for the makers of *The Omega Man* to emphasise the enormity of Neville's solitude. He is not just on his own, but he is also cut off from the community that such a gathering symbolises: the sharing of the burden; the mutual care and support that comes with human society at its best. At one point in *Woodstock*, Wadleigh includes footage of Hugh Romney (aka Wavy Gravy), an activist and professional clown who, along with his Hog Farm collective, took on the unenviable task of trying to feed the crowd during the festival. Looking down from the stage as his friends distribute bowls of vegetables and cereal we see Romney begin to sermonise. It's not clear if he was thinking about bread and fishes but he nonetheless speaks in sacred terms: 'There's no doubt this is heaven, boys and girls, we are feeding each other.' Although the clip does not appear in *The Omega Man* it perfectly sums up Neville's predicament. Alone after the fall of civilisation with no one to count on but himself, Neville is a man cast out of heaven who exists in the limbo of survival. As the film opens he's managed to avoid the fate that has taken so many, but his life of sifting through the remnants of the city, hopefully clinging to the vestiges of his pre-plague routine, is hardly a life at all. Like Lucifer in John

Milton's *Paradise Lost* (1667) Neville traverses a chaotic space; he's stuck between the hell of the world's end and the teasing heaven of what the late 20th century could have been.[3]

He also has the other devils of the piece to contend with. Neville remains heavily armed because there *are* other inhabitants roaming the city, but he doesn't see them as fellow survivors exactly. They are neither his comrades, his disciples, nor a potential army over which he can be imperious. They're an extremely hostile group who all want him dead. As the film details, for a small number, the plague was not fatal but instead had a mutating effect. In an unapologetic act of disablist demonisation, they're pictured as light-sensitive albinos: vampires of a sort who can only come out at night. When they do, they fanatically set about destroying the remains of contemporary culture to expunge traces of modernity from their new world. Led by Jonathan Matthias, a former newsreader who came to see the plague as a form of 'judgement', the mutants are a cult-like group who call themselves 'the Family'. Sounds familiar. Shrinking from daylight like Manson's followers emerging from the bottomless pit, the Family see themselves as the inheritors of the post-apocalyptic landscape. To them Neville is a man with 'nothing to live for but his memories'. He is a relic of the past and their automatic enemy, a living reminder of the technological era that 'destroyed the world'. With their robes, shades, charismatic long-haired leader and Ron Grainer's groovy Hammond organ score playing nearly every time they appear in the film, the Family are every inch the sixties doomsday cult. At the same time, their misanthropic conflict with Neville, and the setting it plays out in, sees *The Omega Man* firmly consign the sixties to the past: whatever the values and beliefs espoused by Woodstock they're nothing but empty gestures in the disastrous ruins of the future.[4]

*

By 1971 Charlton Heston knew these ruins well. As the displaced astronaut Taylor, he had already explored Earth's post-apocalyptic future in *Planet of the Apes* and in Ted Post's surreal, ultra-nihilistic sequel *Beneath the Planet of the Apes* (1970). Alongside a cast of variously humane, militant and intolerant apes, *Beneath* features an apocalypse cult of mutated humans who hide away in the remains of the New York subway. There they worship a still active nuclear bomb which is detonated once the conflicts of the film spiral out of control. As the film closes with a blinding white-out it's made abundantly clear that the explosion has finally destroyed what remained of the Earth. A grim voiceover announces that a 'green and insignificant planet ... is now dead.'[5]

Few films of the period are as utterly annihilating as *Beneath the Planet of the Apes*, and with its terminal end Post certainly had a good go at topping the climatic twist of the preceding film. This spectacular one-upmanship aside, the idea of an entire planet dying would have carried an added charge for audiences of the early seventies. By 1971 depictions of the Earth as a singular and beautiful green planet were well established as part of a growing ecological awareness and an associated political agenda. In 1967 NASA launched ATS-3, a geostationary weather and communications satellite that took a series of photographs charting the Earth's rotation. The resulting film sequence became the first colour images of the world in motion. A year later the *Apollo 8* mission, under the command of astronaut William Anders, was launched with the goal of entering the Moon's orbit. As Anders and his crew cycled around the lunar surface on 24 December 1968, they were able to see the far distant Earth suspended in space. Anders took a photograph of the sight which became known as 'Earthrise'. It depicted the majesty of the planet, the dynamism of its swirling atmospheric systems but also its utter isolation. Alone in the silence of space, the Earth needed to be cared for if it was going to keep on providing a home for its inhabitants. Command Module Pilot Jim Lovell said as much during the live broadcast from the *Apollo 8* flight: 'The vast loneliness is awe-inspiring and it makes you realize just what you have back there on Earth.'[6]

Stewart Brand, a former Merry Prankster and trained biologist, certainly did realise the Earth's value and sanctity. Witnessing the world from space via 'Earthrise' helped to refine his thinking on what he called the 'Whole Earth'. If this isolated, vulnerable globe was 'our' home, then it needed to be cared for, and such care depended on the realisation that we humans are one species among many. Anticipating the work of chemist and ecologist James Lovelock who proposed the Gaia hypothesis – the notion that the Earth's environment functioned as a vast, interconnected intelligence – Brand's 'Whole Earth' concept uprooted the complacent, anthropocentric assumption that humans held dominion over the planet. The idea – now something of a truism – was that 'we' stand alongside other forms of organic life as co-dependents within the matrix of natural, ongoing systems which keep the world habitable.[7]

This is what Brand saw in the ATS-3 footage: the planet as a complex, organic body within which multiple systems interact:

> You see darkness, then a crescent of dawn, then advancing daylight and immense weather patterns whirling and creeping on the spherical surface then the full round mandala Earth of noon, then gibbous afternoon, crescent twilight and darkness again.

To live – and survive – within this delicate environment, Brand saw it as imperative to adopt a lifestyle of ecological awareness and self-sufficiency. To that end Brand began to publish *The Whole Earth Catalog*, a weighty, beautifully designed sourcebook that provided information about and listed for sale all manner of 'tools'. By 'tools', Brand meant anything – books, equipment, machines, ideas – that could help foster a sense of grassroots independence, an alternative to the control exerted by government and large-scale business interests. This 'personal power' would permit the individual to conduct 'his own education, find his own inspiration, shape his own environment, and share his adventure with whoever is interested'. The first edition of the *Catalog* took as its cover image a still from the ATS-3 film, while the Spring 1969 edition carried the 'Earthrise' photograph.[8]

Unlike the $25 'peace dresses' sold in Sears that so depressed Peter Whitehead, Brand's tome offered little in the way of fashion items or luxury goods. Apart from buckskins and beads there are no listings for clothing. Instead, the *Catalog* leads with listings for such books as Hanns Reich's *The World from Above* (1966), John S. Shelton's *Geology Illustrated* (1966) and NASA's *Earth Photographs from Gemini III, IV and V* (1967). Along with the ATS-3 film, these documents provide views of the Earth's surface, topography and complex landform patterns. Together they present a pointedly depopulated view of the world, reminding us as Brand notes, 'that this beautiful place is scarcely inhabited at all'. According to the *Catalog*, Reich's book contains some aerial photography of urban locations, 'good traffic flow pattern shots' that depict the 'surface anatomy of civilization'. Framed from such high altitude though, the images look more like the abandoned cities of *The Omega Man*. So too with NASA's *Earth Photographs*. Although the Gemini shots of California's Imperial Valley carry an undeniable power, it's difficult to see them and not think of the barren Forbidden Zone in *Planet of the Apes*, released the same year as the first *Catalog*, or the desert of Roger Zelazny's post-apocalyptic novel *Damnation Alley* (1969), published the year after. However, unlike these examples, Brand's interest does not lie in trying to preserve human dominance. Instead, in listing books like *Geology Illustrated* or Theodor Schwenk's study of 'flow forms in water' *Sensitive Chaos* (1965), *The Whole Earth Catalog* placed more emphasis on trying to understand the natural systems – atmospheric, geologic, meteorological and aquatic – that enable human life on Earth. If anything, 'man' with all its problematic baggage is pushed to the margins of the *Catalog*. It is an inventory of the human sciences, but one in which the reader is encouraged to use such knowledge to live in concert with the natural world rather than exploit it.[9]

The Whole Earth Catalog and its philosophy was heavily influenced by the work of polymath and public intellectual *par excellence* R. Buckminster Fuller. Variously described as an 'architect, engineer, geometrician, cartographer, philosopher, futurist' and (not least), 'inventor of the famous geodesic dome', Fuller was an expert in a dizzying array of specialist fields. Much of his work though involved the study of 'synergy', what he defined as 'the behaviour of wholes unpredicted by the behaviour of their parts'. Fuller was fascinated by the interplay of natural, human and mechanical systems and believed that society could greatly benefit from a comprehensive knowledge of their operation.

In 1969 Fuller published *Operating Manual for Spaceship Earth*, a manifesto-like distillation of the varied work he had published and lectured on across the 1960s. It was a brief but suitably wide-ranging study of the social and economic problems facing human society. After castigating our 'vanity, short-sightedness, biases and ignorance in general', Fuller offered his simple but significant mission statement: 'we are all astronauts'. His point was that we humans share the same planet, we share the same resources, and we live in an age of unprecedented wealth; and yet inequality, poverty and the possibility of extinction through environmental damage and nuclear war remain as pressing – and ongoing – points of crisis. The main issue then, according to Fuller, related not to wealth or the politics of war but to the stark matter of how to ensure the survival of life on Earth.

Fuller argued that we will survive if we are prepared to harmonise the natural systems of the Earth and the industrial systems of human culture. For Fuller, the wealth of the Earth is not to be understood merely in financial terms. Industrialised capitalism lives in the shadow of the 'vast amounts of income wealth' that come from fossil fuel deposits, solar radiation and lunar gravity, the forces which 'implement our forward success' as a planet. To maximise these reserves for future life and at the same time to properly realise the full, non-exploitative, potential of industrialisation, Fuller argues for the abandonment of a profit-oriented economy. In a world of affluence and overproduction there is, in theory, no need for in-work poverty and economic inequality. With the right distribution of resources and the will to let automation take its course, Fuller argues that we, the 'Earthians', can be set free to '*think* clearly'. This independence of thought will beget a kind of world 'fellowship' permitting humans to 'accelerate scientific exploration and experimental prototype development'. Thanks to this 'unique [...] metaphysical capability', Fuller argues, the Earth and its collective society will then be supercharged towards further evolution.[10]

The argument is wonderfully, if not naively, utopian, but Fuller carries it with conviction. The confidence and erudition of *Spaceship Earth* makes it feel like the science fictional premise of its title – a blast off into a new way of being – is within reach. It is the perfect theoretical text to go with the practical emphasis of *The Whole Earth Catalog*. Together, they offer a forthright response to the type of apocalyptic fantasies that would appear in *The Omega Man* and *Beneath the Planet of the Apes*. The world is precious, argue Brand and Fuller, but with the right steps forward, building on the countercultural efforts of the 1960s, we can move into a bright future. The problem was, not everyone shared their commitment and their optimism. Particularly in the cinema of the period, images of exhaustion, disillusion and destruction proliferated. There was clearly need for change, but it seemed as if the culture of the late 1960s was neither ready for the type of evolutionary step Fuller envisaged, nor willing to embrace it.

One of the most distinctive films to come out of the turning point between the 1960s and the 1970s was Alejandro Jodorowsky's *El Topo* (1970). Shot in Mexico mainly between August 1969 and September 1970, *El Topo* ('The Mole') grew out of Jodorowsky's dramatic work with the Panic Movement and was essentially an attempt to apply to cinema the visceral intensity of 'ephemeral' panic performances like the 'Melodrama Sacramental' (1965). The film focuses on El Topo, a black-clad gunfighter played by Jodorowsky who seeks out and eventually defeats four mystical 'Masters'. Having completed his quest, El Topo engages in a further series of challenges and confrontations that involve betrayal, transformation and a final act of self-immolation. Enlightenment is sought throughout *El Topo* but it is never fully achieved. Instead, over the course of the film the Mole is constantly blinded by the sun that he seeks.

When it was released in America in December 1970, *El Topo* quickly became a cult hit thanks to a series of late-night screenings at New York's Elgin theatre and plaudits from Yoko Ono and John Lennon. As with Anger's work, not least *Lucifer Rising*, *El Topo* was full to bursting with complex, esoteric symbolism. It was also excruciatingly violent. With its rivers of blood, vivid arterial sprays, and destructive gunfights, *El Topo* was a total assault on the senses, which no doubt accounts for its appeal as a midnight movie. According to the writer Ben Cobb, the 'apocalyptic vision' of *El Topo* was viewed as a clear reflection of its times. In his study of Jodorowsky, *Anarchy and Alchemy* (2008), Cobb reads the director's performance and the look of El Topo – long hair, beard, all sinewy and ready to strike – as an echo of Charles Manson's rattlesnake intensity. Cobb's interpretation is based more on coincidence rather than direct influence – Jodorowsky was well into making *El Topo* when the Manson murders came to light – but it nonetheless evokes the lens through which the film was viewed upon its release. The poet Jack Hirschman, for example, wrote a long, glowing review for *The Staff* in early 1971 in which he claimed *El Topo* had made a stronger impression on him than any film he had seen 'since my mind became planetarily engaged through assassinations and the cartographies of war'. Going on to compare the violence of *El Topo* with that of *Gimme Shelter*, Cobb makes clear what Hirschman was pointing to, that in making the film at the end of the decade, Jodorowsky was 'somehow [anticipating] the dark cloud that rolled in over the halcyon sixties'.[11]

What Cobb calls 'the brutal end of the hippy dream' was displayed more directly in Richard C. Sarafian's road movie *Vanishing Point* (1971). Focusing on Kowalski, an ex-racing driver ex-cop who embarks on a cross-country dash in a ferocious Dodge

Challenger, *Vanishing Point* is another failed quest. Driving at high speed from Denver to San Francisco, Kowalski draws the interstate police forces into an elaborate pursuit, one that ends with a bulldozer roadblock in the Californian desert. As with *Easy Rider*, *Vanishing Point* is a road trip that leads to disaster, but where Billy and Wyatt are stopped in their tracks, Kowalski charges headlong into automotive suicide. Thanks to 'Super Soul', a radio DJ who reports on the chase, Kowalski becomes something of a folk hero during his journey, but the role is of little interest to Kowalski himself. Haunted by personal tragedy and bad memories of the past Kowalski is a man burdened with psychic baggage, and he uses his epic, amphetamine-fuelled driving sessions as a way of flushing it out. According to the film's internal timeframe, all Kowalski's misfortune – including the loss of his career and the death of his girlfriend – happened around 1966, some five years before the events of the main story. Moving into the 1970s, Kowalski thus exists in a kind of post-traumatic state and his restless driving is an attempt to leave these experiences behind, first by way of pure acceleration and then via the fireball that erupts as he finally crashes into the roadblock.[12]

El Topo and *Vanishing Point* are portraits of doom. They are cul-de-sac films that feature isolated figures moving through landscapes of personal, social and cultural disaster. Tonally, they echo two other examples of late-1960s ultraviolence, Sam Peckinpah's *The Wild Bunch* (1969) and Ralph Nelson's *Soldier Blue* (1970). *The Wild Bunch* looks at the closure of a certain vision of the American West at the end of the 19th century while *Soldier Blue* uses a massacre of Cheyenne tribespeople to evoke the brutality of contemporary warfare. What *Vanishing Point* depicted and what *El Topo* appeared to symbolise was a more specific sense of cultural eclipse: the dissipation of the energy of the sixties.

Vanishing Point in particular shows a world in which the collective action typically associated with the era of has faded to the point of disappearance. What's more, there's a distinct sense of 'good riddance'. Characters like Kowalski are not looking to revive this spirit but are merely seeking a way out of the scene altogether.[13]

By the time Jeff Lieberman's *Blue Sunshine* (1978) came along with its former LSD users turned murderers, the sixties were not just an era to be lamented but a force to be feared. In the film, 'Blue Sunshine' is the name of a peculiar form of LSD taken by a group of Stanford students in 1967. Ten years later the after-effects of the drug begin to take hold and they start to suffer from migraines, hair loss and, finally, homicidal bouts of psychosis. The conspiracy culture surrounding LSD use would generate numerous horror stories throughout the 1960s, some of which gained extra validation in light of the MK-ULTRA revelations. *Blue Sunshine* takes these urban legends, cautionary tales and speculative half-truths one step further, with the stable middle-class lives of its educated professionals destroyed due to their youthful experimentation. In Lieberman's hands, the culture of the sixties does not lead to the type of evolutionary leap that Fuller sought, nor is it a source of pleasing nostalgia. Instead, the decade becomes a historical spectre that lies heavy on the present, its acid flashbacks conjuring terrible violence rather than roadmaps to new worlds or pleasant memories of blissed-out afternoons.[14]

Although deeply wedded to the images and ideas of the sixties, films like *Blue Sunshine* were also taking the temperature of the seventies. What it portrayed in its images of former hippies turned monsters was a sense of hostility towards the previous decade and its projects. Put another way, *Blue Sunshine* is a post-psychedelic horror movie that connects the afterlife of the sixties with one of the main political banners of the 1970s, 'Law and Order'.

Richard Nixon had campaigned heavily on the matter throughout 1968 and 1969 and, until the Watergate scandal (which saw him flouting both law *and* order), the issue lay at the heart of his domestic policy. This was an easy card to play because, as Andrea Pitzer points out, 'The crime wave seized on by Nixon was not imaginary':

> Beginning in the 1960s, the United States faced a surge in criminal violence. Across the decade, the murder rate rose by 44 percent, and per capita rates of forcible rape and robbery more than doubled.

According to Pitzer, this 'surge' was linked to the number of male baby-boomers coming of age in the 1960s. For 'middle America' though, the traditionalist sector of the lower middle class – 'blue-collar workers, lower-echelon bureaucrats, schoolteachers, and white-collar employees' – the causes were much more specific. Rising crime levels were the inevitable result of the progressivism of the sixties, the decade's countercultural drive and the apparently 'soft' approach to crime taken first by John F. Kennedy and then by Lyndon Baines Johnson. As Karl Fleming writing for *Newsweek* observed, 'middle Americans felt "threatened by a terrifying array of enemies: hippies, Black Panthers, drugs, the sexually liberated, those who questioned the sanctity of marriage and the morality of work"'.[15]

Middle America was a politically valuable demographic, a group who by 1969 made up – in economic terms at least – '55 per cent of the population'. To them, a challenge to the status quo did not mean a potentially liberating change in consciousness or social position but a change in the consensus; a disturbing challenge to 'normality', the 'stability and predictability of established ways'. As Peter Schrag put it in his *Harper's* article 'The Forgotten American' (1969):

> Whatever law and order means, for example, to a man who feels his wife is unsafe on the street after dark or in the park at any time, or whose kids get shaken down in the school yard, it also means something like normality – the demand that everybody play it by the book, that cultural and social standards be somehow restored to their civics-book simplicity, that things shouldn't be as they are but as they were supposed to be.

As well as *Blue Sunshine*, films like Don Siegel's *Dirty Harry* (1971) featuring Clint Eastwood's tough, uncompromising cop Harry Callahan, played directly into these fears. Set in contemporary San Francisco the film features a murderous rooftop sniper who goes by the name 'Scorpio'. Screenwriters Rita and Harry Fink were heavily influenced by the local and then still ongoing case of the 'Zodiac Killer', a masked, heavily armed murderer active in the Bay Area from the late 1960s onwards. By 1971 the investigation had built up a suspect profile of a 'military man, most likely from the Navy or Airforce', aged around 30 but possibly older based on the language of the coded, cryptic letters he sent to the police and the *San Francisco Chronicle*. In *Dirty Harry*, however, Scorpio, played by Andy Robinson, is a young man in his mid to late twenties who, with paisley shirts and a crop of long, scraggly hair, is clearly intended to represent a psychotic hippie. Early in the film it becomes clear that Callahan has form in dealing with *perps* like Scorpio, the apparently antisocial and deviant members of the San Franciscan counterculture. Sometime around 1969–70 he's said to have shot a man 'in the Fillmore district'. In an utterly unsubtle nod to the violence Callahan will soon mete out on Scorpio, he offers an unapologetic defence of his actions: 'When an adult male is chasing a female with an intent to commit rape, I shoot the bastard. That's my policy.' Roving killers, rapists, robbery, drugs, unsafe streets: if middle America entered the seventies with the sense that 'things shouldn't be as they are', it was the shoot first 'policy' of *Dirty Harry* that promised to resolve the crisis in law, order and social values; to put things back 'as they were supposed to be'.[16]

Upon its release *Dirty Harry* generated a certain amount of controversy with film critic Pauline Kael claiming it had fully realised the 'fascist potential' of the action movie genre. But it was precisely the tolerant agenda of these liberal voices that the film, its sequels *Magnum Force* (1973) and *The Enforcer* (1976), as well as the likes of *The French Connection* (1971) and *Death Wish* (1974), were responding to. Their characters belligerently broke the rules because they believed the progressive system that issued them was no longer fit for purpose. These films seemed to accept without irony the image of the boot 'stamping on a human face' from George Orwell's *Nineteen Eighty-Four* (1949), by suggesting that force was necessary to curb the damage done by the political weakness of the previous decade. Others, like Stanley Kubrick's *A Clockwork Orange* (1971), were more ambivalent. While teen gangs like the Droogs revel in the old ultraviolence, the brutalising methods of psychological conditioning used to curb their behaviour are equally disturbing. Neither anarchy nor authority has the upper hand in Kubrick's dystopian portrait of a near-future society. He offered a cautionary tale aimed at liberals and conservatives alike by showing where 'we' in the West might be heading but would not wish to live. By contrast, there's nothing science fictional or even satirical about *Dirty Harry* and *Death Wish*. They're political fantasies that revel in the dream of swift justice. Consciously or not the images of Eastwood clutching his .44 Magnum, 'the most powerful handgun the in the world', and Charles Bronson stalking public parks looking for 'freaks' to shoot in *Death Wish* became avatars for Nixon-era republicanism.[17]

It was easy to make such an analogy because even before these films had reached the screen Nixon – like a frustrated cop defying his chief – had already thrown out the rulebook when it came to legal procedure. Before entering office he had practised as an attorney, but as President, Nixon seemed neither to know nor to care about the need for delicacy when it came to public statements about active cases. On 2 August 1970, at a law enforcement conference in Denver, the President heavily criticised the media and its coverage of the ongoing Manson trial, claiming that it glorified and made 'heroes out of those engaged in criminal activities':

> I noted, for example, the coverage of the Charles Manson case ... Front page every day in the papers. It usually got a couple of minutes in the evening news. Here is a man who was guilty, directly or indirectly, of eight murders. Yet here is a man who, as far as the coverage is concerned, appeared to be a glamorous figure.

'Manson Guilty Nixon Declares' ran the headline in the *LA Times* the following day. Manson's defence team 'moved for a mistrial' because there were concerns members of the jury would be influenced by the story. The White House press secretary then hastily issued a statement claiming that the President had intended to use the word 'alleged'. Whatever the spin, the implication of Nixon's comments was clear. In a foreshadowing of Donald Trump's campaign against 'fake news' Nixon was suggesting that in failing to adopt an automatic and unwavering hard line against this case and others, the media were working against the government's agenda on crime.[18]

It was not just Manson who caught Nixon's attention. Timothy Leary was equally held up as a threat to public order. In January 1970, after much legal wrangling, he had finally been sentenced to a total of twenty years in jail for charges relating to drug possession. This came after two arrests (one in 1965 and one in 1968) for the possession of marijuana. To his supporters it was clear that an example was being made of Leary – the high-profile voice of the psychedelic movement – and the marijuana charges provided the convenient pretext to get him in court. However, if conservative America breathed a sigh of relief as their arch-enemy disappeared behind bars, their satisfaction would be short-lived. In September 1970, a few months after arriving at his low-security prison in San Luis Obispo, Leary was sprung from jail by members of the Weather Underground. Funded by the Brotherhood of Eternal Love, a group of Californian drug distributors, the escape required Leary to scale the prison walls via a precarious wire cable before various Weathermen spirited him away. They helped him get out of the US and travel to Algeria where he joined Eldridge Cleaver and the Black Panther Party in their 'government in exile' before seeking further sanctuary in Switzerland with the arms dealer Michel Hauchard.

Soon after the escape, the Weather Underground 'issued a communiqué claiming responsibility'. According to Stewart Tendler and David May, they saw it as 'another blow against the "belly of the beast" ... a tremendous propaganda coup freeing a political prisoner from the State's POW camp'. But in springing Leary as part of their 'war', the Weather Underground had only really gained victory in a single battle. The real spoils of the propaganda war had gone to the establishment, what the Weather Underground termed 'pig Amerika'. Particularly in the light of Leary's own post-escape statement in which he called for acts of 'sabotage and hijackings' and declared himself 'armed and [...] dangerous', it was easy to paint Leary as a man who *should* be behind bars. Here was the author of *The Psychedelic Experience*, a book that had looked forward to a blissful new age of chemical enlightenment, on the lam with gun runners and armed revolutionaries. In 1968 Leary had declined to take part in the Chicago demonstrations for fear of violence but by late 1970 the man who, according to Nixon, was the most dangerous in America was promising violence against anyone who threatened his 'life and freedom'. Thanks to this language and the circumstances of his escape, Leary's new life as a fugitive easily fed into the emerging narrative that the sixties had yielded a welter of aggression, militarism and terror. Manson, Leary and everyone in between, they were all the same: the product of a decade that was too soft on the younger generation and let them get away with too much. In response, Nixon assumed the role of disciplinarian. His domestic policy was a clean-up job, a battery of measures designed to straighten out the disorder caused by the irresponsibility of the sixties.[19]

'Law and Order', as Pitzer continues, offered subsequent presidents Gerald Ford, Jimmy Carter and Ronald Reagan a guaranteed vote-winning platform, particularly in light of the assassination attempts that each faced during their terms of office. Of these, the most damning for the legacy of the sixties was Lynette 'Squeaky' Fromme's attempt to shoot President Ford in Sacramento on

5 September 1975. Fromme was a member of the Family. Along with another member, Sandra Good, she had remained in contact with the incarcerated Manson and both had continued to do his bidding. At Manson's suggestion they had adopted nun-like roles under the guise of an ecological protest group, ATWA (Air, Trees, Water and Animals). On the day of the alleged assassination attempt, Fromme, wearing a red robe and brandishing a handgun, confronted Ford during a walkabout in Sacramento's Capitol Park. She aimed, pulled the trigger, but the gun failed to go off. Fromme later claimed not to have wanted to kill Ford but to draw attention instead to the aims of ATWA.[20]

Within such an atmosphere of incipient violence, it seemed necessary for politicians to advocate the use of police force as a weapon in the 'war' on crime. Beyond this pragmatism, there was also the need to respond to the 'counter-revolution' of political support mounted by middle America, also known as 'the Silent Majority' or the 'frustrated middle'. As Schrag described it, 'the middle American' who is 'free, white and twenty-one', who 'has a job, a home, a family and is up to his eyeballs in credit', is 'perhaps the most alienated person in America'. While 'he' does 'all the right things, obeys the law, goes to church and insists [...] that his kids get a better education than he had', this same 'he' also sees federal funding go elsewhere. In the late sixties and into the early seventies such funding was spent, says Schrag, on 'the poor, on the inner cities (e.g. Negroes) and the unemployed'. To middle America – the comfortable, reasonably well off, reasonably secure demographic who wanted their lives to go on being comfortable – welfare, public support for marginalised communities and threatening stories of 'positive' discrimination amounted to a toxic mix. Such measures, indicative of a sense of social mission and born, in part, out of the climate of the sixties, symbolised the provision of help given to those who didn't *deserve* it, which made life harder for 'good Americans', who felt they'd *worked* for it. Schrag offers the example of a widow in Chicago 'with three children who earns $7,000 a year' but who can't get her children 'college loans because she makes too much; the money is reserved for people on relief'. In a reverse of the situation in Morningside Heights that sowed the seeds of the Columbia occupation, Schrag adds that 'New schools are built in the ghetto but not in the white working-class neighborhoods where they are just as dilapidated'.

In writing 'The Forgotten American', Schrag was not presenting a manifesto on behalf of white, middle-class entitlement. Rather, he was trying to account for what he saw as a series of major divisions in American society and how a tide of 'resentments' were yielding increasing support for conservative politics. Nixon recognised this and cultivated his base of support via rhetoric aimed at the tensions existing across the boundaries of class and race. In particular, there was a distinct racist undertone carried by the politics of 'Law and Order' which implicitly linked civil rights advances with rising crime rates. Disorder, Nixon's policies suggested, was a 'problem' of black and minority communities. Stokely Carmichael was well aware of this form of prejudice, remarking in 1967 in 'Black Power' that acts of 'rebellion' against institutionalised racism were invariably termed 'riots' by the white press. Journalists like Seymour Hersh and conspiracy theorists like Mae Brussell also argued that the covert activities of Operation Chaos saw black radicalism as an active source of subversion in American society. But, once again, if there was any doubt about the pervasiveness of this thinking in the public imagination you need only look at *Dirty Harry*. In the now iconic scene where Callahan asks the 'punk' if he 'feels lucky', it's a *black* punk he's talking to. The wounded man who lies on the ground as Callahan taunts him is part of a gang of bank robbers made up entirely of young black men. In less time than it takes for Callahan to eat his hot dog lunch, he's killed all but one of them with neither remorse nor consequence. It's worth noting that the scene begins with Callahan getting a whiff that a '211' – a bank robbery – might be 'in progress.' What sparks his finely tuned cop senses? Close to the bank he sees a black man in a parked car with the engine running. He *must* be the getaway driver. Why else would a black man be there?[21]

Stoking fear while promising security, garnering support from the majority by demonising minorities, 'Law and Order' quickly became the mother tongue of 1970s politics in America, a thinly-veiled code by which the liberalism, civil rights advances and countercultural shifts of the 1960s could be castigated and rolled back. In the immediate post-Manson days of December 1969, the *International Times* was already feeling the effects of this change in attitude, which was not just limited to the American cultural agenda. Writing from their London outpost, the 'Editorial Group' used the paper's December 18–31 issue to decry 'the hysterical spate of evil propaganda dished out about Hippies' which 'gives the Maniac American and the English Hypocrite the signal to lynch long-hairs on sight.' Conjuring the reactionary voices of such propagandists, the editorial notes that a particularly intense level of hysteria is directed towards 'the daring drug-heads':

> who are clamoring for Lucifer in Sugar Cubes ... and the evil cannabis resin. We already know that Acid created Satan, and Speed was directly responsible for Pinkville. Next it will be said that those who carried out 'The Moors Murders' were heavy LSD gurus.

Within this climate, a concern for rehabilitation, attention paid to matters of social justice, and an attempt to identify the socioeconomic factors that cause people to offend were seen as concessions that had eroded respect for the law. While films like *Dirty Harry* took the contemporary pulse and argued that something needed fixing here and now, in the 1970s, *Blue Sunshine*, for all its exaggerated horrors, took a longer view. With its scenes of acid-inspired homicide that virtually dramatised 'the hysterical spate of evil propaganda' decried by *International Times*, the film offered an amplified view of what could happen if the liberalism of the sixties was allowed to percolate beyond the bounds of the decade. As its tag line warned, as if evoking the Republican party addressing Middle America: 'It could happen to you.'[22]

Back in 1971, *The Omega Man* had already come up with a plan to 'tackle' such disorder, and it was just as unforgiving as the 'policy' of *Dirty Harry*: kill or cure. Having spent the first part of the film trying to wipe out the Family, Neville encounters a group of survivors living outside the city and gradually modifies his genocidal attitude. With their encouragement he makes a serum from his blood and toys with the idea of offering it to Matthias. However, when one of the survivors dies at the hands of the Family, Neville's humanitarianism evaporates, and he returns to his tried and tested method of extermination with extreme prejudice. Mortally wounded in the final moments of the film, Neville passes the serum on to the band of survivors. Having begun *The Omega Man* as a post-apocalyptic Lucifer cast out of heaven and left alone, raging against his fate, Neville ends it as a Messiah. Shedding blood to bring an end to the plague, he becomes the saviour who sacrifices himself for the good of the world to come. It is into this world that the band of survivors drive as the film ends. Youthful, resourceful and responsible, they are a much more conventional family than Matthias' cult and point to the revival of traditional values amid the ruins. This is what Neville has been fighting for.

Despite lamenting the failed promise of Woodstock, at no point in *The Omega Man* does Neville try to instigate a 'turn-around' to a 'new' or 'alternative' society. That way lies the horror of the Family. Rather, with his memories, his routines and his trappings of contemporary urban life, Neville is self-appointed custodian of pre-apocalypse America, fully prepared to use force to preserve his view of the world. Despite its clear anti-war stance and the progressivism of its interracial kiss between Neville and Lisa, one of the survivors, *The Omega Man* is a conservative fantasy in countercultural clothes. It offered the ultimate riposte to films like *Lucifer Rising*: nobody wants the New Age. If the sixties are going to flower into the Aeon of Horus, this era of the child will need someone around to clear up the mess it makes. Like a parent tidying up after their kid's party, these strong figures will have to make sure that everything is brought back under control.

In a 1993 interview David Jay Brown put it to Robert Anton Wilson that 'The whirlwind ecstasies of the sixties have, for many, settled down into a gentle breeze'. What did Wilson now feel 'were the fleeting and lasting effects of this cultural phenomena'? Largely ignoring the invitation to talk about countercultural trends in the 1990s, Wilson focused his reply on the early 1970s and the work of Buckminster Fuller:

> I think Bucky Fuller hit the nail on the head. He said that around 1972, the brighter people realized that there are more effective ways of challenging the system than going

out in the streets and running their heads against policemen's clubs. So, they got more subtle.[23]

While *The Omega Man* was working through its reactionary bombast and *Dirty Harry* was helping Hollywood to put the old order back together, some of this 'subtlety' could be found in Jodorowsky's follow-up to *El Topo, The Holy Mountain* (1973).

Part-funded by John Lennon, *The Holy Mountain* was based on René Daumal's surrealist novel *Mount Analogue* (1952). In Daumal's book the mountain – the space of enlightenment – is only visible to those who search for it. Ascent requires a process of initiation in which the seeker must map out the spiritual, psychological and deeply personal pathway they intend to follow. In *The Holy Mountain*, a thief and a group of wealthy industrialists join an Alchemist (played by Jodorowsky) on a quest for 'the great secret', the 'secret of immortality: to be like gods.' To embark on the journey each initiate must purge themselves of their material goods, then their inhibitions, and then their anxieties and psychological hang-ups: all the markers of their individual personalities. Free of this baggage, the group travel to the foot of the Holy Mountain where they find a carnivalesque way station full of those who failed to complete the journey. This space – the Pantheon Bar – is full of temptations and sensory pleasures. It is Jodorowsky's decadent version of the Slough of Despond, the classic obstacle that threatens to waylay the quester. It is also overflowing with the conventional trappings of the counterculture: poetry, drugs and 'free' love.

Despite his links to the world of the Beatles, the 'trippy' nature of his films and their unquestionably hip credentials as midnight movies, Jodorowsky often stood at a critical distance from that taken to be the counterculture. Discussing his filmmaking process, he claimed to ask of 'cinema what most North Americans ask of psychedelic drugs', a comparison that suggests Jodorowsky 'uses' cinema *rather than* psychedelic drugs. Judging by the Pantheon Bar, drugs and the wider psychedelic culture stand in the way of true enlightenment. Whether chemical, aspirational or mystical, messiah figures have no place in Jodorowsky's spiritual world. They can only ever be false masters who obscure the true path ahead. Climbing the Holy Mountain does not require these supplements and prosthetics. Ascension is a process that must be activated *within*, when everything else has been stripped away. As Jodorowsky put it when summarising his spiritual outlook: 'I don't believe in god [...] I know god'.[24]

Although its action is anything but subtle and an ominous mood persists throughout, parts of *El Topo* present a similar outlook. Characters use violence to attack and destroy each other, but violence also offers El Topo a means of stripping away the seemingly inauthentic layers of his identity. As in *The Holy Mountain*, the film is full of objects and attributes being jettisoned: clothes, possessions, hair, personalities. Bodies are ruptured and destroyed; identities are taken up and dispensed with seemingly at will. When El Topo burns himself at the climax of the film, the sequence is given the subtitle 'Apocalypse'. It's an appropriate word given the amount of death and destruction on display elsewhere in the scene, but it also calls upon an earlier, biblical use of the word 'apocalypse' that means 'revelation'. It's in this sense that the scene is apocalyptic. El Topo's death in flames is not the end of the character, exactly, but it is revealed as an act of transformation. Unlike Thích Quảng Đức, the Buddhist monk who burnt himself to death in Saigon on 11 June 1963, El Topo's immolation is not intended as a protest. His body is destroyed, but as the film closes another character, Hijo – El Topo's son – exits wearing his father's black clothes. An identity has been passed on. El Topo's death does not involve the type of transcendence seen in *The Omega Man*, nor is there any sign of the spectacular changes experienced by David Bowman in *2001*. Jodorowsky is not interested in such singular transformations. He focuses instead on the intersection of one lifecycle and another. Buried among the atrocities and transgressions, something quietly synergetic takes place as *El Topo* ends.[25]

Spaceship Earth, Fuller argued, was synergetic: its various systems operated together to permit survival. The gases 'given off respiratorily by Earth's green vegetation' are essential to mammal life while the 'gases which they give off respiratorily are essential to the support of the vegetation.' It's an interplay that works perfectly, despite there being nothing about each system to suggest such an outcome. This is how the world operates but we so often fail to see it because 'the business of the whole,' as Fuller notes, is typically given over to figures of singular authority, 'the feudal kings or local politicians,' and is thus understood in such monolithic terms.[26] It is this way of thinking that Jodorowsky's films work against. By destroying his central character, Jodorowsky ultimately removes from *El Topo* his own figure of singular authority. What remains is a pile of charred bones, a clutch of memories, a set of clothes and someone else wearing them. In one sense, El Topo has been annihilated but in another he persists, only in a variety of different forms at once. Elsewhere in *El Topo* Jodorowsky's camera lingers over gravestones covered in honey around which a swarm of bees circulate. While it is easy to see death as a terminal event, in these moments Jodorowsky shows how it is also one biological process that interacts with many others. To transcend in this world means to join with these multiple systems, and Jodorowsky ultimately has El Topo open out to embrace this. More broadly, Jodorowsky's films are quests away from the centre, movements outside the influence of homelands and routines, teachers and leaders. They advocate views that are neither establishmentarian nor 'countercultural'. There's no truth, *The Holy Mountain* suggests, in LSD and psychedelia nor is there any need to put your faith in figures of authority. The 'secret' is to forget yourself and walk on, to the land unmapped. 'Goodbye Holy Mountain', says Jodorowsky at the end of the film when the great quest has been revealed as a cosmic joke, 'Real life awaits'.[27]

Compare this to what Timothy Leary was writing in 1973. Following his escape, Leary's life as a fugitive took him as far as Afghanistan until he was rearrested and sent to California's Folsom prison, what he called 'the Black Hole of American Society'. There, shortly after his arrival, he wrote a strange but optimistic missive which he published as *Starseed: A Psi-Phy Comet Tale* (1973). *Starseed* was, in Leary's words, an essay he 'transmitted' soon after he read a book from the prison library, Bernard Lovell's *The Exploration of Outer Space* (1962). Lovell's final chapter contained 'a drawing of the remnant of a living organism found on a meteorite' and Leary saw this as a 'the first signal from extra-terrestrial life'. At the same time, Leary heard the news that Kohoutek, a newly observed comet, was to pass the Earth during the fall of 1973. He took this as confirmation that 'extraplanetary contact' with Kohoutek, or as he named it 'Starseed', was about to occur. According to Leary such an encounter was necessary in an age of human crisis, one marked by 'Drought. Famine. Shortage. Pollution. Malaise. Disorder. Tyranny. Espionage.' The appearance of Kohoutek marked the arrival of a 'Higher Intelligence' that transcended the politics responsible for these problems. To ensure human survival beyond this time of emergency it was vital that we put aside short-sighted concerns and evolved in its direction. To Leary, Kohoutek was the herald of this change, the signal that it was 'about time to mutate', to '[c]reate and transmit the new philosophy'.[28]

Given Leary's personal circumstances in 1973 it's not surprising that he would begin to imagine a cosmic source of deliverance, a flash of brilliant light that would release him from the black hole of Folsom. That said, his message of 'hope and interstellar love' was not just an over-optimistic response to the bleak prospect of his imprisonment. In essence, Leary was offering the same argument that Anger was outlining in *Lucifer Rising*; *Starseed* spoke with the same anticipation as the astrologers who looked forward to the Age of Aquarius. But it also mirrored the conservative fantasies that gave rise to *The Omega Man* and *Dirty Harry*. Although poles apart politically, what each of these works have in common is the desire for a figurehead, a leader; they each wish for the appearance of a powerful individual who will bring an end to a period of crisis and usher in a new way of thinking. Whether to the benefit of the political left or the political right, and whether directed towards pushing order into liberating chaos or chaos into establishmentarian order, it's a deeply egocentric model. The mess will be sorted out as soon as some kind of modern messiah, superhero or super*cop* shows up. And look, a cynic might reasonably say, where this desire leads to by the end of the sixties: Leary, the Weather Underground, the Black Panthers and other radical factions pushing against the world while Nixon's crusade of Law and Order pushes back the other way.

Meanwhile, alongside this polarisation of culture and counterculture there remained the ecstatic invitation to ego loss that powered Jodorowsky's films. There was also *The Whole Earth Catalog* with its concern for the *eco* not the *ego* and its fascination with the beautiful complexity of the Earth's finely tuned mechanism. As various types of Omega Men were banging their heads together at the start of the 1970s, these projects were following Fuller's lead. They were attempting to open out the head to access the synergistic world around them. The 'last man' was being consigned to history and in his place another way of coming together was mapped out: a future of networks, feedback loops and ecosystems.

CHAPTER X

The New Jerusalem

Time to get away.

In the immediate aftermath of Sharon Tate's death, Roman Polanski mourned in public. Reporters and television cameras turned up *en masse* to Tate's funeral in Culver City on 13 August and Polanski found himself swept up in a rumour mill of speculation and scandal. The media were presenting him as everything from grieving husband to intended target, or even perpetrator, of the murders. Keen to put across his own perspective, Polanski returned to Cielo Drive on 17 August. With him were a writer–photographer team from *Life*, Thomas Thompson and Julian Wasser, as well as the television psychic Peter Hurkos. Hurkos had been a friend of one of those killed at Cielo Drive, the hairdresser Jay Sebring, and he claimed that by using ESP (extrasensory perception) he could glean information about the crime.

Hardly anything had been changed since the evening of the ninth and for Polanski 10050 Cielo Drive, now a crime scene rather than a home, had become utterly uncanny, truly *unhomely*: a disturbing mix of the familiar and the unfamiliar. It was all there, just as he remembered it, but there were other, horrible things too: the vivid marks of murder. Blood stains covered the floor and the walls, much of the furniture was in disarray giving an uneasy impression of the struggles that had ensued, and throughout the house the air was heavy with the chemical traces of forensic analysis. Worst of all, there was an overwhelming sense of absence. Tate was not there, nor were her and Polanski's friends, nor was their child. Weeping in the bedroom, Polanski suddenly realised this attempt at catharsis was too much, far too soon. He left the house, and it wasn't long before he left the country.

Early 1970 found Polanski in Switzerland and from there he went to London. Having abandoned *The Day of the Dolphin*, the film he was preparing at the time of Tate's death, he plunged into a new project. With the theatre critic Kenneth Tynan, Polanski started work on a film version of Shakespeare's *Macbeth* (1603). As 1970 drew on, he moved further out. Location shooting for what became *Roman Polanski's Macbeth* (1971) took the director through North Wales and then on to the borderlands and the ancient sites of pilgrimage: Lindisfarne and the beaches of Northumberland.[1]

Peter Whitehead also made a break for it in late 1969. Although he had not experienced trauma of the magnitude suffered by Polanski, he was nevertheless exhausted after making *The Fall*. After spending the previous two years shuttling between London and New York, deeply embedded in a culture of protest, radicalism and assassination, Whitehead wanted a change of pace. And so, shortly after showing *The Fall* at the Edinburgh Film Festival in September, he retreated into the Scottish Highlands in pursuit of wild falcons.

This desire for a new direction had been bubbling for a while but, by Whitehead's own account, the specific decision to take up falconry was made during the festival. Something changed in him when he encountered an old man feeding a flock of birds. This man seemed to know each bird by name. As Whitehead sat and watched this moment of gentle connection, all his frustrations about filmmaking were brought into sharp relief. Film had made him a voyeur: present, watching but never fully *there*. Whitehead had spent so long looking through the camera that it had affected his view of the world. 'I had become film', he would later say, sounding not unlike a burnt-out YouTuber, 'I could not walk down the street without editing, panning, zooming'. To remedy this, Whitehead decided to bring a 'real, living, breathing' creature into his life. He wanted to experience the Edinburgh man's almost psychic connection with the birds in the square. Whitehead left the festival seized with the urge to train and fly a falcon. Whitehead continued to make films throughout the 1970s. He made live concert films like *Led Zeppelin at the Albert Hall* (1970) and more personal, creative projects like *Daddy* (1973) with the artist Niki de Saint Phalle and *Fire in the Water* (1977) with Nathalie Delon. Falconry remained, though, an abiding obsession. As the 1970s progressed he immersed himself in the mythology of the falcon and travelled across the world tracking and training in the wilds of Morocco, Alaska, Pakistan and Saudi Arabia.[2]

Geographically and psychologically, Whitehead and Polanksi were moving in different directions at the end of the sixties. That they should each perform such radical departures, however, was not an uncommon response to the closure of the decade. In 'The White Album', Joan Didion reflects on this mood, describing at the end of the essay her own move in January 1971 from Franklin Avenue in Hollywood to 'a place on the sea'. Franklin Avenue is where Didion had hosted long sixties parties; it's where she hung out with rock stars and talked about New Age ideas. It's also where she received creepy phone calls, had strange visits from a private detective and where she was living when 'word of the murders on Cielo Drive travelled like bushfire through the community'. While 9 August 1969 was for many in her circle the exact moment when 'the Sixties ended abruptly', the decade truly ended for Didion in 1971 when she made the break and took up residence elsewhere. As she puts it, the house on the sea 'had been very much a part of the Sixties' and it was littered with reminders of its recent history: 'a piece of Scientology literature beneath a drawer lining, a copy of *Stranger in a Strange Land* stuck deep on a closet shelf'. These Manson-era relics are the texts that have haunted the earlier pages of the essay and so, by getting down to some serious house clearing Didion is able to cast them out. The essay and her experience of 'the Sixties' thus end with an act of expulsion. Construction work is done on the house and between 'the power saws and the sea wind', Didion tells us, 'the place got exorcised'.[3]

The end of 'The White Album' reads like a long sigh of relief. Didion moves into her new house seemingly intent on forgetting the old one and the decade it played host to. Part way through Whitehead's film *Daddy*, there's a short scene imbued with a similar feeling of release. Whitehead shot the film during the summer of 1972 on the grounds of a large, isolated chateau in the south of France. For the most part he stayed behind the camera, content to let de Saint Phalle work through her intense psychodrama with 'Daddy', the film's villain, played by Rainer Diez. At one point, though, Whitehead appears on-screen as Daddy's falconer. He is visible swinging a lure as his bird swoops down from above and flies the length of the chateau's palatial garden. Amid all the transgressive strangeness of the film, Whitehead looks a model of calm during this fleeting cameo. He is, to all intents and purposes, alone with his falcon in the French countryside. There are no references to *The Fall* or to its themes of pop, politics and protest. The tumult of the late 1960s seems to have slipped away into planetary recession.[4]

In the case of Polanski, however, making *Macbeth* did not appear to bring him any relief or closure. Nor did it act as a personal exorcism. If anything, the film brought his ghosts into sharper focus. Released in the autumn of 1971, Polanski's *Macbeth* was suffused with the trauma of the Manson murders. Featuring Jon Finch in the title role and Francesca Annis as Lady Macbeth, the film is full of home invasions, brutal killings and an all-pervading atmosphere of witchcraft. All this, of course, is faithful to the original play, but Polanski seemed intent on rendering Shakespeare's material in the bloodiest and most personal way possible. When Finch's young, lithe, long-haired Macbeth creeps into King Duncan's bedchamber and stabs him, it's hard not to see the knives that descended on Tate, her friends and the LaBiancas. In Polanski's hands the horror of the scene comes not from the awfulness of regicide but from the sheer mess Macbeth's knife makes of the King. At one point during the production Tynan questioned the need for such graphic detail, to which Polanski reportedly replied: 'You didn't see my house last summer. I know about bleeding.' Although he was thousands of miles away from Los Angeles there was a big part of Polanski that had never really left Cielo Drive. Publicly he may have been stoically ploughing on with his career, but psychologically Polanski was still weeping in the bedroom.

One of Shakespeare's most affecting scenes in *Macbeth* comes when Macduff learns his house has been 'surprised' and Macbeth's men have killed his wife and children. 'All?' he asks in utter incomprehension, 'All my pretty chickens?' Played by Terence Bayler in Polanski's film, Macduff sinks to his knees upon hearing the news and in a gesture of grief and denial pulls a cowl over his face. The same feeling emanates from one of Julian Wasser's photographs of Polanski taken during the visit to Cielo Drive. Sat alone and inconsolable at the front of the house, the word 'PIG' still visible on the door, he exudes a sense of overwhelming desolation. For Macduff, hearing the news becomes a turning point: it's this moment in the play that he resolves to take revenge and meet Macbeth in battle. Polanski's response to grief, it seems, was to make the film. Rather than taking up arms he projected his bad feelings onto the screen. When he left America, then, and retreated into the British landscape, Polanski was not trying to forget or to cast out the terrible events of 1969. He was attempting to confront them head-on.[5]

*

By the time Whitehead was living with falcons, Polanski had arrived in North Wales and Didion had found her house by the sea, heading out to 'the country' had become something of a trend, almost a rite of passage for those who had made it to the late sixties. As the new decade took hold edgelands, borderlands and other rural landscapes exerted a powerful gravitational pull on the sixties diaspora. For the Rolling Stones, the attraction was mainly financial. Soon after leaving Altamont in their helicopters, the band found they were heavily in debt. The combination of a massive tax bill from the Inland Revenue, plus manager Allen Klein allegedly withholding millions in royalties, meant that the Stones had no funds to run their day-to-day operations. As Robert Greenfield describes it, the solution to this mess was to leave the country and become tax exiles, to 'drop Klein and drop out of England'. In April 1971 they headed off to France with the intention of living there for at least a year. Holed up in the faded luxury of the Villa Nellcôte on the Côte d'Azur, theirs would be a decadent exile, one in which Keith Richards, his partner Anita Pallenberg and their entourage of friends and fixers would give free rein to their infatuation with heroin. The Stones also recorded some music. All the ideas, enthusiasms, mind games, drug highs and comedowns that coloured their residency at Nellcôte found their way into a new collection of songs which would finally give rise to the album, *Exile on Main Street* (1972).

Although the Stones were, as Greenfield points out, the first English band to 'decamp *en masse* for foreign shores', the idea of musicians getting away from it all for business, creative or chemical reasons wasn't new. Steve Winwood's band Traffic had retreated to rural Berkshire to write *Mr. Fantasy* (1967). Led Zeppelin had gone to Bron-Yr-Aur, an isolated cottage in the Welsh mountains, to work out the songs for *Led Zeppelin III* (1970), and when the time came to record *Led Zeppelin IV* (1971), the whole band assembled at Headley Grange, a mansion in rural Hampshire. At the same time the Incredible String Band were experimenting with group living in a farmhouse in Wales and then on a farm on the Scottish borders, while back over in Berkshire, John Lennon and Yoko Ono were becoming JOHNANDYOKO in their country pile, Tittenhurst Park.[6]

Elsewhere, the practical, 'back to the land' philosophy promoted by the likes of *The Whole Earth Catalog* had increasingly found form in a series of rural communes as well as more high-concept community projects like Drop City in Colorado. Established in 1965 by art students Gene and JoAnn Bernofsky, Richard Kallweit and Clark Richert, Drop City was intended as an autonomous, non-hierarchical space for the production of art. With its cluster of geodesic domes, it was an attempt to put into practice the synergy between natural and human systems that Buckminster Fuller would later cite as essential for the functioning of Spaceship Earth. Although courageously ambitious, Drop City was very short-lived. Despite attracting others to join in the community, a series of internal tensions meant that by 1968 many of the core group had left. This set the pattern for similar communes that appeared at the intersection of the 1960s and 1970s: with a few exceptions they were either unsustainable experiments or became cultish hives, as was the case with the Manson Family and Mel Lyman's Fort Hill Community in Boston. Bands probably had more success when living and working communally because they were going on retreat to work on a specific project, one that had an outcome in mind other than the wholesale rejection of the world and its way of life. However, the rock 'n' roll retreat shared a sense of necessity with the utopian commune: when life in the city became too much or the workaday world became too bleak; when all the drugs had gone or the addictions had become too severe; when the money started to run out or things simply became too *heavy*, eco-activists and acid-fried musicians alike made a break for the pleasures of the pastoral. In their yurts, domes, cottages and crumbling mansions they could 'reconnect' and engage in the nebulous art of finding oneself.[7]

There was an air of romanticism about these flights from the city. Like the speaker in William Wordsworth's poem 'Tintern Abbey' (1798) it seemed as if these late-1960s travellers were heading to their retreats in search of 'something far more deeply interfused'. Not everyone thought this was a good idea. According to Abbie Hoffman, 'moving to the country' was a retreat only in the sense of a withdrawal from battle. At one point in *Woodstock Nation* he describes hippies taking to the hills as a kind of abandonment, adding that they've left him 'mighty lonely on the fence'. He was making a wider point about shifts in the political commitments of the burgeoning New Left, but the symbolism was clear: activism and protest belong on the streets and to turn away from this frontline was a dereliction of duty. Other writers like John Michell, author of *The Flying Saucer Vision* (1967), would not have seen things in such polarised terms. Michell was interested in ley lines, UFO phenomena and the ancient, often hidden ritual spaces of the British Isles. *The Flying Saucer Vision* and his other works like *The View Over Atlantis* (1969) contained no references to protest or to left-wing activism, and in contrast to Hoffman's street-smart rhetoric Michell wrote more like a character from an M.R. James short story. That said, when encouraging his readers to explore Britain's old byways he was not advocating for the kind of depoliticised escapism to the country that Hoffman disparagingly refers to. Instead, he was attempting to foster a countercultural interest in archeological sites of historical and spiritual significance.[8]

Michell's writing was well placed to reflect a growing public appreciation of Britain's environmental heritage. Conservation groups like the National Trust were undergoing a profound re-organisation in the 1960s. Their membership was growing, as was their portfolio of protected sites. At the same time the Trust was tortuously working through a set of internal ideological tensions. With more leisure time, more disposable income and with the family car becoming more affordable, day-trippers and holidaymakers were converging in ever increasing numbers on the Trust's nature reserves and recently opened stately homes. In part, this was precisely the type of demand the Trust had been working to foster since its inception in 1895. It aimed for the 'permanent preservation for the benefit of the nation of lands and properties of beauty or historic interest'. That said, mass tourism remained something of an anathema to its governing body, a group that in the 1960s still consisted of what Sean Nixon calls 'a landed elite of aesthetically inclined aristocrats'. Two Labour Prime Ministers – Clement Attlee and Harold Wilson – had passed legislation first in 1949 and again in 1968 designed to increase public access to the countryside and to newly designated national parks. The Trust, however, saw such 'over-consumption' as potentially damaging to the very spaces they were attempting to 'conserve'. As such, their policy of preserving areas for the nation fell back on the tired and tested institution of English snobbery as they sought 'to segregate the discriminating visitor from the mass tourist'.

Thanks to the recommendations of the Benson Report, an internal policy review headed by Sir Henry Benson and launched in 1967, some of these attitudes began to fade. The Trust professionalised and moved in a more commercial direction that very much required a large customer base to fill up its tea rooms. What remained, though, was the picture-postcard version of Britain that the Trust preserved so committedly. Their Britain was another version of England's green and pleasant land: a landscape of fine cultivated gardens in the grounds of magnificent houses, surrounded by Romantic rolling hills and close to spectacular clifftop prospects. By the late 1960s National Trust properties were teeming with visitors but, to the contrary, they marketed the fantasy of depopulated, private land.[9]

Michell speculated on the deeper foundations of this landscape. His focus was on Britain's sacred environment, its traces of ancient ritual sites which map out the places 'where the gods had once revealed themselves to men'. When discussing Stonehenge, the Neolithic stone circle on Salisbury Plain, Michell's concern was not a matter of ownership or access. The land on which the monument stood had been in the care of the National Trust since 1928, but for Michell the site, which to him reflected 'the conventional image of the flying saucer', was *really* in the possession of much older, higher powers. It was an example of the 'sacred engineering' he described in *The View Over Atlantis*, the type of space that exerts a peculiar attraction and fires the imagination:

> A sentiment which frequently occurs, particularly, it seems to English poets and mystics, alludes to some intangible mystery concealed within the landscape, an aesthetic law

> which ever defies formation. Some have attempted to frame this law in poetry, others in works of science and philosophy. Yet we still do not know why it is that certain spots on the Earth's surface are by general agreement more inspiring than others or how it happens that these very places so often coincide with the centres of prehistoric sanctity.

Michell's combination of speculative archeology, history and folklore became known as the study of 'Earth Mysteries', and it was not solely an attempt to connect historic landscapes with secret knowledge and pagan practices. As Janet and Colin Bord put it in their book *Mysterious Britain* (1972), the approach was equally concerned with mapping out that 'which still goes unnoticed, untouched by the clean-sweeping broom of officialdom.' The National Trust were one such 'broom of officialdom.' In focusing on these occult sites, 'occult' in the dual sense of magical and hidden, Michell and his fellow travellers in the Earth Mysteries movement were redrawing Britain's heritage map. Rather than propping up the outlook of the landed gentry, theirs was a landscape of resonant prehistory linked to Druidry, star-maps and sacred geometry.

The major point of influence on this thinking was Alfred Watkins, whose book *The Old Straight Track* (1925) popularised the idea that a system of prehistoric 'leys' traversed the country. According to the book leys are alignments that extend 'across miles of country' that link 'a great number of objects, or sites of objects, of prehistoric antiquity.' For Watkins they marked out ancient footpaths; Michell meanwhile argued that they had 'meaning as lines only to be seen from above.' Both linked leys to acts of pilgrimage, but Michell's pilgrims had potentially much further to travel. In *The Flying Saucer Vision*, he came to see these lines as flightpaths marked out for ancient UFOs, a reading that according to Michell was confirmed by the high frequency of modern UFO sightings in the vicinity of hilltops 'linked by systems of leys'. When compared to Watkins' careful, detailed reflections on mounds, mark stones and water site points, Michell's speculations on 'the old sites of sacrifice to sky-gods' seems like an eccentric departure. However, both writers came to see the ley network as an alternative map of Britain, one that marked out the country as a charged landscape of interconnected ritual sites. To 'ley hunters' like Michell these lines bound the nation together in ways that were far more significant and 'deeply interfused' than the lines of inheritance that brought the country's stately homes into the National Trust.[10]

With its clear challenge to the aristocratic and academic establishment as well as its emphasis on esoteric ideas, the Earth Mysteries movement easily stood alongside and fed into the wider countercultural climate of the 1960s. Indeed, Michell was a frequent contributor to *International Times* as well as to more specialist publications like *The Ley Hunter* magazine, launched in 1965. Although they made for France at the start of the 1970s and not the English wilderness, the Rolling Stones were also very much aware of these ideas. Soon after the publication of *The Flying Saucer Vision*, Brian Jones, Marianne Faithfull and Mick Jagger became friends with Michell who took them on a tour of Stonehenge. There were also excursions to Glastonbury Tor during which Jagger, Faithfull, Richards, Pallenberg and other members of their entourage took LSD and scanned the sky for UFOs. Another jaunt to Herefordshire saw Kenneth Anger join the party and no doubt the evening's conversations on flying saucers and leys complemented his own thinking on the then in progress *Lucifer Rising*.[11]

In 1971 Michell was approached by Andrew Kerr and Arabella Churchill, the organisers of the Glastonbury Fair and consulted on the construction of their Pyramid Stage. Michell suggested a design that would stand above the intersecting Glastonbury–Stonehenge ley, as if intending for the festival to tap into the area's ancient energy. There was more at play here than an interest in matters of heritage and archeology. What Michell was trying to evoke in his writings and field work was a kind of landscape psychedelia. Where writers like Aldous Huxley and Timothy Leary saw the use of LSD as a gateway to enlightenment, Michell, while no stranger to acid, saw such heady wisdom as bound into the soil underfoot. He often presented Alfred Watkins as a man of supreme vision: someone who, in a single flash of insight on a Herefordshire hillside, saw 'a network of lines standing out like glowing wires all over the surface of the country'. There is no direct reference to this revelation in *The Old Straight Track*, but Watkins often spoke in private about perceiving the existence of the ley system as a kind of epiphany. The experience was, according to Michell, an invocation of the *genius terrae britannicae*, the spirit of the British countryside, and in the late 1960s he too was in pursuit of a similarly spiritualised view of the landscape. While some saw the 'end of the sixties' in the horrifying events of the Tate–LaBianca murders and the Altamont concert, for Michell, standing in sight of Glastonbury Tor as the seventies began, there was no sense of catastrophe. The countercultural project was in full swing and the New Jerusalem was in reach. William Blake's Giant Albion was underfoot; it could be sensed all along the pathways and tracks – seen and unseen – that criss-crossed Britain's holy places. With the right kind of eyes, a poetic vision similar to that which fuelled the writing of Michael Horovitz and the Children of Albion, this ancient land of myth and power could be revived in the modern world.[12]

*

With its soundtrack by countercultural stalwarts the Third Ear Band, its vivid sense of the medieval landscape and its supernatural overtones, Polanski's *Macbeth* does at times comes across like Shakespeare retold for the Earth Mysteries crowd. However, as can be expected from the gravitas of its plot and the trauma Polanski brings to the telling, the film carries little trace of Michell's visionary optimism. As in the play, Polanski begins *Macbeth* with the Weird Sisters meeting to cast a spell. They walk across a desolate coastline, what becomes the film's first battlefield, and their magic takes the form of a ritualistic burial. They place a noose, a severed hand and a dagger into the wet sand before sealing the arrangement with blood and covering it over. Just after they melt away into the mist, Macbeth's forces arrive and proceed to spill more blood over the burial spot as they vanquish the Norwegian invasion. Before Macbeth encounters the witches and hears their prophecy, then, he has walked over cursed ground.[13]

Director Piers Haggard dabbled with similar imagery when he made *The Blood on Satan's Claw* (1971). A tale of England's dark side, it features a 17th-century farming community beset by a source of demonic power. In the opening sequence a plough is pulled across a field and out of the churned furrows comes a skull covered in something like animal fur. Recovered and brought back into the village, the remains start to have a sinister effect on the local children. Their bodies and their behaviour begin to change. Led by the adolescent Angel Blake they quickly band together into a pagan cult, a group that delights in sacrifice and, in one deeply troubling scene, gang rape.[14]

Released at opposite ends of 1971, *The Blood on Satan's Claw* and *Macbeth* take place in landscapes saturated in *chthonic* power: it is earthy and subterranean. The influences that flow through the films come from down below and bring with them all the diabolical implications that such a direction implies. This sense of energy – magical or otherwise – emanating from the landscape is, in essence, not too far removed from Michell's view of the countryside. The idea that a network of leys traverses the land like a sacred switchboard does bring a sense of unease. There is something old and powerful just under the surface. That said, Michell's writing proceeds with a sense of awe, and the tone of *The View Over Atlantis* veers more towards the sublime than the horrific. By contrast, Polanski and Haggard present landscapes that pulse with malevolence. When they come into the range of this force, their characters do not experience an epiphanic vision but fall into various forms of physical and moral decline.

In his essay 'Locus Terribilis' (2013), the writer and musician English Heretic neatly encapsulates this ambience via a discussion of another film that finds horror in the countryside, Michael Reeves' *Witchfinder General* (1968). Set during the European 'witch craze' of the 17th century, Reeves' brooding film is based on the brief career of the notorious, self-appointed witch-hunter Matthew Hopkins. Between 1644 and 1647 Hopkins roamed through East Anglia pursuing and prosecuting those accused of witchcraft. He charged each village for his services and his investigations are thought to have resulted in hundreds of executions. Played with icy authority by Vincent Price, Reeves' Hopkins tears through the Suffolk villages of Lavenham and nearby Brandeston making accusations and inflicting terrible acts of torture. Placing Hopkins *in situ* gives Reeves the chance to luxuriate over aspects of the Suffolk landscape and, particularly in the film's opening moments, he treats us to some loving, lingering shots of its fields and farmlands. It isn't long however before these bucolic images give way to a dreadful scene showing a public hanging. For English Heretic, this jarring effect finds Reeves using an established literary device: the *locus terribilis*, the 'bad place', that, in the likes of Ovid's *Metamorphosis*, works as an inversion of the pastoral idyll and the safety it represents.[15]

Witchfinder General is a film that has little faith in humanity. It shows lives and communities torn apart by Hopkins and his crusade: a mission that speaks more of his desire for power that a willingness to purge the land of 'evil'. When Hopkins is eventually attacked by Ian Ogilvy's character, the soldier Richard Marshall, it doesn't come across as a heroic revenge – a righting of wrongs to restore balance and revive the idyll. Reeves instead shows a young man driven into action after suffering the trauma of Hopkins and his men torturing his wife Sara (Hilary Dwyer). In the film's disturbing amoral world violence begets violence with no hope of catharsis. It is this bleak worldview that Reeves conveys through contrasting images of tranquillity and cruelty. When watching *Witchfinder General* it feels as if a world of pain waits behind every sun-dappled copse, just as every calm face seems a moment away from contorting into fear, pain or aggression. As the film's trailer put it, 'Never has England looked so beautiful yet been so violent'. For Reeves, this spirit of brutality is the real face of human nature, the baseline identity that sits beneath a veneer of civility. And so, when the violence of the film spills out into the harmony of the countryside, it does not spoil the idyll so much as reveal the true spirit of those who live there.[16]

When they came to build their own 'bad place' in *The Blood on Satan's Claw*, Haggard and screenwriter Robert Wynne-Simmons focused less on the influence of 'authority' figures like Hopkins and turned instead to the sinister forces of youth. The film looks on the younger generation with deep-seated anxiety. Angel Blake and her followers display horrific amplifications of the changes that occur in the space between childhood and adulthood. Ungovernable and libidinous with unruly bodies and a ferocious desire to upset the existing order, Blake's group makes clear what any number of exhausted parents have long known to be true: teenagers really are inspired by the devil. For Haggard and Wynne-Simmons, though, this characterisation was laden with contemporary relevance. They saw Angel Blake and her disciples as reflections of the Manson Family. Just as Manson, according to the likes of *Life*, had plunged the idyll of the sixties into its own *locus terribilis*, Blake's diabolical followers break with Christian tradition and threaten to destroy their peaceful corner of England rather than inherit it. It is a reactionary vision on the part of the filmmakers in which the malign influence of the skull that bubbles up from the earth reflects the fears of the establishment towards the post-war 'youthquake'.[17]

So too with Polanski's *Macbeth*. As Deanne Williams points out, by casting the youthful Finch and Annis in the title roles, Polanski and Tynan broke with the idea of the play as 'a story of middle-aged aspirants seizing their last chance'. Instead, their version charted an 'untimely decline from starry-eyed youth to disillusioned maturity'. Over the course of the film as the bad vibes accumulate, Finch and Annis become wan and drawn. They lose their physical beauty as the guilt gnaws away at them like a canker. According to Williams, this is Polanski distilling the atmosphere of decline that circulated at the 'end of the sixties', a time in which 'idealistic hopes for personal freedom and positive collective action were answered by violence and conspiracy'. The characters enter the last stages of the film jaded, exhausted and looking for an exit.

Having this drama play out in a landscape so heavily infused with occult power allows Polanski to really intensify the symbolism of Macbeth's decline. In one sense he and Lady Macbeth live in *the* idyll. Their life of feasting in castles set among rolling hills more than matches the pastoral fantasies that coloured the counterculture's hopes for a coming Golden Age. But, with the witches' spell doing its work underground from the outset, Polanski points to the intrusion into the scene of a malign influence. The landscape holds dark, poisonous forces just as Macbeth, with his ability to act like a serpent while looking like a flower, carries a murderous spirit within him. By the end of the film, with Macbeth decapitated and Lady Macbeth's post-suicide corpse seen crumpled on cobblestones, it is as if their bodies have fallen apart in the aftermath of their crimes. Like the optimistic project of the sixties, and like the organic matter built into the witches' buried spell, Macbeth and Lady Macbeth have rotted away.[18]

*

One of the big questions posed by films like *Macbeth* and *The Blood on Satan's Claw* relates to the idea of legacy. Placed right at the point of transition between the 1960s and the 1970s, they ask us to think about what the old decade can pass on to the new. What is going to grow from the seeds sown in the sixties? With all its difficulties, traumas and malevolence, what should we be looking to take from the decade? As Didion seems to suggest at the end of 'The White Album', should the approach be to clear the house and rebuild it: to simply throw out the detritus of the sixties and start afresh as a new decade begins?

Peter Whitehead offered an intense and hallucinatory take on these types of question in the film he went onto make after *Daddy, Fire in the Water* (1977). Featuring actors Nathalie Delon and Edouard Niermans, *Fire in the Water* is another film deeply invested in the mysteries of the natural landscape. Departing from the documentary style of *The Fall*, *Fire in the Water* plots a fictional scenario in which a filmmaker (Niermans) and his partner (Delon) pack up and head off into the Scottish Highlands. As Whitehead did after showing *The Fall* at the Edinburgh International Film Festival, Niermans' character goes into retreat to reflect on his role as a filmmaker. Once there, he hunches over a Steenbeck editing machine and works on an epic film project. Meanwhile, his partner – isolated and cut off from the creative enterprise – drifts into the rugged landscape that surrounds the remote cottage. There she undergoes a radical communion with the natural world and its animal intelligences. Aside from prefiguring aspects of Lars von Trier's *Antichrist* (2009), *Fire in the Water* also works as an updated version of Edgar Allen Poe's 'The Oval Portrait' (1842–5). In this story a self-obsessed artist begins a portrait of his wife which he labours over for so long and with such all-encompassing concentration that when it is finally finished, he finds she has long since died.

Fire in the Water, though, is more than an allegory for artistic creation in the general sense. The character played by Niermans is not a stereotypical 'artist' but is intended to be Whitehead's cinematic double. The footage upon which Niermans works is taken from Whitehead's prior films that cover the period 1965–9: *Wholly Communion*, *Tonite Let's All Make Love in London*, *Benefit of the Doubt*, *The Fall* and various music promos. At one point, frames from *The Fall* showing Whitehead's face on a television screen appear on the editing machine monitor. Niermans is sat in front of the screen replaying footage from the film. It's a brief but brilliantly composed shot in which the monitor becomes a magic mirror. It momentarily reveals Niermans' 'true' identity to the viewer.

The great work that emerges from Whitehead's cinematic archive is a vast summation of the sixties, one in which the pop stylings of *Tonite* are recast in sequences featuring protest imagery from *The Fall*. Elsewhere we see footage of NASA launches, and in Whitehead's hands they look less like great leaps forward than rockets plotting overdriven trajectories towards oblivion. Overall, it's a largely negative, pessimistic view, one that brands the countercultural project of the 1960s a failure. Whitehead made this view clear in the proposal he prepared for *Fire in the Water* in 1974, which at that point carried the title, *Requiem for the Sixties*:

> The decade of the Sixties already seems to be sufficiently lost in the past, for us to be able to cast a historical eye upon it. The nostalgia that brought back the 30s, then the 40s, then the 50s ... is at work. There has been so much gloom, so much emptiness since 1970, that it seems even more necessary now, already to ask the question ... what happened in the Sixties? What did we do to ourselves? Why has it turned out like this? At least we may ask the question and try to propose an answer.

The 'answer' Whitehead proposes is twofold. First, leading on from the events of *The Fall*, he offers the protest culture of the sixties as consumed 'from the start [...] with a dream of violence and revolt'. It was this spirit of insurrection that was 'savagely crushed' during the Columbia occupation and later at Kent State, to the extent that for Whitehead, despite the continued activities of the Weather Underground in the post-1969 period, this 'radical faith' was absent from the 'annihilating Seventies'. Second, by referring in the proposal to the 'work' of nostalgia, Whitehead suggests that the radicalism of the countercultural drive has been smoothed over by the way the 1970s have come to remember the 1960s.[19]

While the likes of *Fear and Loathing in Las Vegas* and the various hymns to Nixon-era politics had very quickly announced the 'death' of the sixties as the new decade began, plenty of other contemporary works – of film and music – were taking a more rose-tinted, celebratory view of the recent past. By the time Whitehead had prepared his proposal, the Who had released *Quadrophenia* (1973), their tribute to mid-1960s mod culture. The band's drummer, Keith Moon had also appeared with David Essex and the Beatles' Ringo Starr in screenwriter Ray Connolly's two eulogies to rock 'n' roll, *That'll Be the Day* (1973) and *Stardust* (1974). The second film, *Stardust*, charts the rise of the rock group the Stray Cats through the 1960s and early 1970s and is not shy about showing the darker, grittier side of the music business. Like the album *Quadrophenia* and its own film version that followed in 1979, *Stardust* is shot through with a sense of inevitable disappointment. They both show that lifestyles of drink and drugs only go so far; the uppers wear off, bands break up and after every bust-up on Brighton beach there's the workaday world to return to. That said, *Stardust* and *Quadrophenia* are both portraits of youth that link the idea of a flourishing youth culture directly to life in the sixties. This sense of ongoing adolescence with its dramas but also its sense of accelerated freedom is what the 1970s seem to call time on. With its tag line 'Do you remember the 60s?', *Stardust* was not just recalling a certain type of music but, like Brian Wilson and the Beach Boys had done with the late 1950s and early 60s, was inviting its audience to see the decade as a kind of halcyon period: one, by implication, far removed from the adult responsibilities of the 1970s. This type of nostalgia echoes what Whitehead describes in his proposal as having been 'unanimously agreed' about the sixties. Because it is impossible to say what really happened, Whitehead argues that the decade has been built into 'a period of optimism', a 'decade of POP, when the culture of the young took root and flowered as a multi-petaled blossoming of pleasure, of music, of art, of fashion ...'[20]

For Whitehead, however, with *The Fall* as his vivid testimonial, the 1960s remained a period not of pleasure but of violence. A similar view was most likely held by his star, Nathalie Delon. Along with her former husband the actor Alain Delon, with whom she appeared in *Le Samourai* (1967), Nathalie Delon had been part of the Tate–Polanski social circle and was particularly close to Sharon Tate. They were in Italy together in the spring of 1969 when Tate was completing what became her last film, *The 13 Chairs* (1969). An odd caper featuring antique dealers pursuing a set of vintage chairs across Europe, the film began shooting in Lavenham, Suffolk, the village Reeves had used for *Witchfinder General* the year before. *The 13 Chairs* then transferred to Rome where Tate and Delon hung out with fellow actor Christopher Jones. According to Jenny Fabian, when the production wrapped Tate invited Delon to visit her in Hollywood over the summer. The suggestion is that Delon – like so many other Hollywood notables who have since claimed to have *almost* been at Cielo Drive in August 1969 – narrowly escaped death at the hands of the Manson Family.[21]

Coincidences aside, the point is that Whitehead and Delon, like Roman Polanski, Joan Didion and the family of Meredith Hunter, the young man killed at Altamont, would have seen the late 1960s as a time of trauma; trauma felt and trauma witnessed. There's no sign of this in the likes of *Stardust*, George Lucas' *American Graffiti* (1973) or the long-running sitcom it gave rise to, *Happy Days* (1974–84). Even films based specifically on the dark side of 1969 veered more towards the realms of fantasy than crime-scene reconstruction. Case in point, the barrage of Manson-inspired exploitation movies that appeared across the 1970s. These ranged from fictionalised accounts of the Tate–LaBianca murders and the Manson trial like *The Love Thrill Murders* (1971), *The Other Side of Madness* (1972) and *Helter Skelter* (1976) to out-and-out horror movies featuring evil hippies and Manson-esque villains like *Deathmaster* (1972) and *The Hills Have Eyes* (1977). The savagery of these films was a world away from the nostalgic comforts of *American Graffiti* but, in sensationalising the events of the late-sixties, *The Other Side of Madness* and its ilk did similar 'work'. The human damage and terrible loss of life at the heart of the Manson case was reduced to a sequence of spectacular violence: grisly entertainment designed for the drive-in horror circuit.

For the sociologist and philosopher Jean Baudrillard, this nostalgia mode was a key characteristic of postmodernism. Writing in *Simulacra and Simulations* (1981), Baudrillard claimed that postmodernism was all about symbols no longer standing in for the things they appeared to represent. In an age of mass reproduction, what do endless postcards of Leonardo da Vinci's 'Mona Lisa' (1503–6) do to the 'original' painting? When we queue in the Louvre to see the small portrait are we there to appreciate an old master or are we checking up on an image we've already seen so many times on posters, T-shirts and jigsaws? And when we shell out for more of that stuff in the gift shop what exactly are we buying? Is the 'original' painting even relevant or important anymore when we come to prefer that T-shirt over the underwhelming oil painting we waited hours to see? This weird phenomenon of the copy replacing the original is what Baudrillard had in mind when he spoke about simulation and its ultimate form: the simulacra, the copy *without* an original. Simulation was in full force in American culture of the 1960s with the rise of Disneyland, the growth of Las Vegas, and the exponential increase in television ownership. In this world of overwhelming spectacle, 'reality' was simply not what it used to be. By inviting us to remember a past that never happened, films like *American Graffiti* and *Stardust* add to this climate. They superimpose 'the sixties' over the 1960s and, once under the cover of this fantasy, the decade's historical reality gradually fades away.[22]

Baudrillard did not limit his analysis to media and culture. He saw the same ideas at play in some of the key social and historical events of the late 20th century. In his essay 'After the Orgy' (1990), Baudrillard wrote, in part, on the revolutionary politics and liberalising drive of the 1960s. Using 'orgy' to conjure up the stereotypical image of 1960s hedonism, he reflects on the limits of a social mood defined by a progressive desire to break down barriers. What next for the spirit of the left when, in Baudrillard's view, all their wishes have been granted? Imagining this crisis as a moment of post-coital awkwardness, Baudrillard asks in yelling capitals: 'WHAT DO WE DO NOW THE ORGY IS OVER?' The answer, according to Baudrillard, is that we *simulate*. When 'everything has been liberated' and all 'the chips are down', the only form of revolt possible is the simulation of revolt, the radical gesture performed as an action replay. Those who witnessed Haight-Ashbury go from countercultural community to hippie theme park would have agreed with this analysis. Although the language is very different, Tom Wolfe covers similar ground in 'The Me Decade'. The narcissistic celebration of the self he saw as characterising the seventies is what started to happen when the protests finished. The counterculture grew up and moved to the suburbs but still wanted to retain the veneer of an 'alternative' lifestyle.[23]

Wolfe and Baudrillard offer powerful arguments, but they both read the apparent *ennui* of the seventies as a sign that for some people there was nothing to protest about. This is the point Whitehead would have taken issue with. *Fire in the Water*, with its recycling of previous works and its navel-gazing characters does carry clear shades of 'The Me Decade' and 'After the Orgy', but for Whitehead the seventies, even by 1974, were shaping up to be a difficult time. In his proposal for the film, he labels the decade as one of 'loss [...] purposelessness and depression' and in doing so he describes a set of responses to the period. In Whitehead's view the culture has not slipped into 'depression' because there's nothing to do, but because it is hard to know exactly how to deal with the decade's problems. By the time the film was being shown in Cannes and Paris in 1977, this negative atmosphere had become even more tangible. Britain's experience of the 1970s was one of deep uncertainty. While the 1970s in America were marked by the politics of 'Law and Order' Britain struggled through a period of cultural and political anarchy. The oil crisis; the three-day week; industrial unrest; unemployment; urban deprivation; massive divides when it came to matters of class, race, gender and wealth. This was the period that gave rise to the spit and anger of British punk rock. Clearly there was much to protest about and plenty of people looking for a way to do it.

Although it steps away from the street-level protest culture of *The Fall*, *Fire in the Water* does give voice to a powerful, insurrectionary spirit. Whitehead suggests that the violent energies of the sixties are still active even in the 'gloom' and 'emptiness' of the seventies, but they are 'hidden and preserved in a sacred garden that can only be entered when the time is right.' Accessing these energies is the task Whitehead set himself in 1974. He intended for *Fire in the Water* to revive the 'radical faith' of the sixties. As the film would show, this recharging occurs not by sifting through the archive on a Steenbeck editing machine but by flinging open the door and lighting out for the wilderness: 'falling away into nature'.[24]

*

On 20 February 2005 English Heretic performed a private ritual in the grounds of Ipswich Cemetery. He wrapped an open compact disc case in transparent plastic and laid it at the base of a tree on the cemetery's February Lawn. Thirty-six years previously, the ashes of Michael Reeves, director of *Witchfinder General* had been scattered at this spot. Reeves had died on 11 February 1969, at the age of just 25, after overdosing on sleeping pills and alcohol. He suffered from manic depression and on hearing the news some in his circle suspected suicide. The official verdict, though, was accidental death. In the intervening years Reeves and his films, particularly *Witchfinder General*, amassed a significant cult following.

In laying his memorial, English Heretic was not just paying his respects, but he was formally instituting his own anti-tradition. The offering he made to Reeves was intended as a 'Black Plaque' with the label of the CD inside the case being 'a subversion of English Heritage's ubiquitous [blue] placements'. Rather than celebrating the life and achievements of 'worthy' historical personages, English Heretic was trying to mark those generally left off the cultural map. With Reeves as the inaugural recipient, the Black Plaques were intended to commemorate those who moved through landscapes very much at odds with the 'packaging of history' and 'souvenir shop approach to leisure' peddled by English Heritage and their co-conspirators, the National Trust. If these institutions put in place an image of England as a pleasant idyll, the East Anglia that Reeves made visible in *Witchfinder General* was the *locus terribilis*, a place that appears beautiful, but which gives way to terrible violence. For English Heretic, this was not just a matter of aesthetics and the *appearance* of the English landscape on-screen, but it also had something to do with the strange effect he believed *Witchfinder General* had on its main shooting location, the Suffolk village of Lavenham.

Reeves used the village marketplace to shoot the film's harrowing witch-burning sequence. According to actor Ian Ogilvy, local residents treated the scene as something of a 'spectacle' but the next day reported hearing noises in the night, 'clanking' and 'crying', the 'awful noise of wind, screams, moans', as if staging the execution had 'woken a lot of the ghosts up'. Inspired by this strange story, English Heretic visited the village and started looking into the other films made there. He quickly came across a series of peculiar synchronicities. 'A week after Reeves' cremation', he explains, shooting began in Lavenham for 'what would turn-out to be Sharon Tate's last film, *The 13 Chairs*'. Appearing as Pat, one of the antique dealers involved in the film's quirky pursuit, Tate plays her scene in a shop that looks out over Lavenham's market square. Following this, in December 1969, the village would welcome John Lennon and Yoko Ono who also made a film in the square. Theirs was *Apotheosis No. 2* (1970) their follow-up to *Apotheosis*, the balloon film they had made earlier in the year on the Hampshire airfield. As with *Apotheosis*, this second instalment consisted of a single shot taken from the balloon as it rose over the countryside. What interested English Heretic was that Reeves, Tate, Lennon and Ono, figures in different ways connected to what he calls 'the darkening end game of the 60s', all occupied the same space in quick succession between 1968 and 1969. It's a purely coincidental overlap, but considering the deaths that affected this group, English Heretic thought it a connection that spoke of darker forces at play in the village. He came up with the conceit that *Witchfinder General* had not just rattled the old bones of Lavenham but had somehow put a curse on the place. Bad things seemed to have happened to those who followed Reeves and made films there.[25]

As an artist, English Heretic focuses on the imaginative potential of coincidence and conspiracy. He is also interested in *psychogeography*, the study of the 'effects of the geographical environment, consciously organized or not, on the emotions and behavior of individuals'. Through writing, music and site-specific performance, English Heretic embarks on creative investigations into the border zones between fact and fantasy. He will look for a point of connection between an artwork and its surroundings and will then play out the lines of association as far as they will go. The result is a form of magickal thinking that purports to reveal the hidden histories of seemingly innocuous locations across Britain. Seen through English Heretic's eyes, quiet villages become centres of conspiratorial intrigue and certain films take on prophetic significance.

Case in point, English Heretic's reading of *Apotheosis No. 2*. On the soundtrack of the completed film you can hear gentle ambient noise as the balloon rises. Suddenly, somewhere off in the distance, the crack of gunfire intrudes into the mix. Although it's obviously the echo of a game shoot or the sound of a Suffolk farmer going about their business, for English Heretic, this brief interruption is irresistibly portentous. The gunshots, as he put it in 'Locus Terribilis' (2013), 'were ricochets across time and space'. He claimed they were the sound of Lennon's death outside New York's Dakota Building haunting him eleven years ahead of time.

There's a fascinating, hypnotic quality to the way that English Heretic builds up his high-concept conspiracy theories, but we might want to ask, what's purpose of this? Such speculation works as way of firing the imagination into a visionary state. His essays often feature a point of psychic ignition when the co-ordinates of geography, coincidence and art become so intertwined that he is *transported*. As he describes in his essay 'The New Geography of Witchcraft' (2013), thinking about Lavenham as a locus of 1960s occult conspiracies had a radical effect on his experience of the village. It was as if one of its winding lanes became a secret passageway to another world. 'I seemed to have found myself trespassing,' he intoned like one of H.P. Lovecraft's doomy narrators, 'in some annex between the hidden corridors of the Dakota Building and Cielo Drive.'[26]

Nathalie Delon's character enters a similar space of imaginative intensity towards the end of *Fire in the Water*. One of the titles used by Whitehead for an early cut of the film was *Apocalypse*, which clearly reflects the nature of the archive footage seen in the film. Another was *The Real World* and this one, more so than *Fire in the Water*, or even *Requiem*, suits the events that unfold. The idea of an artist in retreat, working on his magnum opus is only the opening gambit of the film. As *Fire in the Water* progresses, it becomes clear that Whitehead is much more interested in Delon's experience of the surrounding landscape. Towards the end of the film she immerses herself, Ophelia-like, into the waters of a mountain pool. She swims and then, following a brief cut-away to an enormous, raging waterfall, she sinks under the surface. At this point, the filmmaker arrives and tries in vain to locate his partner. He thrashes around in the water, fails to find her and eventually leaves the area alone. In his eyes she's vanished, but what Whitehead shows is her character taking a sidestep into a different world. After plunging underwater Delon's character finds herself somewhere other, somewhere *beyond*. She's pictured in a transparent box, a sort of crystal sarcophagus as ravens, snakes and reptiles converge around her. Repeated cut-aways to erupting geysers and bubbling mud recall the elemental turmoil at the start of Kenneth Anger's *Lucifer Rising*. The powerful sequence reaches a climax when an enormous falcon appears and, in a swirl of movement and sound, seems to merge with Delon's character.

The scene could be read as one of ego loss, a step into the type of void-state that Timothy Leary mapped out as part of his psychedelic sacrament. Whitehead, however, was keen to emphasise the specific image of the falcon. At this point in the film he's not just giving a nod to his own interest in falconry but is drawing on the rich mythology associated with the bird. For Whitehead, what he called the 'occult meaning' of the falcon related to its appearance in Egyptian myth via the figure of Horus, the falcon-headed god. Horus, god of the morning sun, was the offspring of the goddess Isis and the dismembered god Osiris. According to the myth, Osiris was killed and divided into pieces by his brother Set. To bring Horus into being, Isis gathered Osiris' scattered parts, transformed herself into a falcon and entered into magical copulation with the fragmented god. Horus thus emerged from an act of supernatural synergy: he represented a powerful new whole that exceeded the sum of its parts. For Anger, Horus was the lord of the new aeon, the crowned child who symbolised the coming of a joyous new dawn. By contrast, in Whitehead's reading of the myth he is a figure who transcends the 'normal' orders of time, space and reality. Hovering, not moving, experiencing all moments at once rather than flying into the past or the future, Horus points the way to a mysterious world of simultaneity: 'the crucifixion of several planes of time into one apparent *coincidence*'.[27]

It is this higher state of consciousness, one that exists outside 'normal' concepts of space and time, that Delon's character accesses in *Fire in the Water*. She does not retreat into lamentation for 'the sixties' – as far as *Fire in the Water* is concerned, 'the sixties' are gone, over: they only exist as fleeting film clips. Instead, it is this so-called 'documentary' reality that Delon's character flies from as the film concludes. She pushes at the limits of human experience so as to commune with ecological, elemental and animal forces rather than attempting to recycle images of psychedelia and the short-lived revolutionary projects of the previous decade.[28]

With such an ecstatic focus on the natural landscape, Whitehead's film does recall aspects of John Michell's *The View Over Atlantis*, a book that spoke about making manifest the 'New Jerusalem' by tapping into the buried secrets of structures like Stonehenge. For Michell, decoding England's sacred engineering and its network of mysterious leys held the key to the 'principles of true spiritual science'. It was this wisdom, he argued, that the chaotic modern world needed to hold off its self-destruction. Although Delon's character seems to tap into equally powerful ecological energies, when *Fire in the Water* actually ends, it does so with a long single shot, a slow zoom-out that gradually reveals the isolated cottage seen at the start of the film. This is the point from where the characters embarked on their respective journeys. It is now covered in snow and is dwarfed by the landscape. At first glance, it is a scene of desolation; an appropriate sight given that by the late 1970s there was little-to-no sign in the culture of the type of revelation Michell had hoped for. Perhaps, as Whitehead implied, the time was not right.

When he laid his Black Plaque in tribute to Michael Reeves, English Heretic offered it not just as a memorial but as a '*terma*'. In

Tibetan Bon Buddhism, the *terma* were objects 'secreted in a rock, buried in the ground or lodged in a tree'. They were time capsules, 'hidden teachings that were intended to be discovered sometime in the future'. The *terma* provided a way of preserving and passing on wisdom, a useful strategy in 8th-century Tibet when the Bon religion was subject to persecution. 'The future recipient of the *terma*', explains English Heretic, 'was known as a *tertön*' and, applied to the Black Plaque project, 'the *tertön* was the future creative self'. He buried the *terma* in the hope that its rediscovery would inspire his later work. In *Fire in the Water*, the filmmaker is too consumed with his own recent past to make speculative plans for work yet to come. Instead it is Delon's character who, through her act of transformation, assumes the role of *terma*.[29]

At the start of the film Whitehead had his characters arrive at the cottage in the heat of summer. By ending on a winter scene, he is not presenting the landscape as now absent of life but is suggesting that it has entered a dormant state. With the cycle of the seasons it will, once again, spring into life. The disappearance of Delon's character coincides with this shift in the weather, indicating that she too has gone into some form of hibernation or stasis. Whitehead thus suggests that the forces generated by the character's transformation are now held by the landscape. They are latent and wait for their revival. Built into the myth of the sixties was the promise of a wonderful future. What Whitehead argues with *Fire in the Water* is that by the late 1970s, this version of the future was history. Unlike Didion and Polanski, Whitehead's response is not to try to clear out the ruins or loudly announce the terminal end of the era. Rather, he sets about laying the seeds for something else. The 'radical faith' of the sixties is still there in his film, but it's been ploughed into the ground as a gift of wisdom and a legacy for those who follow on.

⁂

The idea of the 'time capsule' often comes up when we tell ourselves stories about the sixties. It's a phrase that suggests the pleasures of the era can and should be sealed, preserved and passed on for the benefit of future generations. Time capsules take many forms and – whether encountered through exhibitions of psychedelic art, anniversary screenings of classic films or globe-trotting reunion tours – they make the sixties accessible for those who weren't there and for those who can't remember the decade. Currently, stepping back into the sixties is as easy as going to Liverpool to visit the childhood homes of Paul McCartney and John Lennon, two properties owned and maintained by the National Trust. More capsules will be surfacing in the future. In 2010 three 'boxes of vision' were buried to mark what would have been Lennon's 70th birthday. Commissioned by Cleveland's Rock and Roll Hall of Fame, they contained materials covering Lennon's life and work and will be uncovered in 2040 to mark his centenary.[30]

These rituals, sacred spaces and magical objects offer points of psychic refuge. We use them to look back in the hope of re-experiencing the sixties, a period far removed from the *locus terribilis* of 'today'. At the time of writing preparations are underway for Woodstock 50 and Apollo 50; the Rolling Stones are currently touring America; and at a less visible but still resonant level Kenneth Anger – youthful at a mere 92 years old – continues to screen, discuss and promote *Lucifer Rising*. These high-profile events and appearances are invariably packaged so as to remind us that *back then* things – be that films, music, or even scientific achievements – were much better. Watching Woodstock 50 on whatever streaming service gets the rights will offer a brief respite from the horror of Donald Trump, the resurgence of far-right politics, the chaos of Brexit and the general state of economic and ecological disaster that constitutes life in the 21st century.

At the same time there are other time capsules circulating that do not deliver these warm, fuzzy feelings. Charles Manson's death in November 2017 made international headlines and led to a series of lawsuits concerning ownership of his songs, artwork and name. The Manson 'legacy' fought over was essentially a set of merchandising rights. Films like Daniel Farrands' *The Haunting of Sharon Tate* (2019) and Quentin Tarantino's *Once Upon a Time in Hollywood* (2019) – all blood, polyester and lovingly curated soundtracks – show that there's certainly a market for Manson-related media. He continues to have pull as a popular culture icon.[31]

Why do these images keep returning? If the late sixties continue to be linked on the one hand to groundless nostalgia and to terrible personal tragedy on the other, why do we keep on reviving them? In part, the answer lies in the mood of *Fire in the Water* and what Peter Whitehead realised, even as early as 1974: that the future projected by the decade was not going to arrive. Recycling the sixties does not make manifest these promises in the present day but rather reiterates this sense of failure. Whether offering a celebratory or sinister representation of the period, the sixties emerge from these various time capsules as either an idyll lost to the past due to the compromises of the present or a grand project that collapsed under the weight of its own excesses.

At the end of *Bomb Culture*, Jeff Nuttall speaks with a tone of urgency. After having spent the book outlining a climate of violence and nuclear anxiety, he calls on his readers to move forward with defiant optimism. With the world in a state of crisis, he argues, it will not be resolved by waiting for the established institutions of government, industry and culture to do their bit. Dynamic, collective action is required on the part of the young, post-war generation that Nuttall addresses. 'Let's not wait', he says, for 'the administration to hand out money or land [...] let's start thinking in terms of permanence now and build our own damn future'. It is difficult to imagine a statement of such social mission being made in the current climate. Not least because the social media platforms where we might look for a voice equivalent to Nuttall's so often foster discord and intolerance rather than collective action. Also, it is hard to even imagine – let alone bring about – a future of 'permanence' when so many of us currently live, work and think in conditions of continual precarity. As a response to this we might take comfort in Woodstock 50 and the manifold pleasures of the sixties. A better option would be to go further and tap into the streams of left-wing activism that inspired Nuttall's interrogative take on post-war culture and his clarion call to action. In doing so, we would be tearing down the familiar images of Charles Manson, hippies and head shops and bringing back to the surface the true radicalism of the 1960s. The mission is not complete, we're still in a time of crisis, so let's not wander into fantasy and lose our way. Let's go digging instead and get our hands dirty. Somewhere among all the wreckage, we might find a map to a better world.[32]

Epilogue: *Apotheosis No. 2*

When John Lennon and Yoko Ono arrived in Lavenham to make *Apotheosis No. 2* (1970) they had a BBC film crew in tow. Director Paul Morrison shadowed the pair as they glided into the village in their white Rolls Royce and set about preparing for their shoot. His short, *24 Hours: The World of John and Yoko* (1969) shows a small group inflating the balloon in the market square as the village residents gather round to watch the spectacle. Lennon and Ono, meanwhile, are visible in the footage standing off to one side. They have dressed themselves in masks and long black cloaks and as the scene unfolds they look on impassively, like dark monks.[1]

Back in September, their balloon rose through the clouds into a sunny sky. Now, in the very last days of the year, their second flight takes place in the winter half-light over Suffolk's snow-blanketed landscape. It was a different and more ominous atmosphere, but one that seemed to match the mood of late 1969. Strange and troubling things had happened in the few months since Lennon and Ono had begun *Apotheosis*: a Greek astrologer had predicted Lennon's death, Charles Manson had made his presence known and the world seemed an altogether more uncertain place. Twenty-four hours after their arrival in the village, the events at the Altamont Speedway would begin to unfold.

Lennon and Ono had originally planned to be passengers and stand in the balloon's basket as it rose. In the event, it was their friend and cameraman Nic Knowland who embarked on the flight. After scrambling on board with a sound engineer, Knowland repeated the drill from the Hampshire shoot. He focused the camera on Lennon and Ono and left it running until the film ran out. As before, the two figures shrank into the distance as the balloon ascended. In the completed film, the camera moves through the cloud bank, reveals a panoramic view of the countryside and then shortly after, the sound of the gunshot intrudes.

Conspiracies aside, it is hard to watch this material and not think of Lennon's untimely death. His fatal encounter with Mark Chapman outside the Dakota Building is exactly the kind of awful event that confers retrospective significance on the merest of gestures, glances, slip-ups and mistakes. But it is not just knowledge of events to come that gives Lennon's appearance in the footage a ghostly, funereal tinge. Both he and Ono seem to have gone out to create this impression when making *Apotheosis No. 2*. In their shrouds and cloaks they look like lost members of the Process or spectres momentarily made manifest in the village square. That they should be playing roles for the cameras, their own cameras and those of the BBC, is not in and of itself remarkable. What is notable is their choice to appear in such sinister garb. In the absence of the white gowns and almost angelic air they brought to the Bed-Ins for Peace, Lennon and Ono appear in *Apotheosis No. 2* as intense countercultural mavens, the type of characters who would gleefully pull the ripcord on the Beatles and the cultural phenomenon the band had generated. It is as if they have arrived in the English countryside to call time on the sixties.

Despite the ominous undertow of the scene, as the balloon rises, these are the figures who stay on the ground. When the first *Apotheosis* took off in September, leaving Lennon and Ono behind on the runway, it looked like a failed escape attempt. *Apotheosis*

No. 2, seems to present a much more successful getaway, one in which the balloon moves beyond the influence of the film's strange characters.

In another world, Lennon and Ono did get on board with Knowland. They headed out for the clouds while these doppelgängers stayed below in the vortex of Lavenham. Maybe they're still out there looking for somewhere to land. It's nice to think so. In this version of the sixties, they cut away their shadows and with them jettison all the complicated baggage of the era. Unburdened and heading skyward, Lennon and Ono carry on with their voyage to territories new.

Notes

Prologue: *Apotheosis*

1. My account of the making of *Apotheosis* was informed by Peter Doggett's *The Art and Music of John Lennon* (London: Omnibus Press, 2009), 230–32.
2. For details of the last days of the Beatles and the relationship between Lennon and Ono see: Ray Coleman, *Lennon: The Definitive Biography* (New York: Harper Perennial, 1999), 419–88. For a general overview of the Beatles, their work and their career, see Philip Norman, *Shout! The Beatles in their Generation* (USA: Fireside, 1996). For more detailed accounts events such as the rooftop concert, see Tony Barrell, *The Beatles on the Roof* (London: Omnibus, 2017).
3. Definition of 'apotheosis' from the *Oxford English Dictionary* 2nd edition, volume 1. (Oxford: Clarendon Press, 1989), p. 559.

Chapter I: The Devil's Business

1. My account of the Tate–LaBianca murders uses details from Vincent Bugliosi and Curt Gentry, *Helter Skelter* (USA: W.W. Norton, 1974), 21–111; Ed Sanders, *The Family* (New York: E.P. Dutton, 1971), 177–230. John Gilmore and Ron Kenner, *Manson* (New York: Amok Press, 2000), 102–18; Adam Gorightly, *The Shadow Over Santa Susana* (London: Creation, 2009), 313–25; Simon Wells, *Charles Manson: Coming Down Fast* (London: Hodder, 2010), 214–48.
2. This moment is in the film and the novel. See Ira Levin, *Rosemary's Baby* (New York, Dell, 1967), 205–18. Gary Lachman mentions Garretson's musical preferences in *Turn Off Your Mind* [2001] (Finland: Dedalus, 2010), p. 334.
3. Bugliosi and Gentry, p. 71.
4. For more on the link between Charles Manson and Terry Melcher see Wells, 214–48.
5. Manson's enthusiasm for 'The White Album' is discussed in Bugliosi and Gentry, p. 297 onwards. For an analysis of the songs on *The Beatles* see Ian MacDonald, *Revolution in the Head: The Beatles' Records and the Sixties* (London: Pimlico, 1995), 239–55. See also Mark Goodall (ed.) *The Beatles, or 'The White Album'* (Great Britain: Headpress, 2018).

6. Bugliosi and Gentry, 325–34. See also my essay 'Helter Skelter' in Goodall, 89–95.
7. Barney Hoskyns, *Waiting for the Sun: Strange Days, Weird Scenes and the Sound of Los Angeles* (USA: St. Martin's Press, 1996), p. 181.
8. Joan Didion, 'The White Album', in *The White Album* (New York: Simon and Schuster, 1979), 11–48: p. 47.
9. Hoskyns describes the post-Manson Sunset Strip in *Waiting for the Sun*, p. 181. Jann S. Wenner, 'John Lennon: *The Rolling Stone* Interview', *Rolling Stone* (January 1971). Online at: https://www.rollingstone.com/music/music-news/john-lennon-the-rolling-stone-interview-part-one-160194/.
10. Manson's image and the headline 'The Love and Terror Cult' appeared on the cover of *Life*, December 1969. Robert Jones' article, 'Hippie: The Philosophy of a Subculture' appeared in *Time*, July 1967.
11. Manson's incarceration is covered by Gilmore and Kenner, 13–21 and Wells, 38–58.
12. Sanders, p. 27.
13. Manson's exposure to Scientology and other influences during his pre-1967 prison time, is discussed by Wells, 38–58; Sanders, 3–12 and 26–7.
14. For an overview of Haight-Ashbury's development see Charles Perry, *The Haight-Ashbury: A History* (New York: Random House, 1988). See also Hank Harrison, *The Grateful Dead* (London: Star, 1975), 94–118.
15. For more on the internal politics and economics of the Haight see Danny Goldberg, *In Search of the Lost Chord: 1967 and the Hippie Idea* (London: Icon Books, 2017), 15–53.
16. Roszak, 'Youth and the Great Refusal', *The Nation* (March 1968), 400–406: p. 400.
17. Jones, p. 23.
18. The origins of the term 'hippie' is discussed in Arthur Marwick, *The Sixties* (Oxford: Oxford University Press, 1998), 480–86.
19. Roszak and Joseph Berke, *Counterculture: The Creation of an Alternative Society* (London: Fire, 1969), p. 24. My definition of 'culture' draws on Raymond Williams, *Keywords* (London: Fontana), p. 65. I discuss Roszak, Jones, Berke, Williams and others in my essay 'Terminal Data: J.G. Ballard, Michael Moorcock and the Fiction of the Decade's End', *The 1960s: A Decade of Modern British Fiction*, ed. Philip Tew, James Riley and Melanie Seddon (London: Bloomsbury, 2018), 257–85.
20. For an account of the Be-In, see Goldberg, 27–37.
21. Lachman, p. 6.
22. Hesiod, 'Works and Days', *Theogony and Works and Days*, ed. M.L. West (Oxford: Oxford University Press, 1988), 35–63: p. 40.

23. Lachman, 6–8.
24. John Symonds provides an overview of Crowley's work in *The Great Beast: The Life and Work of Aleister Crowley* (Great Britain: Mayflower, 1971). For details of Aiwass, see 81–7. For an overview of Horus in the Egyptian pantheon see Alfred Wiedemann, *Religion of the Ancient Egyptians* (London: H. Grevel & Co, 1897), 27–30.
25. For details of Anger's work in San Francisco see Bill Landis, *Anger: The Unauthorized Biography of Kenneth Anger* (USA: Harper Collins, 1995), 141–6 and 156–7. Lachman briefly discusses the meeting of Anger and Beausoleil, p. 300. Further details are offered by Gilmore and Kenner, 37–65. Lucifer is discussed in John M. Steadman, *Milton's Epic Characters: Image and Idol* (USA: Chapel Hill, 1959), 282–97. See also Judith Lee, 'Lucifer: A Fantastic Figure', *Journal of the Fantastic in the Arts* 8.2 (1997), 218–34.
26. Jay Stevens, 'Night Thoughts About the Sixties', in Peter O. Whitmer and Bruce VanWyngarden, *Aquarius Revisited* (New York: Citadel, 1991), iii–vi: p. iv.
27. For Manson's song lyrics see *The Manson File*, ed. Nikolas Schreck (New York: Amok Press, 1988), 72–80.
28. For background see Grace Slick, *Somebody to Love: A Rock-and-Roll Memoir* (New York: Warner, 1988), 84–6.
29. Gordon Kerr, *A Short History of the Vietnam War* (Harpenden: Oldcastle, 2015), 64–5; James McAllister, 'Who Lost in Vietnam? Soldiers, Civilians and U.S. Military Strategy', *International Security* 35.3 (2010/2011), 95–123: p. 116. See also Norman Mailer, *The Armies of the Night* (New York: New American Library, 1968). For an overview of the protest context circa 1967 as well as commentary on Bernie Boston's photograph see Russell Duncan, 'The Summer of Love and Protest: Transatlantic Counterculture in the 1960s', *The Transatlantic Sixties: Europe and the United States in the Counterculture Decade*, ed. Grzegorz Kosc *et al*, (Bielefeld: transcript Verlag, 2013), 144–73.
30. See Goldberg, p. 184.
31. 'Creepy-crawls' described in Bugliosi and Gentry, p. 149.
32. Didion, 'The White Album', 21, 13, 47. The Black Panther Party was formed in 1966 by two former student activists, Bobby Seale and Huey P. Newton. As Goldberg puts it 'Their core identity was armed citizens' patrols which monitored the behavior of police officers and challenged police brutality in Oakland' (p. 164). In their calls for improved community resources, the Panthers reflected the priorities of the wider Black Power agenda. However, their public image as an armed group, as well as Newton's (eventually dismissed) murder charge discussed by

Didion, led the Panthers to be seen as the extreme, militant wing of the movement.

33. Ibid., p. 47.
34. See Maury Terry, *The Ultimate Evil* (Great Britain: Grafton, 1988); Wells, p. 363; James Parks, *Cultural Icons* (London: Bloomsbury, 1991), p. 278; Martin A. Lee and Bruce Shlain, *Acid Dreams: The Complete Social History LSD* (New York: Grove, 2000), p. 254.
35. The 1971 E.P. Dutton edition of Sanders' *The Family* contained a chapter about Manson and the Process. This was removed from later editions after the Process launched legal action against the publisher on the grounds of alleged defamation. For various points of Manson-related numerological speculation see Gorightly, 238–9

Chapter II: Bomb Culture

1. Mark Donnelly, '*Wholly Communion*: Truths, Histories and the Albert Hall Poetry Reading', *Framework*: *The Peter Whitehead Issue Part 1*, 52.1 (Part 1, Spring 2011), 129–44: p. 133.
2. Daniel Kane, '*Wholly Communion*, Literary Nationalism and the Sorrows of the Counterculture', *Framework* 52.1, 104–27: p. 109.
3. The details in this section come from Jonathan Green, *Days in the Life: Voices from the English Underground, 1961–1971* (London: Heinemann, 1988), 64–74. The 'Invocation' can be found in *Wholly Communion*, ed. Peter Whitehead (New York: Grove Press, 1965), n.p.
4. A description of Fainlight's performance appears in Green, 71–2; Nuttall provides an account of his appearance at the Albert Hall in the documentary, *Days in the Life: A Gathering of the Tribes* (Edmund Coulthart, GB, 2000); in his 'Introduction' in the *Wholly Communion* book, Alexis Lykiard describes the atmosphere and cites the press responses to the event (n.p.).
5. Peter Whitehead, 'Notes on the Filming', *Wholly Communion* (n.p.); Raymond Durgnat, 'Wholly Communion' *Films and Filming* (June 1966), *The Essential Raymond Durgnat*, ed. Henry K. Miller (London: BFI, 2014), 50–51; Jeff Nuttall, *Bomb Culture* [1968], ed. Douglas Field and Jay Jeff Jones (London: Strange Attractor, 2018), p. 195.
6. The website Bombsight.org provides a searchable map of bomb sites across London linked to the period, 1940–41. For further details and commentary see Mark Clapson, *The Blitz Companion* (London: University of Westminster Press, 2019) and Tom Allbeson, 'Visualizing Wartime Destruction and Postwar Reconstruction: Herbert Mason's Photograph of St. Paul's Cathedral', *Journal of Modern History* 87.3 (2015), 532–78.

7. For further details on post-war reconstruction see Peter J. Larkham and Mark Clapson (eds.) *The Blitz and its Legacy: Wartime Destruction to Post-War Reconstruction* (London: Routledge, 2016). New Towns and the post-war context are discussed in Philip Tew, James Riley and Melanie Seddon, 'Surfing the Sixties' and Melanie Seddon, 'Our Troubled Youth: A Literary History of the 1960s', *The 1960s: A Decade of Modern British Fiction*, 1–26; 27–59.
8. Attlee's 'Leader's Speech, Scarborough, 1951' can be read here: http://www.britishpoliticalspeech.org/speech-archive.htm?speech=161. The effects and interpretations of the 1944 Education Act are covered by Arthur Marwick in *British Society Since 1945* (London: Penguin, 1990), p. 55.
9. Robert F. Paul, 'Peter Whitehead Interview: The Wanderer (Part 1)', *Framework* 5.2, 15–30: p. 16.
10. See C.E. Rolph, *The Trial of Lady Chatterley* (Harmondsworth: Penguin, 1961).
11. See Philip Larkin, *High Windows* (London: Faber, 1974) p. 34; Robert Conquest, 'Introduction', *New Lines: An Anthology*, ed. Robert Conquest (London: Macmillan, 1956), xi–xvii: p. xv. The point on housing in this section quotes Christopher Brooker, cited in Tew, Riley and Seddon, 'Surfing the Sixties', p. 4.
12. Sam Selvon, *The Housing Lark* (London: MacGibbon & Kee, 1965). For details of Peter Rachman and the Profumo circle see Richard Davenport-Hines, *An English Affair: Sex, Class and Power in the Age of Profumo* (London: Harper, 2013), p. 182. For more on Britten see, James D. Herbert, 'Bad Faith at Coventry: Spence's Cathedral and Britten's *War Requiem*', *Critical Inquiry* 25.3 (1999), 535–65.
13. Adam Ritchie's images are included in *Barrett*, ed. Russell Beecher and Will Shutes (London: Essential Works, 2011), 54–6.
14. Green, 'The Swinging Sixties? As if', *The Guardian*, 17 April (1999). Online at: https://www.theguardian.com/books/1999/apr/17/books.guardianreview1.
15. Green, *Days in the Life*, p. x. The *OZ* trial was an obscenity trial launched at the underground newspaper *OZ*, which had turned its May 1970 issue over to a guest editorial team of secondary school children.
16. William Blake, 'Milton' and 'Jerusalem: The Emanation of the Giant Albion', *The Complete Poems* ed. Alicia Ostriker (Harmondsworth: Penguin, 1977), 513–607: p. 514; 635–847: p. 799. Michael Horovitz, 'Afterwords', *Children of Albion: Poetry of the Underground in Britain*, ed. Michael Horovitz (Harmondsworth: Penguin, 1969), 316–79: p. 316.

17. Mick Farren, *Give the Anarchist a Cigarette* (London: Pimlico, 2001), 112–13. The social and artistic context surrounding *Sgt. Pepper* is discussed in Derek Taylor, *It Was Twenty Years Ago Today* (London: Bantam, 1987).
18. For images and context regarding *My Own Mag* see Douglas Field and Jay Jeff Jones, 'Primarily for Squares: An Introduction', *Bomb Culture*, xiv–xliv. For Nuttall's discussion of CND see *Bomb Culture*, 35–66.
19. Harold Wilson, 'The New Britain' and 'Our National Purpose', *The New Britain: Labour's Plan. Selected Speeches 1964* (Harmondsworth: Penguin, 1964), 9–23; 125–34. Arthur Marwick, *The Sixties*, p. 10.
20. For background on Whitehead's film and its content see 'Dossier: *Tonite Let's All Make Love in London*', *Framework* 52.1, 246–322.
21. Nuttall, p. 169.
22. Information on the Process and apocalypticism in this section is taken from, R.N. Taylor, 'The Process: A Personal Reminiscence', *Apocalypse Culture*, ed. Adam Parfrey (USA: Feral House, 1990), 159–72; Gavin Baddeley, *Lucifer Rising: Sin, Devil Worship and Rock 'n' Roll* (London: Plexus, 1999), 60–62; Arthur Goldwag, *Cults, Conspiracies & Secret Societies* (USA: Vintage, 2009), 88–91; David S. Katz, *The Occult Tradition* (London: Jonathan Cape, 2005), 185–90; Aleister Crowley, *Magick*, ed. John Symonds and Kenneth Grant [1929] (Great Britain: Guild, 1989), 220; *Sympathy for the Devil? The True Story of The Process Church of the Final Judgement* (Neil Edwards, GB, 2014).
23. Self's 'Guard Dog on a Missile Base, No. 1' (1965) can be viewed at: https://www.tate.org.uk/art/artworks/self-guard-dog-on-a-missile-base-no-1-t01850; Latham's 'Full Stop' can be viewed at: https://www.tate.org.uk/art/artworks/latham-full-stop-t11968; Adrian Mitchell's 'To Whom it May Concern' is included in *Wholly Communion*, 54–5; the making of *Benefit of the Doubt* is covered in 'Dossier: *Benefit of the Doubt*', *Framework* 52.1, 326–43.
24. Nuttall, p. 161.

Chapter III: Surrender to the Void

1. Harry Fainlight, 'The Spider', *Wholly Communion*, 44–8: p. 44; Green, 64–74. I discuss each of these in my essay, 'The Spiderhood: Psychedelic Literature, Literary Psychedelia and the Writing of LSD', *British Literature in Transition, 1960–1980: Flower Power*, ed. Kate McLoughlin (Cambridge: Cambridge University Press, 2019), 182–97.
2. Gerald Moore and Lawrence Schiller, 'The Exploding Threat of the Mind Control Drug that got out of Control', *Life* (March 1966); Various, *LSD* (Los Angeles: Capitol Records, 1996).

3. Aldous Huxley's use of mescaline and then LSD is detailed in Jay Stevens, *Storming Heaven: LSD and the American Dream* (USA: Perennial, 1988), 8–61; H.P. Lovecraft, 'From Beyond' [1934], *Necronomicon: The Best Weird Tales of H.P. Lovecraft*, ed. Stephen Jones (Great Britain: Gollancz, 2008), 387–93: p. 388.
4. Huxley, 'The Doors of Perception', *The Doors of Perception/Heaven and Hell* (Great Britain: Granada: 1977), 9–64: p. 46.
5. The background to LSD is covered in Stewart Tendler and David May, *The Brotherhood of Eternal Love* (London: Panther, 1984), 17–33. See also Andy Roberts, *Albion Dreaming: A Popular History of LSD in Britain* (Singapore: Marshall Cavendish, 2012), 10–22.
6. Coinage of 'psychedelic' and the death of Huxley is covered in Lee and Shlain, 55, 96; Stevens, 48, 29; Tendler and May, 42–4.
7. Timothy Leary, Ralph Metzner and Richard Alpert, *The Psychedelic Experience* [1964] (Great Britain: Penguin, 1964); the Millbrook context is covered in Stevens, 166–75; Leary and Cohen can be heard on the *LSD* album. For further information about Leary, see John Higgs, *I Have America Surrounded: The Life of Timothy Leary* (London: Friday, 2006). As regards the number of LSD users that Leary cites, Tendler and May offer a useful summary: 'In 1962 Leary estimated that some 25,000 Americans had tried psychedelics. Three years later, a study of the drugs by Alpert and others suggested that four million had now tasted LSD; and in 1966 *Life* magazine put the number who had tried mescaline, let alone the other psychedelics, at one million', p. 67.
8. Wells, p. 46.
9. Lee and Shlain provide a good overview of Ken Kesey, 119–38. The classic account is Tom Wolfe, *The Electric Kool-Aid Acid Test* (New York: Bantam, 1969).
10. The production and prohibition of LSD is covered in Lee and Shlain, 141–56; LSD illegality and Manson's trip is described in Wells, 46–7.
11. Gerard DeGroot, *The 60s Unplugged: A Kaleidoscopic History of a Disorderly Decade* (Great Britain: Pan Macmillan, 2008), p. 213. Terry Taylor, *Baron's Court, All Change* [1961] (London: London New Editions, 2011), p. 99. Taylor's brief reference to LSD has been offered as s a marker of the novel's cultural value. Stewart Home's introduction to the 2011 edition, 'Jazz Clubs, Drugs and Proto-Mods', 1–10, emphasises the point as does Andy Roberts in *Albion Dreaming*, 120–22. Roger Harris, *The LSD Dossier* (London: Compact, 1966), 147. I discuss these texts and others in 'The Spiderhood', *British Literature in Transition, 1960–1980: Flower Power*, 187–8.
12. Leary *et al*, pp. 3, 6, 24.

13. Ibid, p. 24. Lee and Shlain, p 56.
14. Mikal Gilmore, 'Beatles' Acid Test: How LSD Opened the Door to *Revolver*', *Rolling Stone* (25 August 2016). Online at https://www.rollingstone.com/music/music-news/beatles-acid-test-how-lsd-opened-the-door-to-revolver-251417/. Leary, 'Instructions for Use During a Psychedelic Session', *The Psychedelic Experience*, 95–124: p. 98.
15. Frank Herbert, *Dune* (USA: Chilton, 1965); *Dune Messiah* (New York: Putnam, 1969); Hari Kunzru, '*Dune*, 50 years on: how a science fiction novel changed the world', *The Guardian* (3 July 2015). Online at https://www.theguardian.com/books/2015/jul/03/dune-50-years-on-science-fiction-novel-world.
16. Nuttall, p. 67. Lee and Shlain, p. 109.
17. Wells, 59–63; Schreck, 126–37.
18. Manson's use of the bus is described in Gilmore and Kenner, 51–66; Beausoleil in Topanga and the birth of Valentine Michael Manson is described in Wells, 103–7; Anger's 'curse' is described in Landis, p. 205. For more on the link between Manson and the Beach Boys see, David Toop, 'Surfin' Death Valley USA: The Beach Boys and 'Heavy' Friends', *The Sound and the Fury*, ed. Barney Hoskyns and David Pringle (London: Bloomsbury, 2003), 399–407. When Dennis Wilson was playing host to the Family, Manson made his musical ambitions clear. Wilson introduced him to producers like Terry Melcher, booked some studio time and tried to help Manson get a project off the ground. Wilson also bought the rights to Manson's song 'Cease to Exist'. He re-wrote the lyrics and it appeared as 'Never Learn Not to Love' on the Beach Boys' album *20/20* (1969). Manson would record his own version of the track which was released on his album *Lie: The Love and Terror Cult* (1970).
19. Bugliosi and Gentry, p. 233. Laura Whitcomb, 'Mel Lyman: God's Own Story', *Apocalypse Culture*, 153–8: 153.
20. Wells describes 3-Star Enterprises, p. 27.
21. Ibid, p. 133–6. Manson's appeal to the so-called 'garbage people' is the key point of Gilmore and Kenner's book Manson, which was originally published as *The Garbage People* (Los Angeles: Omega Press, 1971).
22. Ibid. Gorightly describes Manson's use of group sex, p. 57 and the episode with Paul Watkins, p. 166.
23. Leary, *The Psychedelic Experience*, p. 24.
24. Fainlight, 'The Spider', p. 46.
25. 'Brian' on *LSD* album.

Chapter IV: The Art of Violence

1. This scene is visible in *The Fall* (Peter Whitehead, UK/USA, 1969).

2. The information in this chapter pertaining to the making of *The Fall* comes from three texts by Peter Whitehead included in *Framework* 52.1: '*The Fall* Dossier', 484–497; 'Two Film Treatments: *Protest* and *The Fall*, 498–524. '*The Fall* Dossier' is a long, diaristic text Whitehead kept during the making of *The Fall* which covers the period 1967–1969. *Protest* and *The Fall* are film treatments written to raise funding for the projects in question. *Protest* was written in 1967 before Whitehead started work on *The Fall* but shares various themes with the later protect.
3. Whitehead, '*The Fall* Dossier', pp. 486–7.
4. Ibid, pp. 489–90; 'Protest', p. 502.
5. Whitehead, '*The Fall* Treatment', p. 503.
6. Ibid, p. 510. Albert Samaha, 'The Rise and Fall of Crime in New York City: A Timeline', *The Village Voice* (7 August 2014). Online at https://www.villagevoice.com/2014/08/07/the-rise-and-fall-of-crime-in-new-york-city-a-timeline/.

   J. Anthony Lukas, 'The Two Worlds of Linda Fitzpatrick', *New York Times* (16 October, 1967); Bruce Porter, 'Trouble in Hippieland/Gentle Marcy: A Shattering Tale', *Newsweek* (October 30, 1967).
7. Whitehead, '*The Fall*, Treatment', p. 503.
8. Whitehead, '*The Fall* Dossier', pp. 486–90.
9. Raphael Montañez Ortiz, 'Destructivism: A Manifesto' [1962], *Theories and Documents of Contemporary Art: A Sourcebook of Artists' Writings*, ed. Kristine Stiles and Peter Selz (Berkeley: University of California Press, 1998), 722–3: p. 722.
10. Sergio Guzik *et al*, 'A Mass Changes Me More: An Interview with Alejandro Jodorowsky', *The Drama Review* 14.2 (Winter 1970), 70–76: p. 76.
11. For information on the Vienna Actionists see Malcolm Green (ed.), *Writings of the Vienna Actionists* (London: Atlas Press, 1999); Stephen Barber, *The Art of Destruction: The Films of the Vienna Action Group* (London: Creation Books, 2004) and Eva Badura-Triska, *Vienna Actionism: Art and Upheaval in 1960s Vienna* (Germany: Walther Koing, 2012).
12. Nuttall, p. 161. See also my essay 'Terminal Data', *The 1960s: A Decade of Modern British Fiction*, p. 261.
13. For a useful survey of Marxist thought – one published contemporaneously with the rise of the New Left – see C. Wright Mills, *The Marxists* (USA: Dell, 1962).
14. For more context see John Lewis Gaddis, *The Cold War* (Great Britain: Penguin, 2005), 5–47.
15. Ibid, 48–83.
16. Daniel Bell, *The End of Ideology* (New York: The Free Press, 1960); Carl Oglesby, 'The Idea of the New Left', *The New Left Reader* (New York:

Grove Press, 1969), 1–23: p. 3; John Summers 'Daniel Bell and The End of Ideology', *Dissent* (Spring 2011). Online at https://www.dissentmagazine.org/article/daniel-bell-and-the-end-of-ideology. Mills, 'Letter to the New Left', *New Left Review* 1.5 (September– October 1960). Online at https://www.marxists.org/subject/humanism/mills-c-wright/letter-new-left.htm. Mario Savio's speech is discussed in Mark Kurlansky, *1968: The Year that Rocked the World* (London: Jonathan Cape, 2004), 90–93.

17. David Cooper, 'Introduction', *Dialectics of Liberation*, ed. David Cooper (Harmondsworth: Penguin, 1968), 7–13: p. 10.
18. Mills, Letter to the New Left'; Herbert Marcuse, *One Dimensional Man* (USA: Beacon, 1964).
19. Kurlansky, 94–7. For more detail on the March Against Fear, see Aram Goudsouzian, 'If the March Cannot Be Here, then Where?': Memphis and the Meredith March', *An Unseen Light: Black Struggles for Freedom in Memphis Tennessee*, ed. Aram Goudsouzian and Charles W. McKinney (USA: University Press of Kentucky, 2018), 254–78.
20. Stokely Carmichael, 'Black Power', *The Dialectics of Liberation*, 150–75: pp. 160–61.
21. For an indication of the range of radical interests at play in the late 1960s, see Peter Stansill and David Zane Mairowitz, *BAMN (By Any Means Necessary): Outlaw Graphics and Ephemera* (Harmondsworth: Penguin, 1971).
22. Gustav Metzger, 'Manifesto Auto-Destructive Art' (1960). Online at http://radicalart.info/destruction/metzger.html. For further information on the Destruction in Art Symposium see *Art & the 60s: This Was Tomorrow*, ed. Chris Stephens and Katherine Stout (London: Tate, 2004).
23. Whitehead, '*The Fall* Dossier', p. 487.
24. *Apocalypse Now* (Francis Ford Coppola, US, 1979).
25. Whitehead, '*The Fall* Treatment', pp. 516–18.
26. Whitehead, 'I Destroy Therefore I Am', *Films and Filming* (January 1969), *Framework* 52.1, 536–46: p. 540.
27. Kurlansky, 178–208: pp. 195–7.
28. Whitehead documents his involvement in the Columbia occupation in 'The Fall Dossier', 490–96. It is a long, single entry in the diary that covers the period 24 April to 1 May. All the quotes in this section are taken from this text.
29. For further detail and context see, Patrick Seale and Maureen McConville, *French Revolution 1968* (Harmondsworth: Penguin, 1968). Whitehead discusses possible CIA interference in his film in his interview with Robert F. Paul, 'The Inadvertent Agent', *Peter Whitehead: A Singular Vision*, ed. Peter Whitehead (Pytchley: Hathor, 2001), n.p. and

his interview with Gareth Evans and Ben Slater, 'The Falconer: Three Lives of Peter Whitehead', *Entropy* 1.1 (June 1997), 10–22: p. 12.

30. Whitehead's meeting with Mansraven and his return to the UK is discussed in Evans and Slater, p. 12; his filming of Robert Kennedy is described in '*The Fall* Dossier', p. 487; his reaction to the death of Kennedy is outlined in 'I Destroy Therefore I Am', p. 543.
31. Evans and Slater, p. 12; Whitehead, 'I Destroy Therefore I Am', p. 543.
32. Paul Cronin, 'The Ceremony of Innocence', *Sight and Sound* (March 2007). Online at http://old.bfi.org.uk/sightandsound/feature/49359.

Chapter V: The Dark Side

1. Carl Gustav Jung, *Dreams* trans. R.F.C. Hull [1974] (Routledge: London, 2002), p. 122; p. 279.
2. For a comprehensive history of NASA see Joan Lisa Bromberg, *NASA and the Space Industry* (USA: Johns Hopkins University Press, 2000), 16–45. For an account of the Moon landing see Andrew Smith, *Moon Dust* (London: Bloomsbury, 2005) 6–25 and Rob Kirkpatrick, *1969: The Year Everything Changed* (USA: Skyhorse, 2009), 114–29.
3. Smith, p. 90.
4. Michael Moorcock, *The Final Programme* [1969] (London: Fontana, 1979), p 148; Smith, p. 90; J.G. Ballard and George Petros, 'Seconds Chance', *Seconds* 40 (1996). Online at http://www.jgballard.ca/media/1996_seconds_magazine.html.
5. Smith, p. 23; viewing figures and 'Voyage to the Moon' referenced in Kirkpatrick, p. 125.
6. Michael Crichton, *The Andromeda Strain* (USA: Knopf, 1969). Smith and Kirkpatrick both refer to Crichton, p. 10 and p. 118. Buzz Aldrin described the moonscape as a scene of 'magnificent desolation'.
7. For more details on the murder of Gary Hinman; its background, circumstances, repercussions and Manson's announcement of 'Helter Skelter' see Wells, 201–19.
8. Stevens, 275–83.
9. The events of the 1968 Chicago Democratic Convention are covered by Kurlansky, 269–86. A detailed account of the Days of Rage can be found in Kirkpatrick, 216–31.
10. Dave Williams and Ron Bailey, 'An Open Letter to the Underground from the London Street Commune' *International Times* (October 1969), pp. 10–12.
11. Chris Evans, 'J.G. Ballard: The Space Age is Over', *Penthouse* 14.1 (1979). Viewable at http://www.jgballard.ca/media/1979_january_UKpenthouse_magazine.html.

12. Mike Kaplan, 'Kubrick: a marketing odyssey', *The Guardian* (2 November 2007). Online at https://www.theguardian.com/film/2007/nov/02/marketingandpr.
13. Yvonne Salmon, 'Black Holes and Blown Minds: Psychedelic Science Fiction, 1968–1984'. Public Lecture. Institute of Continuing Education, Cambridge. 25 October 2015.
14. For Whitehead on Syd Barrett see Robert F. Paul, 'The Inadvertent Agent', n.p. For Storm Thorgerson's images of Barrett see *Barrett*, 114–19.
15. J.G. Ballard, 'A Question of Re-Entry', *The Terminal Beach* (Great Britain: Gollancz, 1964), 7–40; 'The Dead Astronaut', *Memories of the Space Age* (USA: Arkham House, 1988), 68–90.
16. Didion, 'Slouching Towards Bethlehem', *Slouching Towards Bethlehem* (New York: Farrar, Straus and Giroux, 1968), 72–113. W.B. Yeats, 'The Second Coming', *W.B. Yeats: Selected Poetry*, ed. Norman Jeffares (Great Britain: Pan, 1990), pp. 99–100.
17. Moorcock, 'A New Literature for the Space Age', New Worlds, 142 (May–June 1964), 2–4: p. 2: Ballard, 'Author's Note', *The Atrocity Exhibition* [1970] (London: Harper, 2006), p. vi.
18. Roland Barthes, 'The Death of the Author'; Michel Foucault, 'What is an Author?', *The Norton Anthology of Theory and Criticism*, ed. Vincent B. Leitch et al (New York: Norton, 2001), 1466–70; 1622–36.
19. John Storey, 'Introduction: Postmodernism', *Cultural Theory and Popular Culture: A Reader*, ed. John Storey 2nd ed. (Great Britain: Prentice Hall, 1998), 343–50.
20. Jean-François Lyotard, *The Postmodern Condition* (Manchester: Manchester University Press, 1986); Storey, p. 346.
21. For details of the reach of the British Empire, an account of its links to slavery particularly in the West Indies and the use of troop deployments, see Robert Johnson, *British Imperialism* (Great Britain: Palgrave, 2002), 1–12; 13–23, 77–90 and Ronald Hyam, *Britain's Imperial Century: 1815–1914* (Basingstoke: Palgrave, 1976), 74–133. Britain's technological and capitalistic development is covered in Andrew Porter, 'Britain and Empire in the Nineteenth Century', *The Oxford History of the British Empire*, ed. Andrew Porter, vol. 3 (Oxford: Oxford University Press, 1999), 1–31. The era of 'British Peace' is discussed in detail in Barry Gough, *Pax Britannica: Ruling the Waves and Keeping the Peace before Armageddon* (Great Britain: Palgrave, 2014). For a discussion of 'Rule Britannia' see Oliver J.W. Cox, 'Frederick, Prince of Wales, and the First Performance of 'Rule, Britannia!', *The Historical Journal* 56.4 (2016), 931–54.
22. For further detail on the context of post-war decolonisation and the Suez crisis, see, Saul Dubow, 'Macmillan, Verwoerd, and the 1960 "Wind

of Change" Speech', *The Historical Journal* 54.5 (2011), 1087–1114; John Darwin, *The Empire Project: The Rise and Fall of the British World System 1830–1970* (Cambridge: Cambridge University Press, 2009), 528–40 and 590–609; Gaddis, p. 128.

23. Graham K. Riach, 'Ways of Staying, Ways of Saying: From Black Writing in Britain to Black British Writing', *The 1960s: A Decade of Modern British Fiction*, 137–65: p. 137.
24. Origins of 'Helter Skelter' discussed in Barry Miles, *Paul McCartney: Many Years from Now* (London: Vintage, 1998), 487–88; 'Ruins of Rome' from Piers Brendon, *The Decline and Fall of the British Empire, 1781–1997* (London: Vintage, 2008) p.xv.
25. The article that accompanied the cover story 'Is God Dead?', 'Toward a Hidden God' was written by the magazine's religion editor, John T. Elson.
26. Jung, *Flying Saucers: A Modern Myth of Things Seen in the Skies*, trans. R.F.C. Hull (London: Routledge & Kegan Paul, 1959), p. xii. Lachman discusses Jung in *Turn Off Your Mind*, 138–9, as does John Michell in *The Flying Saucer Vision* (Great Britain: Sidgwick & Jackson, 1967), 19–20.

Interlude: *Island of Death*

1. A video of the conversation, 'Interview with Yoko Ono (2000)' can be found here: https://www.youtube.com/watch?v=LsDHee4Fv34. 'Paul is Dead' conspiracy theories are discussed in Goldwag, 185–6.
2. Coleman provides a detailed overview of Lennon's death in *Lennon*, 1–63.
3. For an example of this see Erkki Rautio's essay 'Rosemary: The Connection Between Mia Farrow, Sharon Tate, Charlie Manson and The Beatles' (2011). Online at: http://www.phinnweb.org/livingroom/rosemary/index2.html.

Chapter VI: The Rebirth of Dionysus

1. See *Cain's Film* (Jamie Wadhawan, UK, 1969); Stewart Home, *Tainted Love* (London: Virgin, 2006). The most detailed account of the State of Revolt event can be found in Home's essay, 'A Walk on Gilded Splinters', *London: City of Disappearances*, ed. Iain Sinclair (London: Penguin, 2006), 398–409.
2. Peter Biskind, *Easy Riders, Raging Bulls: How the Sex, Drugs and Rock 'n' Roll Generation Changed Hollywood* (London: Bloomsbury, 1999), 52–80; p. 74.
3. My account of Woodstock in this chapter – particularly the details regarding logistics and traffic – comes from Rob Kirkpatrick, *1969: The Year Everything Changed* (USA: Skyhorse, 2009). His chapter 'Heaven in a

Disaster Area' (171–195) offers a detailed overview of the festival. Further, specific points of quotation from Kirkpatrick will be identified in notes below. Lennon and Ono's Bed-In is described in Coleman, 494–7. For the UPI report see 'Thousands flee Woodstock chaos, mud' (UPI, 16 August 1969), online at: https://www.upi.com/Archives/1969/08/16/Thousands-flee-Woodstock-chaos-mud/5321502589701/. Elliot Tiber provides details of Raymond Mizak's death in a useful online narrative: http://www.woodstockstory.com/how-woodstock-happened-5.html. Tiber and Tom Monte also provide a more personal account of the festival's background as well as its wider context in *Taking Woodstock* (New York: Square One, 2009).

4. See *Woodstock: 3 Days of Peace and Music* (Michael Wadleigh, US, 1970). Kirkpatrick discusses *Woodstock*, 179–91; the Barry Melton quote comes from Kirkpatrick also, p. 191. The concession stand incident is recounted in James Parker, 'Woodstock Nation', *The Atlantic* (September 2009). Online at: https://www.theatlantic.com/magazine/archive/2009/09/woodstock-nation/307611/. 'Dark Star' can be heard on the Grateful Dead, *Live/Dead* (Warner, 1969). For documents and a critical overview of this period in the Vietnam conflict see Robert Griffiths and Paula Baker (eds.), *Major Problems in American History Since 1945* (Boston: Houghton Mifflin, 2001), 281–320. On Nixon see: David F. Schmitz, *Richard Nixon and the Vietnam War: The End of the American Century* (USA: Rowan and Littlefield, 2014), 41–76; Melvin Small, *The Presidency of Richard Nixon* (USA: University of Kansas Press, 1999), 59–97 and Gregory A. Daddis, *Withdrawal: Reassessing America's Final Years in Vietnam* (Oxford: Oxford University Press, 2017), 45–76.
5. Andy Cush, 'Remember When Jimi Hendrix Protested the National Anthem on a National Stage?', *Spin* (September 2016). Online at https://www.spin.com/2016/09/remember-when-jimi-hendrix-protested-the-national-anthem-on-a-national-stage/; the performance is discussed Kirkpatrick who quotes Al Aronowitz, 189–90. A further account of the Woodstock concert can be found in Charles R. Cross, *Room Full of Mirrors: A Biography of Jimi Hendrix* (Great Britain: Sceptre, 2005), 270–72.
6. Abbie Hoffman, *Woodstock Nation* [1969] (New York: Pocket Books, 1971); quotes regarding a 'youth colony', a lifestyle defence and the 'psychedelic liberation front' come from Lee and Shlain's discussion of Hoffman and *Woodstock Nation*, 254–5. Where Hoffman was linked, as founder, to the Yippies, the Youth International Party, John Sinclair founded the radical, anti-racist group the White Panther Party as a counterpart to the Black Panthers. In 1969 Sinclair was sentenced to ten years

in prison for offences relating to marijuana. This was the issue Hoffman attempted to highlight during the Who's set at Woodstock.

7. It took Woodstock Ventures eleven years to pay off their creditors. See John Robinson, 'Interview with the organisers of Woodstock festival', *The Telegraph* (12 August 2009). Online at: https://www.telegraph.co.uk/culture/music/rockandpopfeatures/6017442/Interview-with-the-organisers-of-Woodstock-Festival.html.
8. 'Medley' can be heard on the 5th Dimension, *The Age of Aquarius* (Soul City, 1969). For more on *Hair* (1967) see Eric Grode, *Hair: The Story of the Show That Defined a Generation* (London: Goodman, 2010).
9. David Jay Brown and Rebecca McClen Novick, 'Robert Anton Wilson: Firing the Cosmic Trigger', *Mavericks of the Mind* [1993] (USA: MAPS, 2010), 132–52: p. 140.
10. This exchange is visible in *Woodstock*; For details of cloud seeding see Sam Kean, 'Climate Control', *Air & Space* (July 2010). Online at https://www.airspacemag.com/history-of-flight/climate-control-181122. See also A.B.C. Whipple, *Storm* (USA: Time / Life, 1982), 153–4; H.E. Willoughby *et al*, 'Project STORMFURY: A Scientific Chronicle 1962–1983', *Bulletin American Meteorological Society*, 66. 5 (May 1985), 505–14. For a more conspiratorial take see Jerry E. Smith, *Weather Warfare* (USA: Adventures Unlimited, 2006).
11. For details of Hurricane Debbie see R.C. Gentry, 'Hurricane Debbie Modification Experiments, August 1969', *Science* 168. 3930 (24 April 1970). For an interesting contrast see Kirkpatrick's description of another storm system, Hurricane Camille, 178–90.
12. Robert Anton Wilson, 'The Illuminatus Saga Stumbles Along' (1990). Online at: http://rawilsonfans.org/the-illuminatus-saga-stumbles-along. For more on *Playboy* and its context see Barbara Ehrenreich, *The Hearts of Men: American Dreams and The Flight From Commitment* (Great Britain: Pluto Press, 1983).
13. Wilson, 'The Illuminatus Saga Stumbles Along'. For more on *The Gemstone File* see Kenn Thomas and David Hatcher Childress, *Inside the Gemstone File* (USA: Adventures Unlimited, 1999). Definition of 'classic conspiracy theory' from Vankin and Whalen, p. 225.
14. Robert Shea and Robert Anton Wilson, *Illuminatus! Part I: The Eye in the Pyramid* (Great Britain: Sphere, 1976), 12,14,15,17,20. For background to Wilson', Shea and the writing of *Illuminatus!* see John Higgs, *The KLF: Chaos, Magic and the Band Who Burned A Million Pounds* (London: Phoenix, 2012), 40–54. For brief overviews of the historical Illuminati see Whalen and Vankin, 199–205; Goldwag, 260–61, Katz, 83–4 and David Southwell and Sean Twist, *Conspiracy Theories* (Great Britain: Carleton,

1999), 215–17. Examples of the *Playboy* 'Forum' letters, some alleged to have been written by Wilson himself can be found at http://rawilsonfans.de/en/letters-to-the-playboy-forum/.

15. Richard J. Hofstadter, 'The Paranoid Style in American Politics', *The Paranoid Style in American Politics and Other Essays* (Harvard: Harvard University Press, 1964), 3–40: pp. 3, 23, 25, 29, 32.
16. Shea and Wilson, *The Eye in the Pyramid*, p. 51.
17. The phrase 'Never trust anyone over 30' or 'Don't trust anyone over 30' is generally attributed to Jack Weinberg, a member of the Berkeley Free Speech Movement. Shea and Wilson, *Illuminatus! Part II: The Golden Apple* (Great Britain: Sphere, 1976), 180–83.
18. Seale and McConville, 227–229. For more detail on Kent State see Howard Means, *67 Shots: Kent State and the End of American Innocence* (Boston, Da Capo, 2016).
19. See George Robertson, 'The Situationist International: Its Penetration into British Culture', *What is Situationism: A Reader* ed. Stewart Home (Stirling: AK Press, 1996), 107–34; Gordon Carr, *The Angry Brigade: A History of Britain's First Urban Guerilla Group* (London, Gollancz, 1975); Richard English, *Armed Struggle: The History of the IRA* (Oxford: Oxford University Press, 2003), 81–147: p. 107; Stefan Aust, *The Baader-Meinhof Complex* [1987] (London: The Bodley Head, 2008); Robert C. Meade, *Red Brigades: The Story of Italian Terrorism* (Great Britain: Palgrave, 2014). Broader contextual surveys can be found in Jack Sargeant (ed.), *Guns, Death Terror: An Illustrated History of 1960s & 1970s International Terror* (London: Creation, 2003) and Stewart Home, *The Assault on Culture: Utopian Currents from Lettrisme to Class War* (Stirling: AK Press, 1991).
20. Nuttall, 'Snipe's Spinster' [1975], *An Aesthetic of Obscenity: 5 Novels by Jeff Nuttall*, ed. Douglas Field and Jay Jeff Jones (Singapore: Verbivoracious Press, 2016), 3–89: p. 22; Field and Jones, 'Introduction', *An Aesthetic of Obscenity*, vii–xx: pp. xii–xiii; English, p. 92.
21. See Carl Bernstein and Bob Woodward, *All The President's Men* (London: Quartet, 1974); Seymour Hersh, 'Huge CIA Operation Reported in U.S. Against Antiwar Forces, Other Dissidents in Nixon Years', *New York Times* (22 December 1974). Online at https://www.nytimes.com/1974/12/22/archives/huge-cia-operation-reported-in-u-s-against-antiwar-forces-other.html. *The Village Voice* quote is from *Illuminatus!*, back cover copy, Sphere edition (1976).
22. Mae Brussell, 'From Monterey Pop to Altamont: Operation Chaos – The CIA's War Against the Sixties Counter-Culture' (November 1976), n.p. Online at: http://www.maebrussell.com/Mae%20Brussell%20Articles/Operation%20Chaos.html. Jimi Hendrix played at Madison Square

Garden with the Band of Gypsys on 22 January 1970. The event was cut short when Hendrix left the stage after two songs. It is claimed that he had taken LSD during the evening. Overall, though, the concert's premature end and the dissolution of the Band of Gypsys that followed is generally attributed to existing tensions within the group rather than to any deep state, conspiratorial intrigue. See David Henderson, *'Scuse Me While I Kiss the Sky: The Life of Jimi Hendrix* [1978] (London: Omnibus, 2002), p. 343.

23. See John D. Marks, *The Search for the Manchurian Candidate* (New York: Dell, 1978); Brussell, 'From Monterey Pop', n. p.
24. For and overview of Lennon and FBI surveillance see Vankin and Whalen, 325–31. For details of the War Council see Lee and Shlain, 257–8.

Chapter VII: Pandemonium '69.

1. The astrological references in this section and the general background to Altamont comes from Ralph J. Gleason, 'Aquarius Wept: The Rolling Stones at Altamont 1969', *Esquire* (August 1970) and 'Rolling Stone', 'The Rolling Stones Disaster at Altamont: Let It Bleed', *Rolling Stone* (January 1970). Both are online at: https://www.esquire.com/news-politics/a6197/altamont-1969-aquarius-wept-0870/ and https://www.rollingstone.com/music/music-news/the-rolling-stones-disaster-at-altamont-let-it-bleed-71299.

   The *Rolling Stone* article was a collective effort involving reports from twelve journalists 'and the first-hand accounts of dozens of others'. The named journalists included Lester Bangs, Greil Marcus and Michael Goodwin. The article does not identify individual contributions and so as per the magazine's by-line it will be attributed here to 'Rolling Stone'. For Booth's account see Stanley Booth, *The True Adventures of the Rolling Stones* [1984] (Edinburgh: Canongate, 2012), p. 151.
2. Tony Sanchez, *Up and Down with the Rolling Stones* (London: John Blake, 2010), p. 188. Details of the atmosphere and sequence of events from Gleason and 'Rolling Stone' as well as from *Gimme Shelter* (Albert Maysles, David Maysles and Charlotte Zwerin, US, 1970). Other useful accounts can be found in A.E. Hotchner, *Blown Away: The Rolling Stones and the Death of the Sixties* (New York: Simon and Schuster, 1990); Philip Norman, *Mick Jagger* (London: Harper Collins, 2013) and Sam Cutler, *You Can't Always Get What You Want* (Canada: ECW Press, 2008).
3. Etymological information regarding the name 'Altamont' can be found in Keith C. Lee's study of Altamont, New York, *Images of America: Altamont* (USA: Arcadia, 2014), p. 10. Topographic information and a brief history of Altamont, California can be found in

David Durham, *California's Geographic Names* (USA: Word Dancer Press, 1998), p. 593. For Owens' images see Bill Owens, *Altamont 1969* (Italy: Damiani, 2019). His account, 'The Altamont Story' can be found online at: https://trivalleycahistoryblog.wordpress.com/2009/08/27/the-altamont-story-by-bill-owens-altamont-photographer/.

4. For details of the Who concert see Chet Flippo, 'Rock & Roll Tragedy', *Rolling Stone* (January 1980). Online at: https://www.rollingstone.com/music/music-news/rock-roll-tragedy-why-11-died-at-the-whos-cincinnati-concert-93437/. See also Joel Selvin, *Altamont: The Rolling Stones, the Hells Angels and the Inside Story of Rock's Darkest Day* (USA: Dey Street Books, 2017).
5. For details on the making of *Gimme Shelter*, see Michael Sragow, '*Gimme Shelter*: The True Story', *Salon* (August 2000). Online at: https://www.salon.com/2000/08/10/gimme_shelter_2/.
6. Gleason, 'Aquarius Wept'; critical responses discussed in Sragow.
7. In Stephen Barber's *Abandoned Images: Film and Film's End* (London: Reaktion Books, 2010), he describes *Gimme Shelter* as having 'cancelled' the future promised by the counterculture. For an impression of the enduring status of Gimme Shelter see Richard Brody, 'What Died at Altamont?', *The New Yorker* (March 2015). Online at: https://www.newyorker.com/culture/richard-brody/what-died-at-altamont.
8. For further details see Harvey Kubernik, *A Perfect Haze: The Illustrated History of the Monterey International Pop Festival* (USA: Santa Monica Press, 2011).
9. For background on the making of *Invocation* see Landis, 170–74 and Baddeley, 43–53; Anger's description of *Invocation* as a 'fragment made in fury' is from Carel Rowe, 'Illuminating Lucifer', *Film Quarterly* 27.4 (Summer 1974), 24–33: p. 31. The detailed analysis cited here is from Deborah Allison, 'Magick in Theory and Practice: Ritual Use of Colour in Kenneth Anger's *Invocation of My Demon Brother*', *Senses of Cinema* (February 2005). Online at: http://sensesofcinema.com/2005/feature-articles/invocation_demon_brother/.
10. For further details on the technicalities of *Invocation*, see Allison. Anger's discussion of film and demons is quoted in Mikita Brottman, 'Introduction: Force and Fire', *Moonchild: The Films of Kenneth Anger*, ed. Jack Hunter (London: Creation Books, 2002), 1–18 p. 2. For a detailed discussion of magick, see Aleister Crowley, *Magick in Theory and Practice* [1929] (New York: Castle Books, 1992), 130–32. Anger's thoughts on *Invocation*, banishment and the coming of a 'joyful' time are quoted in Baddeley, p. 52.
11. Zachary Lazar, *Sway* (London: Vintage, 2008), p. 221.

12. John Milton, *Paradise Lost* [1667], ed. John Leonard (Great Britain: Penguin, 2003), p. 228.
13. Chris Petit, *Back from the Dead* [1999] (London: Pan, 2000), 221–2. At one point in the novel Petit describes a screening of a film by Alexander Blackledge that contains a scene not unlike the 'Henny Penny Piano Destruction Concert' sequence from Whitehead's *The Fall*.
14. Kevin Fagan, 'Seeking Shelter from a Memory/Nostalgia absent on Altamont's 30th Anniversary', *San Francisco Chronicle* (6 December 1999). Online at: https://www.sfgate.com/bayarea/article/Seeking-Shelter-From-a-Memory-Nostalgia-absent-2891015.php.
15. Norman, 219–28. For a useful overview of the Rolling Stones during this period and Peter Whitehead's involvement with the band see, Victor Coelho, 'Through the Lens, Darkly: Peter Whitehead and the Rolling Stones', *Framework* 52.1, 174–92.
16. Norman, p. 290.
17. The press-conference is visible in *Gimme Shelter*. Throughout the *Rolling Stone* report it is implied that the band are out of step with the attitudes of San Francisco groups like the Grateful Dead.
18. For details of the Rolling Stones and management issues, see Fred Goodman, *Allen Klein: The Man Who Bailed Out the Beatles, Made the Stones and Transformed Rock & Roll* (New York: Houghton Mifflin, 2016). See Sragow for details of the making of *Gimme Shelter*.
19. Norman, 379–80; Gleason and 'Rolling Stone' both cover these logistical matters in detail. The scene described is visible in *Gimme Shelter*. Kirkpatrick discusses it as part of his account of Altamont in *1969*, 'The Hippie Apocalypse', 248–66.
20. Gleason and 'Rolling Stone'; Kirkpatrick describes the Hells Angels as 'one-percenters', 258–9; Owens, 'The Altamont Story'.
21. Gleason, 'Aquarius Wept'; *Rolling Stone*, 'The Rolling Stones Disaster at Altamont'. For details of Phun City see http://www.ukrockfestivals.com/phun-city-menu.html.
22. The KSAN interview is covered in 'Rolling Stone', 'The Rolling Stones Disaster at Altamont'; 'New Speedway Boogie' can be heard on the Grateful Dead, *Workingman's Dead* (Warner, 1970); the KSAN sample can be heard on Black Cab, *Altamont Diary* (2004); their work with Cutler is described in Kate Hennessy, 'The Cab Effect', *Mess + Noise* (July 2009). Online at http://www.thesmallestroom.com.au/the-cab-effect/. For more details on The Lords of Altamont, see https://lordsofaltamont.com/.
23. For details of New Order at Glastonbury see Al Horner, '20 sets that shook Glastonbury', *NME* (September 2017). Online at: https://www.nme.com/features/20-sets-that-shook-glastonbury-the-stories-

behind-worthy-farms-most-memorable-ever-performances-757137. For the interview with Primal Scream see: https://www.youtube.com/watch?v=P6HRo-1wsJw.

24. *Gimme Shelter: Outtakes* (Albert Maysles, David Maysles and Charlotte Zwerin, US, 2000); *Performance* (Donald Cammell/Nicolas Roeg, UK, 1970). This clip is discussed in Rebecca and Sam Umland, *Donald Cammell: A Life of the Wild Side* (Great Britain: Fab Press, 2006), p. 147.
25. For a detailed overview of Cammell and the making of *Performance* see Rebecca and Sam Umland, 87–145. *David Bailey's Box of Pin-Ups* (London: Weidenfeld and Nicholson, 1964). For details on the Krays see John Pearson, *The Profession of Violence: The Rise and Fall of the Kray Twins* (London: Weidenfeld and Nicholson, 1972).
26. For details of Litvinoff and the social circle surrounding *Performance*, see Paul Buck, *Performance: A Biography of the Classic Sixties Film* (London: Omnibus, 2012), 43–60.
27. Michael Goodwin, 'A Heavy Trip Inside Mick Jagger's Head', *Rolling Stone* (September 1970). Online at: https://www.rollingstone.com/music/music-news/a-heavy-trip-inside-mick-jaggers-head-184328/.
28. Cammell quoted in Rebecca and Sam Umland, p. 147.
29. Iain Sinclair, 'Who Cares for the Caretaker?', in Iain Sinclair and Rachel Lichtenstein, *Rodinsky's Room* (Great Britain: Granta, 2000), 131–51: p. 141.
30. Paul Kantner quoted in Fagan.

Chapter VIII: The Cataclysm

1. *The Virgin Sacrifice* ('J.X. Williams', US, 1969). See *Experiments in Terror* (The Other Cinema, 2003).
2. See Tony O'Neill, *Sick City* (New York: Harper, 2010), p. 7. For more on John Aes-Nihil see http://www.aes-nihil.com/aes.html. A useful overview of Manson-related films can be found in Jim Morton, 'Manson Movie Madness', in Jim Van Bebber, *Charlie's Family* (London: Creation, 1998), 164–85.
3. Nikolas Schreck, *The Satanic Screen* (London: Creation, 2001), 133–40: p. 138.
4. Ibid, 136–44.
5. Anton LaVey, 'Nine Satanic Statements', *The Satanic Bible* [1969] (New York: Avon, 1992), p. 25; Nat Freedland, *The Occult Explosion in America* (London: Michael Joseph, 1972), p. 14; 'Fire' can be heard on *The Crazy World of Arthur Brown* (Atlantic, 1968); 'Black Mass' can be heard on Coven, *Witchcraft Destroys Minds & Reaps Souls* (Mercury, 1969). Freedland discusses the *Time* article in *The Occult Explosion*.

6. Hunter S. Thompson, 'To Jim Silberman, Random House. January 13, 1970', *Fear and Loathing in America: The Brutal Odyssey of an Outlaw Journalist 1968–1976*, ed. Douglas Brinkley (London: Bloomsbury, 2000), 257–69: p. 258. See also, Thompson, *Hell's Angels: The Strange and Terrible Saga of the Outlaw Motorcycle Gangs* (New York: Random House, 1967).
7. Thompson, 'To Jim Silberman', 258–63.
8. Thompson, *Fear and Loathing in Las Vegas* [1972] (Great Britain: Flamingo, 1993), 3–4.
9. Thompson, 'To Jim Silberman, p. 264.
10. Thompson, *Fear and Loathing in Las Vegas*, 5, 22–3, 66–8.
11. Ibid, p. 68.
12. This incident is described in detail in Edwards' film *Sympathy for the Devil? The True Story of The Process Church of the Final Judgement*. See also Lachman, *Turn Off Your Mind*, 261–79.
13. Polanski sticks close to the dream sequence as it is narrated in Levin's novel, 79–82. Sea images are described in Jung, *Dreams*, p. 122.
14. For an indicative critical response, see Jonathan Rosenbaum, '*Zabriskie Point*, 1984 review', online at: https://www.jonathanrosenbaum.net/2018/12/zabriskie-point-1984-review.
15. Nuttall, *Snipe's Spinster*, 23–34.
16. *Tuesday's Child* is briefly discussed in Lee and Shlain, p. 257. Nuttall, 25–33. Nuttall quotes from Thompson's 'wave speech' in this section.
17. Thompson, *Fear and Loathing in Las Vegas*, p. 145.
18. Baddeley, p. 67.
19. Ibid, 66–77. Baddeley's analysis of and interviews with LaVey focus on his attitude towards the San Francisco counterculture. For further information see Blanche Barton, *The Secret Life of a Satanist: The Authorized Biography of Anton Szandor La Vey* (New York: Feral House, 2014).
20. This version of the pantheon is taken from 'The Hierarchy', a Process text issued in December 1967 and reproduced as part of the supplementary materials accompanying Edwards' film. The documentary contains footage of Process members discussing 'John Grey'.
21. See Betty Puttick, *Supernatural England* (Great Britain: Countryside Books, 2002), 9–12.
22. Françoise Strachan, *Aquarian Guide to Occult, Mystical, Religious, Magical, London and Around* (Great Britain: Aquarian Press, 1970), p. 38.
23. Tom Wolfe, 'The 'Me' Decade and the Third Great Awakening', *New York* (August 1976). Online at: http://nymag.com/news/features/45938. Leary *et al*, p. 124.

24. Landis describes the making of *Lucifer Rising*, 178–83. See also, James Magrini, 'Lucifer Rising', *Senses of Cinema* (March 2015). Online at: http://sensesofcinema.com/2015/cteq/lucifer-rising.
25. Lachman, 'Kenneth Anger: The Crowned and Conquering Child', p. 17, DVD booklet.

Chapter IX: The Omega Men

1. In 1970 Bobby Beausoleil was sentenced to death for murder. In 1972 this was commuted to life imprisonment. A portrait of Beausoleil's prison life can be found in 'Then it All Came Down', an interview he did with Truman Capote in 1972. See Truman Capote, *Music for Chameleons: New Writing* [1975] (London: Penguin, 2000), 211–24. Details of the later stages of *Lucifer Rising* can be found in Landis, 181–211. Beausoleil's own account of recording the soundtrack can be found online: http://bobbybeausoleil.com/the-lucifer-rising-suite-a-journey-out-of-darkness.html. The full piece can be heard on Bobby Beausoleil, *The Lucifer Rising Suite* (CD Baby, 2014). Jimmy Page's version can be heard on *Lucifer Rising and Other Soundtracks* (Jimmy Page, 2012).
2. *The Omega Man* (Boris Sagal, US, 1971). The film is based on Richard Matheson's novel *I Am Legend* (1956) and was previous adapted as *The Last Man on Earth* (Ubaldo Ragona and Sidney Salkow, US/Italy, 1964).
3. Wavy Gravy is visible in *Woodstock*. See Milton, *Paradise Lost*, ed. John Leonard, 24–52.
4. *The Omega Man*. In his essay 'Manson Movie Madness', Jim Morton talks about *The Omega Man* and the Manson milieu. See Van Bebber, 174–5.
5. *Beneath the Planet of the Apes* (Ted Post, US, 1970).
6. Smith provides an account of the *Apollo 8* mission and Anders' photographing 'Earthrise' in *Moondust*, p. 160. The image can be seen here: https://www.nasa.gov/multimedia/imagegallery/image_feature_1249.html.
7. Stewart Brand (ed.) *The Whole Earth Catalog: Access to Tools* (Fall 1968), 2–5. 'Earthrise' was used as the cover image for the Spring 1969 edition of *The Whole Earth Catalog*. Other key texts of 1960s environmentalism include Rachel Carson, *Silent Spring* (1962); Edward Abbey, *Desert Solitaire: A Season in the Wilderness* (1968) and Charles A. Reich, *The Greening of America* (1970).
8. For the Gaia hypothesis see James Lovelock, *Gaia: A New Look at Life on Earth* (Oxford: Oxford University Press, 2000).
9. Brand, *The Whole Earth Catalog: Access to Tools*, 5–7.
10. R. Buckminster Fuller, *Operating Manual for Spaceship Earth* [1969] (Switzerland: Lars Müller, 2014), pp. 55–6; 94; 124–6. Description of Fuller's expertise from back cover copy used on this edition.

11. *El Topo* (Alejandro Jodorowsky, US, 1970). For further details on the making and release of *El Topo* see Alejandro Jodorowsky, *The Spiritual Journey of Alejandro Jodorowsky: The Creator of El Topo* (Rochester: Park Street Press, 2008), 220–38; Ben Cobb, *Anarchy and Alchemy: The Films of Alejandro Jodorowsky* (London: Creation, 2007), p. 114. Jack Hirschman, 'Breaking down walls of corporeal and narcotic sleep', *The Staff* (1971). Online at: https://cinephiliabeyond.org/1971-interview-alejandro-jodorowsky-el-topo-psychedelic-genre-bending-midnight-movie.
12. Cobb, p. 144; *Vanishing Point* (Richard C. Sarafian, US, 1971).
13. *The Wild Bunch* (Sam Peckinpah, US, 1969); *Soldier Blue* (Ralph Nelson, US, 1970); *Vanishing Point.*
14. *Blue Sunshine* (Jeff Lieberman, US, 1978).
15. Andrea Pitzer, 'The Bitter History of Law and Order in America', *Longreads* (April 2017). Online at: https://longreads.com/2017/04/06/the-bitter-history-of-law-and-order-in-america/. Karl Fleming, quoted in *A History of Our Time: Readings on Postwar America*, ed. William Chafe *et al* (Oxford: Oxford University Press, 2008), p. 287.
16. Peter Schrag, 'The Forgotten American', *Harper's Magazine* (August 1969), in Chafe *et al* (Oxford: Oxford University Press, 2008), 287–300: 289–90; Robert Graysmith, *Zodiac: The Socking True Story of America's Most Elusive Serial Killer* [1976] (London: Titan, 2007); *Dirty Harry.*
17. Pauline Kael, '*Dirty Harry*: Saint Cop', *The New Yorker* (January 1972). https://scrapsfromtheloft.com/2017/12/28/dirty-harry-saint-cop-review-by-pauline-kael/. George Orwell, *Nineteen Eighty-Four* [1949] (London: Penguin, 2000), p. 280. *Dirty Harry* (Don Siegel, US, 1971); *Death Wish* (Michael Winner, US, 1974).
18. This is described in Bugliosi, 439–40.
19. Tendler and May describe the circumstances of Leary's prison escape, 188–93. For a wider overview of Leary in the Nixon era, see Bill Minutaglio and Steven L. Davies, *The Most Dangerous Man in America: Timothy Leary, Richard Nixon and the Hunt for the Fugitive King of LSD* (New York: Twelve, 2018).
20. See Jess Bravin, *Squeaky: The Life and Times of Lynette Alice Fromme* (USA: St. Martin's Press, 1997), 226–30.
21. Schrag, 288–93; Carmichael, 'Black Power', p. 152; *Dirty Harry.*
22. Editorial Group, 'Editorial', *International Times* 70 (December 1969), p. 2; *Blue Sunshine.*
23. David Jay Brown and Rebecca McClen Novick, 'Robert Anton Wilson: Firing the Cosmic Trigger', p. 150.
24. *The Holy Mountain* (Alejandro Jodorowsky, US, 1973); For details of the making see *The Spiritual Journey of Alejandro Jodorowsky*, 179,

220–37. Jodorowsky's spiritual views are discussed in 'Alejandro Jodorowsky: A Mystical Treat', 52 *Insights* (December 2016). Online at: https://www.52-insights.com/alejandro-jodorowsky-a-mystical-treat-interview-film-holy-mountain/.

25. *El Topo*. For more on Thích Quảng Đức see Ellen J. Hammer, *A Death in November: America in Vietnam, 1963* (New York: E.P. Dutton, 1987), p. 149.
26. Fuller, 79–80.
27. *El Topo*; *The Holy Mountain*.
28. Timothy Leary, *Starseed: A Psi-Phy Comet Tale* (San Francisco: Level Press, 1973), 20–24.

Chapter X: The New Jerusalem

1. Sharon Tate's funeral and Polanski's return to Cielo Drive is recounted in Wells, 280–3.
2. Whitehead's post-*Fall* experience is described in Evans and Slater, 'The Falconer', p. 15. Cronin recounts the story of the Edinburgh man in 'The Ceremony of Innocence'. His career as a falconer is covered at length in 'Dossier: Falcon', *Framework* 52.2, 689–773.
3. Didion, 'The White Album', p. 47.
4. *Daddy* (Peter Whitehead, UK/FR, 1973). For background details on the production see 'Dossier: *Daddy*', *Framework* 52.2, 599–655.
5. *Macbeth* (Roman Polanski, US / UK, 1971). For details of the film's production see Deanne Williams, 'Mick Jagger Macbeth', *Shakespeare Survey* 57 (2008), 145–58; p. 145. For the passage featuring Macduff see William Shakespeare, 'The Tragedy of Macbeth', *The Norton Shakespeare* ed. Stephen Greenblatt *et al* (New York: W.W. Norton, 1997), 2555–2619: 4.3. 219–20.
6. See Robert Greenfield, *Exile on Main Street: A Season in Hell with the Rolling Stones* (USA: Da Capo, 2006), p. 37. For more on Traffic, the Incredible String Band and Led Zeppelin see Rob Young, *Electric Eden: Unearthing Britain's Visionary Music* (London: Faber, 2011), 285–6; 405–8; 347–76. For Lennon and Ono see Coleman, 419–88.
7. For more on Drop City see, https://www.dropcitydoc.com/. For a brief overview of Mel Lyman see Laura Whitcomb, 'Mel Lyman: God's Own Story', *Apocalypse Culture*, 153–8.
8. William Wordsworth, 'Lines Written a Few Miles above Tintern Abbey', *Romanticism: An Anthology* ed. Duncan Wu (Great Britain: Blackwell, 1998), 265–9: p. 268; Hoffman, *Woodstock Nation*, p. 76. John Michell, *The Flying Saucer Vision*; *The View Over Atlantis* (London: Sago Press, 1969).

9. The information on the National Trust in this section comes from Sean Nixon, 'Trouble at the National Trust: Post-War Recreation, the Benson Report and the Rebuilding of a Conservation Organization in the 1960s', *Twentieth Century British History*, 26. 4 (December 2015), 529–50: pp. 531–7.
10. Michell, *The Flying Saucer Vision*, p. 23, 12, 135; *The View Over Atlantis*, pp. 15–6; Janet and Colin Bord, *Mysterious Britain* [1972] (Great Britain: London, 1974), p. 2; Alfred Watkins, *The Old Straight Track* [1925] (London: Abacus, 1970).
11. For more on Michell and the Rolling Stones see Paul Screeton, *John Michell: From Atlantis To Avalon* (Avebury: Heart of Albion Press, 2010).
12. Michell's link to Glastonbury is described in Screeton, p. 30. Michell described Watkins' visionary experiences in his introduction to *The Old Straight Track*, 1–6: p. 2.
13. *Macbeth*. For details of the production see Williams.
14. *The Blood on Satan's Claw* (Piers Haggard, UK, 1971).
15. English Heretic, 'Locus Terribilis', *The New Geography of Witchcraft* (Suffolk: New English Heretic Library 2005/2013), n.p.
16. *Witchfinder General* (Michael Reeves, UK, 1968); English Heretic, 'Locus Terribilis'.
17. *The Blood on Satan's Claw*. In *The Satanic Screen*, Schreck provides a useful discussion of the film's link to the popular image of the Manson Family, circa 1971, pp. 148–9.
18. Williams, pp. 145–8, 157. In *Macbeth* 1.5 Lady Macbeth tells Macbeth, as they welcome King Duncan to their home to 'Look like th' innocent flower / But be the serpent under't'.
19. For an overview of the making of *Fire in the Water* see 'Dossier: *Fire in the Water*', *Framework* 52.2, 655–76. Specifically, see: Peter Whitehead, '*Requiem for the Sixties*: Film Proposal (1974)', 667–76: p. 667.
20. *Stardust* (Michael Apted, UK, 1974); *Quadrophenia* (Franc Roddam, UK, 1979); Whitehead, 'Requiem for the Sixties', p. 668.
21. For details of the Delon/Tate connection, see Jenny Fabian, 'Peter's Friends', *Harper's and Queen* (1996), 130–140: 131. A slightly more salacious account can be found in Lina Das, 'The final affair of Roman Polanski's murdered wife Sharon Tate', https://www.dailymail.co.uk/femail/article-478867/The-final-affair-Roman-Polanskis-murdered-wife-Sharon-Tate.html.
22. See Jean Baudrillard, 'The Precession of Simulacra', *Simulacra and Simulation* [1994], trans. Sheila Faria Glaser (USA: University of Michigan Press, 1994), 1–43.

23. Baudrillard, 'After the Orgy', *The Transparency of Evil: Essays on Extreme Phenomena* [1990], trans. James Benedict (London: Verso, 1993), 3–15: p. 3.
24. Whitehead, '*Requiem for the Sixties*', p. 668.
25. English Heretic, 'Locus Terribilis'.
26. English Heretic, 'Locus Terribilis'; 'New Geography of Witchcraft', *The New Geography of Witchcraft*, n.p. Definition of psychogeography from Guy Debord, 'Introduction to a Critique of Urban Geography', *Situationist International Anthology*, ed. and trans. Ken Knabb (Berkeley: Bureau of Public Secrets, 1996), 8–12: p. 9.
27. Whitehead discusses the mythological aspects of falconry in Evans and Slater, p. 17. A longer, more detailed discussion can be found in Robert F. Paul, 'Peter Whitehead Interview: The Wanderer (Part 1)', 25–30.
28. Whitehead, '*Requiem for the Sixties*', p. 673.
29. English Heretic, 'Locus Terribilis'.
30. See https://www.nationaltrust.org.uk/beatles-childhood-homes. For details of the 'Boxes of Vision', see https://www.beatlesinternational.com/index.php/releases/john/101-john-lennon-time-capsule.
31. For details see: https://www.woodstock.com/; https://www.nasa.gov/specials/apollo50th/; https://www.forbes.com/sites/trialandheirs/2018/01/16/the-charles-manson-estate-battle-is-the-fight-worth-it/#3efa162ed765.
32. Nuttall, p. 259.

Epilogue: *Apotheosis No. 2*

1. See Doggett for details on the making of the *Apotheosis* project, 230–232. See also English Heretic, 'Locus Terribilis', n.p. Paul Morrison's *24 Hours: The World of John and Yoko* appeared on BBC television on 15 December 1969.

Bibliography

I. Books and Articles

Abbey, Edward, *Desert Solitaire: A Season in the Wilderness* (USA: McGraw-Hill, 1968)

Allbeson, Tom, 'Visualizing Wartime Destruction and Postwar Reconstruction: Herbert Mason's Photograph of St. Paul's Cathedral', *Journal of Modern History* 87.3 (2015)

Allison, Deborah, 'Magick in Theory and Practice: Ritual Use of Colour in Kenneth Anger's *Invocation of My Demon Brother*', *Senses of Cinema* (February 2005)

Aram Goudsouzian and Charles W. McKinney (eds.), *An Unseen Light: Black Struggles for Freedom in Memphis Tennessee* (USA: University Press of Kentucky, 2018)

Aust, Stefan, *The Baader-Meinhof Complex* [1987] (London: The Bodley Head, 2008)

Baddeley, Gavin, *Lucifer Rising: Sin, Devil Worship and Rock 'n' Roll* (London: Plexus, 1999)

Badura-Triska, Eva, *Vienna Actionism: Art and Upheaval in 1960s Vienna* (Germany: Walther Koing, 2012)

Bailey, David, *David Bailey's Box of Pin-Ups* (London: Weidenfeld and Nicholson, 1964)

Ballard, J.G., *The Terminal Beach* (Great Britain: Gollancz, 1964)

______, 'Terminal Documents' *Ambit* 27 (Spring 1966)

______, *Memories of the Space Age* (USA: Arkham House, 1988)

______, *The Atrocity Exhibition* [1970] (London: HarperPerennial, 2006)

Ballard J.G. and George Petros, 'Seconds Chance', *Seconds* 40 (1996)

Barber, Stephen, *The Art of Destruction: The Films of the Vienna Action Group* (London: Creation Books, 2004)

______, *Abandoned Images: Film and Film's End* (London: Reaktion, 2010)

Barrell, Tony, *The Beatles on the Roof* (London: Omnibus, 2017)

Barton, Blanche, *The Secret Life of a Satanist: The Authorized Biography of Anton Szandor LaVey* (New York: Feral House, 2014)

Baudrillard, Jean, *Simulacra and Simulation* [1994] trans. Sheila Faria Glaser (USA: University of Michigan Press, 1994)

______, *The Transparency of Evil: Essays on Extreme Phenomena* [1990] trans. James Benedict (London: Verso, 1993)

Beecher, Russell and Will Shutes (eds.), *Barrett* (London: Essential Works, 2011)

Bell, Daniel, *The End of Ideology* (New York: Free Press, 1960)

Berke, Joseph, *Counterculture: The Creation of an Alternative Society* (London: Fire, 1969)

Bernstein, Carl and Bob Woodward, *All The President's Men* (London: Quartet, 1974)

Biskind, Peter, *Easy Riders, Raging Bulls: How the Sex, Drugs and Rock 'n' Roll Generation Changed Hollywood* (London: Bloomsbury, 1999)

Blake, William, *The Complete Poems*, ed. Alicia Ostriker (Harmondsworth: Penguin, 1977)

Booth, Stanley, *The True Adventures of the Rolling Stones* [1984] (Edinburgh: Canongate, 2012)

Bord, Janet and Colin, *Mysterious Britain* [1972] (Great Britain: London, 1974)

Brand, Stewart (ed.), *The Whole Earth Catalog: Access to Tools* (Fall 1968)

Bravin, Jess, *Squeaky: The Life and Times of Lynette Alice Fromme* (USA: St. Martin's Press, 1997)

Brendon, Piers, *The Decline and Fall of the British Empire, 1781–1997* (London: Vintage, 2008)

Brody, Richard, 'What Died at Altamont?', *The New Yorker* (March 2015)

Bromberg, Joan Lisa, *NASA and the Space Industry* (USA: Johns Hopkins University Press, 2000)

Brown, David Jay and Rebecca McClen Novick, *Mavericks of the Mind* [1993] (USA: MAPS, 2010)

Buck, Paul, *Performance: A Biography of the Classic Sixties Film* (London: Omnibus, 2012)

Bugliosi, Vincent and Curt Gentry, *Helter Skelter* (USA: W.W. Norton, 1974)

Capote, Truman, *Music for Chameleons: New Writing* [1975] (London: Penguin, 2000)

Carl Oglesby (ed.), *The New Left Reader* (New York: Grove Press, 1969)

Carmichael, Stokely and Charles V. Hamilton, *Black Power: The Politics of Liberation* (New York: Random House, 1967)

Carr, Gordon, *The Angry Brigade* (Oakland: PM Press, 2010)

Carson, Rachel, *Silent Spring* (USA: Houghton Mifflin, 1962)

Clapson, Mark, *The Blitz Companion* (London: University of Westminster Press, 2019)

Cobb, Ben, *Anarchy and Alchemy: The Films of Alejandro Jodorowsky* (London: Creation, 2007)

Coleman, Ray, *Lennon: The Definitive Biography* (New York: Harper Perennial, 1999)

Conquest, Robert (ed.), *New Lines: An Anthology* (London: Macmillan, 1956)

Cox, Oliver J.W., 'Frederick, Prince of Wales, and the First Performance of 'Rule, Britannia!', *The Historical Journal* 56.4 (2016)

Crichton, Michael, *The Andromeda Strain* (USA: Knopf, 1969)

Cronin, Paul, 'The Ceremony of Innocence', *Sight and Sound* (March 2007)

Cronin, Paul, James Riley and Drake Stutesman (eds.), *Framework 52: The Peter Whitehead Issue* 2 volumes (Spring 2011)

Cross, Charles R., *Room Full of Mirrors: A Biography of Jimi Hendrix* (Great Britain: Sceptre, 2005)

Crowley, Aleister, *Magick*, ed. John Symonds and Kenneth Grant [1929] (Great Britain: Guild, 1989)

______, *Magick in Theory and Practice* [1929] (New York: Castle Books, 1992)

Cush, Andy, 'Remember When Jimi Hendrix Protested the National Anthem on a National Stage?', *Spin* (September 2016)

Cutler, Sam, *You Can't Always Get What You Want* (Canada: ECW Press, 2008)

Daddis, Gregory A., *Withdrawal: Reassessing America's Final Years in Vietnam* (Oxford: Oxford University Press, 2017)

Dalton, David, 'Altamont: The End of the Sixties', *Gadfly* (November/December 1999)

Darwin, John, *The Empire Project: The Rise and Fall of the British World System 1830–1970* (Cambridge: Cambridge University Press, 2009)

Davenport-Hines, Richard, *An English Affair: Sex, Class and Power in the Age of Profumo* (London: Harper*Press*, 2013)

DeGroot, Gerard, *The 60s Unplugged: A Kaleidoscopic History of a Disorderly Decade* (Great Britain: Pan Macmillan, 2008)

Didion, Joan, *Slouching Towards Bethlehem* (New York: Farrar, Straus and Giroux, 1968)

______, *The White Album* (New York: Simon and Schuster, 1979)

Doggett, Peter, *The Art and Music of John Lennon* (London: Omnibus Press, 2009)

Dubow, Saul, 'Macmillan, Verwoerd, and the 1960 'Wind of Change' Speech', *The Historical Journal* 54.5 (2011)

Durham, David, *California's Geographic Names* (USA: Word Dancer Press, 1998)

Ehrenreich, Barbara, *The Hearts of Men: American Dreams and The Flight From Commitment* (Great Britain: Pluto Press, 1983)

'English Heretic', *The New Geography of Witchcraft* (Suffolk: New English Heretic Library 2005/2013)

English, Richard, *Armed Struggle: The History of the IRA* (Oxford: Oxford University Press, 2003)

Evans, Chris, 'J.G. Ballard: The Space Age is Over', *Penthouse* 14.1 (1979)

Evans, Gareth and Ben Slater, 'The Falconer: Three Lives of Peter Whitehead', *Entropy* 1.1 (June 1997)

Fabian, Jenny, *A Chemical Romance* [1971] (London: Do-Not Press, 1998)

______, 'Peter's Friends', *Harper's and Queen* (1996)

Fabian, Jenny and Johnny Byrne, *Groupie* [1969] (London: Mayflower, 1971)

Fagan, Kevin, 'Seeking Shelter from a Memory/Nostalgia absent on Altamont's 30th Anniversary', *San Francisco Chronicle* (6 December 1999)

Farren, Mick, *Give the Anarchist a Cigarette* (London: Pimlico, 2001)

Feldman, Gene and Max Gartenberg, *Protest* (London: Panther, 1962)

Flippo, Chet, 'Rock & Roll Tragedy', *Rolling Stone* (January 1980)

Freedland, Nat, *The Occult Explosion in America* (London: Michael Joseph, 1972)

Fuller, Buckminster, R., *Operating Manual for Spaceship Earth* [1969] (Switzerland: Lars Müller, 2014)

Gaddis, John Lewis, *The Cold War* (Great Britain: Penguin, 2005)

Gentry, R.C., 'Hurricane Debbie Modification Experiments, August 1969', *Science* 168. 3930 (24 April 1970)

Gilmore, John and Ron Kenner, *Manson* (New York: Amok Press, 2000)

Gilmore, Mikal, 'Beatles' Acid Test: How LSD Opened the Door to *Revolver*', *Rolling Stone* (25 August 2016)

Gleason, Ralph J., 'Aquarius Wept: The Rolling Stones at Altamont 1969', *Esquire* (August 1970)

Goldberg, Danny, *In Search of the Lost Chord: 1967 and the Hippie Idea* (London: Icon Books, 2017)

Goldwag, Arthur, *Cults, Conspiracies & Secret Societies* (USA: Vintage, 2009)

Goodall, Mark (ed.), *The Beatles, or 'The White Album'* (Great Britain: Headpress, 2018)

Goodman, Fred, *Allen Klein: The Man Who Bailed Out the Beatles, Made the Stones and Transformed Rock & Roll* (New York: Houghton Mifflin, 2016)

Goodwin, Michael, 'A Heavy Trip Inside Mick Jagger's Head', *Rolling Stone* (September 1970)

Gorightly, Adam, *The Shadow Over Santa Susana* (London: Creation, 2009)

Gough, Barry, *Pax Britannica: Ruling the Waves and Keeping the Peace before Armageddon* (Great Britain: Palgrave, 2014)

Graysmith, Robert, *Zodiac: The Shocking True Story of America's Most Elusive Serial Killer* [1976] (London: Titan, 2007)

Green, Jonathon, *Days in the Life* (London: Heinemann, 1988)

______, 'The Swinging Sixties? As if', *The Guardian*, 17 April (1999)

______, *All Dressed Up: The Sixties and the Counterculture* (London: Pimlico, 1999)

Green, Malcolm (ed.), *Writings of the Vienna Actionists* (London: Atlas Press, 1999)

Greenblatt, Stephen *et al* (eds.), *The Norton Shakespeare* (New York: W.W. Norton, 1997)

Greenfield, Robert, *Exile on Main Street: A Season in Hell with the Rolling Stones* (USA: Da Capo, 2006)

Greer, Germaine, *The Female Eunuch* (Great Britain: MacGibbon and Kee, 1970)

Griffiths, Robert and Paula Baker (eds.), *Major Problems in American History Since 1945* (Boston: Houghton Mifflin, 2001)

Grode, Eric, *Hair: The Story of the Show That Defined a Generation* (London: Goodman, 2010)

Groes, Sebastian, *British Fiction of the Sixties* (London: Bloomsbury, 2016)

Guzik, Sergio, *et al*, 'A Mass Changes Me More: An Interview with Alejandro Jodorowsky', *The Drama Review* 14.2 (Winter 1970)

Hammer, Ellen J., *A Death in November: America in Vietnam, 1963* (New York: E.P. Dutton, 1987)

Harris, Roger, *The LSD Dossier* (London: Compact, 1966)

Harrison, Hank, *The Grateful Dead* (London: Star, 1975)

Henderson, David, *'Scuse Me While I Kiss the Sky: The Life of Jimi Hendrix* [1978] (London: Omnibus, 2002)

Hennessy, Kate, 'The Cab Effect', *Mess + Noise* (July 2009)

Herbert, Frank, *Dune* (USA: Chilton, 1965)

______, *Dune Messiah* (New York: Putnam, 1969)

Herbert, James D., 'Bad Faith at Coventry: Spence's Cathedral and Britten's *War Requiem*', *Critical Inquiry* 25.3 (1999)

Hersh, Seymour, 'Huge CIA Operation Reported in U.S. Against Antiwar Forces, Other Dissidents in Nixon Years', *New York Times* (22 December 1974)

Hesiod, *Theogony and Works and Days*, ed. M.L. West (Oxford: Oxford University Press, 1988)

Hewison, Robert, *Too Much: Art and Society in the Sixties, 1960–1975* (Oxford: Oxford University Press, 1987)

Higgs, John, *I Have America Surrounded: The Life of Timothy Leary* (London: Friday, 2006)

______, *The KLF: Chaos, Magic and the Band Who Burned A Million Pounds* (London: Phoenix, 2012)

Hoffman, Abbie, *Woodstock Nation* [1969] (New York: Pocket Books, 1971)

Hofstadter, Richard J., 'The Paranoid Style in American Politics', *The Paranoid Style in American Politics and Other Essays* (Harvard: Harvard University Press, 1964)

Home, Stewart, *Tainted Love* (London: Virgin, 2006)

______, *The Assault on Culture: Utopian Currents from Lettrisme to Class War* (Stirling: AK Press, 1991)

Horner, Al, '20 sets that shook Glastonbury', *NME* (September 2017)

Horovitz, Michael (ed.), *Children of Albion: Poetry of the Underground in Britain* (Harmondsworth: Penguin, 1969)

Hoskyns, Barney, *Waiting for the Sun: Strange Days, Weird Scenes and the Sound of Los Angeles* (USA: St. Martin's Press, 1996)

Hotchner, A.E., *Blown Away: The Rolling Stones and the Death of the Sixties* (New York: Simon and Schuster, 1990)

Hunter, Jack (ed.) *Moonchild: The Films of Kenneth Anger* (London: Creation Books, 2002)

Huxley, Aldous, *The Doors of Perception/Heaven and Hell* (Great Britain: Granada: 1977)

Hyam, Ronald, *Britain's Imperial Century: 1815–1914* (Basingstoke: Palgrave, 1976)

Jodorowsky, Alejandro, *The Spiritual Journey of Alejandro Jodorowsky: The Creator of El Topo* (Rochester: Park Street Press, 2008)

Johnson, Robert, *British Imperialism* (Great Britain: Palgrave, 2002)

Jones, Robert, 'Hippie: The Philosophy of a Subculture', *Time* (July 1967)

Jones, Stephen, *Necronomicon: The Best Weird Tales of H.P. Lovecraft* (Great Britain: Gollancz, 2008)

Jung, C.G., *Flying Saucers: A Modern Myth of Things Seen in the Skies*, trans. R.F.C. Hull (London: Routledge & Kegan Paul, 1959)

______, *Dreams*, trans. R.F.C. Hull [1974] (Routledge: London, 2002)

Kael, Pauline, 'Dirty Harry: Saint Cop', *The New Yorker* (January 1972)

Kaplan, Mike, 'Kubrick: a marketing odyssey', *The Guardian* (2 November 2007)

Katz, David S., *The Occult Tradition* (London: Jonathan Cape, 2005)

Kean, Sam, 'Climate Control', *Air & Space* (July 2010)

Kerr, Gordon, *A Short History of the Vietnam War* (Harpenden: Oldcastle, 2015)

Kirkpatrick, Rob, *1969: The Year Everything Changed* (New York: Skyhorse, 2009)

Kosc, Grzegorz *et al* (eds.), *The Transatlantic Sixties: Europe and the United States in the Counterculture Decade* (Bielefeld: transcript Verlag, 2013)

Knabb, Ken (ed.), *Situationist International Anthology* (Berkeley: Bureau of Public Secrets, 1996)

Kubernik, Harvey, *A Perfect Haze: The Illustrated History of the Monterey International Pop Festival* (USA: Santa Monica Press, 2011)

Kunzru, Hari, '*Dune*, 50 years on: how a science fiction novel changed the world', *The Guardian* (3 July 2015)

Kurlansky, Mark, *1968: The Year that Rocked the World* (London: Jonathan Cape, 2004)

Lachman, Gary, *Turn Off Your Mind* [2001] (Finland: Dedalus, 2010)

______, 'Kenneth Anger: The Crowned and Conquering Child', *Kenneth Anger: The Magick Lantern Cycle* (London: BFI, 2011). DVD Booklet.

Landis, Bill, *Anger: The Unauthorized Biography of Kenneth Anger* (USA: Harper Collins, 1995)

Larkham, Peter J. and Mark Clapson (eds.), *The Blitz and its Legacy: Wartime Destruction to Post-War Reconstruction* (London: Routledge, 2016)

Larkin, Philip, *High Windows* (London: Faber, 1974)

LaVey, Anton, *The Satanic Bible* [1969] (New York: Avon, 1992)

Lazar, Zachary, *Sway* (London: Vintage, 2008)

Leary, Timothy *et al*, *The Psychedelic Experience* [1964] (Great Britain: Penguin, 1964)

______, *Starseed: A Psi-Phy Comet Tale* (San Francisco: Level Press, 1973)

Lee, Judith, 'Lucifer: A Fantastic Figure', *Journal of the Fantastic in the Arts* 8.2 (1997)

Lee, Keith C., *Images of America: Altamont* (USA: Arcadia, 2014)

Lee, Martin A. and Bruce Shlain, *Acid Dreams: The Complete Social History LSD* (New York: Grove, 2000)

Leitch, Vincent B., *et al* (eds.), *The Norton Anthology of Theory and Criticism* (New York: Norton, 2001)

Levin, Ira, *Rosemary's Baby* (New York, Dell, 1967)

Lovelock, James, *Gaia: A New Look at Life on Earth* (Oxford: Oxford University Press, 2000)

Lukas, Anthony, J., 'The Two Worlds of Linda Fitzpatrick', *New York Times* (16 October 1967)

Lyotard, Jean-François, *The Postmodern Condition* (Manchester: Manchester University Press, 1986)

MacDonald, Ian, *Revolution in the Head: The Beatles' Records and the Sixties* (London: Pimlico, 1995)

Magrini, James, 'Lucifer Rising', *Senses of Cinema* (March 2015)

Mailer, Norman, *The Armies of the Night* (New York: New American Library, 1968)

Marcuse, Herbert, *One Dimensional Man* (New York: Beacon Press, 1964)

Marks, John D., *The Search for the Manchurian Candidate* (New York: Dell, 1978)

Marwick, Arthur, *British Society Since 1945* (London: Penguin, 1990)

______, *The Sixties* (Oxford: Oxford University Press, 1999)

McAllister, James, 'Who Lost in Vietnam? Soldiers, Civilians and U.S Military Strategy', *International Security* 35.3 (2010/2011)

McLoughlin, Kate (ed.), *British Literature in Transition, 1960–1980: Flower Power* (Cambridge: Cambridge University Press, 2019)

Meade, Robert C., *Red Brigades: The Story of Italian Terrorism* (Great Britain: Palgrave, 2014)

Means, Howard, *67 Shots: Kent State and the End of American Innocence* (Boston, Da Capo, 2016)

Michell, John, *The Flying Saucer Vision* (Great Britain: Sidgwick & Jackson, 1967)

______, *The View Over Atlantis* (London: Sago Press, 1969)

Miles, Barry, *Paul McCartney: Many Years from Now* (London: Vintage, 1998)

Miller, Henry K. (ed.), *The Essential Raymond Durgnat* (London: BFI, 2014)

Mills, C. Wright, *White Collar: The American Middle Classes* (Oxford: Oxford University Press, 1951)

______,'Letter to the New Left', *New Left Review* 1.5 (September–October 1960)

______, *The Marxists* (USA: Dell, 1962)

Milton, John, *Paradise Lost* [1667] ed. John Leonard (Great Britain: Penguin, 2003)

Minutaglio, Bill and Steven L. Davis, *The Most Dangerous Man in America: Timothy Leary, Richard Nixon and the Hunt for the Fugitive King of LSD* (New York: Twelve, 2018)

Moorcock, Michael, 'A New Literature for the Space Age', *New Worlds* 142 (May–June 1964)

______, *The Final Programme* [1969] (London: Fontana, 1979)

Moore, Gerald and Lawrence Schiller, 'The Exploding Threat of the Mind Control Drug that got out of Control', *Life* (March 1966)

Nixon, Sean, 'Trouble at the National Trust: Post-War Recreation, the Benson Report and the Rebuilding of a Conservation Organization in the 1960s', *Twentieth Century British History*, 26. 4 (December 2015)

Norman, Philip, *Shout! The Beatles in Their Generation* (USA: Fireside, 1996)

______, *Mick Jagger* (London: Harper Collins, 2013)

Nuttall, Jeff, 'Snipe's Spinster' [1975], *An Aesthetic of Obscenity: 5 Novels by Jeff Nuttall*, ed. Douglas Field and Jay Jeff Jones (Singapore: Verbivoracious Press, 2016)

______, *Bomb Culture* [1968] ed. Douglas Field and Jay Jeff Jones (London: Strange Attractor, 2018)

O'Neill, Tony, *Sick City* (New York: Harper, 2010)

Ortiz, Raphael Montañez, 'Destructivism: A Manifesto' [1962], *Theories and Documents of Contemporary Art: A Sourcebook of Artists' Writings*, ed. Kristine Stiles and Peter Selz (Berkeley: University of California Press, 1998)

Orwell, George, *Nineteen Eighty-Four* [1949] (London: Penguin, 2000)

Owens, Bill, *Altamont 1969* (Italy: Damiani, 2019)

Parfrey, Adam (ed.), *Apocalypse Culture*, ed. (USA: Feral House, 1990)

Parker, James, 'Woodstock Nation', *The Atlantic* (September 2009)

Parks, James, *Cultural Icons* (London: Bloomsbury, 1991)

Pearson, John, *The Profession of Violence: The Rise and Fall of the Kray Twins* (London: Weidenfeld and Nicholson, 1972)

Perry, Charles, *The Haight-Ashbury: A History* (New York: Random House, 1988)

Petit, Chris, *Back from the Dead* [1999] (London: Pan, 2000)

Porter, Andrew (ed.), *The Oxford History of the British Empire* (Oxford: Oxford University Press, 1999)

Porter, Bruce, 'Trouble in Hippieland/Gentle Marcy: A Shattering Tale', *Newsweek* (October 30, 1967)

Puttick, Betty, *Supernatural England* (Great Britain: Countryside Books, 2002)

Reich, Charles A., *The Greening of America* (New York: Random House, 1970)

Roberts, Andy, *Albion Dreaming: A Popular History of LSD in Britain* (Singapore: Marshall Cavendish, 2012)

Robertson, George, 'The Situationist International: Its Penetration into British Culture', *What is Situationism: A Reader*, ed. Stewart Home (Stirling: AK Press, 1996)

Robinson, John, 'Interview with the organisers of Woodstock festival', *The Telegraph* (12 August 2009)

'Rolling Stone', 'The Rolling Stones Disaster at Altamont: Let It Bleed', *Rolling Stone* (January 1970)

Rolph, C.H., *The Trial of Lady Chatterley* (Harmondsworth: Penguin, 1961)

Roszak, Theodore, 'Youth and the Great Refusal' *The Nation* (March 1968)

______, *The Making of a Counterculture* (USA: Anchor/Doubleday, 1969)

Rowe, Carel, 'Illuminating Lucifer', *Film Quarterly* 27.4 (Summer 1974)

Samaha, Albert, 'The Rise and Fall of Crime in New York City: A Timeline', *The Village Voice* (August 2014)

Sanchez, Tony, *Up and Down with the Rolling Stones* (London: John Blake, 2010)

Sanders, Ed, *The Family* (New York: E.P. Dutton, 1971)

Sargeant, Jack (ed.), *Guns, Death Terror: An Illustrated History of 1960s & 1970s International Terror* (London: Creation, 2003)

Screeton, Paul, *John Michell: From Atlantis To Avalon* (Avebury: Heart of Albion Press, 2010)

Schmitz, David F., *Richard Nixon and the Vietnam War: The End of the American Century* (USA: Rowan and Littlefield, 2014)

Schrag, Peter, 'The Forgotten American' [1969], *A History of Our Time: Readings on Postwar America* ed. William Chafe *et al* (Oxford: Oxford University Press, 2008)

Schreck, Nikolas (ed.) *The Manson File* (New York: Amok Press, 1988)

______, *The Satanic Screen* (London: Creation, 2001)

Seale, Patrick and Maureen McConville, *French Revolution 1968* (Harmondsworth: Penguin, 1968).

Selvin, Joel, *Altamont: The Rolling Stones, the Hells Angels and the Inside Story of Rock's Darkest Day* (USA: Dey Street Books, 2017)

Selvon, Sam, *The Housing Lark* (London: MacGibbon & Kee, 1965)

Shea, Robert and Robert Anton Wilson, *Illuminatus!* (Great Britain: Sphere, 1976)

Sinclair, Iain (ed.), *London: City of Disappearances* (London: Penguin, 2006)

Sinclair, Iain and Rachel Lichtenstein, *Rodinsky's Room* (Great Britain: Granta, 2000)

Slick, Grace, *Somebody to Love: A Rock-and-Roll Memoir* (New York: Warner, 1988)

Small, Melvin, *The Presidency of Richard Nixon* (USA: University of Kansas Press, 1999)

Smith, Andrew, *Moon Dust* (London: Bloomsbury, 2005)

Smith, Jerry E., *Weather Warfare* (USA: Adventures Unlimited, 2006).

Southwell, David and Sean Twist, *Conspiracy Theories* (Great Britain: Carlton, 1999)

Sragow, Michael, '*Gimme Shelter*: The True Story', *Salon* (August 2000)

Stansill, Peter and David Zane Mairowitz, *BAMN (By Any Means Necessary): Outlaw Graphics and Ephemera* (Harmondsworth: Penguin, 1971)

Steadman, John M., *Milton's Epic Characters: Image and Idol* (USA: Chapel Hill, 1959)

Stephens, Chris and Katherine Stout (eds.), *Art & the 60s: This Was Tomorrow* (London: Tate, 2004)

Stephens, Julie, *Anti-Disciplinary Protest: Sixties Radicalism and Postmodernism* (Cambridge: Cambridge University Press, 1998)

Stevens, Jay, *Storming Heaven: LSD and the American Dream* (New York: Grove, 1988)

Storey, John (ed.), *Cultural Theory and Popular Culture: A Reader* (Great Britain: Prentice Hall, 1998)

Strachan, Françoise, *Aquarian Guide to Occult, Mystical, Religious, Magical, London and Around* (Great Britain: Aquarian Press, 1970)

Summers, John, 'Daniel Bell and The End of Ideology', *Dissent* (Spring 2011)

Symonds, John, *The Great Beast: The Life and Work of Aleister Crowley* (Great Britain: Mayflower, 1971)

Taylor, Derek, *It Was Twenty Years Ago Today* (London: Bantam, 1987)

Taylor, Terry, *Baron's Court, All Change* [1961] (London: London New Editions, 2011)

Tendler, Stewart and David May, *The Brotherhood of Eternal Love* (London: Panther, 1984)

Terry, Maury, *The Ultimate Evil* (Great Britain: Grafton, 1988)

Tew, Philip, James Riley and Melanie Seddon (eds.), *The 1960s: A Decade of Modern British Fiction* (London: Bloomsbury, 2018)

Thomas, Kenn and David Hatcher Childress, *Inside the Gemstone File* (USA: Adventures Unlimited, 1999)

Thompson, Hunter, S., *Hell's Angels: The Strange and Terrible Saga of the Outlaw Motorcycle Gangs* (New York: Random House, 1967)

______, *Fear and Loathing in Las Vegas* [1972] (Great Britain: Flamingo, 1993)

______, *Fear and Loathing in America: The Brutal Odyssey of an Outlaw Journalist 1968–1976*, ed. Douglas Brinkley (London: Bloomsbury, 2000)

Tiber, Elliot and Tom Monte, *Taking Woodstock* (New York: Square One, 2009)

Toop, David, 'Surfin' Death Valley USA: The Beach Boys and 'Heavy' Friends', *The Sound and the Fury*, ed. Barney Hoskyns and David Pringle (London: Bloomsbury, 2003)

Umland, Rebecca and Sam, *Donald Cammell: A Life of the Wild Side* (Great Britain: Fab Press, 2006)

Van Bebber, Jim, *Charlie's Family* (London: Creation, 1998)

Watkins, Alfred, *The Old Straight Track* [1925] (London: Abacus, 1970)

Wells, Simon, *Charles Manson: Coming Down Fast* (London: Hodder, 2010)
Whipple, A.B.C., *Storm* (USA: Time/Life, 1982)
Whitehead, Peter (ed.), *Wholly Communion* (New York: Grove, 1965)
______, *Peter Whitehead: A Singular Vision* (Pytchley: Hathor, 2001)
Whitmer Peter O., and Bruce VanWyngarden, *Aquarius Revisited* (New York: Citadel, 1991)
Wiedemann, Alfred, *Religion of the Ancient Egyptians* (London: H. Grevel & Co, 1897)
Williams, Dave, and Ron Bailey, 'An Open Letter to the Underground from the London Street Commune', *International Times* (10 October 1969)
Williams, Deanne, 'Mick Jagger Macbeth', *Shakespeare Survey* 57 (2008)
Williams, Raymond, *Keywords* (London: Fontana, 1976)
Willoughby, H.E. *et al*, 'Project STORMFURY: A Scientific Chronicle 1962–1983', *Bulletin American Meteorological Society*, 66. 5 (May 1985)
Wilson, Harold, *The New Britain: Labour's Plan. Selected Speeches 1964* (Harmondsworth: Penguin, 1964)
Wolfe, Tom, *The Electric Kool-Aid Acid Test* (New York: Bantam, 1969)
______, 'The 'Me' Decade and the Third Great Awakening', *New York* (August 1976)
Wu, Duncan (ed.), *Romanticism: An Anthology* (Great Britain: Blackwell, 1998)
Yeats, W.B., *Selected Poetry*, ed. Norman Jeffares (Great Britain: Pan, 1990)
Young, Rob, *Electric Eden: Unearthing Britain's Visionary Music* (London: Faber, 2011)

II. Films

2001: A Space Odyssey (Stanley Kubrick, UK/US, 1968)
13 Chairs, The (Nicolas Gessner, IT/FR, 1969)
24 Hours: The World of John and Yoko (Paul Morrison, UK, 1969)
American Graffiti (George Lucas, US, 1973)
Apocalypse Now (Francis Ford Coppola, US, 1979)

Apotheosis (John Lennon and Yoko Ono, UK, 1970)
Apotheosis No. 2 (John Lennon and Yoko Ono, UK, 1970)
Army Medicine in Vietnam (US Army, US, 1970)
Beatles at Shea Stadium, The (Robert Precht, UK/US, 1966)
Beneath the Planet of the Apes (Ted Post, US, 1970)
Benefit of the Doubt (Peter Whitehead, UK, 1967)
Blood on Satan's Claw, The (Piers Haggard, UK, 1971)
Blow-Up (Michelangelo Antonioni, UK/IT/US, 1966)
Blue Sunshine (Jeff Lieberman, US, 1978)
Cain's Film (Jamie Wadhawan, UK, 1969)
Clockwork Orange, A (Stanley Kubrick, UK/US, 1971)
Charlie is My Darling (Peter Whitehead, UK, 1966)
Conquest of Space (Byron Haskin, US, 1955)
Cream's Farewell Concert at the Albert Hall (Sandy Oliveri, Tony Palmer, UK/US, 1969)
Daddy (Peter Whitehead, UK/FR, 1973)
Days in the Life: A Gathering of the Tribes (Edmund Coulthart, GB, 2000)
Death Wish (Michael Winner, US, 1974)
Deathmaster (Ray Danton, US, 1972)
Dirty Harry (Don Siegel, US, 1971)
Dunwich Horror, The (Daniel Haller, US, 1970)
Easy Rider (Dennis Hopper and Peter Fonda, US, 1969).
El Topo (Alejandro Jodorowsky, Mexico, 1970)
Enforcer, The (James Fargo, US, 1976)
Eye of the Devil (J. Lee Thompson, UK, 1966)
Fall, The (Peter Whitehead, UK/USA, 1969)
Fall of the Roman Empire, The (Anthony Mann, USA, 1964)
Fearless Vampire Killers, The (Roman Polanski, USA/UK 1967)
Fields of Sacrifice (Donald Brittain, Canada, 1964)
First Man into Space, The (Robert Day, UK, 1959)
French Connection, The (William Friedkin, US, 1971)
Fire in the Water (Peter Whitehead, UK, 1977,)
Gimme Shelter: Outtakes (Albert Maysles, David Maysles and Charlotte Zwerin, US, 2000)
Green Slime, The (Kinji Fukasaku, IT/Japan/US 1968)
Guns at Batasi (John Guillermin, UK, 1964)

Harvest of Shame (Fred W. Friendly, US, 1960)
Hells Angels on Wheels (Richard Rush, US, 1967)
Helter Skelter (Tom Gries, US, 1976)
Hills Have Eyes, The (Wes Craven, US, 1977)
Holy Mountain, The (Alejandro Jodorowsky, Mexico/US, 1973)
I Drink Your Blood (David E. Durston, US, 1970)
Inauguration of the Pleasuredome (Kenneth Anger, US, 1954)
Invocation of My Demon Brother (Kenneth Anger, US, 1969)
Island of Death (Nico Mastorakis, Greece, 1976)
Journey to the Far Side of the Sun (Robert Parrish, UK, 1969)
Kustom Kar Kommandos (Kenneth Anger, US, 1965)
Led Zeppelin at the Albert Hall (Peter Whitehead, UK, 1970)
The Love Thrill Murders (Bob Roberts, US, 1971)
Lucifer Rising (Kenneth Anger, UK/US/Germany, 1980)
Macbeth (Roman Polanski, UK/US, 1971)
Magnum Force (Ted Post, US, 1973)
Omega Man, The (Boris Sagal, US, 1971)
Other Side of Madness, The (Frank Howard, US, 1971)
Performance (Donald Cammell/Nicolas Roeg, UK, 1970)
Planet of the Apes (Franklin J. Schaffner, 1968)
Pop Gear (Frederic Goode, UK, 1965)
Quadrophenia (Franc Roddam, UK, 1979)
Quatermass Experiment, The (Val Guest, UK, 1955)
Ramrodder, The (Van Guylder, US, 1969)
Rosemary's Baby (Roman Polanski, US, 1968)
Satan's Sadists (Al Adamson, US, 1969)
Scorpio Rising (Kenneth Anger, US, 1963)
Soldier Blue (Ralph Nelson, US, 1970)
Stardust (Michael Apted, UK, 1974)
Sympathy for the Devil? The True Story of The Process Church of the Final Judgement (Neil Edwards, UK, 2014)
That'll be the Day (Claude Whatham, UK, 1973)
Trip, The (Roger Corman, US, 1967)
Virgin Sacrifice, The ('J.X. Williams,' US, 1969)
Wild Angels, The (Roger Corman, US, 1966)
Wild Bunch, The (Sam Peckinpah, US, 1969)
Wild One, The (László Benedek, US, 1953)

Tonite Let's All Make Love in London (Peter Whitehead, UK, 1967)
Vanishing Point (Richard C. Sarafian, US, 1971)
Wholly Communion (Peter Whitehead, UK, 1965)
Witchfinder General (Michael Reeves, UK, 1968)
Woodstock: 3 Days of Peace and Music (Michael Wadleigh, US, 1970)

III. Albums

5th Dimension, The, *The Age of Aquarius* (Soul City, 1969)
Beach Boys, The, *20/20* (Capitol, 1969)
Beatles, The, *Please Please Me* (Parlophone, 1963)
______, *Revolver* (Parlophone, 1966)
______, *Sgt. Pepper's Lonely Hearts Club Band* (Parlophone, 1967)
______, *The Beatles (The White Album)* (Apple, 1968)
______, *Abbey Road* (Apple, 1969)
______, *Let it Be* (Apple, 1970)
Syd Barrett, *The Madcap Laughs* (Harvest, 1970)
______, *Barrett* (Harvest, 1970)
Black Cab, *Altamont Diary* (Interstate 40, 2004)
Bobby Beausoleil, *The Lucifer Rising Suite* (CD Baby, 2014)
Crazy World of Arthur Brown, The, *The Crazy World of Arthur Brown* (Atlantic, 1968)
Coven, *Witchcraft Destroys Minds & Reaps Souls* (Mercury, 1969)
Grateful Dead, The, *Live/Dead* (Warner, 1969)
______, *Workingman's Dead* (Warner, 1970)
Jefferson Airplane, *Surrealistic Pillow* (RCA Victor, 1967)
______, *Volunteers* (RCA Victor, 1969)
Jimmy Page, *Lucifer Rising and Other Soundtracks* (Jimmy Page, 2012)
John Lennon and Yoko Ono, *Unfinished Music No. 1: Two Virgins* (Apple, 1968)
Led Zeppelin, *III* (Atlantic, 1970)
______, *IV* (Atlantic, 1971)
Charles Manson, *Lie: The Love and Terror Cult* (Awareness Records, 1970)
Pink Floyd, *Piper at the Gates of Dawn* (EMI, 1967)
______, *A Saucerful of Secrets* (EMI, 1968)
______, *The Dark Side of the Moon* (Harvest, 1973)
Rolling Stones, The, *Aftermath* (Decca, 1966)

______, *Their Satanic Majesties Request* (Decca, 1967)
______, *Let it Bleed* (Decca, 1969)
______, *Exile on Main Street* (Rolling Stones, 1972)
Traffic, *Mr. Fantasy* (Island, 1967)
Various, *LSD* (Capitol Records, 1966)
Who, The, *Quadrophenia* (Track, 1973)

IV. Online Sources

Beausoleil, Bobby, 'The Lucifer Rising Suite' http://bobbybeausoleil.com/the-lucifer-rising-suite-a-journey-out-of-darkness.html
Brussell, Mae, 'From Monterey Pop to Altamont: Operation Chaos – The CIA's War Against the Sixties Counter-Culture' (November 1976) http://www.maebrussell.com/Mae%20Brussell%20Articles/Operation%20Chaos.html
Das, Lina, 'The final affair of Roman Polanski's murdered wife Sharon Tate' (undated posting) https://www.dailymail.co.uk/femail/article-478867/The-final-affair-Roman-Polanskis-murdered-wife-Sharon-Tate.html
Hirschman, Jack, 'Breaking down walls of corporeal and narcotic sleep', *The Staff* (1971), reproduced on 'Cinephilia and Beyond' https://cinephiliabeyond.org/1971-interview-alejandro-jodorowsky-el-topo-psychedelic-genre-bending-midnight-movie/
Metzger, Gustav, 'Manifesto Auto-Destructive Art' (1960) http://radicalart.info/destruction/metzger.html
Owens, Bill, 'The Altamont Story' https://trivalleycahistoryblog.wordpress.com/2009/08/27/the-altamont-story-by-bill-owens-altamont-photographer/
Pitzer, Andrea, 'The Bitter History of Law and Order in America', (2017) https://longreads.com/2017/04/06/the-bitter-history-of-law-and-order-in-america/
Rosenbaum, Jonathan, '*Zabriskie Point*' (1984) https://www.jonathanrosenbaum.net/2018/12/zabriskie-point-1984-review
'Thousands flee Woodstock chaos, mud' (UPI, 16 August 1969) https://www.upi.com/Archives/1969/08/16/Thousands-flee-Woodstock-chaos-mud/5321502589701/
Tiber, Elliot, 'How Woodstock Happened' http://www.woodstockstory.com/how-woodstock-happened-5.html

Wenner, Jann S., 'John Lennon: *The Rolling Stone* Interview' (*Rolling Stone*, January 1971) https://www.rollingstone.com/music/music-news/john-lennon-the-rolling-stone-interview-part-one-160194/

Wilson, Robert Anton, 'The Illuminatus Saga Stumbles Along' (1990) http://rawilsonfans.org/the-illuminatus-saga-stumbles-along

Other useful websites:

www.52-insights.com
www.aes-nihil.com/aes.html
www.beatlesinternational.com
www.Bombsight.org
www.britishpoliticalspeech.org
www.dropcitydoc.com
www.forbes.com
www.nationaltrust.org.uk
www.nasa.gov
www.phinnweb.org
www.ukrockfestivals.com
www.woodstock.com
www.youtube.com

Acknowledgements

It's been a long, strange trip. Thankfully, I've had a wonderful team of people around me with whom I could share this journey. With them on board writing *The Bad Trip* has been, despite its title, a real pleasure.

For his guidance and foresight, I would like to thank my agent Donald Winchester. Wise and enthusiastic, he had faith in this project from the start and continued to wave the flag at every stage of its development. Everyone at Icon Books has been fantastic, particularly Kiera Jamison. I could not have asked for a better editor. Donald and Kiera are, quite simply, magicians: they take *ideas* and transform them into *books*. Ruth Killick, meanwhile, is the one who helps get the books *out there*. Many thanks to her for such brilliant work in banging the drum.

The seeds of *The Bad Trip* were sown at a number of conferences, symposia and events including 'Decades: The 1960s' at Brunel University, London; 'Subcultures, Popular Music and Social Change' at London Metropolitan University; 'Visions of Enchantment' at the University of Cambridge and 'Weekend Otherworld' at the Cinema Museum, London. I am particularly grateful to Nottingham Contemporary for the opportunity in 2012 to curate the film season 'Film, Counterculture and the Death of the Sixties'. The ongoing sequences of seminars mounted by the Cambridge Counterculture Research Group and the Alchemical Landscape have been an invaluable forum for discussing ideas in progress.

Some of the ideas used in Chapters two and three as well as other points dotted around the book were rehearsed in the essays I wrote for *The 1960s: A Decade of Modern British Fiction* (Bloomsbury, 2018), *The Beatles, or the 'White Album'* (Headpress, 2018) and *British Literature in Transition, 1960–1980: Flower Power* (Cambridge, 2019). My thanks to the editors Philip Tew, Melanie Seddon, Kate McLoughlin and Mark Goodall.

Lots of other friends and colleagues contributed in various ways as *The Bad Trip* took shape. For conversation, suggestions, tips and interviews I am very grateful to:

> David Ashford, Brian Baker, Jo Brooke, John Calder, Jenny Fabian, Douglas Field, Jake Fior, Hannah Gilbert, Jonathon Green, Malcolm Guite, Spike Hawkins, Richard Herland, the late John Hopkins, Michael Horovitz, Rod Mengham, Barry Miles, Judith Noble, Alastair Reid, Andy Sharp and Iain Sinclair.

Extra special thanks in this regard go to my co-conspirator Yvonne Salmon: I know of no better guide to the highways and byways of underground culture.

For their unfailing support I would like to thank Charlotte, Simon, Johnny and Eden. Most of all I would like to thank Mum and Dad: thank you for *Sounds of the Sixties* on Saturday mornings; thank you for all the great first-hand stories; thank you, of course, for everything.

Index

H

I

J

K